AF600309

CROWNING GLORIES

Netherlandish Realism and the French Imagination during the Reign of Louis XIV

HARRIET STONE

Crowning Glories

Netherlandish Realism and the French Imagination during the Reign of Louis XIV

UNIVERSITY OF TORONTO PRESS
Toronto Buffalo London

© University of Toronto Press 2019
Toronto Buffalo London
utorontopress.com

ISBN 978-1-4875-0442-7

Library and Archives Canada Cataloguing in Publication

Title: Crowning glories : Netherlandish realism and the French imagination during the reign of Louis XIV / Harriet Stone.
Names: Stone, Harriet Amy, 1953– author.
Description: Includes bibliographical references and index.
Identifiers: Canadiana 20189067381 | ISBN 9781487504427 (hardcover)
Subjects: LCSH: Louis XIV, King of France, 1638–1715 – Art patronage. | LCSH: Arts, French – 17th century. | LCSH: Painting, Dutch – 17th century – Influence. | LCSH: Painting, Flemish – 17th century – Influence. | LCSH: Realism in art – History – 17th century. | LCSH: Art and society – France – History – 17th century. | LCSH: France – Courts and courtiers – History – 17th century.
Classification: LCC DC128 .S76 2019 | DDC 944/.033—dc23

University of Toronto Press acknowledges the financial assistance to its publishing program of the Canada Council for the Arts and the Ontario Arts Council, an agency of the Government of Ontario.

Canada Council for the Arts Conseil des Arts du Canada

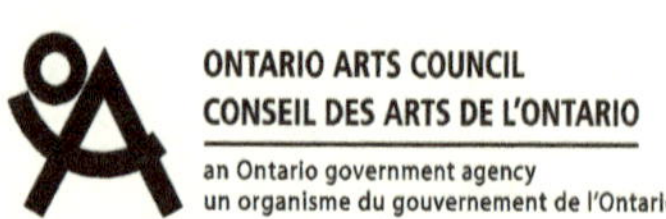

Funded by the Government of Canada | Financé par le gouvernement du Canada | Canada

Contents

Images

French titles are followed by the English translation. I provide only English titles for Netherlandish works held outside of France. To view images in colour, use the URL provided with the captions.

Chapter 1

Chapter 2

Chapter 3

Chapter 4

Chapter 5

Chapter 6

Coda

Acknowledgments

It is a sign of the interdisciplinary academic times in which we live that my interests in seventeenth-century French literature have continued to engage the equally vibrant but very different world of Netherlandish art of the same period. I have come to believe that this art held a special place in French court culture as an unsuspecting agent of change. *Crowning Glories* represents my exploration of what it would have meant, intellectually as well as aesthetically, for French court society to have had Northern realism, dedicated to portraying daily life, as a foil to the allegorical fullness of the art and literature with which Louis XIV surrounded himself. There was much more to the arts in Paris and at Versailles than met the eye, and nothing better than Flemish and Dutch paintings to encourage us to take a closer look.

I examine how the production of art and literature grounds the structuring of knowledge in the early modern period, arguing that this vital connection explains not only how the arts support the French monarchy but also their potential to destabilize the court's efforts to control the flow of ideas. My project benefitted from the contributions of many scholars pursuing collaborative study. I am indebted to Tili Boon Cuillé for her generous support from the inception of this project through its final (and oft-revised) paragraphs. Her insightful readings have proved invaluable. Other colleagues and friends have made incisive contributions in the course of my study, including Faith Beasley, Iver Bernstein, Elizabeth Childs, Dominique de Courcelles, Alexandre Dubé, Sarah Dunant, Richard Goodkin, Emma Kafalenos, Hélène Le Dantec-Lowry, Janice Liebowitz, Joseph Loewenstein, Judy Mann, Ashley Ray, Elzbieta Sklodowska, Andrew Schoenholtz, Lynne Tatlock, William Wallace, Betha Whitlow, Gerhild Williams, and Carla Zecher.

Special thanks go to members of Washington University's Eighteenth-Century Interdisciplinary Salon, for their rigorous feedback, and to the continued stimulation of another salon, this one a circle of friends, for thought-provoking discussions about the arts. In that group I especially recognize the contributions of Linda Skrainka, whose intellectual vitality is sorely missed, and Mary Reid Brunstrom, who remains a model of artistic engagement.

I am deeply grateful for the calm and steady encouragement of Milica Banjanin, to whom this book is dedicated.

My students have challenged me to share my passion for Dutch art along with French literature in ways that resonate with their interests and their discovery of the world of ideas, a process that I have very much enjoyed and that has enriched me as well. The anonymous and generous readers of my manuscript challenged me in other ways. They provided excellent suggestions that have greatly improved the final product. Their validation of my research means a great deal to me.

For the continued support from Washington University in St. Louis for my research, I thank the Dean of the Faculty of Arts & Sciences and Mary-Dell Chilton Distinguished Professor Barbara Schaal; the Center for the Humanities; and Professor Michael Sherberg in the Department of Romance Languages and Literatures. I also thank Rita Kuehler, our Office Manager, for her constant care and efficiency. Kyle Young stepped into the breach with dedicated bibliographic assistance.

I remain most appreciative of Suzanne Rancourt at University of Toronto Press for believing in this project. I thank her and her able production team for shepherding the book, with its many images, to publication.

All translations are my own.

An earlier version of portions of chapter 3 appeared as "Points de vue héroïques: Perspectives sur *Suréna*" in *Héros ou personnages: Le personnel du théâtre de Pierre Corneille*. Ed. Myriam Dufour-Maître. Mont-Saint-Aignan, France: Presses Universitaires de Rouen et du Havre, 2013. 111–28.

An earlier version of portions of chapter 4 appeared as "A Battle for Hearts and Minds: Turenne and Louis XIV." *Introduction à l'éventail européen aux XVIIe et XVIIIe siècles*. Ed. Katherine Ibbett. Spec. Issue *Seventeenth-Century French Studies* 36, no. 1 (June 2014): 71–80.

CROWNING GLORIES

Netherlandish Realism and the French Imagination during the Reign of Louis XIV

Introduction: Hiding in Plain Sight

Court culture during the reign of Louis XIV (1643–1715) was expansive. The arts formed an integral part of France's efforts to extend the king's influence and to consolidate his power. Artists, musicians, dramatists, and other apologists for the crown produced an impressive body of work that constituted a veritable propaganda campaign for Louis XIV. The king's patronage enabled the production of significant numbers of paintings, sculptures, tapestries, prints, concerts, plays, ballets, architectural works, and orations celebrating his reign.[1] Nobles and bourgeois admired the French decor at the Louvre; at Versailles, where the idea of grandeur assumed new proportions; and at the king's other chateaux. Royal art collections featured many important French works, but they also included paintings by Northern artists. In France examples of Northern art were likewise found in private collections, in art dealers' shops, and in travellers' accounts. They were discussed in academic circles as well as among prospective buyers and admirers of fine art. Along with the more commanding French court style, Northern realism was therefore familiar to the upper classes. This book explores what it would have meant for the French elite to consider examples of Dutch and Flemish realism along with French images and texts that paid tribute to Louis XIV. More specifically, I investigate how the French, who were subject to the monarchy's concerted efforts to impose the king's image, constructed knowledge in ways that reflected both the predominant influence of the arts and letters supporting the crown and the realism of Netherlandish paintings.

I study the effects of the arts on the French imagination, examining the world of ideas that the French elite developed in response to the State spectacle that defined court culture under the Sun King. During the reign of Louis XIV, the court's magnificence was evident in the splendid palace decors; the grand equestrian statues of the king and his many portraits; the ceremonies performed to commemorate marriages, victories, and deaths; and the exceptional fêtes organized to awe his subjects. Louis XIV organized the Plaisirs de l'Ile Enchantée [Pleasures of the Enchanted Island] at Versailles on 7–13 May 1664 in honour of his mother, Anne d'Autriche, and his wife, Queen Marie-Thérèse. This remarkable celebration at the palace where, nearly two decades later, the king would relocate the court, exemplifies his capacity to impress. The theme of the six-day event was based on the story of Alcine, a sorceress who held Roger and his valiant knights prisoner in her enchanted palace. On the second evening, Louis XIV performed the role of Roger in *La Princesse d'Elide* [*The Princess of Elide*], a comedy-ballet that Molière and Lully created for the occasion, which combined theatre, music, and dance. The king dancing onstage at Versailles, a performer in the performance that he orchestrated to impress the court, is a fitting image for the spectacle devoted to his persona that would mark his reign.

Courtiers sought the monarch's favour through service in the army, the royal administration, and more personal relations. Service to the king was so deeply ingrained in the life of the nobles and bourgeois that even highly mannered rituals would have appeared unexceptional. Louis codified etiquette well beyond the practices of previous monarchs. The various roles assigned to individuals as part of the king's daily routines as well as during state ceremonies were the equivalent of so many privileges, marks of distinction that were selectively awarded to some members of the court, and therefore explicitly denied to others. The rules of etiquette thus reinforced the precise hierarchy through which the king controlled his subjects.[2] Nobles and bourgeois, ministers and valets, family and mistresses all assumed their identity in relation to others and, most critically, to Louis XIV. From his rising in the morning (levée) to his going to bed at night, and including his meals, walks, and receptions of ambassadors, court rituals affirmed Louis's authority.[3]

Netherlandish art also contributed to French culture during Louis's reign. Louis XIV kept both Flanders and Holland, with its prosperous global trade, firmly in his sights. Holland's economy included a vast market for art, with artists and dealers selling works at various price points, and in different styles.[4] Not only Northern paintings but also Northern artists came to France to decorate the royal palaces. Nonetheless, scholars of French Cultural Studies seldom attend to Netherlandish realist art as it mediates the monarchy's power during Louis XIV's reign. The French style under Louis XIV remained distinctly un-Dutch and, given the contemporaneous academic ideal that privileged noble subjects, anti-Dutch.[5] Rather than narrate histories of kings and gods, Netherlandish realist art describes the everyday. Yet we cannot fully appreciate the French monarchy's promotion of Louis XIV's image without examining Netherlandish realism as a countervailing intellectual force within France.

I use the designations *Northern realism* and *Netherlandish realism* to refer to the naturalistic style of art prevalent during the Renaissance and the Dutch Golden Age. Dates for Dutch Golden Age art vary, but discussions typically begin in 1585, when Antwerp fell to Spain, provoking the migration of many artists and intellectuals from that city to the Dutch Republic, and extend throughout the seventeenth century and the first decades of the eighteenth century.[6] Many of the masterworks associated with this movement were produced between 1650 and 1680. The large span of the Dutch Golden Age correlates closely with Louis's XIV's birth in 1638 and his death in 1715, and the peak years of Dutch artistic production correspond with some of the most remarkable years of his reign.

Netherlandish indicates art from both Flanders and the Dutch Republic (the *Low Countries*), which comprises a subset of Northern Renaissance art that also includes art from Germany. I limit my examples to Flemish and, principally, Dutch works. *Holland* (*La Hollande*, in French) here refers to the Dutch Republic, also called the *United Provinces*, meaning the independent Northern Netherlands. The Dutch Republic was a confederation of seven individual states that rebelled against Spain in 1568; declared their independence from Spanish control in stages over the period 1579 (date of the signing of the Union of Utrecht treaty, which founded the Republic of the Seven United Provinces) through 1581 (date of the Act of Abjuration renouncing the King of Spain); and achieved status as an independent state in 1648 at the conclusion of the Eighty Years War. *Flanders* (the *Spanish Netherlands*), in the south, remained part of Spain.[7] The most specific designation to *Holland* was and remains the region of the country that includes Amsterdam. I reserve the designations *Flemish* and *Fleming* for artists from Flanders, including those working in Paris.

I also use the term *Dutch realism* as a general reference to Netherlandish art from both the north and south because the history of the sixteenth and seventeenth centuries redrew frontiers.[8] As a consequence of wars, the Reformation, and changing fortunes in commerce, many artists and tradesmen migrated. This movement affected urban populations of Amsterdam, Antwerp, Delft, Haarlem, Leiden, and Utrecht, as well as Paris. In the seventeenth century, moreover, the Dutch School continued to develop the realistic emphasis of Flemish masters Jan van Eyck, Robert Campin, Hieronymus Bosch, and Pieter Brueghel. *Crowning Glories* contrasts this realism with the cultural production in France during Louis XIV's reign dedicated to promoting his image.

The rise of science in the seventeenth century and the rationalism that characterized the classical period in France had no real equivalent in the myths, histories, and allegories that French artists and writers used to bolster the image of the king. Painters and playwrights who benefitted from the court's patronage composed their works with an eye to balance and order, certainly. The various elements of their compositions, however, conformed to a unique ideal of Louis's glory. I use *unique* to convey a singular quality, or oneness, of elements that cohere to produce an image of the king's power. In contrast, Northern realist art focused on the specific identities of different things. Artists depicted exceptional objects of rare beauty as well as ordinary objects that formed part of daily life. They described their world with exacting detail.

Important differences between the Flemish School, which included many court painters, and the Dutch School notwithstanding, both traditions developed a considerable body of work devoted to secular subjects. The emphasis that these artists placed on precise description has profound implications for the formation of knowledge in France during the reign of Louis XIV. Recording objects in ways that valued the observer function, the Northern tradition was decidedly unlike the art and literature that the French court championed as part of its propaganda campaigns for the Sun King. Netherlandish realism engaged the viewer in a process of interpreting the world that was at odds with the monarchy's efforts to fashion an idea/ideal of the king's absolute authority through a reliance on grand historical and literary narratives. Flemish and Dutch artists offered the French unfamiliar views, scenes of other lands and traditions. They also presented the French elite with an alternative way of organizing information. Examining images and texts that typify French court culture during Louis XIV's reign and the Northern realist tradition of the same period, I study how each work functions as a map, or grid, for knowledge. Netherlandish realist painting offered a different aesthetic and, even more important for my study, a different epistemological orientation than the arts and literature produced to celebrate Louis XIV. Dutch art, in particular, opened lines of intellectual inquiry that the French monarchy might have found threatening, if only it had looked beyond the value, both aesthetic and monetary, that Northern works held as collectors' items.

Northern art entered France's royal palaces and private residences throughout Louis XIV's years in power.[9] Despite the many points of contact between the France and both Flanders and Holland during this period, however, scholars who examine the culture of the Sun King pay scant attention to the integration of Netherlandish art in France as part of the State's exploitation of the arts to build the king's image.[10] Art historians have studied the lines of transmission and economic forces that situate Northern and French art within a larger European network. Literary scholars and cultural historians of the court of Louis XIV have analysed the relationship between court spectacle and the exercise of power via the arts. In this context, however, the specific connection with Northern realism has not claimed the attention that it deserves. This book aims to rectify that omission.

In the seventeenth century Holland emerged as a major economic presence within Europe, while France became the single most important political and military power. Wars in the Spanish Netherlands and Holland expanded France's territories and prestige. Louis XIV's increased control, however, came at a serious cost for France, as calculable in both lives and debts. The cultural production that I explore takes place against the backdrop of French dominance, on the one hand, and persistent political, religious, and economic strife, on the other. I focus on the contribution of Northern realism to cultural life in France during the years of Louis XIV's reign and its aftermath.

Resplendent with mythical figures and historical allusions, the arts in France were instrumental in transforming the man who became king into an imposing figure. The aura of the king seemed to permeate the court unrestrainedly. Jean-Baptiste Colbert relied on the "Petite Académie" for propaganda, which operation oversaw the production of the king's image in various media.[11] Louis's contemporaries did not witness this process uncritically, however. Modern historians and literary scholars have interrogated the nature of power that the king wielded, examining his failures along with his accomplishments. To the weight of this historical opposition, I add one silent source: Netherlandish realism.

I describe what it would have been like for members of the aristocracy and the bourgeoisie to experience the art and literature produced, collected, and discussed in France during Louis XIV's long reign as this cultural activity included Netherlandish realist painting. I study images and texts supportive of the monarchy's efforts to consolidate power as these efforts are in turn mediated by the integration of Northern realism into French court culture. *Crowning Glories* expands our sense of the diverse factors at play in the French imaginary during this period of intense cultural production by the court.[12] *Imagination* here denotes a system of thought conditioned by images and texts; it is a cognitive schema. The *imagination*, or *imaginary*, a term I also use in this context, does not refer to any person's or group's thoughts. Individuals had differing opinions about what they saw and read. Focusing instead on how the visual arts and literature shape possibilities for knowledge, I examine how the court's propaganda fashioned not only a message but also as a way of thinking, that is, a system for classifying and understanding. Like the proverbial round peg that does not fit into a square hole, some thoughts are inconsistent with the formal system organizing images and texts. One cannot locate difference in a system that tolerates only similarity. The French monarchy cultivated Louis's likeness, whereas Netherlandish realist art emphasized differences. This conflict, I argue, has significance for the history of ideas in early modern France.

Cultural historians have addressed the topic of knowledge and knowledge systems with renewed vigour, including studies of libraries, collections, and the systems used to organize them. For the early modern period in Europe this research involves natural histories and encyclopedias as well as literary texts. From Michel Foucault's groundbreaking studies, through Peter Burke's social histories of knowledge, Ann Blair's study of "information management" as related to the design of reference books, and Jacob Soll's analysis of Colbert's library and organization of information for the French State, scholarly interest in patterns of thought has broadened our understanding of the early modern period.[13] In my study the locus for knowledge is not a library or a reference source but rather the minds of French viewers who contemplate the appeal of Northern realism at the same time as they experience images and texts that the French court produced to celebrate Louis XIV.

I examine the compositional design of paintings, plays, and other cultural artefacts. More specifically, I analyse the patterns of elements in images and texts, arguing that these patterns order knowledge.[14] I propose two fundamental models of thought. Whereas the arts in France stress analogy and similarity, Northern realist images emphasize the defining characteristics of objects. The Northern tradition in effect reverses the logic of the French court's propaganda. Dutch images rely on an open system of relations, an order of things as varied as the eclectic objects that the artists chose to paint. Dutch artists designed their compositions in ways that inventoried their lives. Describing the various things that people produced, used, and admired, their images constituted an expansive and heterogeneous system of knowledge. French artists and writers created an integrated system; they exalted Louis XIV by comparing him to historic figures and gods, that is, by developing a single paradigm of heroic glory.

Official court painting, theatre, and prose in France share few commonalities with Northern realist art of the same period. I use the term *official* to refer to works celebrating the king or otherwise sanctioned by the crown. In France the arts produced in conjunction with the powerful monarchy had little in common with the art market in Holland and the estimated millions of images that entered private homes of all social classes, taverns, and other public spaces there as well as in collections abroad.[15] To the degree that it constituted a record of the things in the world, Netherlandish realist art was an anomaly in the French court, where the king's glorious image shone so brilliantly and abundantly. Northern painters assembled objects in order to emphasize their individual characteristics, much as a collector assembled items within a cabinet. Northern realist paintings thus defied the French monarchy's totalizing impulse. Northern artists frequently accentuated the naturalness of what they described by positioning objects within their images in an apparently random fashion. Such studied efforts to record the world at it really was, but with a heightened sense of beauty, stood in marked opposition to exquisite French works that portrayed the king with an elevated sense of drama and grandeur.

Dutch art further represented the kind of thinking about knowledge that would assume a major role during the second half of the eighteenth century with Denis Diderot and Jean le Rond d'Alembert's *Encyclopédie* [*Encyclopedia*] (1751–72). To explain the arc of intellectual history that led from French absolutism to the Enlightenment, we must appreciate the empirical emphasis of Northern realism. This book traces that history, beginning with court art produced during Louis XIV's reign and extending through the conception of the *Encyclopédie*. Individual chapters explore how the Northern realist tradition would have inflected the French response to the monarchy's propaganda and the brilliant spectacle of Versailles. *Crowning Glories* thus expands our notions of power, systems of representation, and the formation of knowledge in classical France.

The Culture Wars

Netherlandish art comprised a relatively small but nonetheless significant aspect of French culture during the years of Louis's reign. The influence of Renaissance Italy on the arts in France was far more dominant during this period. Northern art, however, was not new to France in the seventeenth century. Prominent artists worked at courts throughout Europe, and many, including French, Flemish, and Dutch artists, trained in Italy. The persistent presence of Northern realism within the culture devoted to the Sun King is arresting nonetheless. Viewed alongside the allegories, commemorative art, and works of theatre representing royal power, Northern realist art seems out of place.

To appreciate the mindset of the French living in the king's orbit we cannot attend only to the *portrait du roi* [king's portrait] and the "fabrication" of Louis XIV's image, as two seminal works refer to this critical phenomenon.[16] The perfection of oil paints in the Netherlands allowed artists to depict the world with unprecedented precision, and their influence was recognized throughout Europe. The French had long prized the most esteemed Northern artists, and the taste for Netherlandish art in France continued to be felt over the course of Louis's reign in privately held as well as in royal collections. The French were aware of the exceptionally vibrant visual culture taking place in Holland, and some sought out particular artists' works. Balthasar de Monconys, a French diplomat and art connoisseur, included in a journal entry for 1663 a reference to a visit he made to Johannes Vermeer during a stay in Delft.[17] Although Vermeer had no painting to show him, Monconys viewed one of Vermeer's works in the home of a Delft baker. The ambassador's account demonstrates the French elite's awareness of the Dutch art market. His taste for genre paintings included Vermeer and also Gerrit Dou, one of whose works Monconys purchased during the same trip.[18] As many artists inspired others to work on similar themes and compositions, we can assume that Monconys knew not only the paintings of Vermeer and Dou but also certain works by Gerard ter Borch, Pieter de Hooch, Gabriel Metsu, Frans van Mieris, Caspar Netscher, and Jan Steen.[19] Monconys would likely have shared his interests with associates in Paris. The influence of Netherlandish realist art in Louis's France thus extends beyond a history of the numbers of paintings purchased and catalogued in inventories. It surpasses even the equivocal judgments of those devoted to French and Italian influences who looked down upon Netherlandish artists.[20] Such negative opinions, too, demonstrate that Northern realist art was very much part of the French world of ideas during Louis's reign. *Crowning Glories* takes the measure of that idea.

With its emphasis on accurate description, Northern realist art presented French court society with an alternative way of organizing knowledge. The logic inherent in such realist art had more in common with knowledge based on a universal, mathematically formulated science than it did with the art decorating French royal palaces.[21] Committed to cataloguing identities of diverse things in the world, Dutch Golden Age art correlates with important tenets of French Enlightenment thought. Artists and authors who identified with the court did not anticipate the changes that would occur in the decades following Louis XIV's death that marked the decline of the monarchy. Yet some of the early signs were there, in the form of Northern images that were framed and hung in palaces and private homes belonging to France's elite. *Crowning Glories* contributes to our understanding of the rise of empiricism in the early modern period by taking into account the unsung role of Northern realism in shaping French court culture during Louis's reign.

Art, knowledge, and power intersect in the exceptional presence of Netherlandish painting in France, where it was the enemy hiding in plain sight. Many Flemish artists formed part of the vast operations to decorate royal residences and, as part of that project, to memorialize the king's glory. In Holland cultural production was associated primarily with urban centres rather than with the court, and with the wealthy burghers who controlled the cities rather than with a monarch. In Amsterdam and other Dutch cities, the bourgeoisie had already "risen," and art had become a widely accessible commodity. Dutch art informs the viewer about domestic space; the marketplace; international trade; the appetites for food, drink, sex, and the moral codes designed to limit indulgences. It exposes the viewer to the fruits of a modern economy, the growth of other urban centres, and land that the Dutch recovered from the sea. Dutch paintings collectively represent a cultural archive; they present a compendium of Dutch life, a record of Dutch society's values as reflected in the activities of families in their canal houses, in city streets, and in nature.

In France Northern realist art contributes to the "Ludovican episteme," a term I coin to refer to the system of knowledge that artists and writers set in place during Louis's reign and its aftermath. The French were aware of the different "look" of Northern realist images.

Northern realism bore scant resemblance to the allegories that adorned French royal palaces. The images of homes, canals, and other urban views in Dutch works contrasts markedly with the myths that elevate Louis XIV's actions to the level of the gods. *Crowning Glories* will allow the reader to gauge the impact of Northern realism as French nobles and bourgeois in Paris and Versailles would have experienced it, side by side with the expansive art, theatre, and orations celebrating Louis XIV's victories and his legacy. Chapters are designed as composites of French and Northern realist works, in keeping with the two strains of cultural influence that members of French court society would have experienced together, in varying measures, during Louis XIV's years in power.

Official French court art designed to promote the king's power relies on the principle of analogy likening the king to the divine. Relations of similitude reinforce the notion of a political hierarchy in which Louis's subjects submit, in ascending order by rank, to Louis XIV. This concept served to unify under one ideal of monarchic power a society in which divisions between individuals, religions, and ideas were never really erased. Conflicts between the king and his challengers and critics; class distinctions, notably between the nobility and the bourgeoisie; tensions between Catholics and Protestants; the need to reconcile the search for truth in science with acts of faith, and acts of faith with the monarchy's prerogatives – these differences marked the long reign of Louis XIV. For all the court's success in elaborating an idea of Louis's glory and power via the arts, therefore, we cannot imagine that the public's response to specific works of art and theatre was either uniform or static. Further contributing to that unease, I argue, was Northern realism, which went against the grain of the cultural production in France that championed the king's authority.

It is possible to associate French allegory with Dutch allegory; French religious painting with Dutch religious painting; French history painting with Dutch history painting, and so forth, in a discussion of French and Dutch mentalities, but I adopt a different approach. *Crowning Glories* contrasts official French court art – images and texts that support the interests of the monarchy in France – with Northern realism as competing epistemological systems. I analyse the patterns that take shape within the artist's or writer's work. A viewer or reader absorbs the patterns (series of identical objects; series of similar objects of different values; series of different objects, etc.) along with the description of individual objects (a king on horseback; a woman feeding her child, etc.). The process of perceiving the work is not fully conscious. A viewer who contemplates a portrait of Louis XIV in a decor punctuated with fleurs-de-lis that also includes an Apollonian motif would no doubt associate the flowers and Apollo with Louis and with France. The same viewer, however, would not dwell on the relations of analogy, the function of the triple references to the king (Apollo, fleur-de-lis, France) on which the composition is based. Similarly, a viewer seeing a Ming vase and tobacco in a Dutch image might appreciate that both objects are imports, exotic items from different continents. The individual characteristics of each object – the colours and forms that identify it – also capture the viewer's attention. The juxtaposition of objects enhances their singularity. The Asian porcelain contrasts with the product from the English colony of Virginia; the enduring value of the ornate vessel contrasts with the impermanence of the commodity that the Dutch traded, processed, and smoked, and in some areas successfully planted.[22] The viewer who identifies these objects as things belonging to Dutch daily life, i.e., as specific content, would not likely pause to consider these same objects as elements that exist in particular relation to other elements, that is, as identities within a classificatory system, or taxonomy. Yet the repetitive French and the varied Dutch patterns reveal different foundations for organizing knowledge. I argue that such divergence in conceptual systems has profound implications for the consolidation of information during Louis XIV's reign, his use of cultural production to control his subjects, and the potential for Northern realist art to interrupt that process.

Patterns of interconnected elements function within the mind as taxonomic categories; they comprise the classification system for cataloguing information. While I am building here on Foucault's analysis of the episteme, my approach deviates from his in significant ways. Foucault associates relations of similitude with the Renaissance; he associates relations of difference – contiguous relations – with the classical episteme. I show that during the classical period French court culture, through its inclusion of Netherlandish realist paintings, evidences both types of relations. In a further distinction from Foucault's treatment of the classical episteme, I focus attention on the formal design of images and texts, on visual language as well as written language and discursive power.[23] I am concerned with how ideas are "filtered" in the viewer's and reader's mind, how ideas fit within categories of knowledge. In the seventeenth century philosophers, notably Descartes, debated what it meant to perceive the world and to represent the world as thoughts.[24] I study paintings and texts as examples of integrated systems of thought, as these order what viewers and readers understand about the world.[25]

Patterns of similarity create a sense of stability and inevitability. French artists and writers therefore rely on likenesses to depict the king's absolute power. Resemblances might include two portraits of Louis XIV in the same work; images and speeches that provide portraits of both the king and his heir; or, in the theatre, situations that mirror each other, including serial confessions or deaths. Other elements exist within French works destined for the court audience, of course, but these are typically symbols of Louis, signs of his glory, and thus parts of the same paradigm. The more versions of Louis's power one sees, the more the analogic model appears harmonious and true. The Northern model, however, turns that idea on its head. Realist artists from Flanders and Holland emphasize specific attributes of objects to create a vast compendium of the world. These artists assemble a visual catalogue of different shapes, textures, and materials that identify things within urban and country settings. Compared to this aggregate knowledge of disparate elements, the French court's singular dedication to signs of Louis's glory seems restricted and artificial.

Dutch Golden Age painters are particularly interesting in this regard. Dutch artists embed moral themes tied to Calvinist admonitions against indulging in earthly pleasures within images that also celebrate Holland's tremendous commercial success.[26] Describing homes with a focus on people and their possessions, Dutch images bear witness to the achievements of the bourgeoisie, the burgher class. Artists depict material wealth with a dignified restraint, balancing attention to luxury items with depictions of utensils and ordinary foodstuffs. They oppose suggestions of licentiousness with the harmonies of elegantly clad musicians. Dutch paintings capture the world of things, even in more modest settings. Through scenes of private homes, courtyards, taverns, cities, as well as in still lifes, Dutch artists transform ordinary experiences into images whose richness reflects both Holland's material success and the enduring appeal of art that celebrates it.

French artists and writers construct a narrative of Louis XIV's glory that extends from ancient heroes through his reign, that of his heirs, and into the future. They compare Louis to the Greeks, Louis to the Romans, and, inevitably, Louis to himself in order to create, via such iterations, a sense of his ineluctable and inexhaustible power. Conversely, Dutch artists reveal a fascination with description and the display of objects that is consistent with a scientific, empirical approach.[27] Research on

Dutch art looks beyond iconography to consider the image as a record of what the eye observes.[28] Scholars have correlated the visual emphasis of Dutch art, which captures the appearance of objects absent a predominant narrative emphasis, with advances in science in seventeenth-century Holland, especially improved lenses that made visible previously invisible things.[29] What Dutch artists record has particular resonance in France not only because they describe a foreign culture but also, and most consequentially for the history that I trace, because Dutch art oriented French perceptions away from grandiose myths towards a more empirical understanding of the world. As a result, the monarchy's control of information appears less inevitable, less inexorable.

Assembling a Collection: Bearing Witness to the Effects of Dutch Art on the French Imagination

In the chapters that follow I frequently associate a single Dutch painting with a French image or text. These pairings are not intended to suggest the influence of the Dutch work on the French work. The paintings are representative of genres of Netherlandish realist art with which French courtiers would have had some familiarity. Apart from works in royal and elite collections, I focus on the attributes of realistic painting outside the acquisition history in France of Netherlandish paintings. Rather than present a linear study, I analyse the disruptive effects of Northern realism within the French context. The French art and literature that I incorporate into my discussions exemplify key features of court culture associated with the monarchy's devotion to the cult of the king. My chapters bring Netherlandish realist art, predominantly Dutch works, to bear in several discrete contexts that define cultural production during Louis XIV's reign. I argue that Dutch images would have acculturated the French to think beyond the limits that the monarchy imposed.

My notion of opposed French and Dutch models builds on art historical distinctions. I do not refer to mentalities, tastes, or world views. Rather, I situate, from the French perspective, the simultaneously alluring and menacing presence of Northern realism within French court society. I argue that Netherlandish realist art had the subtle effect of presenting a different aesthetic valued as part of a long art historical tradition of transnational exchanges but undervalued for its potential to destabilize the collective imaginary in France. Dutch art represented the interests of a powerful merchant class, an alternative class and economic structure that, given tensions between the nobles and the bourgeois in France, had the potential to weaken Louis XIV's relations with his subjects. This threat is all the more apparent given the ways in which the logic, or basic formal relations, of Northern realist art countered the logic of the propaganda that the court developed via the arts in France. The Northern emphasis on empirical observation focused attention on the reality behind the appearances, and thus subverted the allegorical cover that the crown adopted to impose the image of Louis XIV's eternal glory.

Much was made in seventeenth-century France of the play of appearances. Writing to his son and heir, Louis XIV observed: "Les peuples sur qui nous régnons, ne pouvant pas pénétrer le fond des affaires, règlent d'ordinaire leurs jugements sur ce qu'ils voient au dehors, et c'est le plus souvent sur les séances et les rangs qu'ils mesurent leur respect et leur obéissance" [The people over whom we rule, being unable to penetrate the depth of things, normally base their judgment on what they observe on the surface, and most often they base their respect and obedience on privileges and rank].[30] We have no reason, however, to believe that the French were so gullible. Political and literary debates regularly tested their critical acumen.[31] The French had come to identify power and beauty with elaborate images and ubiquitous tributes to the king. Insofar as the French associated the court's manipulation of appearances, including the production of painting, theatre, and other media, with value for France and for themselves, they had reason to accept court spectacle as worthy of their admiration.[32] Those who were intent on securing access to Louis to advance their own careers were inclined to accept the "staging of power" at court as Louis intended, with obedience. The rituals and performances were signs of the king's majesty and examples of his will to exert control. Louis's subjects were not, however, uncritical, incapable of seeing the manipulations. As La Rochefoucauld's *Maximes* attest, the principle of self-interest was alive and well at court: "L'amour-propre est le plus grand de tous les flatteurs" [Self-interest is the greatest of all flatterers].[33] The point is telling: moralists, satirists, memorialists, and others were quick to expose the negative interests, that is, the costs for individuals of the court's regulations and refinements. The feigned behaviour of courtiers seeking the king's favour meant that they lived what La Bruyère characterized as *une fausse vie*, a false life: "Il y a une fausse modestie qui est vanité; une fausse gloire qui est légèreté; une fausse grandeur qui est petitesse; une fausse vertu qui est hypocrisie; une fausse sagesse qui est pruderie"

[There is a false modesty, which is vanity; a false glory, which is levity; a false grandeur, which is pettiness; a false virtue, which is hypocrisy; a false wisdom, which is prudery].[34]

These writers called into question the foundations of court life. Other voices directly challenged the power of the monarchy and Louis XIV's own efficacy as king.[35] One of the unintended consequences of Northern realist art in France during Louis's reign, however, was that it, too, represented a challenge to the order of things imposed by the crown. Flemish and Dutch artists depicted nothing that directly challenged the monarchy or France. The king and those whom he appointed to oversee his projects valued the realistic techniques of the Flemish artists whom they employed. Nonetheless, the Flemish and Dutch artists' commitment in their native countries to ordinary scenes of daily life fell well short of the French academic standards for noble subjects. Netherlandish realist art therefore posed no threat to the prominence of French art, or to the court's efforts to promote French products, including art and other decorative pieces. During Louis's reign, however, Northern realist art allowed the French to see, literally and figuratively, that much was to be gained by looking beyond the studied effects of court culture.

Here the Dutch vanitas is instructive. Still lifes displaying objects such as skulls, watches, hourglasses, and partly consumed pies and cheeses evoke death and the fragility of life. They caution the viewer against worldly indulgences. Yet the viewer's pleasure in contemplating the objects displayed counters the painting's moral message. The visual appeal of such images suggests that ambiguity had its own value, that of authenticity. Dutch paintings serve as repositories of knowledge. Northern artists' depictions of flowers, shells, insects, and assorted objects feed the human ambition to catalogue, to assemble knowledge about the world. In these images beauty serves a different master than it does in France, where the will to power trumps the will to know.

In the chapters that follow I assemble a range of visual and textual examples that are as eclectic as they are revealing. I mean to recreate the experience of Northern realism as it existed, unobtrusively but consequentially, in the French imagination. Individual works of art and of literature (theatre, memoirs, orations, inscriptions, and documents) serve to define two major strains of thought in the early modern period, as they extend from the French court of Louis XIV through the Enlightenment. I do not exhaustively survey either the arts in France or the

Netherlandish realist tradition, and many important figures in the respective histories of these cultures are elided. I do not discuss individual works by Peter Paul Rubens, arguably the most sought-after Flemish painter of the seventeenth century. Known for the grand manner of history painting that typified much official French court art, including mythological scenes and allegories, Rubens died in 1640, when Louis XIV was only two years old, and three years shy of becoming king. While Rubens's art exerted a sustained influence within the French court, particularly at the end of the seventeenth century, his work offers no real(ist) counterpoint to the court style under Louis XIV. Nor do I discuss the French artist Georges de La Tour, whose paintings in the early decades of the seventeenth century reveal the intimacy and the naturalism of the Northern artists as well as a strong Caravaggesque influence. His 1630s nocturnes, images of figures captured in candlelight, suspend the viewer between the real and the ideal, the worldly and the spiritual. In the last decades of La Tour's life until his death in 1652 the artist's renderings of candlelight often diminish the sharpness of bodies and objects, emphasizing the simplicity of geometric forms. Although it evidences qualities of the Netherlandish works that I discuss, La Tour's style is not as explicitly empirical as this art.[36] I include two paintings by Rembrandt Harmensz. van Rijn but much of his vast oeuvre lies beyond the descriptive emphasis of my study. The celebrated landscapes of Claude Lorrain are likewise excluded from the collection of paintings that I analyse. I rely on Nicolas Poussin's work for my comparison with the landscape techniques of Jacob van Ruisdael.[37] We find exceptions to the descriptive art that I associate with Northern realism in Rembrandt's histories and in the work of other Dutch Golden Age artists devoted to allegory, myth, and the Bible. Many more examples than I can analyse, however, confirm the tendency to catalogue the world that I ascribe to Netherlandish realist art.

The paintings and texts that I study are representative of the styles and the themes of the dominant systems of knowledge operating in French court culture and Northern realist art. The French elite need not have directly viewed any work that I present to have had an idea of Netherlandish art. A very general sense of what separated French art from Netherlandish art and what distinguished French society from Dutch society was enough to engage members of Louis's court in basic comparisons of art and literature produced for the French court's admiration, on the one hand, and the visual culture of the Dutch Republic and its depictions of the exceptional character of ordinary lives, on the other. I have selected paintings whose subjects ultimately matter less, however, than the compositional design of the images. The latter enables us to appreciate the systems of knowledge that individual artists and authors set in place to describe the world.

Part 1 of my study establishes the interplay of French court art and Northern realism through a series of critical encounters between France, Flanders, and Holland. Adopting a comparative approach common to interdisciplinary studies and the notion of *histoire croisée*, I "correct," or compensate, for the emphasis in French Cultural Studies on Louis XIV's image through an examination of points of intersection of French visual and textual production with Northern realism.[38] Referencing Holland's urban culture as it contrasts with cultural production in Louis's France, I develop two models to explain the orientation of ideas in French and Northern art. Similitude grounds the court's message in France; difference marks the power and richness of Northern realism.

French artists worked in consort with the monarchy to support the king's political ambitions. In Holland artists expressed the values of the merchant class. Both traditions produced objects of beauty and enduring significance. In each culture the viewer or reader assembled knowledge consistent with the specific ordering of elements within the artist's or writer's composition. The question becomes: How were individual works structured? What objects were included? Were they placed symmetrically or randomly? Were objects grouped in pairs or set off individually? Are we looking at images within images? If so, are they similar or different? The answers to these questions and others like them allow us to see the patterns of relations that define how parts of the image or text connect to other parts, and those parts to the whole of the work. They create the infrastructure, the set of rules regulating how individual identities relate to each other within a coherent system. A viewer who understands that the painting describes a landscape with people going about their daily lives, or soldiers going into battle, and a reader who recognizes the content of a scene to include a king being celebrated or mourned, has absorbed the logic of these patterns: what repeats, what varies, how categories relate to other categories. While the viewer and the reader focus on the content rather than on the structures through which artists and authors develop the content, the forms tell a critical story about the construction of knowledge. Within individual works discrete patterns of elements shape meaning. The fact that similar patterns recur from work to work within the respective French and Northern realist traditions, moreover, serves to reinforce the sense of a dominant discourse or epistemic norm.

Chapter 1 presents the French and Netherlandish realist models within a sociohistorical context. I contrast portraits of Louis XIV with Dutch still lifes and genre paintings to illustrate the system of knowledge that informs each artistic tradition.

Chapter 2 further analyses the exceptional status of Northern realist art in France. I offer detailed readings of a series of paintings by Adam Frans van der Meulen, Jan van der Heyden, Pierre Patel, Gerard ter Borch, Vermeer, and Charles Le Brun, including the latter's magnificent family portrait of Everhard Jabach, who sold large portions of his collection to Louis XIV. I analyse three different ways in which the French assimilated Northern realism: through inspiration/imitation; through a redirection of the viewer's perceptions; and through the expansion of the royal collection. History paintings that the French monarchy commissioned from the Flemish artist van der Meulen, images whose overt theme is Louis XIV triumphant, situate the victorious French king within a natural setting typical of Northern realism. I argue that the descriptive elements of these commemorative works engage the viewer in identifying and classifying individual elements within the image. Such an interpretive process is antithetical to that created through mythological or allegorical images of official French painting celebrating the king, whose principal elements are integrated into a single paradigm of royal authority. With the Jabach painting the idea of historical portraiture takes yet another turn, for this wealthy German-born collector assumed a critical position in Louis's France.

Part 2 pairs images with texts in ways that emphasize the connections between politics and aesthetics in France. Whereas the first two chapters concern art almost exclusively, the third chapter, on the theatre, forms a bridge to the remaining sections of the book, which integrate prose texts with discussions of art. Proposing that the audience's perceptions of theatrical productions resemble the beholder's perceptions of art, chapter 3 explores classical theatre with an eye to the king's authority. I consider implications of the structures of Dutch genre painting for interpretations of the dramatic performances, as these in turn relate to court spectacle. In chapter 4 that spectacle concerns representations of Louis XIV's death. The monarchy sought to transform the mortal Louis into an immortal sign, the king's body into the king's idealized image. At the French court Northern realism "unthinks" this process. Within the French imaginary, Flemish and Dutch realistic depictions occupy an intermediary space separating the king's material existence and the more spectacular and monumental image of Louis XIV that the monarchy constructs.

Chapter 3 studies how Dutch art, with its open frames and multiple narrative threads, challenges the notion of order and resolution traditionally associated with the denouements of French classical theatre. The association of painting and theatre would have been natural, as both involve a beholder. Reading Molière's *Tartuffe*, Corneille's *Horace* and, as the centrepiece of my analysis, *Suréna*, along with Racine's *Phèdre*, I argue that the French audience familiar with Dutch art would be armed with a different logic for interpreting the theatrical performance, one that resists the notion of closure through which the playwrights artfully and artificially quell the revolt. Dutch art did not encourage the French viewer directly or implicitly to question the king's legitimacy. It did, however, provide, at times quite literally, another window onto that world. Northern realism tolerates divergent ideas and incongruous pairings. Genre paintings by Emanuel de Witte and Vermeer involve competing registers of meanings as well as indefinite boundaries. Applied to classical tragedy, the Dutch model encourages the audience to register not only the sovereign's law as it excludes difference but also the voices and thoughts that his law would suppress. I show that Dutch genre painting, by assembling heterogeneous elements within an "open" design, attenuates the effects of the French theatre that support monarchic ideals. The Dutch model effectively foils the French classical tradition's emphasis on integration, that is, the dramatist's elimination of elements that challenge the king.

Chapter 4 examines official commemorations, beginning with an almanac that celebrates Louis XIV's recovery following a dramatic illness as it contrasts with Steen's more raucous celebration in *The Dancing Couple*. Although it honours the king's life, the almanac also evokes his eventual demise. Building on this notion, I design the remainder of the chapter to resemble the five-act structure of a classical tragedy featuring Louis XIV. This chapter thus mirrors my study of classical theatre. I begin with the Franco-Dutch War, also called the Dutch War [Guerre de Hollande] (1672–78), and the king's loss of the Maréchal de Turenne (Henri de La Tour d'Auvergne, Vicomte de Turenne) and continue through the written record of Louis's death. Louis's image serves here as the sole referent for the narrative of his glory, as this narrative depends on and appropriates the role of Turenne, his military commander. I analyse descriptions of the king's death in light of

Rembrandt's painting of the anatomist Dr Tulp to consider the status of the royal corpse, and the rituals associated with it, as they sustain an ideal of France increasingly at odds with science. My final "act" in this tragedy compares a domestic scene by de Hooch with a French portrait of the royal family, *Louis XIV et sa famille* [*Madame de Ventadour with Portraits of Louis XIV and His Heirs*], which reflects the intimacy of Dutch genre paintings. Despite its dynastic emphasis, this royal portrait conveys both the glory and the decline of the Bourbons, just as it evidences the limits of the French analogic model for structuring knowledge.

Considering objects and ideas that define court culture both during Louis XIV's reign and following his death in 1715, part 3 develops the issue of his legacy. *Legacy* here refers to the production of art that conveys the grandeur of Louis's reign at Versailles and through it, France's relation to Holland. In the Franco-Dutch War Louis set out to annex land to expand his empire and to end Dutch competition with French trade. There would be more wars following the 1678 peace, and more competition. The flamboyant, propagandistic style of the French court, including the expansive art of Le Brun at Versailles, would lose considerable ground during the latter half of the eighteenth century. Those years marked a period of the Enlightenment in which the desire to "tout connaître" [know everything] won out over the monarchy's efforts to sustain, intact, the image of Louis's glory. Measured against that standard, the visual culture of Holland came closer than Le Brun's ceiling to predicting what France would inherit from the royal collections.

The sweep of material in chapter 5 is deliberately broad, extending from Poussin's *Un temps calme et serein* [*Landscape with a Calm*], painted 1650–51, a decade before the start of Louis's self-government in 1661, through Le Brun's ceiling for the Galerie des Glaces [Hall of Mirrors], completed 1679–84, which features Louis XIV's personal history and rise to power. Poussin's painting and Ruisdael's *View of Haarlem with Bleaching Grounds* provide reference points for contrasting the French style as it developed during Louis XIV's expansion of Versailles. In Le Brun's ceiling the Dutch appear frequently as the enemy. I compare the allegorical model that Le Brun uses to support the image of a victorious king with Dutch realism, arguing that Louis XIV's decision to appear as himself, rather than as a god, in Le Brun's ceiling images raises important questions about allegorical and empirical systems of representation.

Chapter 6 studies the pervasive influence of Northern realism on the French imagination that follows Louis XIV's decline. Beginning with La

Bruyère's depiction of the French version of Tulip Mania, I compare the moralist's art with Northern still lifes.[39] The taxonomic emphasis of the moralist's text invites further comparisons with the article on tulips and articles on Northern art, notably the Dutch School, in the *Encyclopédie* (1751–72). These articles confirm, even more than the authors intend, that Northern realism contributed to both the art and the science of description, a topic vital to Diderot's conception of the encyclopedia project.

Crowning Glories explores how Northern realism posed a challenge to the French monarchy's hold on ideas. The Dutch did not declare war on France with their art, but they contributed to a revolution in French thought a century later. The Dutch artists' emphasis on observation and recording combined the specificity of description with an open compositional format for establishing the relations between elements. It is remarkable that this art continued to have a place in the French imagination during the very years in which Louis XIV vigorously campaigned to impose his image on his subjects and throughout Europe. French artists and writers offered a model of continuity: references to ancient glories ensured continuity in the present and predicated a similarly glorious future for Louis and the nation. Northern realist art instead exposed, and made beautiful, the world as it was and as it would continue to be assembled during the eighteenth century, part of a vast knowledge project, one piece of evidence at a time. As that century progressed Enlightenment ideals replaced practices supporting the absolute monarchy, and the popularity of Dutch works grew. This art historical development was perhaps unsurprising, since the subjects and smaller scale of these works were so antithetical to the grand ambitions of the monarchy that Louis XIV fashioned. I argue that these collector's items not only contributed to the allure of genre paintings by eighteenth-century French artists, including Jean-Baptiste-Siméon Chardin, whom I discuss in my concluding pages, but also attest to the continuity of empirical thought from the Northern realist images that populated the imagination of French courtiers viewing seventeenth-century collections through the publication of the *Encyclopédie*.

We can trace a line, albeit oblique, within cultural history from the Dutch Golden Age painters in Holland, via the court of Louis XIV, through French artists of the second half of the eighteenth century. We begin to determine the importance of empirical observation and realistic description in the arts in France in the seventeenth century, where it existed as a decidedly foreign presence and where it exerted a decidedly foreign influence. Northern realist art that entered the French imagination in Paris and at Versailles during the reign of Louis XIV for the most part existed without attracting undue attention, yet it was a force of intellectual change. Along with images of Louis, his victories, and his progeny, Flemish and Dutch realistic images presented the French with a record of things whose individual properties could be measured, described, and classified. Northern artists mastered imitation, the perfect rendering of objects, both ordinary and precious. They also mastered the *in medias res* experience, glimpses of people's lives for which there was no beginning and no end, and for which there was often no single interpretation. These artists thus captured the *in medias res* of knowledge always deferred. That was a message for posterity.

PART ONE

Divergent Patterns

1 Two Models in Context: Northern Realist Art in France

Fruits et riche vaisselle sur une table [*A Table of Desserts*] by Dutch artist Jan Davidsz de Heem formed part of Louis XIV's collection. It received broad acclaim in France. That response was understandable, as the painting is a masterpiece of the still life genre and an example of the venerable tradition of Northern art. De Heem's painting was, quite simply, both beautiful and valuable. Moreover, the theme of abundance would have resonated well with the French court, devoted to its own magisterial style. The painting is full to the brim.

Nonetheless, de Heem's painting represents an intriguing addition to the French royal patrimony for a number of reasons. French artists also produced many still lifes, but the genre was less popular in France during Louis's reign than it was in Northern Europe, where it had been flourishing since the sixteenth century.[1] French still life painters, moreover, were greatly influenced by the works of Northern artists. Two areas in Paris supported French still life painters in the first half of the seventeenth century: the streets around the Pont Notre-Dame and Saint-Germain-des-Prés. Artists in these parts of the city would have encountered Flemish and Dutch artists who visited the capital. The Saint-Germain area, moreover, was home to several artists who were also merchants, including both the French Protestant Louise [Louyse] Moillon and Jean-Michel Picart, born in Antwerp, to whom I refer below, who sold Dutch, Flemish, and Italian works in their shops.[2]

Alexis Merle du Bourg notes that images featuring still lifes from the first half of the seventeenth century reflect the dual influences of Flemish and French traditions, as evident in the *La marchande de fruits* [*The Fruit Seller*] (ca. 1635–45) by Pieter van Boeckel, called "van Boucle" in French. To the left of a table featuring many baskets of fruits and

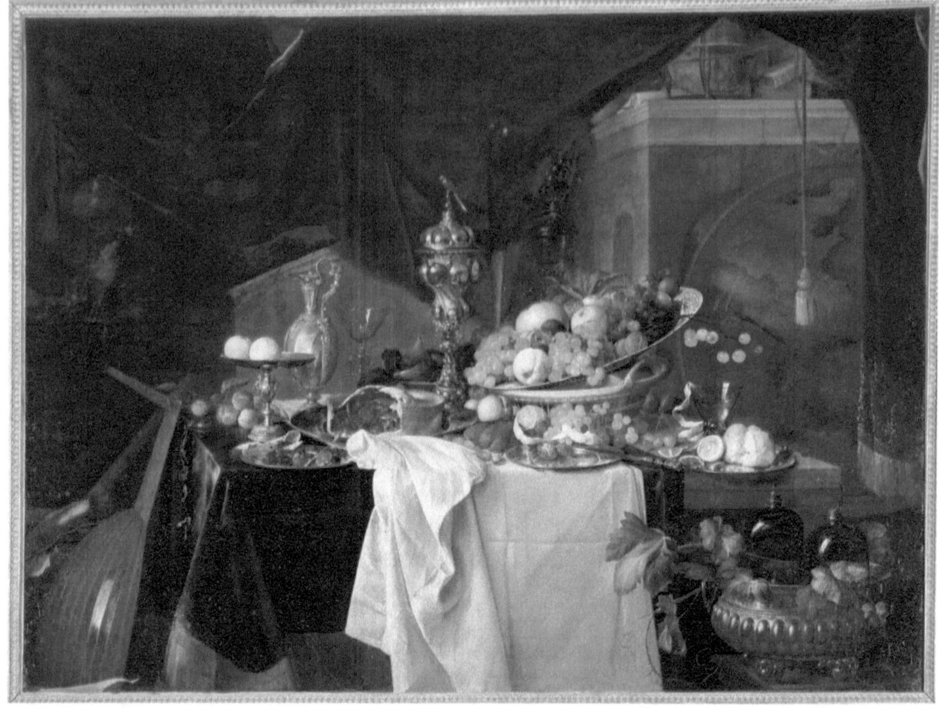

1.1. Jan Davidsz. de Heem. *Fruits et riche vaisselle sur une table* [*A Table of Desserts*]. 1640. 149 × 203 cm (58.7 × 79.9 in). Musée du Louvre. Photo courtesy Louvre, Paris, France/Bridgeman Images. https://www.louvre.fr/en/oeuvre-notices/table-desserts.

vegetables stand a young gentlewoman in French clothing and an old woman merchant in Flemish dress.[3]

If French society was familiar with Northern still life techniques, the genre was still considered inferior to historical subjects closely associated with the French court. French art commissioned to decorate Louis's palaces and to commemorate his victories had a different focus: the cultivation and promotion of Louis XIV's image. How then do we explain the French excitement for de Heem's painting, which makes no reference to Louis? De Heem's image invokes the notion of mortality that pervades many still lifes, and the consequent need to be reserved in one's worldly indulgences. The watch with the blue strap draped

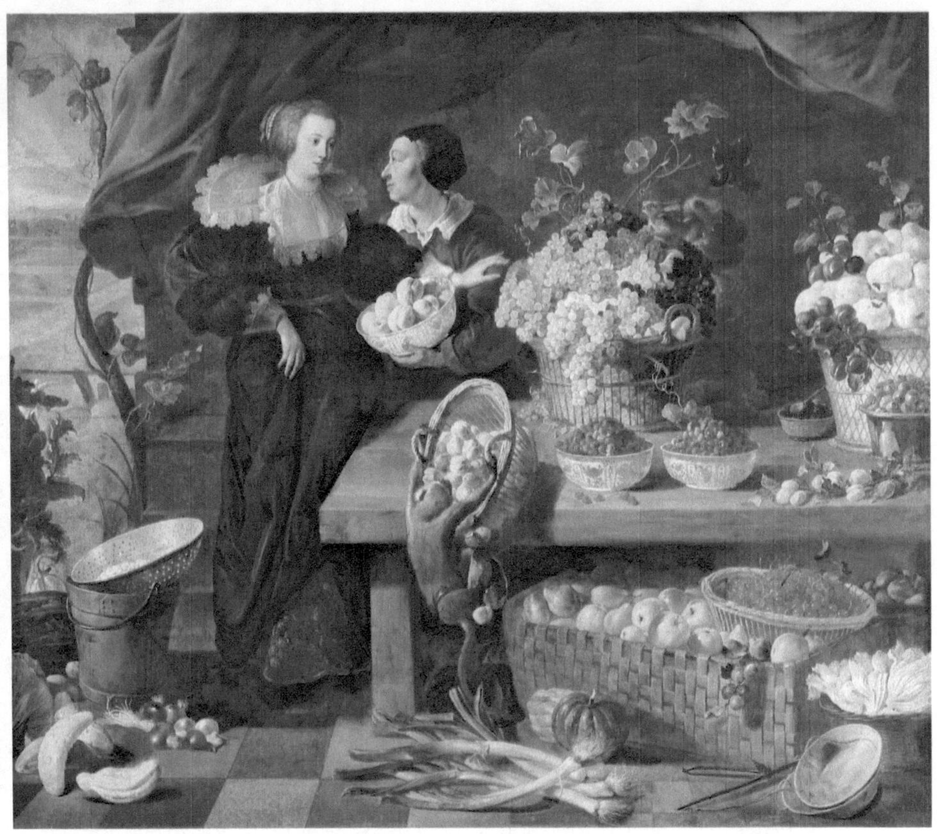

1.2. Pieter van Boucle. *La marchande de fruits* [*The Fruit Seller*]. Ca. 1635–45. 199 × 238 cm (78.3 × 93.7 in). Musée des Beaux-Arts, Arras. Image courtesy Musée des Beaux-Arts, Arras, France/Bridgeman Images. http://webmuseo.com/ws/musenor/app/collection/record/12388?vc=ePkH4LF7w6yelEhJFfqYAYMU-NA84JOokJtYlJyRCCwqFYAoragos6QYXEHDAgQAtkgvrQ$$.

down the left side of the table signals time passing. The partially eaten pie indicates that life is being consumed. On the upper right a globe and pile of books suggest the inevitable decay of all physical things, including texts, their authors, and the knowledge that they record. The bright yellow lemons from warmer climes attract the eye but remain sour to the tongue. A lute and a recorder similarly resonate both positively and negatively: they evoke a distinct sensual pleasure but also the idea that the instruments produce harmonies whose chords and rhythms are fleeting. The bread and wine evoking the Eucharist; the cherries symbolizing paradise; the peaches and apples, both forbidden fruits; and the shrivelling apple peel all suggest mortality and the impermanence of life. Such signs of mortality are counterbalanced by religious allusions to Christ's redemption, via the bread and wine, and also the grapes. Prosperity and the satisfaction of earthly delights is expressed here through the variety of fruits, painted with exquisite textural precision, as well as by the blue and white porcelain bowl, silver platters, and other costly serving pieces.[4]

De Heem captures the beauty of objects, masterfully integrating the bounty of nature within a richly ornate display of acquired wealth and prestige. Whatever their status as cultural symbols, however, the various objects that appear in the image function as discrete elements whose identities the artist captures via exacting depictions of their shapes, colours, and textures. Incorporating both iconographic and realistic details, the artist evokes the need to abandon earthly pleasures in pursuit of spiritual transcendence even as he offers for the beholder's pleasure a scene of sensorial delights within a palatial setting. The items on the table include many different categories of things: foods, drinks, serving pieces, sensory perceptions, with an emphasis on the plurals, multiples. No single idea, even that of the vanitas, unites all elements in the image.

De Heem's painting multiplies associations between the many items it sets out for the viewer's contemplation. The ambiguity of double messages, however, was decidedly not the *modus operandi* of the arts under Louis XIV. In France, Louis was the patron and privileged subject of all royal commissions, from the visual arts and architecture, including the all-important expansion of Versailles and its magnificent gardens, through the theatre, and more. Artists, architects, and writers did not equivocate on issues of Louis's authority.

The Dutch referred to lavish still lifes as *pronkstilleven* (*pronk* means sumptuous or ostentatious). The Dutch context, which Simon Schama has aptly described as an "embarrassment of riches," moderates one's obvious pleasure as a viewer and consumer of things with moral warnings against worldly desire.[5] We can well imagine how the sumptuousness of this image pleased Louis XIV and members of his court, who were devoted to extravagant depictions celebrating the king's authority and magnificence. The French monarchy, too, enjoyed baroque excesses before yielding to the rational, proportional, and symmetrical classicist aesthetic. The viewer of de Heem's painting perceives the studied randomness of a meal in progress. What stands out in the Dutch image is less its lack of restraint, therefore, than the concentrated assemblage of things. Although the elements of the image are realistically detailed, the artist implausibly brings together fruits from different seasons, along with an assorted collection of wine glasses and vessels, and a combination of foods available to eat and foods partially eaten. The artist distributes many different objects throughout the image, accentuating their individual identifying characteristics. This formal arrangement encourages the viewer to consider each object separately rather than as integral parts of a master narrative of a great meal. To a French court accustomed to narratives of kingly accomplishments, the still life was oddly still. The clock is hanging over the edge; time is running out. For the French, however, the arts served to master time, to immortalize history, the master history of Louis's glory.

The dramatic difference between heroic narratives in France, on the one hand, and the tendency to catalogue life in Holland, on the other, motivates my decision to consider what it would have meant to French viewers to perceive Northern realist art during Louis XIV's long reign. My pairing of France and Holland is not arbitrary. The two countries were enemies in war and rivals for foreign markets. Their societies, moreover, held to very different cultural practices. Netherlandish art nevertheless enjoyed a place of distinction in France during the years in which Louis ruled. The French admired, collected, and displayed Northern paintings along with their more extensive collections of Italian and French art.[6] Flemish and Dutch images were aesthetic objects appreciated for their beauty and their status. Yet their decorative function and value as investments, as precious items within royal and other elite collections, tell only part of the story of the place of Northern realism within French culture during Louis's reign. I explore how Northern realism, as a system of thought, had the potential to influence French perceptions and to affect the formation of knowledge in France. I argue that Northern realism mitigated the effects of French court art devoted to the cult of the Sun King.

Collecting Art

The flourishing of the arts during Louis XIV's years in power owed much to Jean-Baptiste Colbert, who oversaw France's finances and cultural affairs (1661–83).[7] As minister in 1661, Colbert served as patron of the

Académie royale de peinture et de sculpture [Royal Academy of Painting and Sculpture] founded 1648, for which institution he selected Le Brun to serve as director and *premier peintre du roi* [first painter to the king]. Under Colbert's direction French manufactories received State support for luxury goods, with Versailles serving as the ultimate setting for the furniture and tapestries produced at the Manufacture royale des Gobelins [Gobelins Manufactory] in Paris.[8] France "became a showcase for the inventions, precious merchandise, artifacts, and works of art that were the aesthetic models of the European market."[9] Colbert thus instituted a system for State support of the arts, which he viewed with an eye not only to benefitting France economically but also to promoting the authority of the French monarchy at home and abroad.[10] The principal subject of the vast cultural production that Colbert and his successors oversaw was Louis XIV.

Virtually nothing in this elaborate cultural campaign recommended Netherlandish art to the French. Yet the French continued to collect it throughout Louis's reign. The Northern Renaissance tradition, including Flemish, Dutch, and German art, also produced fine allegorical and religious painting. By the seventeenth century, however, Dutch painters specialized in other genres, retaining the attention to realistic details characteristic of the Northern school since the fifteenth century, and consistent with recent advances in optics that supported a visual culture devoted to seeing more and better.[11] Their craft stood in stark contrast to the more flamboyant style of French official art during Louis XIV's reign, with its deep Italian roots. While the political and religious orientations of Holland (majority Protestant) and Flanders (majority Catholic) were different in this period, and although painterly styles could vary significantly, the realistic description common to the art of these two nations meant that they resembled each other (and German art) more than either resembled official French art in this period. Netherlandish artists elevated the ordinary into an aesthetically pleasing experience, whereas artists in the service of the French crown (not only painters but also playwrights and other writers) elided the ordinary in favour of elaborate tributes to Louis XIV's extraordinary status.

In France the *grande manière* refers to the most elevated style of narrative painting, which Leon Battista Alberti defined as *historia* in his fifteenth-century treatise *De pictura*.[12] French court art incorporated ancient history, mythology, and scripture to depict a morally significant action capable of revealing universal truths. Artists and writers relied on all manner of historical figures to translate the eternal glory of Louis XIV. In 1667 André Félibien continued to place history at the top of the hierarchy of subjects, emphasizing that artists must not merely copy nature; they should idealize events to reveal their universal essence (*imitare*, in Italian).[13] Valorizing the painter's intellectual expression over his mechanical copying of appearances (*ritrarre*), Félibien's hierarchy made no mention of genre painting. The Dutch artist and theorist Gerard de Lairesse stressed the superiority of historical painting in his 1707 *Groot schilderboek* [*Great Book on Painting*]. No less an artist than Rembrandt produced historical, allegorical, and biblical paintings. Much Dutch Golden Age art, however, concerned scenes of everyday life rendered in a naturalistic style. This art went against French style, which was supported by academic criteria. Netherlandish art received its share of criticism in France for this reason. Yet these realist images formed part of the life of the French elite during Louis XIV's reign. It remains a curious fact that this art, too, had a place in the French imagination during the period that devoted so much attention to myths and symbols. Unlike Dutch society, members of the French elite did not collect large number of images demonstrating the artist's careful execution of an expanding array of things in the world. They did, however, know of this art and its emphasis on the familiar, knowable world.

Although Netherlandish painters devoted themselves to copying life and therefore to mastering appearances through a superior technique (perspective, colour), they conveyed far more than the simple imitation of objects. The best artists found in such subjects, if not the nobility of history painting, then certainly the refined nobility of aesthetic perfection. The latter does not conform to traditional art historical criteria, which in France at this time decry art that relies on technical proficiency rather than the expression of an ideal.[14] Yet the beauty that Flemish and Dutch artists convey is, I argue, inseparable from an empirical appreciation of the world. In their work description is both an art and a science. In France, where the standards for judging art were so dramatically different, the visual pleasure associated with Dutch art brought the French further into knowledge, for their art also served as a repository of the things of the world.

Since the sixteenth century, when the oversupply of paintings in Antwerp helped to develop the Parisian market, the demand for Northern art continued to grow.[15] Antoine Schnapper provides an elaborate account of individual collections. He describes the transactions of particular Flemish merchants selling art in Paris, including Picart, originally from Flanders but later naturalized a French citizen. Picart supplied French buyers with many Northern paintings, including copies of Dutch and Flemish originals. The inventories of Nicolas Estienne, *dit* Perruchot, similarly attest to the range of artists, genres, and prices of Northern works available in Paris.[16]

Northern art entered Louis XIV's royal palaces as well as the city and country homes of distinguished French collectors, princes, *parlementaires*, financiers, and bourgeois.[17] Le Brun's 1683 inventory of the royal collection lists ninety-eight paintings belonging to the "Ecoles du Nord" [Northern schools], including paintings by Antoon van Dyck and Rembrandt.[18] The royal imprimatur only added to the value of these works and their growing influence among the Parisian elite.

By the end of Louis's reign wealthy Parisians had accumulated substantial collections of Flemish and Dutch art. Studying *inventaires après décès* [post-mortem inventories], Olivier Bonfait records that financiers (80 per cent of this group were nobles, but only 46 per cent were "nobles au premier degré") imitated the collections of the king and princes.[19] The financiers were more "modern" in their tastes than the *parlementaires*: the distribution of works in their collections resembles that of later eighteenth-century collections. Referring to statistical tabulations by genre and class as well as by "écoles" of inventories registered 1710–20, Bonfait confirms the significant presence of Netherlandish art in private homes. Inventories for *financiers* contained an impressive number of paintings by Flemish and Dutch artists: "Dans trois inventaires sur six, les œuvres de peintres nordiques constituent l'essentiel ou la totalité des œuvres attribuées" [In three inventories out of six, works by Northern artists comprise the principal or total number of attributed works].[20] These inventories presumably contain works collected throughout the owners' lifetimes. They reflect the steady gain in popularity of Northern art in France.[21]

Inventories show that the French tastes included major genres, notably landscape, history, still life, and genre paintings.[22] Paintings, prints, and drawings were available at different price points, which helped to develop the taste for art among both nobles and bourgeois.[23] Dutch works became increasingly popular purchases in the final years of Louis XIV's life and well into the next century. After 1700 art writers recommended "as a matter of course" that French collectors acquire Dutch and Flemish painting, and by 1750 the price of Golden Age Dutch genre painting in Paris had increased significantly.[24] By the mid-eighteenth century Dutch genre paintings and still lifes were all the rage in Paris. Copies of Flemish and Dutch originals, including both paintings and engravings, which, being less expensive and easier to reproduce in significant numbers, had a wider circulation, and were persistent features in fairs, lotteries, and auctions as well as via specific art dealers.[25]

History of Strife

While the transnational circulation of art ensured that the French nobles and bourgeois maintained contact with Northern art during Louis's reign, it is curious to think of Netherlandish realism, with its distinctive subjects and painterly style, displayed in French palaces and private residences, many of which also included portraits of Louis XIV.[26] Numerous points of contact existed between the French, the Flemish, and the Dutch during Louis XIV's reign. As discussed above, the international art market contributed to the French elite's awareness of Northern art generally, and the worldliness of Dutch culture more particularly.[27] Other encounters between the two cultures were conflictual, the result of Louis's determined attempts to conquer Holland.

The French monarchy's sponsorship of the arts occurred against the backdrop of political and economic tensions between the two nations and within Holland itself.[28] The Dutch Republic steadily surpassed the commercial success of Flanders and Brabant in the Southern Netherlands. From early in his reign the French king saw a rival in the Dutch Republic and an opportunity for expansion in Flanders, which remained in Spanish hands.

The War of Devolution (1667–8) proved to be but an opening gambit for the young, ambitious king. Louis took advantage of Spain's failure to pay the dowry promised to France in exchange for Queen Marie-Thérèse's renouncement of the territories belonging to her father, Philip IV. Led by the distinguished military commander, the Maréchal de Turenne, whose many successful battles garnered the king's support, the French entered the Spanish Netherlands on 24 May 1667 and occupied much of Flanders and Hainault. The following year Louis, Prince de Condé invaded Franche-Comté. The Dutch joined forces with England and Sweden, and this "Triple Alliance" pressured Louis to negotiate peace. The Treaty of Aix-la-Chapelle signed in May 1668 obliged the French to return all of Franche-Comté and most of the Spanish Netherlands. France did retain some of the fortified towns it had acquired, but Louis failed in his efforts to eliminate all Spanish territories on France's eastern border, which situation led in part to the Franco-Dutch War.

The later war engaged France, along with her allies England, Sweden, Munster, and Cologne, in a struggle against the Dutch Republic, which formed a "Quadruple Alliance" with the Holy Roman Empire, Spain, and the Electorate of Brandenburg. The Dutch and their allies clearly saw Louis as a threat. Louis clearly saw the Dutch Republic as an opportunity for increasing his control within Europe. France's decision to go to war in 1672 reflects Louis's expansionist goals. The king was intent on reducing Dutch competition and expanding the market for French goods. Religious tensions between Catholic France and the Protestant Dutch Republic also fuelled this conflict. The Treaty of Nijmegen, which ended the war on 10 August 1678, called for Spain to cede to France Franche-Comté and cities in Flanders and Hainaut, while France ceded Maastricht and the Principality of Orange to the Dutch Republic. Louis XIV continued to pursue the dynastic claims of earlier wars for territory in the Spanish Netherlands in a brief war with Spain, the War of the Reunions [Guerre des Réunions] (1683–4).

The Dutch faced significant challenges, enduring internal political and religious tensions. In the Glorious Revolution of 1688 William III, known as William of Orange (descendent of William I, who fought for independence from Spain), supported by Protestants in England, deposed James II, a Catholic, and William's father-in-law. William and his wife (and first cousin) Mary, the new heir to the throne, became king and queen of England in the aftermath of this revolution. James, meanwhile, took refuge in Louis's France.

The change in rulers did not mark end of conflict between France and Holland. From 1688 to 1697 Louis XIV engaged in the Nine Years' War [Guerre de la League d'Augsbourg or Guerre de neuf ans] against the Grand Alliance led by the Anglo-Dutch Stadtholder-King William III, the Holy Roman Emperor Leopold I (Austrian Habsburgs), King Charles II of Spain, Victor Amadeus II of Savoy, and the princes of the Holy Roman Empire. The succession to the Spanish throne was not secure, as Charles II had produced no heir. Believing that through marriage alliances France could make a claim for the throne against Leopold I, Louis crossed the Rhine in September 1688. The king's ambitions were thwarted, however, as the Europeans joined forces against him. The war extended into the overseas colonies of the major powers. England and France fought in the Americas and in India.[29] Louis thus became engaged in a nine-year global war for which his army was ill prepared.

The War of Spanish Succession [Guerre de succession d'Espagne] began in 1701. Louis placed his grandson Philip on the Spanish throne, where he reigned as Philip V. In 1712 Philip renounced any claim to the French throne but retained control of Spain and the Spanish colonies. In 1714 Emperor Charles VI signed the Treaty of Rastatt with France under which the Spanish Netherlands became the Austrian Netherlands. Louis XIV was by then an old man. He would die approximately eighteen months later on 1 September 1715.

Long and costly wars had weakened France in the final decades of Louis XIV's reign, but his legacy does not rest entirely with his defeats.[30] I focus in this book on the glory decades and the propaganda that accompanied them because the culture that developed around the king during these years has masked to some degree the impact of Netherlandish realist art during the early modern period. France's unmet territorial ambitions represent the collapse of a certain ideal of power. Yet in French court society an enhanced intellectual power, the ability to fashion a world of ideas based on empirical observation, remained a strong foundation on which to continue to build. The route from the culture of Versailles towards Enlightenment thought unexpectedly takes us through the visual production of Holland and the realism that marks Golden Age still lifes, genre paintings, landscapes, and cityscapes. This route required no detour, however, as French court society was familiar with the style and subject matter of these paintings.

The French under Louis XIV had learned to associate power with lavish art celebrating the image of the king. The logic of that association inevitably faltered, however, when the French admired examples of Northern realism, which equated power with commercial success and, most importantly for my study, with knowledge, the artist's ability to describe the world. We can imagine that for court society during Louis's reign Dutch art compelled interest because it offered views of a society whose practices were unlike those of the monarchy. If the French were all too clear about socio-economic differences between the two nations, however, they were less likely to have registered another critical element of Northern realism that challenged the presumptions of the monarchy. The French crown cultivated the arts to exert influence as much as it did for aesthetic reasons. Northern realist art represents a different episteme, that is, a different way of ordering knowledge. What made Dutch paintings seductive from the French perspective, although they would not have characterized it in this way, was that these paintings appeared foreign but unthreatening; they were examples of an art historical tradition long recognized in the courts of Europe. The Dutch, however, were not only France's enemies in war; they were her enemies in thought. Dutch artists presented the French with a different mode of recording history. Their images therefore challenged the monarchy's efforts to "control the message," and impose its will on its subjects and rival nations. Northern realist artists favoured descriptions independent of any grand narrative. That was the science of their art, which relied on the same empirical principles as would later ground the *Encyclopédie*. The presence of realist Flemish and Dutch art in France during the reign of Louis XIV, I am suggesting, did not launch but certainly contributed to the social and intellectual shifts that would mark the Enlightenment.

City Crossings

While wars between France, Spain, and Holland were the most dramatic and politically consequential events of this period, other divisions mark the prevailing cultural influences in each society. In France power emanated from the court, which moved from Paris to Versailles in 1682. Cities were the major commercial and cultural centres of the Netherlands, including Antwerp, in the south, in the previous century until its fall to the Spanish in 1585, and thereafter Amsterdam in the north. Amsterdam received a large influx of migrants from Antwerp, many of whom were Protestants.[31] Religion played a critical role in these years, aligning entire nations under majority Catholic or majority Protestant rule. While France and Flanders were both predominantly Catholic, the Dutch Republic was predominantly Protestant. French Huguenots, including many trained artisans, fled north in different waves over the course of two centuries, seeking a safe haven in which to practise their religion, with the Dutch Republic being a choice exile for them after the Revocation of the Edict of Nantes in 1685.

Based on the divine right of kings, the French monarch's power was believed to be absolute. Louis XIV controlled military decisions and tax collection as well as patronage of the arts. In France the creation of academies and a patronage system meant that not only the material conditions for promoting the arts but also efforts to control the message, to restrict the flow of information that challenged the crown, were matters of the State. In the Dutch Republic the titular head of state, the *stadholder* [city holder], belonged to the princes of the House of Orange. The stadholder's power, however, was primarily asserted in times of war.[32] Government was largely decentralized, located in semi-autonomous cities, where a group of influential merchants and bankers known as regents protected their commercial interests. In the Dutch Republic, therefore, power lay not with the princes but rather with prosperous individuals, many enriched through global trade to Asia, Africa, and the Americas.

Following the Reformation, the Calvinists, who favoured unadorned churches, did not support artists through commissions as the Catholic Church had done earlier. In Holland a market for art grew for wealthy burghers, who bought paintings and prints that reflected their own lives and their own power. Images of acquired wealth were tempered by Calvinist teachings against vanity and earthly pleasures.[33] In this new environment landscapes, seascapes, domestic scenes, portraits, and still lifes depicted people in familiar domestic and public settings. Artists recorded objects, places, and social practices. Scenes of daily life, moreover, were produced in a naturalistic style that stressed authenticity even though artists frequently idealized their subjects. The proliferation of art within private homes included not just the wealthy but also butchers, innkeepers, blacksmiths, and other tradespeople, who acquired works available at lower price points. Describing their world in exquisite detail, artists engaged their patrons in seeing anew. Dutch homes were notoriously full of art. This art encouraged viewers to examine a wide range of observable phenomena, to empower themselves by cataloguing the world. The French, too, would have looked to see what they could identify in these images, a reading strategy that was unlike the skills they practised when identifying the parts of the allegory or myth celebrating Louis XIV.

Cultural borders were porous, and markets for artworks, as for other goods that collectors and consumers valued, regularly crossed them, even as wars continued to modify national frontiers. Not only things but also people crossed borders. René Descartes spent the years 1628–49 thinking and writing in the Netherlands, primarily in Leiden, but also Amsterdam. Rubens painted for courts in Flanders, England, and Spain. Van Dyck also achieved fame as a court painter in England. Both Flemish painters enjoyed an international reputation that garnered commissions from the Catholic Church and sales in major markets throughout Europe. Some artists fled religious persecution; others travelled throughout Europe for inspiration and for work. Rubens, van

Dyck, and Samuel van Hoogstraten, like several of their French counterparts, most notably Poussin, travelled to Rome (Rembrandt, Frans Hals, van Ruisdael, and Vermeer, however, did not). Cultural transference from the North to France is evident in paintings by the Le Nain brothers, who in the first half of the century assimilated qualities of both Dutch genre artists and Caravaggio. When we speak of national artistic traditions, therefore, we must acknowledge repeated borrowings and a certain transnational formation within each culture, although we continue to ascribe certain stylistic traits and thematic preoccupations to Northern realist art that differ from those prevalent in French court art of the period. France, moreover, had been employing French weavers from Flanders, a major European centre for tapestry production since the sixteenth century. Colbert and Le Brun relied on Flemish artisans to decoratethe royal residences. Some Flemings established their own tapestry workshops (*ateliers*) in France, as the demand for their skills was strong.[34]

French Court and Dutch Realist Traditions

Northern artists not only presented different themes but also different formal designs, that is, different ways of organizing elements within the image. In a text or painting the arrangement of elements into patterns determines the range of possible meanings that the reader or viewer is able to conceive.[35] The French monarchy relied on allegory, metaphor, and relations of similarity to reinforce a singular identity of the majestic king, leader in war as in the arts. Northern realism emphasized differences, relations of contiguity, and, frequently, the multivalence of things in the world.[36]

In France, Louis's eternal glory depended on the persistent reproduction of his image. French artists and writers established a paradigm of greatness through a reliance on analogy, likeness. Louis's extended reach from the past into eternity, from the imitation of ancient heroes via his resemblance to their gods, created a vast cultural production by means of an extended metaphor. Northern realist artists concentrated instead on capturing the world as it existed in nature and in culture, as visible to the eye that recorded it.[37] Paintings and sculptures of Louis XIV dressed as a Greek god and as a Roman hero differ dramatically from scenes of Dutch life, a culture awash in things. The French narrative pattern is what I will call motivated, oriented inviolably towards Louis's apotheosis. In this iterative narrative the end replicates the

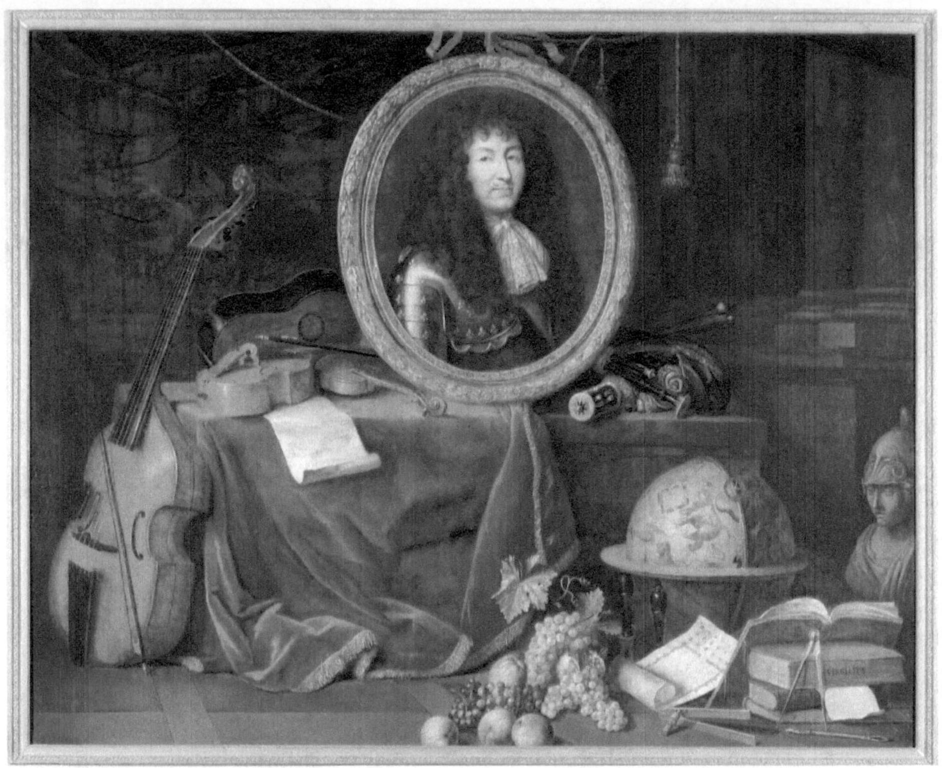

1.3. Jean Garnier [portrait based on work by Claude Lefebvre]. *Louis XIV parmi les attributs des arts et des sciences* [*Louis XIV with the Attributes of the Arts and the Sciences*]. 1670–2. 174 × 223 cm (68.5 × 87.8 in). Château de Versailles. Image courtesy Château de Versailles, France/Bridgeman Images. http://collections.chateauversailles.fr/?%20permid=permobj_07439656-094e-4168-8012-5b23682adedd#53dc26c5-3732-44fe-939d-9ae3c8427c13.

beginning; Louis was, is, and will remain glorious. Conversely, Dutch images of daily life appear to unfold *in medias res*; they are unmotivated. Dutch artists typically present the viewer with a moment of suspended animation – a glimpse of activity minus either a historical referent (mythic, literary, biblical) or clues as to what exactly happened before or will happen after the depicted scene.[38]

A classic example evidencing the French pattern is *Louis XIV parmi les attributs des arts et des sciences* [*Louis with the Attributes of the Arts and the Sciences*] by Jean Garnier, a standard-issue allegory. The king appears in an oval frame, surrounded by fruit, which suggests abundance, and musical instruments, which evoke the harmony of his reign.[39] The globe with the signs of the zodiac refers to the founding of the Académie royale des sciences [Royal Academy of Sciences] in 1666 and the Observatory in 1667.[40] The bust of Athena represents the wisdom and justice of Louis's rule, while the other objects such as the books, one bearing the name of Virgil on its spine, references the heroism of Aeneas.[41] No object, therefore, exists merely as itself; each conveys an attribute of Louis's glorious reign in the *grande manière*.

Louis XIV's image was developed through associations with ancient gods and heroes, resplendent settings, victorious battles. The crown cultivated his glory via metaphors, series of similar images. Louis is like Apollo, like the ancients, like the sun. He imitates in the present the glory of Greece in the past; history is a series of imitative acts that reaffirm his image. The power of the monarchy reflects its efforts to control knowledge, the circulation and currency of ideas, by integrating similar elements into a single paradigm of Louis's glory. In Hyacinthe Rigaud's official portrait of Louis, to take an obvious example, the crown, the sceptre, the sword used in coronation ceremonies ("sword of Charlemagne"), and the royal robes embroidered with fleur-de-lis and lined with ermine are signs that affirm Louis's power. Although he has aged, his legs retain his dancer's youthful appearance.[42]

In the central panel of Le Brun's ceiling for the Galerie des Glaces celebrating the beginning of his self-rule in 1661 (*Le roi gouverne par lui-même* [*The King Governs by Himself*]), Louis XIV, dressed as a Roman military hero, peers at his reflection in Minerva's shield. Minerva, the goddess of wisdom, (wisely) shows him Glory, seated on a cloud. Directing Louis's gaze, and that of the viewer, towards the heavens, the allegory balances an iterative pattern with dynamic movement to suggest the eternal glory of his command. Louis recognizes his glory in his image, as does the viewer.

Similarly, Antoine Coypel's *Louis XIV couronné par la gloire* [*Louis XIV Crowned by Glory*] (ca. 1684–5), an allusion to the Truce of Ratisbon signed on 15 August 1684, celebrates a major foreign policy achievement for Louis XIV in which he secured the eastern and northeastern borders following the War of the Reunions [Guerre des Réunions]. Dressed in ancient imperial robes, the king is crowned by Victory. On

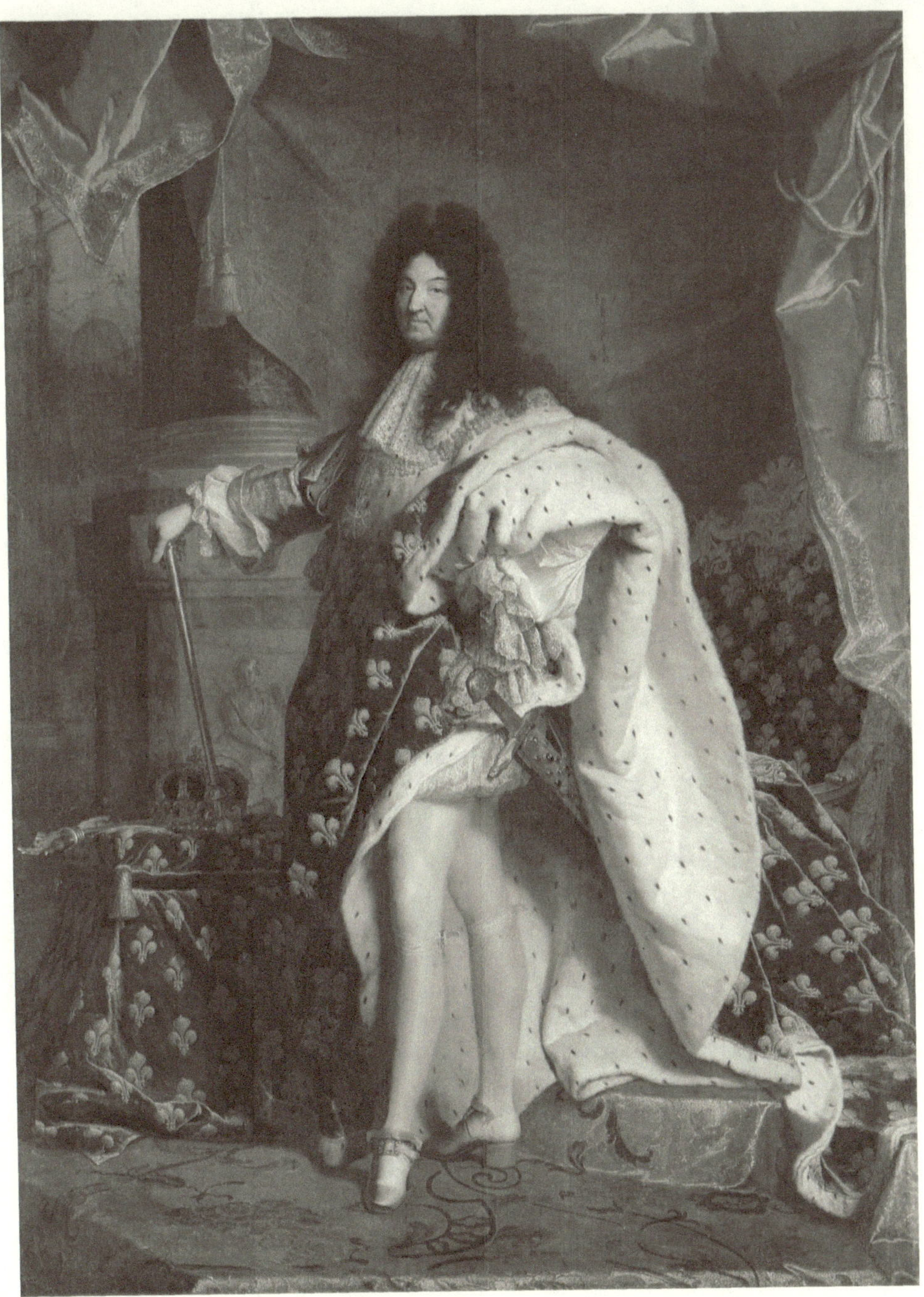

1.4. Hyacinthe Rigaud. *Louis XIV*. 1701. 277 × 194 cm (109 × 76.4 in). Musée du Louvre. Image courtesy Louvre, Paris, France/Bridgeman Images. https://www.louvre.fr/en/oeuvre-notices/louis-xiv-1638-1715.

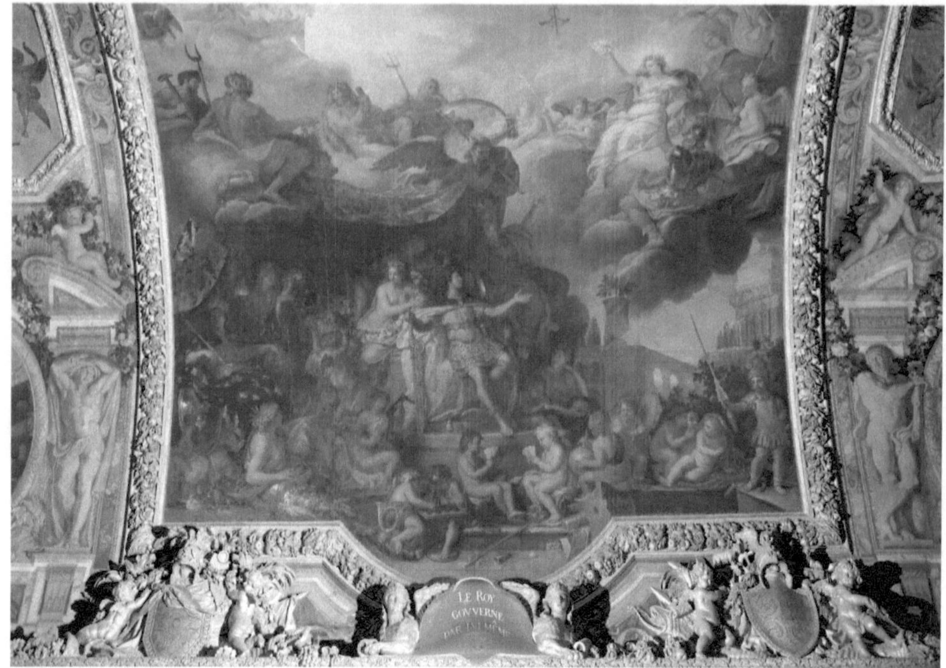

1.5. Charles Le Brun. *Le roi gouverne par lui-même, 1661* [*The King Governs by Himself, 1661*]. Ca. 1680. 103.5 × 99.5 cm (40.75 × 39.17 in). Château de Versailles. Image courtesy Château de Versailles, France/Bridgeman Images. http://www.galeriedesglaces-versailles.fr/html/11/collection/c17.html.

the left, Peace offers the fruits of its horn of plenty, while on the other side of the throne War stands over two lions, symbolizing Spain and Holland, with the eagle representing the Holy Roman Empire.[43] Despite the historic specificity of these elements, it can be argued that as figured here Louis XIV does not compel the viewer to think strategically about the war and its truce so much as to be awed by his presence. Seated on the throne, Louis commands the viewer through his majestic presence in the image just as he imposed his will on Europe via the truce.

Allegories and other images of Louis that rely on his resemblance to ancient gods and heroes contrast dramatically with Dutch still lifes, as evident in the painting by de Heem that forms part of the royal collection. Such paintings not only display an assemblage of diverse things.

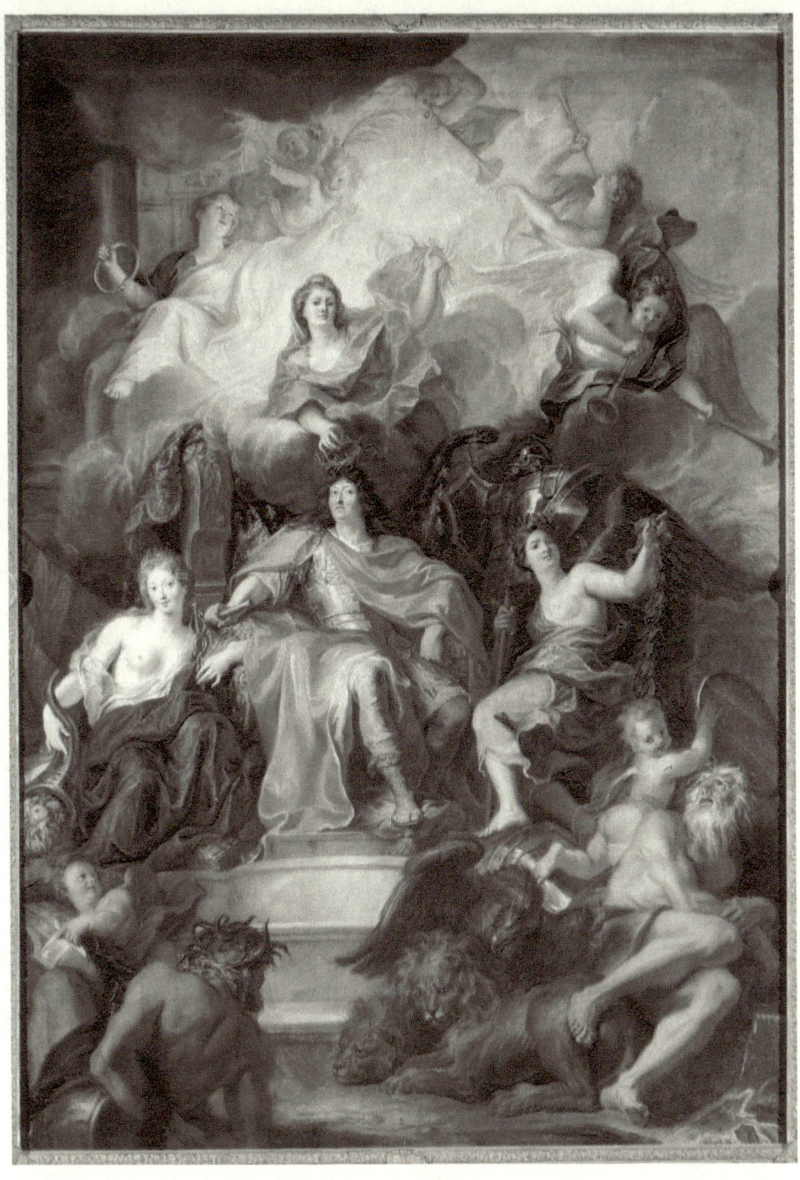

1.6. Antoine Coypel. *Louis XIV couronné par la gloire* [*Louis XIV Crowned by Glory*]. Ca. 1684–5. 197.5 × 136 cm (77.8 × 53.5 in). Château de Versailles. Image courtesy Château de Versailles, France/Bridgeman Images. http://collections.chateauversailles.fr/#0526b6cd-b4a7-41e4-88f4-9531dcda4252.

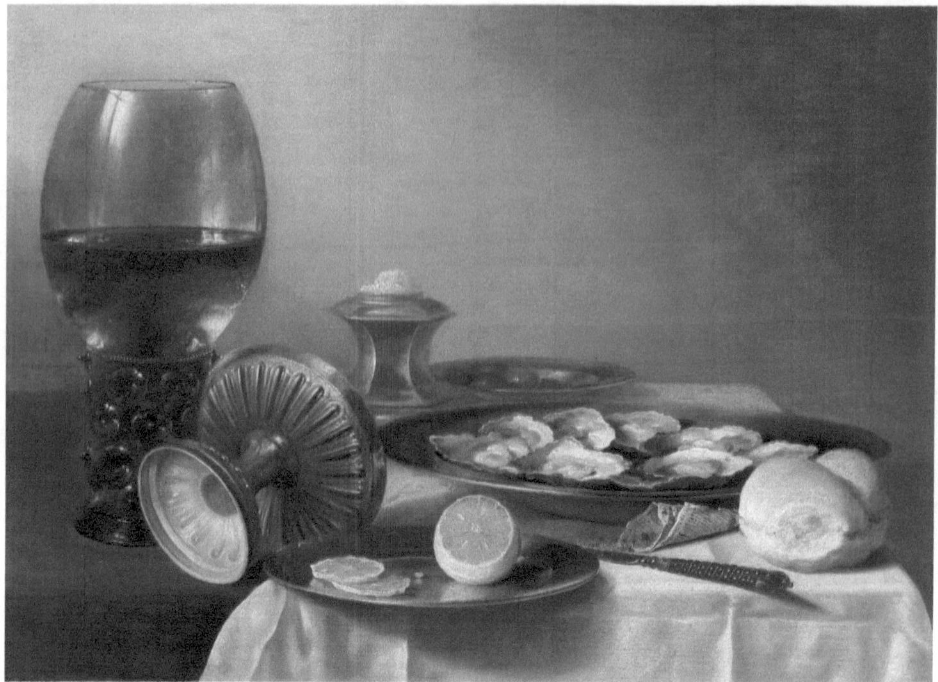

1.7. Pieter Claesz. *Still Life with Wine Goblet and Oysters*. 1639. 50.2 × 70.1 cm (19.8 × 27.6 in). Museum of Fine Arts, Boston. Image courtesy Museum of Fine Arts, Boston/Bridgeman Images.https://www.mfa.org/collections/object/still-life-with-wine-goblet-and-oysters-33570.

They also integrate several layers of meaning that do not cohere into a single history. Pieter Claesz's *Still Life with Wine Goblet and Oysters* resembles the French allegories to the extent that they assemble a variety of objects. Unlike the French examples, however, the meanings of Claesz's still life cannot be unified around a single idea, even though it offers many references to the vanitas theme.

The overturned tazza (serving bowl with short legs) was considered an admonitory reference to the impermanence of earthly life. The bread symbolizes the Eucharist. Oysters represent the Virgin, who protects the baby Jesus in her body like a pearl, and they also have erotic connotations with the female body and aphrodisiacs. Period physicians' treatises, reflecting the medieval theory of the four humours, advised people to balance the consumption of oysters, which are cold and unctuous, with something hot and dry, such as black pepper. The latter, pictured here in a paper roll, is an exotic import of the Dutch East India Company (Vereenigde Oost-Indische Compagnie, known as the VOC).[44] Claesz's painting, therefore, does more than evoke mortality and the concomitant warning of the vanity of earthly pursuits.

Images like Claesz's celebrate life, financial success, and beauty, while proffering moral preachings against indulging human appetites. The careful placement of objects suggesting different seasons, including rare and exotic items, emphasizes the act of displaying, or the art of description, as process of discovery and identification. These images reveal the prosperity that trade brought to those whose ships successfully navigated the seas, and the acquired tastes of a society that saw far more self-determination among the wealthy urban middle class than had existed previously under Spanish rule. Like many still lifes, moreover, this one invites the viewer in with the angled table and the plate that extends into the viewer's space. Meticulously painted, it encourages the viewer to perceive objects as they taste, feel, touch, smell, and, as is the case here, even sound as the knife cracks the shell, revealing the viscous oyster in its luminous essence within the nacre-lined interior.

Thus, while we note the fragility of life as the unifying theme in the vanitas, we also appreciate the image as a palimpsest that presents many layers of meaning. The still life records the importance of secular life, notably commercial success, and the value ascribed to collecting, the acquisition of objects and the knowledge they afford, including many exotic items. A discrete, refined modesty balances the depiction of riches. Dutch artists used fruits and vegetables as symbols, but they also stressed human cultivation of nature – cut fruits, citrus peels artfully draped, prepared cheeses and pies, imported pepper spilling onto the cloth, and decorative salt cellars.[45] Even less sumptuous breakfast or banquet scenes, characterized by their more subdued colour palate, set out objects for the viewer's admiring inspection. Things are arranged with care to suggest accidental and contingent relations, signs of the fragility of life. These Dutch images offer no equivalent to the singular emphasis of French official art. The many portraits and history paintings of Louis XIV meld elements into a single narrative of triumphant heroism. In Dutch paintings the story is precisely that the theme requires no comparable story, no elaborate plot. The viewer delights less in recognizing the moral teaching of a still life than in identifying the various things that appear in the image.[46] That non-story appeals to

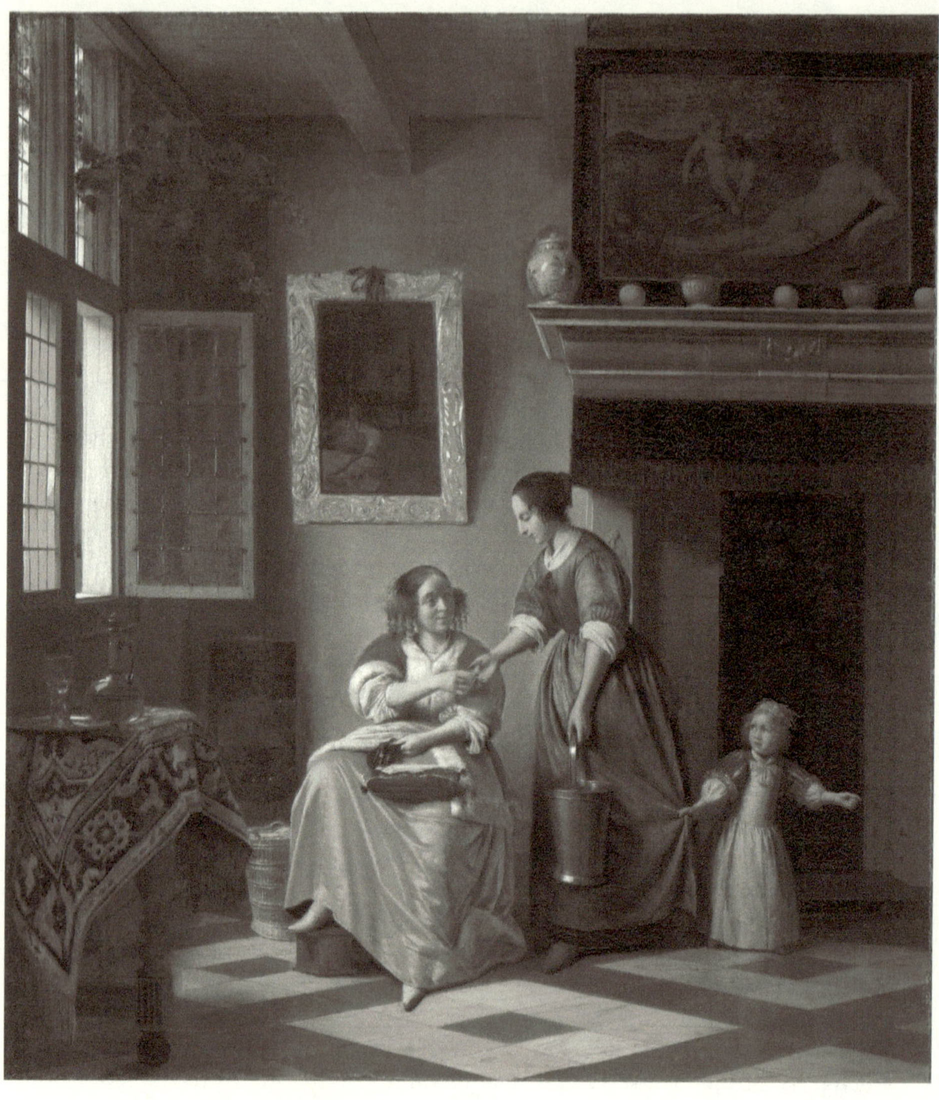

1.8. Pieter de Hooch. *Woman Giving Money to a Servant*. 1670. 67.5 × 59 cm (26.6 × 23.2 in). Private Collection. Digital Image © 2019 Museum Associates/ LACMA, Licensed by Art Resource, NY. https://www.wikiart.org/en/pieter-de-hooch/woman-hands-over-money-to-her-servant-1670.

the economic success of wealthy merchants and those who would imitate them, just as it does to the mind hungry for knowledge. Dutch images offer a catalogue of objects to behold and to identify.

The viewer easily determines the theme of genre paintings. Popular subjects include domestic interiors that define a feminine space by referring to the virtues of women; illicit lovers; and the innocence of children. These themes are by no means mutually exclusive. In de Hooch's *Woman Giving Money to a Servant*, we cannot know the proper context for the primary action depicted: a mistress has interrupted her lacemaking to remove money from her purse, which she hands to her servant, whom a child tries to lead in the opposite direction. Is the mistress paying for the milk in the pail that the servant carries? Is the servant going out to buy milk, or has she just received a delivery from someone still at the door? What does the child want? Have musicians come to sing in exchange for money? Where is the husband? Does the framed image of the nude Venus and Cupid over the mantel suggest anything untoward in the mistress's behaviour? The sense of suspension created by these questions is furthered by the design of the image whose elements draw the viewer in different directions. Intriguingly, leafy branches in the upper left corner appear to enter the room. In seventeenth-century Dutch homes a window cross divided the window into two fixed upper parts and two lower parts that could be opened inside. Is this foliage but an illusion that extends the natural world into the home, and, reciprocally, the home into the world outside? One cannot both look out the window to the left and follow the child's gaze to the right. The viewer does not have a single perspective through which to interpret all the elements of this scene.[47] The compositional design of the image favours the reconfiguration of individual components. The entire scene, moreover, occurs *in medias res*, as part of a narrative that has no clear starting point and no clear resolution.

The image projects a diagonal line extending from the objects on the table (a still life), to their reflection in the mirror, which also includes a canvas on an easel, and then to the framed image over the chimney. In the foreground the glass goblet (*roemer*) used for drinking wine and beer rests on the pewter plate next to a carafe, each about a third full. These objects are viewed from the opposite side in the mirror, where they appear at a different angle because mirrors were hung angled forward to reflect better the evening candlelight. Our gaze travels from the objects on the table, to the somewhat blurred mirrored image of them,

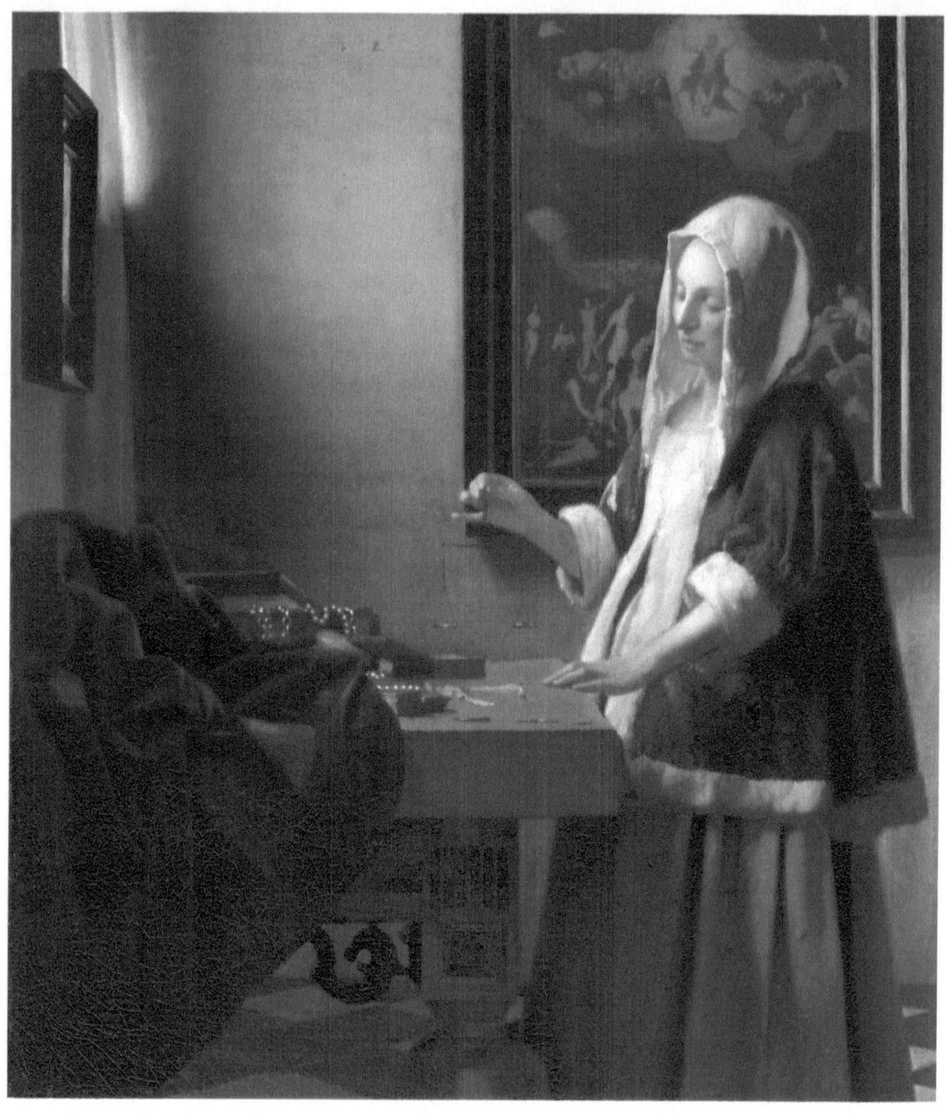

1.9. Johannes Vermeer. *Woman Holding a Balance*. Ca. 1664. 39.7 × 35.5 cm (15.6 × 14 in.). National Gallery of Art, Washington, DC. Image courtesy National Gallery of Art. https://www.nga.gov/content/ngaweb/Collection/art-object-page.1236.html.

and then to the voluptuousness of the female nude over the chimney. The household objects – a glass and carafe, with their associations of wine and pleasure – propel the viewer's perspective all the way to a potentially titillating, but appropriately mythological, and therefore decorous, subject: Venus and Cupid. In this context the voyeuristic gaze is rewarded with an image of love. The painting conveys a double message: the moral rectitude of the lady of the house as it contrasts with the pleasures of the senses and the potential for sin, and the role that money plays in such cases.[48]

Dual and contradictory-seeming messages are a regular feature of Dutch genre painting. Inserted paintings often invite double readings. In *Woman Holding a Balance* Vermeer incorporates a painting of the *Last Judgment*, which at first glance appears as an admonishment to the viewer not to be preoccupied with vain, mortal pursuits like the woman in the foreground, who weighs her jewels. The painting resembles a vanitas. Vermeer's image, however, also invites appreciation for the grace and beauty of this female in her stunning blue fur-lined jacket, a Marian figure who does not look into the mirror hanging on the wall to see her image. She stops short of self-absorption, unlike Vermeer's *Woman with a Pearl Necklace*, who lifts up her necklace in obvious pleasure, the better to study how it affects her appearance.

The woman holding the balance instead appears absorbed with the act of weighing, pondering not only the monetary value of the gold pieces but also the aesthetic value of the objects that artists craft. She invites the viewer to consider the transformative powers of art, and to reflect on the Church rule that would categorically condemn the human urge to take pleasure in material possessions. A viewer cannot know how Vermeer intends us to judge her, only that he covered Saint Michael in the inserted painting, allowing those who study her more latitude to weigh their sins against the value they assign to art. Indeed, if we look closely at the exquisite sparseness of the whitewashed rear wall before which the woman stands in the other painting with her pearl necklace, we are moved to consider how the artist's ability to register the variations of the light beaming through the window makes the wall a work of art in its own right.[49]

By drawing attention to how French and Dutch models organize information in different ways, I am not suggesting that when the French looked at Dutch works they had to learn to exercise their minds in new ways. All humans have the capacity to recognize both similarities, which structure French works, and differences, which ground Dutch

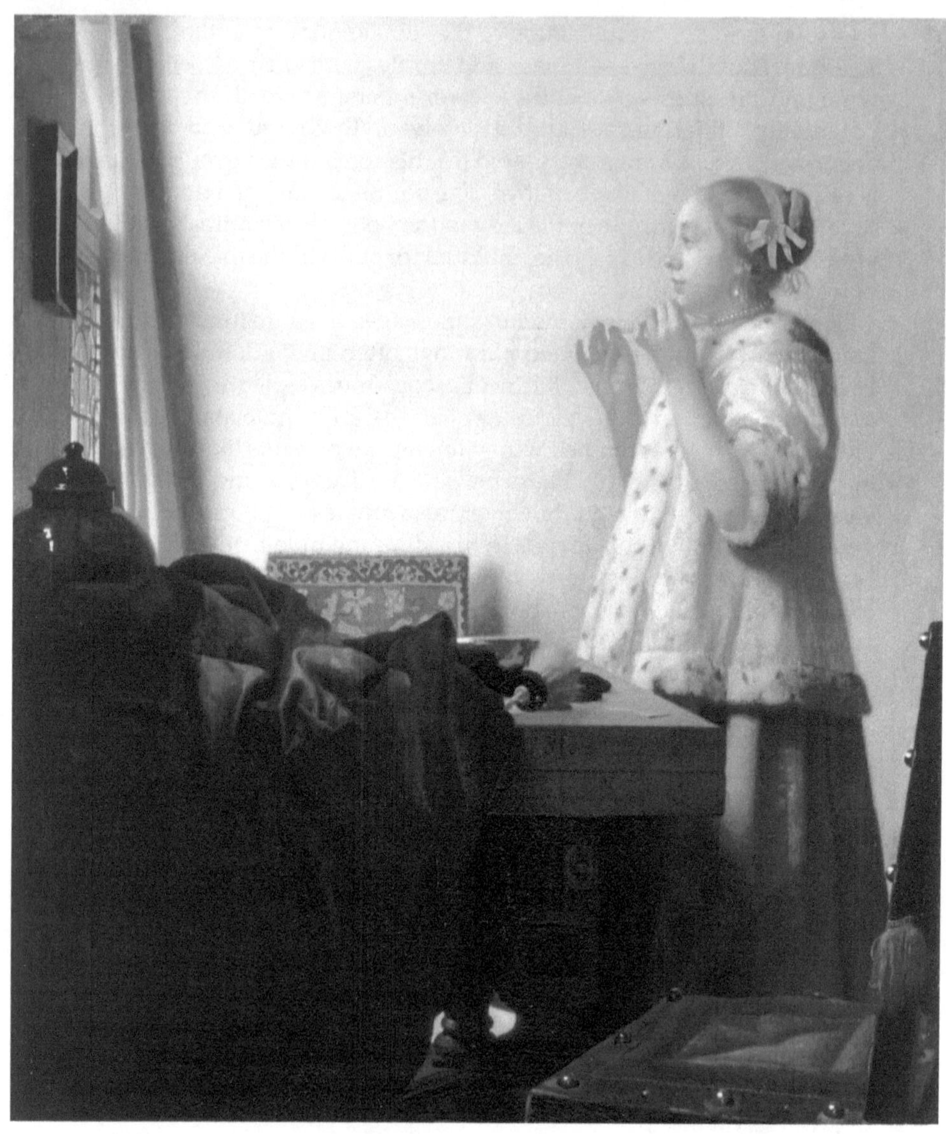

1.10. Johannes Vermeer. *Woman with a Pearl Necklace*. Ca. 1663–4. 56.1 × 47.4 cm (22.1 in × 18.67 in). Gemäldegalerie. Berlin. Photo bpk Bildagentur/Gemäldegalerie/Jörg P. Anders/Art Resource, NY. http://www.smb-digital.de/eMuseumPlus?service=ExternalInterface&module=collection&objectId=863178&viewType=detailView.

images. Rather, what would have seemed radical, from the French perspective, with Northern realism, and especially art from Holland, was the presentation of a different epistemological model. In France the impact of official art was a direct function of its capacity to reassert the singular narrative of Louis's assertion of power. The Dutch genre painters challenged this model by presenting alternative themes through an eclectic array of objects, emphasizing the properties of the objects rather than the origin or the conclusion of the action that takes place within the scene.

Whatever the nobles and the bourgeois really thought of Louis XIV in France, they knew that their own status depended on the king. The exercise of power rested firmly in his hands and those whose authority he chose to recognize. The magnificence of court spectacle did not blind Louis's subjects to the authority that he exerted over them. Artists who participated in the production of the decor and performances celebrating the king in Paris and at Versailles were attuned to the propagandistic function of court art; they accepted commissions with the understanding that the monarchy was intent on celebrating the idea of Louis's majesty. Nobles anxious to retain their place and aspiring bourgeois knew that it was better to assume a role in the spectacle of court life than to live "in exile" outside it. Those in Louis's orbit did not need to suspend disbelief in devotion to the crown. They clearly saw the virtues of courtly spectacle, and they came to associate official art with real power. Thus, when courtiers went to Versailles, watched a play by a dramatist supported through the court's patronage, saw a painting by an artist honoured to be decorating the palace, or viewed an image of Louis XIV engaged in battle within a beautiful Northern landscape, they discerned one clear theme – Louis's glory – and one clear narrative – the king consolidates his power and France celebrates his success – and many analogies for describing it. In contrast, Dutch art had, from the French point of view, the surprising effect of associating power with an empirical model that supported continuous inquiry and discovery. Dutch art was structured in ways that were antithetical to the court's reiteration of the story of Louis's greatness. The coexistence of both artistic traditions during Louis's reign raises an intriguing question. If, as Louis Marin famously stipulated, "le roi n'est roi que dans son image" [the king is only king in his image], then the question becomes: What is the king when his subjects view his image alongside Northern realist images?[50]

2 France at the Intersection: Configuring the French Response to Northern Realism

The French appreciation of Netherlandish art encompassed works in the royal collection and the homes of wealthy collectors and other members of court society. In the city markets, moreover, Parisians were able to look at art dealers' images with no obligation to buy. The influence of the Northern realist tradition on French artists was also noteworthy. Such recognition, however, does not imply that either the French nobles or the bourgeois would have envied even the affluent Dutch or wanted to trade places with them. The king and his court remained the centre of power for French of all classes. A French noble dependent on the crown's favours and a bourgeois eyeing Holland's profitable commerce, however, could be forgiven for thinking that the Dutch were living very well, and that they were fortunate not to be beholden to Louis XIV. French aristocrats would tend to look down at the Dutch burghers, as they would the bourgeois in France, who wanted to share the privileges of the aristocracy. Dutch burghers lacked the culture, the elite breeding, through which the French identified themselves as *honnêtes hommes*. From the French aristocratic perspective, even when France and Holland were not engaged in war, Dutch merchants had the double disadvantage of being of a lower class, and, in most cases, Protestant. Nobles in France felt threatened by the wealthy bourgeois who insinuated themselves into court life by satisfying the king's and the courtiers' needs for luxury items. Prosperous bourgeois were able to provide the cash-strapped crown with necessary funds to pursue expansive projects despite costly wars. The roles that members of the bourgeoisie held in the French administration cost the nobles some of their political influence. Although more restrained, the displays of Dutch burghers' wealth and privilege thus had the potential to fuel the anxiety that French nobles were experiencing: the burghers were the enemy outside who could inspire the enemy within.[1]

New Aesthetic, New Narrative, New Option

Official French art consistently asserts that Louis XIV is the one, and that there is no other. Courtiers who walked through the royal palaces and gardens were repeatedly reminded of Louis's authority. The king was their hero, their master, and the arbiter of their fates. Artists and writers expressed this idea in virtually every work that the monarchy commissioned. Louis was not, of course, immune to verbal attacks and plots by those who resisted his authority, including both individuals and nations seeking to better their own positions. Netherlandish realism presented a subtler challenge to the order that the monarchy sought to impose through the arts. Northern artists no more intended their art to be subversive than French collectors, including the king himself, believed that the acquisition of Netherlandish art was an expression of discontent with French artists or the French style. Yet the empirical emphasis of Northern realism stands opposed to the French reliance on allegory. When only one king, one glorious narrative, and only similar identities are tolerated, any viable alternative to that model, any systematic inclusion of different identities, constitutes a challenge. Netherlandish realism represented such a threat, for it took the viewer from a singular, concentrated system of thought to a more expansive and diffuse ordering of knowledge.

Art did not shut down the viewer's critical capacities. Whatever members of court society thought of the king, and whatever they thought of the court's patronage system, however, the art that surrounded them in Paris, at Versailles, and other royal palaces had to have impressed them. The French came to associate value, status, and influence with history painting, and particularly with allegory. They were conditioned, in other words, to associate power and beauty with a certain order of things. The combination of power and beauty was effective, since any negative thoughts one might associate with the exercise of power were mitigated through its association with the beautiful. Courtiers might not have liked being manipulated by the lavish imagery, but no one could deny that artists went to exceptional lengths to please the eye. The stately decor was punctuated by symbolic narratives and inspiring mythological and historical figures. Versailles was a veritable theatre for the king, whose proclamations, ceremonies, and leisure activities took place within walls and gardens decorated with images of ancient history, myth, and religion. The affairs of state relied on many of the same themes that the playwrights Corneille, Molière, and Racine used to celebrate the power of the sovereign on the classical stage.

A courtier might have preferred something simpler and less grand, of course, but the context for court art was imposing. Anyone who entered a royal palace, and, most spectacularly, Versailles, had to be awed by the sheer number, size, and scale of the works displayed. Visitors acknowledged Louis's exclusive rights to this art, his royal privilege. Power and beauty seduced the viewer into recognizing Louis's image, whatever one thought of his person or his rule.

Part of the appeal of official art involved the use of harmonizing patterns to project Louis's glory. Artists relied on relations of similarity to construct a regular, predictable, and cohesive narrative. With Netherlandish realism, on the other hand, the French came to associate beauty and power with a very different world, and with a very different way of imagining that world. By *imagining* I refer not just to the content of images (a visualization of people, places, and things), but also to structures of knowledge.[2] The themes of Dutch images (battle scenes, landscapes, domestic scenes of maternal love, filial devotion, musical trios, etc.) capture the viewer's attention. Equally important are the irregular patterns of elements that order the compositions into sets of knowable relations.[3] Allowing for more permutations, Dutch images create possibilities for knowledge that the French analogic model actively suppresses. At stake with the French exposure to Dutch art, therefore, is the freedom that comes with a more open and complex system for building knowledge.[4]

French artists and writers serving the crown relied on similar elements to establish a shared identity or reflexivity: Louis resembles the sun and he resembles the sun god Apollo. Likeness also conveys coherence and an inviolable character: Louis consistently triumphs. Two different elements, on the other hand, may suggest tension or negative relations; the passage from one state to another over time; or an increase or reduction in value. The viewer of a painting identifies specific objects: this is an orange; that is an apple. Equally important is the relationship of each object to the others around it: together these fruits convey the earth's bounty, but only the orange suggests warmer climates and the trade responsible for bringing such products to Holland. By emphasizing analogic relations, official French art systematically ruled out the possibility of difference. Politically, this model involved the elimination of opposition and the consolidation of power. Art and literature, however, present systems of thought: they are governed not by armies or commerce but rather by logical relations. In this context the elimination of difference means the creation of an artifice, the act of will responsible for selecting out certain meanings that support the idea of the king's authority at the expense of others. As is evident from the French monarchy's cultivation of the arts to promote Louis XIV's image, the ability to influence thoughts is an effective political tool. Within the context of the French court, however, the realist images of Flemish and Dutch artists represent the obverse relationship. Northern realism exposed the viewer to a far more diverse and inclusive system for knowledge. The empirical orientation of Netherlandish painting encouraged the viewer to think and to process information in ways that challenged the relations that the French court used to ground its mission for the arts, as it in turn supported the ambitions of the king.

To assess the impact of Dutch realism on seventeenth-century French court culture, this chapter examines two works by Flemish artist van der Meulen commemorating Louis XIV's military engagements. In this context van der Meulen produces French art, art in service of the French crown. I consider how van der Meulen's application of Northern landscape techniques affects the construction of Louis XIV's image. I then analyse how, through exposure to Dutch images intended for a Dutch audience, and based on the underlying logic of these paintings, the French would have assembled different patterns of information than with official court art. Mapping techniques inform my readings of Dutch cityscapes, suggesting further deviations. A final section on Le Brun's exquisite portrait of Everhard Jabach studies the influence of Northern realist techniques in Paris circles, and the implications of blended Northern and French styles both for the expanding royal art collection and for the history of knowledge in the early modern period.

Painting for the Record: The Historiography of Louis's Battles

In his native Flanders van der Meulen mastered the finely coloured and detailed landscapes for which his countrymen were known, which skill recommended him to Le Brun. After van der Meulen arrived in Paris, he contributed to the natural settings of commissioned works by documenting topographical features and horses as well as cityscapes, while Le Brun concentrated on the figures and supervised the overall design.[5] Van der Meulen contributed to tapestries commemorating Louis's achievements, including a series of works that Le Brun had organized at the Gobelins factory beginning in 1662 as part of Colbert's vast Histoires du roi [The King's Histories] project, which celebrated the king's diplomatic successes, his military victories, and his support of the arts.[6] Van der Meulen had accompanied Louis XIV during his military campaigns in Flanders during the War of Devolution, and the artist's drawings were used to create the tapestries. Van der Meulen completed a series of paintings on the same theme known as the Conquêtes du roi [The King's Conquests] for the new Marly chateau, a residence that Louis XIV build for leisure, in the 1680s.[7] With the Marly commission van der Meulen depicted the sites of the sieges in a realistic style, consistent with Louis's directives. The Flemish artist rendered these scenes so faithfully that the paintings garnered praise both as royal histories and as landscapes.

Van der Meulen's images allow us to consider how the French monarchy exploited the Northern realist style as part of its propaganda campaigns. Van der Meulen's military images undeniably championed Louis's victories. The question of factual accuracy relates more directly to topographical verisimilitude than to warfare, however. These images often feature the anticipation of Louis's triumph as he enters the city of an already conquered enemy. They create the illusion of battle with an emphasis on France's offensive position. The realistic silhouettes of the cities and the detailed landscapes present empirical elements against which to measure the constructed reality of Louis's military engagement.

Vue de la ville de Lille assiégée, prise du côté du Prieuré de Fives, août 1667 [*View of the City of Lille Under Attack, Showing the Priory of Fives, August, 1667*] bears the unmistakable mark of the artist who documents the scene by attending to the natural setting as well as to the figures. The battle for Lille, which Louis XIV led himself despite the objections of his commanders, was the great conquest of the War of Devolution. As the privileged viewer of this scene once it was displayed at Marly, Louis would have held the long view, literally, as he gazed at the artist's portrayal of his engagement in the battle. In van der Meulen's image Louis stands prominently, although off to the left side, within a vast pastoral setting. Louis and the figure representing him in the painting thus share the same panoramic view through which to "take in" the city

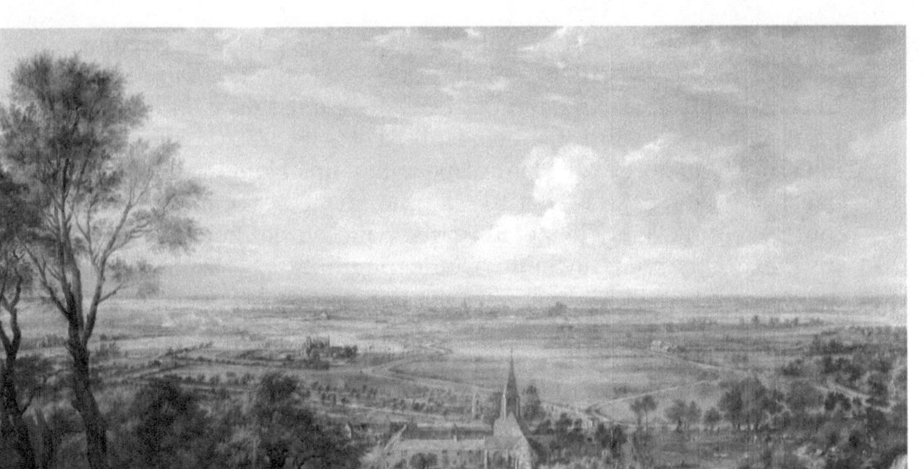

2.1. Adam Frans van der Meulen. *Vue de la ville de Lille assiégée, prise du côté du Prieuré de Fives, août 1667* [*View of the City of Lille Under Attack, Showing the Priory of Fives, August, 1667*]. Ca. 1667–1700. 230 × 328 cm. (90.55 × 129.13 in). Château de Versailles. Image courtesy Château de Versailles, France/ Bridgeman Images. http://collections.chateauversailles.fr/#4e675cc0-b297-460c-a4c5-107178e209ea.

as he moves to "overtake it." Scholars attribute van der Meulen's bird's-eye views to his Flemish training. These views allow the beholder to consider the city from a privileged perspective and also to map it via monuments and other recognizable features. Here the ability to map, or to know, Lille is synonymous with conquering it. The clouds, realistic atmospheric effects, billow in ways that enhance the military mission by contributing a sense of France's destiny.[8] The image balances realism and idealism in ways intended to authenticate the king's role as victorious military commander.

The roads carry the viewer's gaze across the countryside to the city beyond, and away from the sovereign. The extended vista allows the real Louis, and his admiring viewers, to think big. The artist impresses the viewer, however, by also thinking small. As in other paintings in van der Meulen's battle series, the Lille scene offers a faithful reproduction of the area: "le moindre hameau et le moindre bosquet y sont reproduits" [every little hamlet and thicket is recorded].[9] Van der Meulen's ability to portray the landscape with painstaking accuracy has the effect of inviting the viewer to read the image at the micro level in a more scientific vein. The details in the painting flesh out a view of the diversity of the scene, including both topographic and architectural elements, in addition to describing the arrival of the French army as it makes its way towards the city.

Louis's guests at Marly would not weigh the merits of allegory vs the scientific method. The artist's simple intent may well have been, as Isabelle Richefort suggests, to "varier ses compositions" [to vary his compositions].[10] Nonetheless, in the Lille image, the painter's meticulous representation of multiple foci for the horses and figures in the foreground, his detailing of the Prieuré de Fives [Priory of Fives], beyond which lies the city of Lille, as well as his exact rendering of the countryside, invites the viewer's scrutiny. The viewer studies the scene for knowledge about individual figures, including not only the king and those who ride with him but also the riders going down the embankment and across the bridge; the other soldiers crossing via the water; and what appears to be a base camp off to the right. The landscape contains trees of different heights, leaves of different colours, dead branches, and a prominently fallen dead tree in the foreground on the right. Even as the dominant story of Louis's command of the siege comes together in the viewer's mind, and even with the knowledge that the battle of Lille brought a decisive victory to the young king, the painting impresses because it sets out many elements to admire. The hills and the fields; the dogs and riders on horses of different colours; the white horse without a rider; the three men standing; and the man kneeling are so many elements that make this image read like a catalogue of possible permutations of various categories of things: topography, humans, sovereign, soldiers, horses, postures, colours, etc. Once the impulse to observe and to classify enters the culture – once the urge to "tout connaître" [know everything] becomes part of the court's celebration of Louis XIV – it is difficult to imagine how allegory can satisfy the public's desire to know even (or especially) the king.

Van der Meulen's most famous, and arguably most beautiful, image of the king's early war efforts to strengthen France's northern border is *Entrée de Louis XIV et de Marie-Thérèse à Arras, 30 juillet 1667* [*Entry*

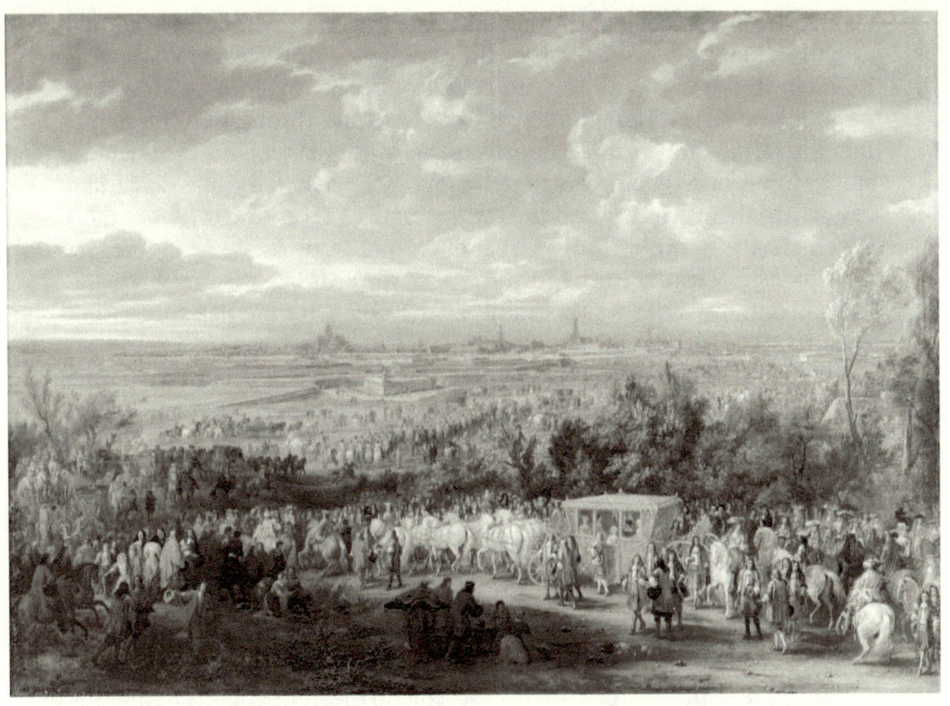

2.2. Adam Frans van der Meulen. *Entrée de Louis XIV et de Marie-Thérèse à Arras, 30 juillet 1667* [*Entry of Louis XIV and Marie-Thérèse in Arras, 30 July 1667*]. Ca. 1685. 232 × 331 cm (91.37 × 130.31 in). Château de Versailles. Image courtesy Château de Versailles, France/Bridgeman Images. http://collections.chateauversailles.fr/#4ead45d1-e2d1-443b-81cd-d4799ccf4c27.

of Louis XIV and Marie-Thérèse in Arras, 30 July 1667], with its exquisite gilded carriage and expansive landscape. Yet the man in the tree wearing the red coat also captures the viewer's gaze – or rather, the *men* in the trees. If we look closely, we see two figures in this largely denuded tree. Lower down, on the right behind some foliage, another pair of heads appears: one male, hatless, and one female, with a cap on the back of her head. These figures, particularly the most prominent man in red, constitute a story within the story. The viewer enjoys observing these figures, three of whom direct their gaze towards Queen Marie-Thérèse, the king, Turenne (French army commander), Monsieur

(Louis XIV's brother), and other members of the royal entourage. An attentive viewer would see that the woman with the cap looks up at the man in the tree with the red coat, not at the royal procession. The painter contrasts different perspectives here and throughout the painting, including French and Flemish, royals and villagers, movement and stasis, foregrounded and ancillary events. As a result, the classical ideal of a world that turns around the central figure of the king is here unbalanced. That disequilibrium in turn encourages the viewer to look further, to seek stability in the form of a more complete idea of what the image contains. The viewer examines the details of the painting along with its major features, breaking down the image into its individual components and aligning them according themes, or types. The latter serve as categories within the larger knowledge system that the image constructs.

Louis XIV's arrival in Arras is presented as court spectacle marking France's victory over Spain. In this history Louis himself serves as the primary actor, although here the queen, seated at the centre of the magnificent carriage, assumes pride of place. The king's presence adds value to the rest, but he commands less attention than the carriage transporting the queen, whose marriage contract, as noted above, occasioned the War of Devolution. The man in red and the other figures in the trees are subordinate to this history. Yet they are by no means inconsequential for the viewer's experience of the painting. The figures in the trees demonstrate will, not fate: they have chosen to climb into the branches. They have done so for a better view of the king, certainly. These spectators, like the others assembled, bear witness to Louis and the triumphal procession. Such contingent actions, however, break the sense of inevitability, of Louis's undisputed dominance over this region, which the image of the royal entry serves to establish. The men might not have climbed the trees; Louis might have gazed up at them, rather than at the royals gathering to his left. Other noblemen accompanying the royal carriage are also looking in the direction from which they have come, while the main action concerns the movement of the royal procession towards the city. This dual orientation creates dramatic suspense. In the foreground groups of royals gather and appear to converse, waiting, perhaps, for the signal to enter Arras, while the villagers gather to watch the French king lay claim to the city.[11] The scene is lively: horses are moving, including the one that the king is riding just behind the queen's carriage. That placement, moreover, requires the viewer to locate the king in front of the group gathered there, whereas Marie-Thérèse's carriage is immediately visible. Van der Meulen thus engages the viewer in surveying the details of the scene through a fluid composition involving many discrete elements that do not centre directly on the king.

Despite the elaborate staging, the royal procession acquires a naturalness, which the presence of the men in the trees underscores. The red coat of the most visible and largest figure atop the tree repeats the red attire of the royal entourage, including the king's hat and the carriage interior, conflating the obvious hierarchy intended to privilege the royal couple and the well-appointed nobles.[12] Furthermore, van der Meulen encourages viewers to admire his own cleverness in placing these bystanders aloft; such details emphasize his role as the image-maker responsible for commemorating the king. The men and woman in the trees validate the king's authority from their perch above the royal carriage. They reinforce the power of the court from the rather awkward angle of the tree branches. These figures, however, constitute a pleasant distraction in an image commemorating Louis's conquests and his subjects' obedience to him.

The French monarchy intends the viewer to experience art as a support for its political mission. The aesthetic appeal of this image, however, does more than enhance the king's military goals. Van der Meulen's realistic depiction privileges observation at the expense of myth. The empirical emphasis equates beauty both with imitation, a record of what exists in the world, and classification, the mind's capacity to order the elements of the image as thoughts. This way of fashioning identities constitutes a real but hidden danger for the French. The danger is *real* because all humans have the native ability to see details and to perceive differences as well as likeness. It is *hidden* because viewers focus on content: they identify the French king via a string of elements that celebrate him. Viewers do not commit to understanding the qualities of all details in the image as part of a query into the order of things in the world. Yet the design of the image encourages viewers to examine the distinctiveness and variety of the objects and figures depicted. The experience is *dangerous* because attention to individual details has the potential to disrupt the iterative process through which the crown projects the king's authority. Louis is like a triumphant god; Louis's military battles help to establish France as the new Rome; Louis's entries evoke other triumphal entries, including those of Roman emperors to whom cities paid homage and promised loyalty; present victories resemble ancient glories. Louis's entry into Arras, however, takes place in a real setting that includes many elements that viewers need to identify if they are really to understand what they see. Measured against the multitude of individual figures, the richness of the topographical description, and the individualized architectural features included in the image, the analogic relation ("Louis resembles") seems not only predictable but also deficient, incapable of explaining all that the image contains.[13]

Van der Meulen's paintings clearly honour Louis XIV's victories in Flanders. Nonetheless, the details of his images engage the viewer in a discovery process that ultimately challenges the methodological underpinnings of the court's attempts to glorify Louis's image. The landscape vistas help to develop the viewer's sense of Louis's exceptional accomplishments. Van der Meulen's naturalistic descriptions, however, bring more to the celebration than a setting for Louis's success. The patterns of elements that structure the image – groups of people, trees, and fields – imprint themselves in the viewer's mind as part of an essential taxonomyof social conditions, natural elements, and historic commemorations. The latter category does not suffice to explain the two other classifications. The descriptive elements in the painting extend, quite literally, the viewer's gaze beyond the artful history of royal propaganda to an appreciation of all that lies outside the royal procession, and the analogies that make the history of that event cohere.

Applying Flemish techniques to art championing the king's ambitions, van der Meulen accomplishes more than a sense of Louis's victory. The viewer enjoys the majestic sweep of the land, a sign of all that Louis wished to conquer, but also the precision with which the artist renders the setting. The viewer assembles the information contained in the image element by element, group by group, and then, with the series of paintings that van der Meulen created for Marly, image by image. Northern artists described what they observed so as to make the world intelligible, and van der Meulen brought that intelligibility to a world caught up in the illusions of grandeur. Nowhere is that relation better imagined, perhaps, than in the image of Louis XIV at Marly contemplating his image in van der Meulen's series of paintings.

Once the relationship of art and truth intrudes upon the relationship of art and power that the monarchy cultivates, the inviolable character of Louis XIV's image is compromised. The monarchy's use of the arts to extend the king's influence continued unabated during Louis's campaigns. Northern realism did not threaten to destroy the propaganda machine that Louis and Colbert developed. Netherlandish art, however, privileged the accurate description of things as they appear in nature, thereby engaging viewers to think analytically about the world they perceive. This interpretive process operates very differently from court spectacle. The viewer looks at van der Meulen's scenes of Lille and Arras not only as royal theatre commanding respect and subservience to the king but also in order to identify and to understand the details of the image and, by extension, the working of the monarchy. The artist's dedication to observing and recording the real means that another force, that of empiricism, is stirring within the arts in France. Art serves more than one master even within the palace walls. The Enlightenment and the *Encyclopédie* are yet to come, but the ground, and the grounding of knowledge, is already shaking a bit under the hooves of Louis's cavalry as he pushes north in van der Meulen's battle scenes.

Water Marks: Van der Heyden and Patel

As Louis XIV's power and influence expanded, Holland occupied more space, both territorial and intellectual, in France. Part of this exposure involved the thriving Dutch art market, with its urban focus. Dutch art brought the French into another society and also into another mode of thought. A view of Amsterdam painted by Jan van der Heyden provides an example of the distinctive Dutch style. Interpreting this image in relation to Pierre Patel's celebrated painting of Versailles, I call attention to important variances in theme and design that would have impressed a French viewer.

With cityscapes of Holland, French viewers confront not only a different socio-economic situation and a different aesthetic but also a more open structure for knowing the world. Patel's painting of Versailles and van der Heyden's view of Amsterdam were completed at roughly the same time. At Versailles engineers would turn a less than desirable, swampy site into a magnificent palace, complete with a Grand Canal constructed 1668–79.[14] Also built during the seventeenth century, Amsterdam's Canal Ring (Grachtengordel) is a network of intersecting waterways developed through the drainage and reclamation of land. The contrast between the single canal at Versailles and the network of canals, plural, in Amsterdam is a historic contingency that sets the stage for my reading. I contrast the singular focus on Louis XIV with the diffuse patterning of elements evident in Dutch paintings.

Patel records Louis XIV's arrival as an imprint on the landscape. While architecturally faithful, Patel fills in a vision that in 1668 still involved three future building campaigns for the chateau. The landscape was even more idealized. The hills enhance a terrain that was in fact very

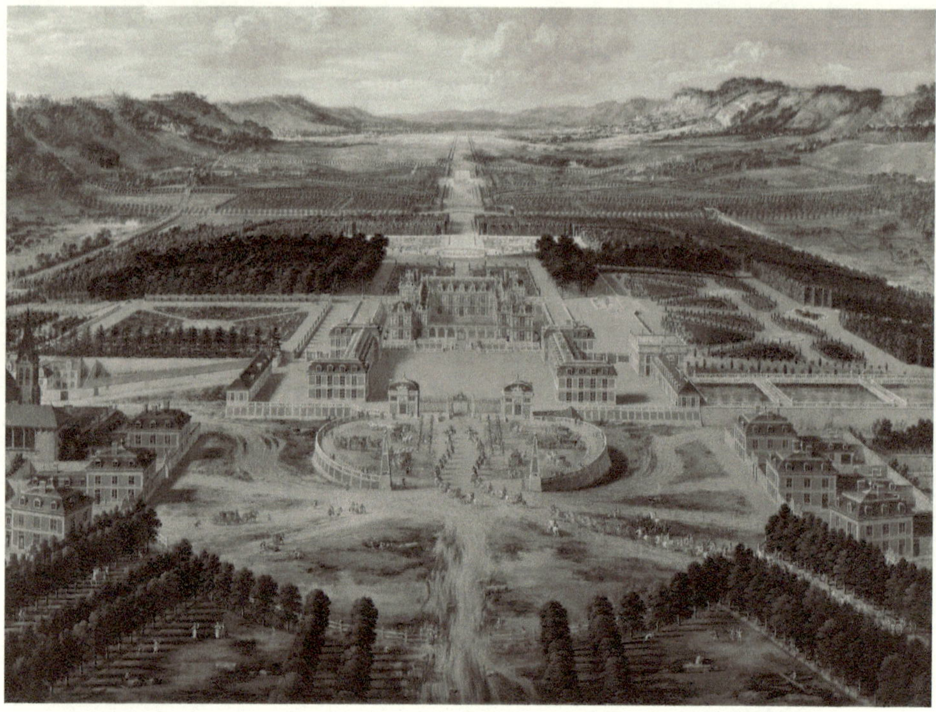

2.3. Pierre Patel. *Vue du château et des jardins de Versailles, prise de l'avenue de Paris* [*View of the Chateau and the Gardens of Versailles, as Seen from the Avenue de Paris*]. 1668. 115 × 161 cm (45.28 × 63.39 in). Château de Versailles. Image courtesy Château de Versailles, France/Bridgeman Images. http://collections.chateauversailles.fr/#365da80c-b84a-4cf0-b250-6f2535f4a2f0.

flat. The sight line of the image begins with the tree-lined road in the lower right and extends via the royal procession into the courtyard and, via the canal, to the horizon, to infinity. We cannot see Louis, but the royal carriage accompanied by many men on horseback confirms his arrival. The king's presence unifies the image not only because the enlarged chateau is "the house that Louis built" and was still expanding but also because the route of the procession into the chateau takes the court that bears his name from Paris to Versailles, and from Versailles, via the canal, into history forever.

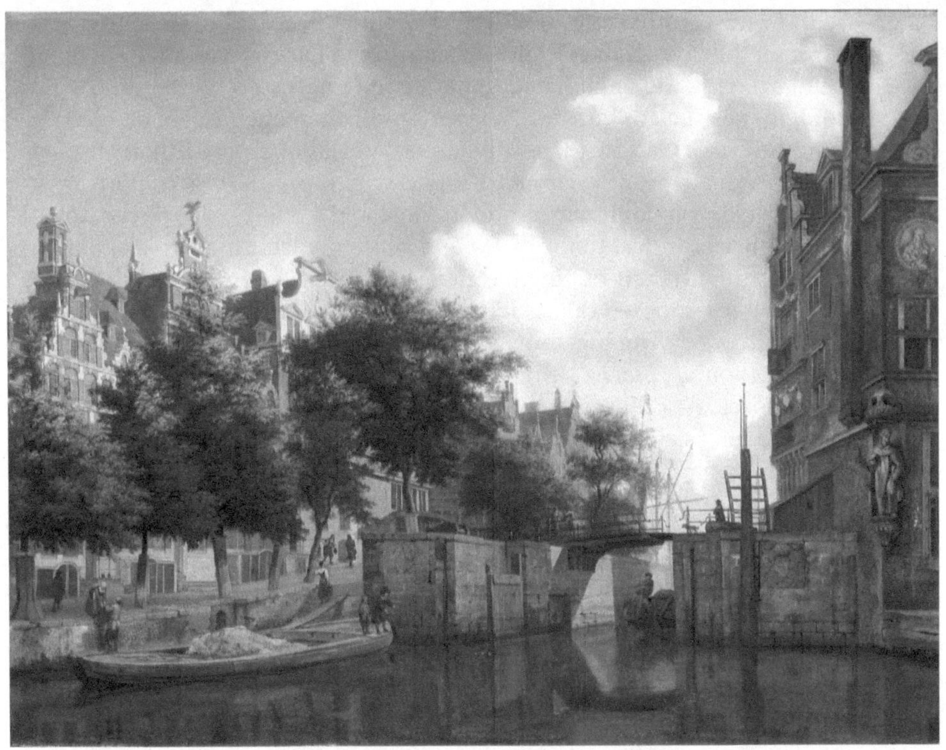

2.4. Jan van der Heyden. *Amsterdam City View with Houses on the Herengracht and the Old Haarlemmersluis*. Ca. 1670. 44 × 57.5 cm (17.32 × 22.64 in). Rijksmuseum. Image courtesy Rijksmuseum. https://www.rijksmuseum.nl/en/search/objects?q=van+der+heyden&f=1&p=1&ps=12&type=painting&st=Objects&ii=0#/SK-A-154,0.

Van der Heyden's painting never entered France, but it is representative of Dutch urban life and the compositional organization of Dutch paintings. With the canal winding through its centre, the serene image of the Dutch city would have impressed any viewer with its uncomplicated elegance. This quality, however, offers a clear counterpoint to the exuberance of much French art serving the crown. Van der Heyden's image compels because the city, unlike the court in France, requires no spectacle, no royal entry, no accoutrements of power to make its mark on the viewer. The pace is unhurried as people go about their business.

With France's influence, political as well as decorative, expanding in Europe, the French likely felt superior to the Dutch in all matters of life and art. Still, the French had to have been impressed by the skilfulness of images such as van der Heyden's, with its meticulously painted facades and trees, and expansive clouds, typical of the Northern tradition. Intrigued by a quiet canal scene where ordinary activities of unnamed citizens complete mundane tasks, the viewer is moved to examine closely individual figures and objects, including the elegant brick houses with their distinctive gables, the trees lining the canal, the two boats – one moored on the left, the other pushing under the bridge in the centre – and the big ships whose masts loom behind the bridge. On the left a man places peat, used for heating, from his boat into a woman's sack. Another woman, her sack already full, walks away. On the street a man strides behind the first woman, while further along two more men stop to chat. Standing on the edge of the boat, a father gestures and his son watches something in the canal. Another man walks with his dog across the bridge. The viewer knows little about the individuals pursuing their activities, other than the colour and style of their clothing as it reveals their gender, size, and posture.

Van der Heyden captures Amsterdam's city dwellers in situ, with many incidental events punctuating the scene. The canal itself and the buildings along it are the true subject of this painting. Reflections in the water give the impression that the canal preserves the city, recording its structures as it registers the movements of its citizens. The flowing water captures time in the forms and shadows of daily life. Shown at is widest angle at the base of the image, the canal draws in the viewer to explore. The play of light on the water emphasizes surfaces, observable phenomena. Art mirrors life, down to some of its finest details.[15]

The canal holds a story that the viewer wants to decipher. What are those two white dots, followed by brown, white, and then more brown dots all in a row? The first dot is a ball, and the rest belong to a brown and white spotted dog with floppy ears. These details give meaning to the man's gesture on the canal bank: he and his son are playing a game of fetch with the dog. The viewer, too, is encouraged to fetch, or seek out, the details in this composition so as to imagine the city as the working day unfolds. The various elements of the painting can be read in different configurations: starting on the left with the peat delivery; on the right with the building's architectural features; or in the centre with the boat slipping under the bridge. One can move back and forth across the canal and then deep into the image. The different configurations of

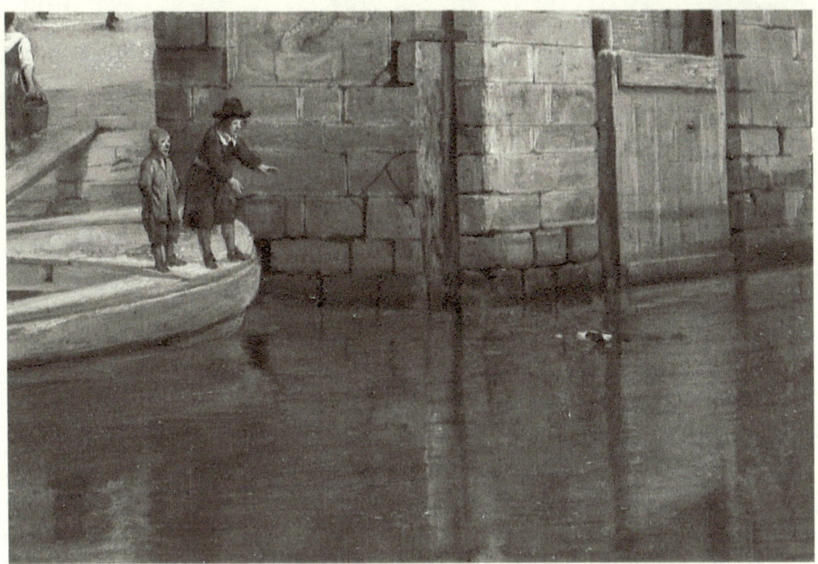

2.5. Jan van der Heyden. *Amsterdam City View with Houses on the Herengracht and the Old Haarlemmersluis*. Ca. 1670. Detail. 44 × 57.5 cm (17.32 × 22.64 in). Rijksmuseum. Image courtesy Rijksmuseum. https://www.rijksmuseum.nl/en/search/objects?q=van+der+heyden&f=1&p=1&ps=12&type=painting&st=Objects&ii=0#/SK-A-154,0.

people alone and together suggest many narratives, and yet no particular narrative.

Patel also distributes figures throughout the fields in front of the chateau, a sign that the village has a stake in Louis's expansion project. The symmetry of the architecture, however, tells the history of record, one requiring the arrival of the king to set it in motion. Patel documents the chateau and the chateau's vast grounds, emphasizing the order of the design through a central vertical axis. His image contrasts with the sweeping curve that van der Heyden extends from the boat on the lower left and across the bridge. The Dutch artist presents a different sense of harmony that rests not with perfectly balanced views of both sides of the canal but rather with the calmness of the scene. In van der Heyden's depiction of Amsterdam the absence of a dramatic narrative, like the absence of a central figure comparable to the sovereign making his royal entry, and his claim, on Versailles, locates meaning in the Dutch city as it lies open before the viewer, there to be discovered.

Mapping Knowledge

Emphasizing the relations between individual objects and the patterns they form, Dutch paintings read much like maps.[16] Maps allow us to know a city by showing where streets intersect; they show the city grid. The Dutch were outstanding mapmakers. Given the prevalence of maps in the Dutch Republic, and given the fact that detailed street maps had been available since the sixteenth century – Amsterdam appeared in the first volume (1572) of the *Civitates Orbis Terrarum* (Cologne) – it is noteworthy that many painters of Dutch cityscapes did not concern themselves with the street grid.[17] Maps were themselves works of art containing vignettes of various sites, figures, and even outlines of (typically generic) houses lining the canals. In cityscapes, however, artists do not customarily represent a nexus of streets. They present individual streets; streets and canals; and one street connecting with the next. They do not, however, offer an extensive view of intersecting streets, or a broad city plan.

With the *View of Delft*, the viewer knows that streets exist where the steeples pop up and the rooftops glow in the light behind the buildings that line the far bank of the River Shie. The agglomeration of structures, including the tower of the Oude Kerk [Old Church], the tower of the Nieuwe Kerk [New Church] basking in the sun, the ramparts, and the two gates on either side of the stone bridge that spans the canal winding through the city engage the viewer searching for landmarks. These details give the impression that Vermeer's image replicates a mapmaker's accuracy, although the artist in fact adjusted the buildings to achieve a more balanced composition. The play of light and shadow; the horizontal lines of the quay in the foreground; the water, with its reflections; the dense city; and the vast expanse of sky reveal the hand of the master who knows how to create the illusion of a moment of time interrupted. The clouds that distribute bands of light and shadow across the scene impress far more readily than do the figures in the foreground. These bodies are so small that they appear as mere placeholders, indicators of the scale of the buildings behind them as they are of the commerce that exists within the vast natural setting. Despite the limited size of the figures, a viewer

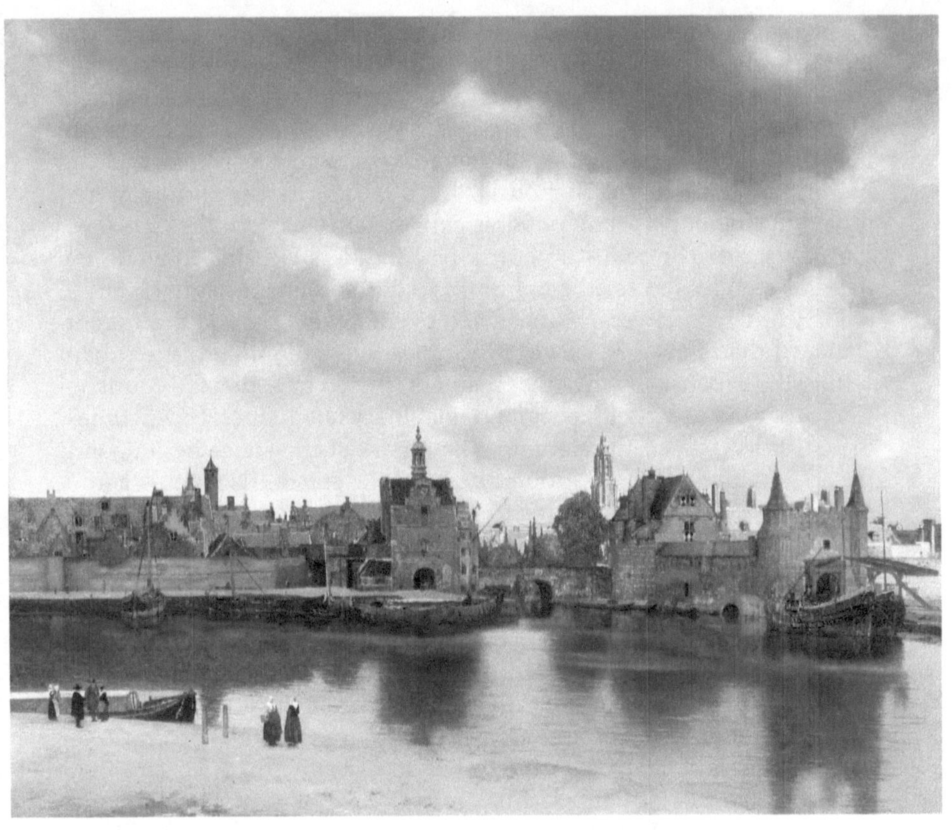

2.6. Johannes Vermeer. *View of Delft*. Ca. 1660–1. 96.5 × 115.7 cm (38 × 45.55 in). Mauritshuis. Image courtesy Mauritshuis, The Hague, The Netherlands/ Bridgeman Images. https://www.mauritshuis.nl/en/explore/the-collection/artworks/view-of-delft-92/.

whose gaze moves from left to right discerns a mother holding a child, a group of two men and a woman talking, and then another pair of women engaged in conversation. Vermeer maps a vision of a city in suspended animation. Delft here exists as a place whose receding spaces draw the viewer in, but that exposes nothing of the pathways connecting its buildings to its streets and the streets to each other. The figures in the foreground seem quite removed from the city across the river, even though the waterway serves both banks.

Cityscapes offer exquisitely detailed renderings of urban spaces, yet artists rarely show more than one street, or two banks of the same canal, connecting either to a bridge or to a corner leading to the next street. The view presented is local, restricted.[18] We note the persistent elision in art of what is arguably one of the most characteristic signs of urban life in the Dutch Republic, both as lived by its citizens and as represented in city maps. Many possible explanations exist for the cityscape *sans* city grid. The maps accomplished the detailed street layout, so there was no reason for the paintings to do the same. Moreover, landscapes, of which cityscapes form a subgenre, were held to a different standard than maps. Artists of cityscapes often adapted to the urban setting the expansive views that painters created to depict the countryside, mountains, winter scenes, and imaginary landscapes.[19] Sometimes the cityscape served to celebrate a landmark such as a cathedral, and the activity that occurred around it. Aesthetic standards for this genre seemed to favour a perspective from the periphery, whether that of the entire city viewed from across the water or that of dwellings along a single canal.

It is noteworthy that so many artists, including van der Heyden in this and other of his appealingly detailed cityscapes, chose to reproduce the urban environment without underscoring the urban network, the connections between various squares and markets that composed the city's vital commercial base along with the quays. After all, the unprecedented success of the Dutch in trade was itself a story of routes, one that provoked the envy of and ultimately war with other nations, among them France. The Dutch had developed global markets from the Mediterranean through the Indies, the Far East, and the New World. Whatever the artists' motives, the contrast between maps and cityscapes highlights a critical difference. Whereas maps allow the viewer to plot routes along known pathways, artists encourage the discovery of (intellectual) pathways by displaying a precise view of the city that alludes to areas situated outside it.[20] Contemplating the features of the image one by one, the viewer inventories the city, identifying the various elements displayed for no other purpose than to render the scene appealing and knowable. Rather than follow a history of the king whose parameters were fixed, to which reading of art the French were accustomed, the French discovered in Dutch cityscapes a world still open to interpretation. That leap was significant: the empiricism genie had escaped from the royal bottle.

From the French Perspective: More than Scenes of Ordinary Life

The role of history paintings in idealizing Louis XIV's image underscores the French court's recognition of the transformative power of art. The documentary evidence of battles won ultimately yielded to the celebration of a heroic figure, a victorious and indomitable king, a figure more myth than man. Dutch art also idealized the success of its citizens through images that perfected the spaces in which their families, possessions, and lands were displayed. Yet these images enhance not to distort or to blind the viewer to the truth but rather to call attention to the material existence of things. The Dutch took pride in what they were able to create on their land in their lifetime, including the art that bore witness to their efforts. The fact that Dutch visual culture reached all social classes suggests that the artist studios, fairs, bookshops, and other venues for paintings allowed Dutch citizens to participate in a vast archival project of their society.

Dutch genre painting exploits the technical finesse required to imitate the real as a process of documentation. Along with exceptional objects, artists record seemingly insignificant things, gestures, and details that heighten the viewer's awareness of their intrinsic value to the vast cultural production of their lives. These works do more than describe "ordinary" experiences; they describe "observable" experiences. Dutch artists inform a view of the world based on direct observations of fleeting moments. From the French perspective, the ordinary themes of Dutch genre paintings appeared inferior to the "noble" subjects favoured at court, the narratives of Louis's victories that were buoyed by myth and ancient history, a sense of unending, infinite time. Dutch genre paintings, however, open a process of discovery. Realistic description grounds the viewer in the here and now of knowable phenomena, as that knowledge includes not only the positive identification of objects and the relations that bind them but also ambiguities, incongruous pairings, and physical changes that qualify those relations. Dutch images embolden the viewer by exposing the need to look more deeply into the image so as to notice the small details as well as the imposing forms. To appreciate the image fully the viewer must consider manifest as well as latent meanings, competing messages, and open-ended situations. The process of identification and cataloguing in these paintings engages the viewer in ways that Louis XIV's glorious portrait, the image of the king as an immutable force, forecloses.

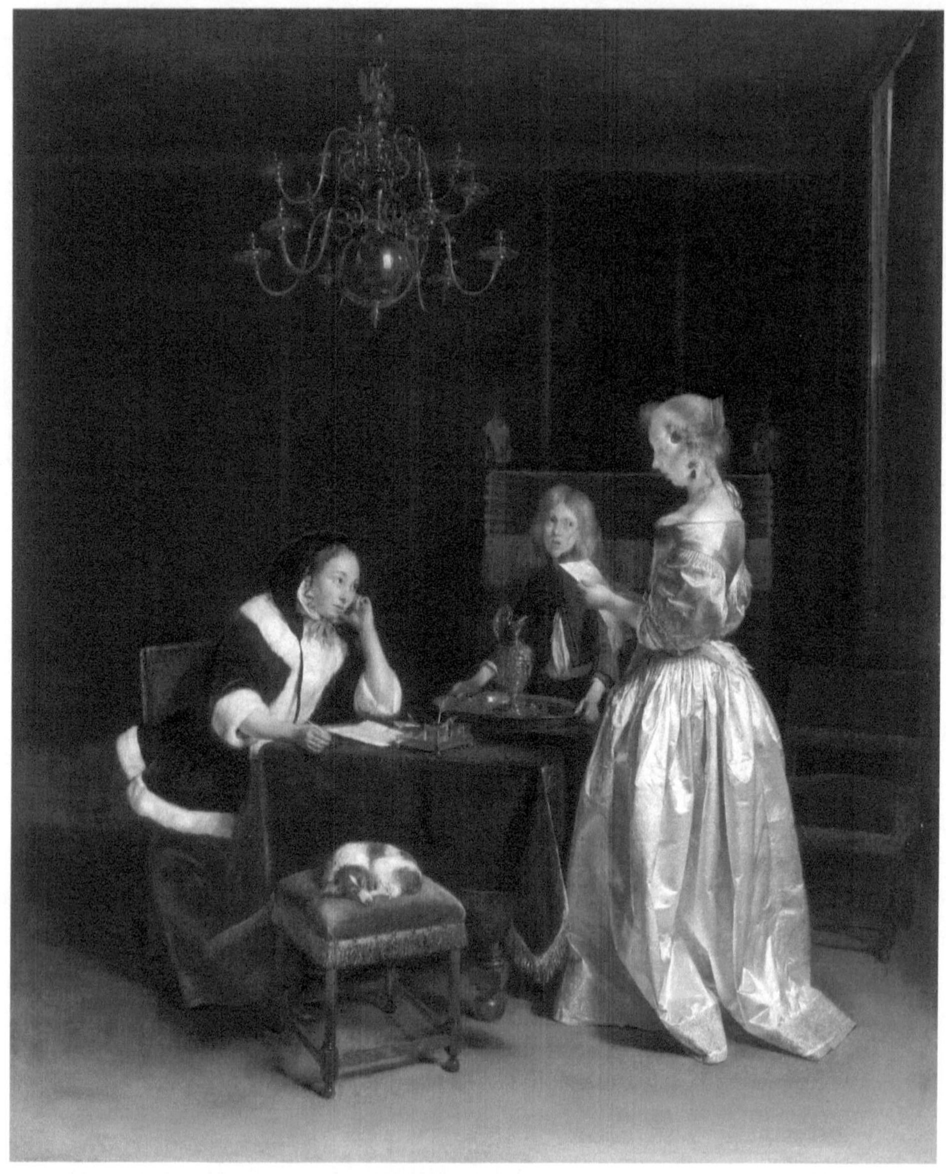

2.7. Gerard ter Borch. *The Letter*. Ca. 1660–5. 81.9 × 68.4 cm (32.25 × 26.93 in). Royal Collection, London. Image courtesy Royal Collection Trust © Her Majesty Queen Elizabeth II, 2018/Bridgeman Images. https://www.royalcollection.org.uk/collection/405532/the-letter.

As exemplified by ter Borch's *Letter*, Dutch genre paintings frequently offer an indeterminate narrative. The viewer arrives *in medias res*, ignorant of what transpired before the depicted scene occurred and what took place following it. Clearly love is in the air. The letter occasions a study of a young woman surrounded by her mother, who defines the home as a feminine space; the young attendant holding a tray, indicating the affluence of the household; and the pet dog, suggesting devotion and loyalty. The most dramatic element in the image, the daughter's exquisite silk dress with its rich blue top and shimmering grey and metallic-trimmed skirt, captures the light, as does the chandelier.

While it describes the prosperous middle class via luxury fabrics and other furnishings, the painting appears unmotivated, that is, suspended from any larger history. Standing before the image, the beholder remains curious about the details of the letter, quite possibly from a suitor, the young woman's response, and its consequences for her love relationship. This painting requires that we understand order to be an effect of description and not action. Indeed, the impact of the painting depends on the individual elements of the scene whose action is remarkably undramatic: a young woman reads a letter while her mother and a page watch and the dog sleeps.[21] The dress is far more engaging than the plot. The mother studies her daughter somewhat expectantly, and the page looks to see the young woman's reaction to the letter. Both communicate suspended action. We will never know how the scene ends, any more than we know how the story began. While such uncertainty is unimaginable for the French court's portrait of the king, here it serves to accentuate description as an end in itself. It moves the viewer away from myth and towards science based on observation.

Le Brun's Jabach Family Portrait

The impact of Dutch Golden Age art on French court society is perhaps no more evident than in the portrait of Everhard Jabach (1618–95) with his family painted by Le Brun around 1660. Le Brun was in good company. Van Dyck had already completed two portraits of Jabach when he was a young man. Everhard Jabach was a prominent banker, second-generation businessman, and art connoisseur widely recognized as having amassed one of the most important art collections in Europe. His ambitions brought him to France, where he set his sights on Paris and the court.[22] In 1664 Jabach was appointed director of the French Compagnie des Indes orientales [East India Company], the same year that Louis

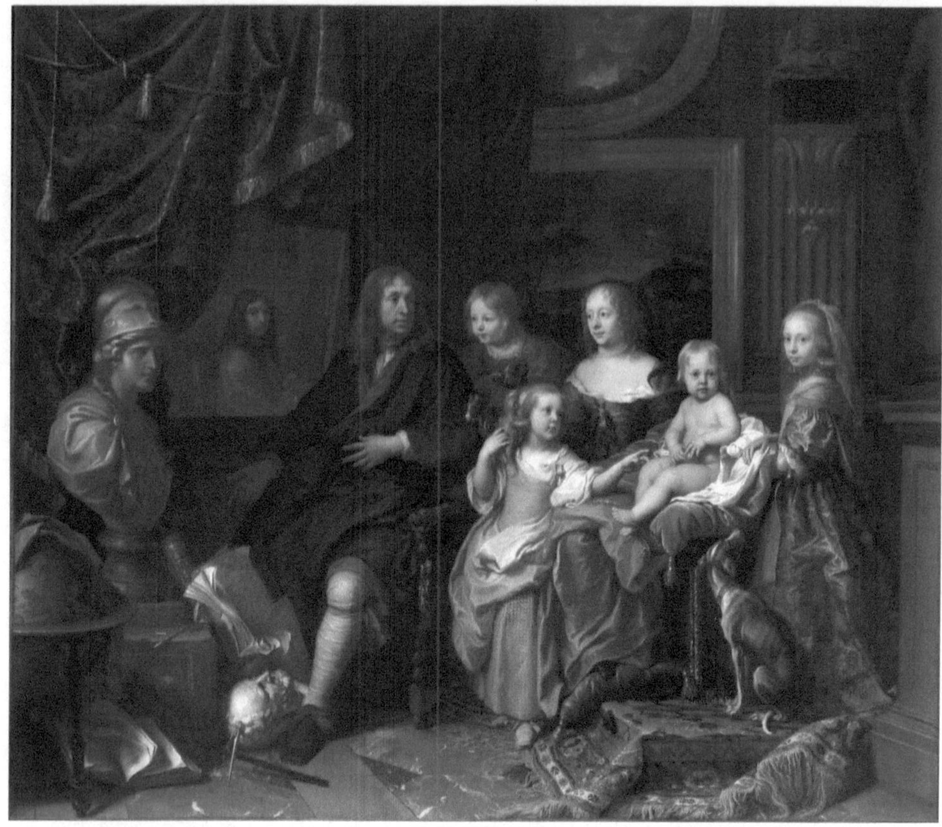

2.8. Charles Le Brun. *La famille Jabach* [*Everhard Jabach (1618–1695) and His Family*]. Ca. 1660. 280 × 328 cm (110.25 × 129.1 in). Metropolitan Museum of Art. Image © The Metropolitan Museum of Art/Art Resource, NY. https://www.metmuseum.org/art/collection/search/626692.

XIV named Le Brun Premier Peintre du Roi [First Painter to the King] and ennobled him. Jabach bought and sold art, which activities brought him into contact with influential artists and collectors, including not only van Dyck and Le Brun but also Rubens, van der Meulen (Jabach was the godfather of one of van der Meulen's daughters), Pierre Mignard, Rigaud, and Nicolas de Largillière, with whom he enjoyed extended friendships.[23]

Le Brun's image of the Jabach family privileges the idea of collecting by featuring the art dealer and financier surrounded by precious objects selected from his cabinet. Jabach confers a sense of dynasty via this family portrait, including his wife and four children, and their pet whippet. Beyond personal fortune, the painting communicates some of the authority with which Jabach would shape French tastes to feature works of Northern art in addition to impressive Italian works, which had long held sway in French circles. Jabach acquired an extensive collection of Italian Renaissance works. Through his business dealings in London, Amsterdam, and Antwerp he also brought to Paris some of the finest examples of Northern art available in Europe, including works by Albrecht Dürer, Hans Holbein, and Paul Bril, as well as by Rubens and van Dyck. Jabach accumulated an outstanding collection of drawings as well as paintings.

Jabach had become Cardinal Mazarin's banker, and, in a complex story that involved death, disgrace, debt, and deferred payment, one hundred of Jabach's works entered the royal collection of Louis XIV in 1662. Le Brun had arranged for several fine Italian paintings to be removed from Jabach's home and displayed in Mazarin's palace prior to their actual purchase for the crown. Mazarin had deeded the paintings to Louis XIV, and had arranged for Fouquet, then Surintendant des finances [Superintendant of Finances], to make the payment to Jabach. Mazarin, however, died, and Fouquet was imprisoned before Nicolas Doublet, whom Fouquet had engaged to advance the funds, was reimbursed. Seeking restitution, Doublet approached Colbert, the future Contrôleur général des finances [Comptroller General of Finances], via Le Brun, whose action in removing the paintings from Jabach's home was potentially compromising: "Le Brun se trouva fort gêné: sa responsabilité était gravement engagée puisque c'était lui qui avait fait déposer les tableaux chez Mazarin sans l'accord de Doublet et que celui-ci lui en avait fait signer un récépissé" [Le Brun was in an awkward situation: he was implicated because he was the one who had the paintings delivered to Mazarin without Doublet's consent, and Doublet had made him sign a receipt].[24] The selected paintings, busts, and bronzes were eventually purchased for the crown from Jabach for 330,000 livres. In 1671 when bankruptcy forced his hand, Jabach sold Louis XIV another hundred paintings and over fifty-five hundred drawings from his collection. These works from Jabach dominate the Louvre Renaissance and seventeenth-century holdings to this day.

This background provides a valuable context for appreciating Le Brun's stunning portrait. Not only did Jabach assume an influential role with respect to the arts in France, but he also commissioned a family portrait commensurate with his wealth, his aspirations, and his influence in Paris. Keith Christiansen, curator at the Metropolitan Museum of Art, observes that Le Brun "combines the domestic intimacy and descriptive richness of Dutch and Flemish art, which Jabach collected and admired, with the measured formal organization and allegorical allusions characteristic of French portraiture."[25]

The setting is lavish, and the prominence of the financier paterfamilias is set off by his central position in his home, a *hôtel particulier* [townhouse]. Jabach is surrounded by his family on his left, and, on his right, by objects that in another context, namely, in a portrait of the king, would be simply allegorical, so many claims to power that, like the theatrical curtain, signal a regal presence. Several objects have those resonances as well, but they likely represent Jabach's actual possessions. Christiansen identifies a Bible; a cast of a bronze lion attacking a horse by Florentine sculptor Giovanni Francesco Susini; a bust of Minerva; an open book that is a famous architectural treatise of 1545; a celestial globe, perhaps by the famous Dutch atlas maker Willem Jansz. Blaeu; an oriental carpet; and a marble floor. On the other side of the painting the family's wealth is evident in Madame Jabach's brocaded silk satin dress and in the rich fabrics that the daughters wear. The younger son, whose nudity identifies him as male, appears Christlike in his splendour.[26] Paintings on the wall include two landscapes. A mirror reflects a self-portrait of Le Brun at work, à la Diego Velázquez, but with the artist occupying the space reserved for the king's reflection in the Spanish masterpiece, the conceit on which that image is constructed.[27]

The toppled head of the philosopher's statue in the foreground and the placement of other objects near it recall a still life. Here, however, the collection of books, rolled drawing, statues, and porte-crayon with three colours of chalk all celebrate Jabach's refined interests in the arts. Together the various objects serve as a counterweight to the bust of Minerva that dominates so forcefully the left side of the painting representing Jabach's cultural interests. If the Minerva statue provides a massive support for Jabach's art collection, this symbol of wisdom is also designed to be balanced by his love for and protection of his family. The latter includes his legacy via the eldest son and heir who, with his eyes fixed on Jabach, holds a small dog and a toy horse.[28] The juxtaposition of Jabach with Le Brun, the impressive collector with the distinguished artist, suggests that authority lies with him who assembles the collection, as with him who paints. Wisdom is the domain of the goddess;

knowledge requires the hand, the mind, and, we might add, the commerce of men.

Le Brun does not upstage the court. Complete with dramatic curtain, however, the Jabach portrait relies on the powerful setting within the family's elegant home on the rue de Merri in the 4th arrondissement. The German-born bourgeois did not triumph over the French crown: financial troubles forced him to sell his collection to Louis XIV at a disadvantageous price, another victory for the French monarch. Art commands an audience, however, and this exquisite work by the painter who was destined to decorate much of Versailles is no exception. The painting was commissioned for display in Jabach's Paris residence (a second portrait went to Germany), which also housed his extensive collection. Not only friends and family but also prospective buyers and others whom Jabach wanted to impress came to view these works. They included collectors and artists, most notably Bernini during his ill-fated trip to Paris in 1665 to work on the Louvre expansion (his design was not accepted). Le Brun's portrait undoubtedly reaffirmed in royal circles and among the Parisian elite Jabach's bona fides as a discerning and influential specialist in painting and drawing, and his role in generating interest in the Northern realist style among the French.

Collecting and the display of collections relate directly to questions of taste and style. Collecting also concerns issues of property and ownership, market forces that operate in conjunction with, but often outside of, court privilege. Here the German bourgeois banker's influence on the history of art and power in France is noteworthy. If we further consider the activity of art collecting as the ordering of objects by type (French School, Northern School, etc.), then we see how Dutch images form part of a classification system for art that situates the French in relation to foreign cultures. Individual works of Dutch realism, moreover, evidence the classificatory function through a meticulous display of objects. I have shown that the descriptive emphasis of Dutch painting ran against the French predilection for allegory. Still, Dutch art did not cry out to make science, not war; nor did it side with the French bourgeoisie against the nobility. Here, too, Jabach's example is instructive, as he played a prominent role among France's elite, including the king. Science would continue to make inroads in France. French philosophers collaborated with the Dutch and other Europeans via the Académie des sciences [Academy of Sciences], which Louis founded in 1666 at the suggestion of Colbert, and other learned societies abroad, as well as independently via private correspondence. The status of Dutch art within French culture during Louis's reign was nevertheless remarkable. Perfection in the Northern realist tradition was an idea associated with fabrics and furnishings, and also with rotting fruits evocatively rendered. Such images suggest the vanity of worldly goods and the inevitable decay of all living things, but they also convey the enduring beauty of art. Most significantly from the French perspective, which sought to create an enduring image of Louis's authority, Dutch realism demonstrates a far more comprehensive system for ordering knowledge. Displaying objects for the viewer's delectation, these works assign a positive valuation to the science of classification, a system whose emphasis on individual identities disrupts the monarchy's attempts to concentrate power through art uniquely devoted to Louis's glory.

Jabach acquired and lost large segments of his collection, and his loss was decidedly the court's gain. Louis XIV knew that he had obtained beautiful and valuable objects from Jabach. The king could not have suspected, however, that these objects supported a way of thinking that would, over the course of the next century, redefine how the French saw their world and his own place in it. The mind's ability to assemble identities, to describe and thereby define the order of things, proved a powerful tool for counteracting the effects of propaganda. It was knowledge that no king, and no market, could eliminate.

PART TWO

Transformations

3 Fractured Spaces: Staging the King's Portrait

Classical theatre, one of the crown jewels of seventeenth-century French culture, reflects the values of the monarchy through the role of the sovereign: kings, generals, fathers, and patriarchal figures incarnate a principle of law. Molière's comedy about bourgeois values shares this orientation with the tragedies by Corneille and Racine. When they were performed onstage, these dramas contributed another dimension to the visual culture of the period. Much research on these plays, my own included, has considered them primarily as texts. Scholars with background in theatre studies are more inclined to see the plays as spectacle. I adapt that position, arguing that the audience viewed the staged drama much as it viewed paintings. The organization of space into clusters of elements within a painting directly parallels the organization of events and characters within the five-act structure of classical tragedy. The theatre audience, like the beholder of a painting, must consider the relations of each element in the performance to all other elements. Those connections comprise the memory traces, or ideas, that the audience retains after the play concludes.

Did drama exist independently of painting? Certainly, but when we consider the multiple influences operant in French court culture during this period, Dutch genre painting presents another theatre of interest. The French audience familiar with the intimate Dutch scenes would be able to relate these images to scenes of plays that show the tensions and realignments of players confronting a crisis. I am not describing an overtly conscious or deliberate process on the part of the spectators but rather the cumulative effects of cultural production over decades. The theatre audience accustomed to the openness of Netherlandish realism would be apt to experience a lingering uncertainty as the action draws to a close through the exercise of sovereign law. I argue that the denouements of French classical theatre impose a *forgetting* that visual language belies.

Portraits of the sovereign in Molière's *Tartuffe* (1664), Corneille's *Horace* (1640) and *Suréna* (1674), and Racine's *Phèdre* (1677) reinforce the ideal of the State as a monolithic power. Rulers are challenged by foreign enemies who would defeat them, by rebels at home who reject their authority, by heroes struggling with an overwhelming desire, and by unfaithful wives. In the end the sovereign's intervention sets things right. In Molière the king represents a beneficent presence. Judgment, however, comes at a price for many rulers.[1] Some, like Corneille's Tulle in *Horace*, can reconcile their decisions only by imposing an order to conceal the crime, the deliberate choice to ignore the evil that transpired. Others, like Orode in *Suréna*, kill off the generous and creative forces within their realms. In Racine's *Phèdre*, Thésée errs tragically before recognizing the truth that would have saved his son. Rule, however, these sovereigns all do in the end. With tragedy the audience, like the characters onstage, discovers the uncomfortable truth of irreparable loss. Classical theatre emphasizes a final release from a state of confusion or unknowing, even though that release brings regret, remorse, and/or a sense of the sovereign's inadequacies. Politically and psychologically rich, these plays depend on the sovereign's exercise of power. While it registers the grief sustained by society, the imposition of law assures an end to the crisis and the submission of all subjects to the king's authority. The French audience was acculturated to appreciate the order that seals the action, as well as the sense that the profound losses were counterbalanced through catharsis, the positive effects of emotions purged.[2]

The present chapter challenges the order implicit in that loss by invoking the idea of competing Dutch and French knowledge systems. Exposure to Netherlandish realism would have made the French more susceptible to interpreting the theatre in ways that supported incongruity, multivalence, and ambiguity, three characteristics of Dutch genre painting.The playwrights enact the singular authority of the king and the law through which he excludes rebellious elements.[3] Dutch art, however, informs a more comprehensive knowledge based on discrete, and sometimes competing, identities. Familiarity with the Dutch art thus broadens the context for viewing the plays.

I study critical aspects of classical theatre that cannot be explained through a traditional respect for its harmonious, symmetrical, and synthetic forms.[4] The audience recognized and respected how the playwrights depicted the sovereign's exercise of judgment. The audience, however, also retained elements of the plays that could not be explained away by the final outcome. I describe these residual thoughts as visual memories because they refer to powerful scenes that the audience observed and of course remembered. The question becomes: How were those residual images processed by the spectators, integrated into a broader knowledge?[5] Dutch Golden Age art is as rational in its use of space and perspective as the French theatre is in its reliance on balanced forms. Familiarity with Dutch images, however, would have encouraged the French audience to recognize – to identify and retain – the differences that classical playwrights eradicate.

Two genre paintings, one by Emanuel de Witte and the other by Vermeer, provide entry points to my discussion. As the previous chapters have shown, Dutch artists concentrate on precisely detailed renderings. They present scenes whose varied objects attract as much attention as the figures with whom they are associated. Most revealingly, while they cohere with a general theme or setting (maternal love within domestic space, for instance), the objects and figures do not lose their integrity as discrete elements within the work. In contrast, the classical theatre, consistent with official court art generally, reinforces the king's authority by demonstrating his power to harmonize discordant elements of society. The latter process amounts to the erasure of difference. Dutch genre paintings would inhibit the audience from suppressing aspects the conflict performed onstage.

In France statecraft and stagecraft were closely aligned. In collaboration with Colbert, Louis XIV became the principal patron of the arts in France. His financial support and praise were essential to the playwrights' prestige and survival. Unsurprisingly, therefore, the theatre presents some of the most resolute examples of kingship in the arts during Louis's reign because so many different plots similarly revolved around the performance of a powerful sovereign. My analysis in this chapter, however, moves from an integrated court model with *Le Tartuffe*; to a dual model with *Horace*, where the hero kills first Curiace and then, problematically, his sister Camille; to a triple model with *Suréna* that incorporates the sublime into the tragic experience opposing the hero/lover and the king. With each permutation the consolidation of sovereign power seems more equivocal.

In *Phèdre* different objects, colours, and sounds play a critical role in the final act. This descriptive emphasis takes on added value when considered in light of the careful detailing of individual objects in Dutch paintings. The record of observable phenomena that these works present contrasts markedly with the French reliance on myth to idealize the king.

The King's Image

Robert Nanteuil's 1664 portrait of Louis XIV establishes the context for the role of the sovereign in the plays written during his reign, continuing the tradition begun under his father, Louis XIII.

Nanteuil's portrait evidences the technical precision of his training with Flemish painter Philippe de Champaigne and French engraver and theoretician Abraham Bosse. Recognized as one of the greatest portraitists of his time, Nanteuil captures the regal presence of the king, who had announced his self-rule only three years earlier. While appropriately confident and assertive, the engraving of the king, especially his eyes and mouth, with his long wig and lace collar, describes the more intimate character and essential humanity of the royal subject. The real, flesh and blood Louis XIV is absorbed into the official portrait, complete with sash and armour, along with the coat of arms within the centred cartouche. The inserted oval frame bearing the Latin inscription *Ludovicus XIIII dei gratia franciae et navarrae rex* [By the Grace of God, Louis XIV King of France and Navarre] contains and concentrates the energy of the figure under the sign of God, literally. Louis's image appears under the frame with the words of God's blessing. These words, moreover, affirm that the king derives his authority from God. The portrait thus conveys the sense of historic mission as Louis, in military dress, looks out at the viewer.

In the same year that Nanteuil completed his portrait of Louis XIV, Molière wrote and produced for the sumptuous Versailles *fêtes*, the *Plaisirs de l'Île Enchantée*, a first version of *Le Tartuffe* about a falsely devout spiritual director and real libertine who dupes the gullible bourgeois paterfamilias, Orgon, attempting to exploit both his wife and his fortune.[6] This version of the play consisted of only three acts, including the eventual unmasking of Tartuffe. The final five-act version of the comedy is very familiar to scholars and students of the period. Molière introduces a positive image of the king consistent with Nanteuil's portrait.

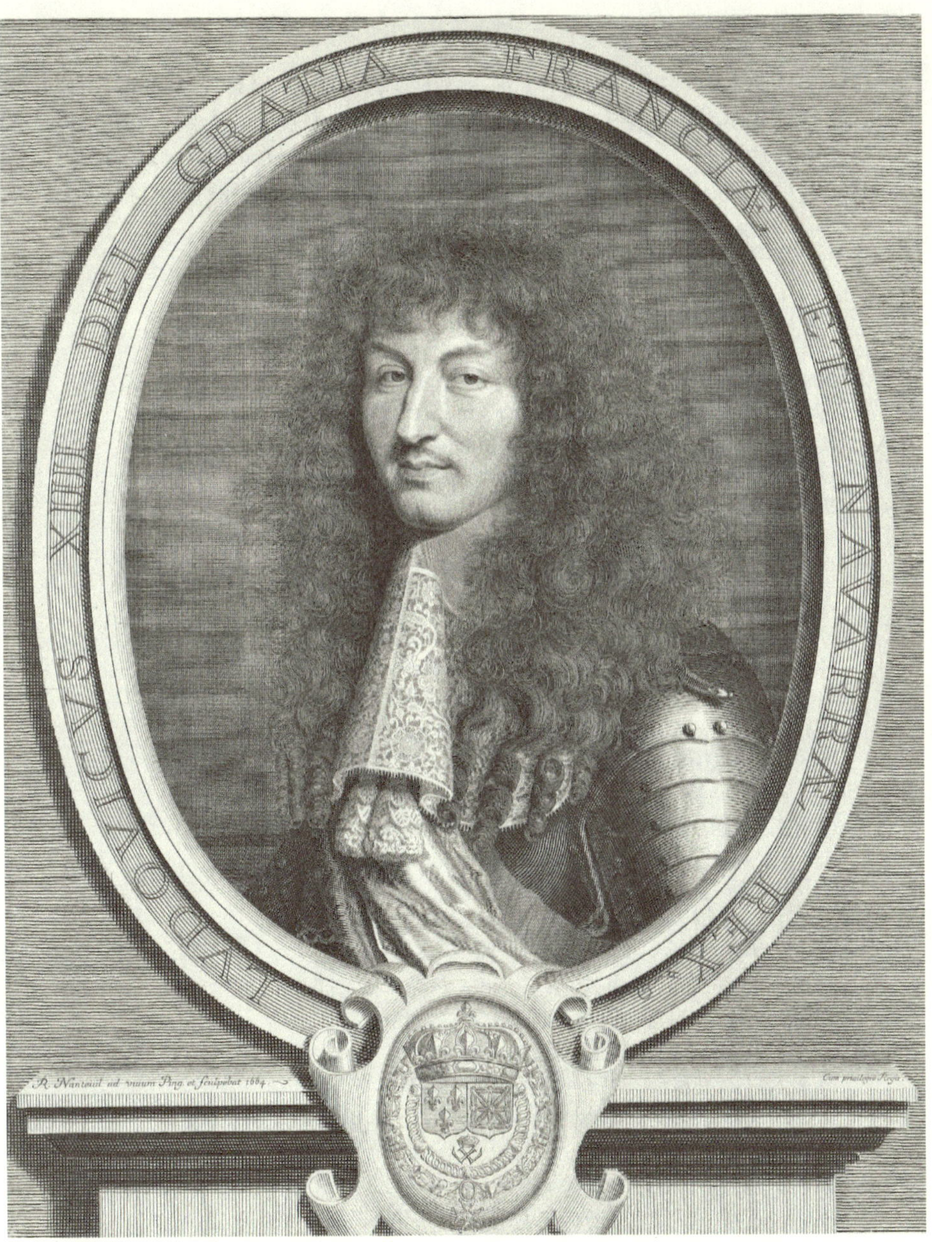

3.1. Robert Nanteuil. *Louis XIV*. 1664. Private Collection. Photo HIP/Art Resource, NY. http://pudl.princeton.edu/objects/00000010z.

Molière Onstage and Off

Orgon's understanding of the threat that Tartuffe poses is long in coming. It follows the hypocrite's persistent overtures to Elmire, Orgon's wife. Tartuffe's lines are hypocritically laced with religious references intended to justify his manipulative and lascivious behaviour:

L'amour qui nous attache aux beautés éternelles
N'étouffe pas en nous l'amour des temporelles;
Nos sens facilement peuvent être charmés
Des ouvrages parfaits que le Ciel a formés.
Ses attraits réfléchis brillent dans vos pareilles;
Mais il étale en vous ses plus rares merveilles;
Il a sur votre face épanché des beautés
Dont les yeux sont surpris, et les cœurs transportés,
Et je n'ai pu vous voir, parfaite créature,
Sans admirer en vous l'auteur de la nature,
Et d'une ardente amour sentir mon cœur atteint,
Au plus beau des portraits où lui-même il s'est peint.
D'abord j'appréhendai que cette ardeur secrète
Ne fût du noir esprit une surprise adroite;
Et même à fuir vos yeux mon cœur se résolut,
Vous croyant un obstacle à faire mon salut.
Mais enfin je connus, ô beauté toute aimable,
Que cette passion peut n'être point coupable,
Que je puis l'ajuster avec la pudeur,
Et c'est ce qui m'y fait abandonner mon cœur.
Ce m'est, je le confesse, une audace bien grande
Que d'oser de ce cœur vous adresser l'offrande;
Mais j'attends en mes vœux tout de votre bonté,
Et rien des vains efforts de mon infirmité;
En vous est mon espoir, mon bien, ma quiétude,
De vous dépend ma peine ou ma béatitude,
Et je vais être enfin, par votre seul arrêt,
Heureux si vous voulez, malheureux s'il vous plaît.

[Love, which attaches us to eternal beauties,
Does not stifle in us a love of temporal things.
Our senses can be easily charmed
By the perfect works that Heaven has formed.

The divine traits of our Creator are reflected in you.
But to you He has awarded his most rare marvels.
He has placed such beauties on your face
That eyes are amazed and hearts transported;
And I cannot see you, you perfect creature,
Without admiring in you the author of nature,
And feel my heart overcome with a deep passion,
You who are the most beautiful of the portraits in which
He has painted his image.
At first I feared that this secret passion
Was a clever surprise of a black spirit,
And my heart even resolved to flee your eyes,
Believing that you were an obstacle on my path to salvation.
But I finally realized, you lovely beauty,
That this passion could not be a guilty pleasure;
That I could reconcile it with a commitment to decency,
And this is what made me abandon my heart.
This is, I confess, a very audacious move
To dare to come to you offering this heart full of love;
But I am, in all my vows, appealing to your goodness,
And depend not at all on my poor vain efforts.
In you rests my hope, my well-being, my peace;
On you depends my suffering, or my delight:
And in the end I am going to be, by your word alone,
Either satisfied, if you wish, or miserable, if you so desire.] (3.3.933–60)[7]

Elmire is no dupe; she understands full well that Tartuffe's declarations betray all sense of religious or moral decency. Affirming that he will submit to her will, Tartuffe uses language that Elmire turns against him. She not only refuses his advances but also orchestrates his disgrace. In attempting to claim for himself all the pleasures of Orgon's household, including his food, wine, daughter, wife, and possessions, Tartuffe pretends to be a "dévot" [devout man] and, unproblematically, also a man of healthy appetites. In seeking to satisfy the latter, however, he reveals his corruption to Elmire, who sets about righting things within Orgon's household. She will prove the hypocrisy of Tartuffe's claim to guide the family, particularly its patriarch, to salvation while the hypocrite attends to his own very mortal desires: "Ah! Pour être dévot, je n'en suis pas moins homme"

[Oh! Although pious, I am nonetheless a man of flesh and blood] (3.3.966).

Elmire will expose Tartuffe to Orgon, whom the imposter has successfully wooed into complying with his excessive demands. The task proves a challenge: Orgon requires Elmire's direction to comprehend how Tartuffe has belittled and insulted him. Her superior understanding and control of the scene are further signs of Orgon's degraded position as head of the family. Obstinately refusing to recognize Tartuffe's efforts to subjugate him, Orgon is made to hear the imposter's seduction from a concealed spot under the table. In this position Orgon literally cannot see, which state of "blindness" reflects his inability to perceive his victimization by Tartuffe. Elmire intends, however, that once he hears Tartuffe's advances to her, Orgon will be able to reassume his role as "master" of the situation:

Vous n'aurez, que je crois, rien à me repartir.
À son mari qui est sous la table.
Au moins, je vais toucher une étrange matière:
Ne vous scandalisez en aucune manière.
Quoi que je puisse dire, il doit m'être permis,
Et c'est pour vous convaincre, ainsi que j'ai promis.
Je vais par des douceurs, puisque j'y suis réduite,
Faire poser le masque à cette âme hypocrite,
Flatter de son amour les désirs effrontés,
Et donner un champ libre à ses témérités.
Comme c'est pour vous seul, et pour mieux le confondre,
Que mon âme à ses vœux va feindre de répondre,
J'aurai lieu de cesser dès que vous vous rendrez,
Et les choses n'iront que jusqu'où vous voudrez.
C'est à vous d'arrêter son ardeur insensée,
Quand vous croirez l'affaire assez avant poussée,
D'épargner votre femme, et de ne m'exposer
Qu'à ce qu'il vous faudra pour vous désabuser:
Ce sont vos intérêts; vous en serez le maître.

[You will, I believe, have nothing to reproach me for.
To her husband who is under the table.
At least, as I am going to enter a strange matter,
Do not be at all scandalized.
Whatever I may say, you must allow me to continue,

For it is in order to convince you, as I promised.
I am going to expose the real ambitions of this hypocrite's soul
By various sweet encouragements, because I am reduced to doing so.
I will flatter his love's brazen desires,
And give free rein to his boldness.
As it is for you alone, and all the better to confound him,
That my soul will pretend to respond to his wishes,
I will have reason to stop as soon as you see what is happening,
And things will only go as far as you allow.
It is up to you to stop his offensive advances,
When you believe that the affair has gone far enough,
In order to spare your wife, and to expose me
To no more than you need in order to be convinced.
This is happening in your house,
  and you will be the master here.] (4.4.1369–85)

The idea of Orgon ruling from his inferior and obscure place under the table, however, merely accentuates the audience's sense of his demise, and the extent to which, blinded by Tartuffe's promises of eternal salvation and a heavenly reward, this paterfamilias has abandoned his role as protector and provider for the family.[8] Tartuffe was decidedly not there "by the grace of God" to whom he pretends to pray.

The question of true and false piety played out offstage as well. Molière's comedy famously involved the king and the playwright in a censorship battle. Despite his enjoyment of the play, Louis XIV ultimately ceded to pressure from those whom it offended. The king, who was sincerely devout, initially supported Molière, who claimed to mock only the falsely devout (*faux dévots*). Louis needed to reconcile his satisfaction with the play and his wish to crush the influence of certain powerful individuals, especially members of the Compagnie du Saint-Sacrement [The Company of the Blessed Sacrament], created in 1627 and composed largely of noble and bourgeois *parlementaires*, which by 1664 functioned as a secret society. Members of this group maintained rigid religious views and were intent on rooting out behaviour that they considered blasphemous or impious; they condemned adultery, libertinage, and irreligious acts, as well as Protestants. This group found Louis's behaviour with his mistress Mademoiselle de la Vallière to be scandalous. Its members were thus poised to oppose the king via Molière, whose comedy left too much room for his opponents to claim that he did not mock imposters, but rather all good Christians. The playwright vigorously defended himself.[9] Wishing to stave off further controversy from those who condemned the play, with the support of his mother, Anne d'Autriche, Louis agreed to ban the play. While the king's actions were somewhat equivocal, he gained in stature by asserting his right to decide the case. That is, Louis's mediation with the playwright served to enhance his own standing, even though he effectively ceded authority in censoring a play that he truly enjoyed.[10]

In 1669 Molière revised the original three-act play into the five-act version that we now possess. In it the king (who is never directly associated with Louis XIV) is literally but his image: the king never appears onstage. Nonetheless, the king's influence remains critical to the resolution of the conflict between Orgon's family and Tartuffe. The revised play concludes not only with the hypocrite Tartuffe unmasked and imprisoned but also with Orgon's life, possessions, and honour restored. This favourable outcome results from the intervention of the sovereign, whose portrait his officer, the Exempt, elaborates:

Nous vivons sous un prince ennemi de la fraude,
Un prince dont les yeux se font jour dans les cœurs,
Et que ne peut tromper tout l'art des imposteurs.
D'un fin discernement sa grande âme pourvue
Sur les choses toujours jette une droite vue;
Chez elle jamais rien ne surprend trop d'accès,
Et sa ferme raison ne tombe en nul excès.
Il donne aux gens de bien une gloire immortelle;
Mais sans aveuglement il fait briller ce zèle,
Et l'amour pour les vrais ne ferme point son cœur
À tout ce que les faux doivent donner d'horreur.
Celui-ci n'était pas pour le pouvoir surprendre,
Et de pièges plus fins on le voit se défendre.

[We live under a prince who is the enemy of fraud,
A prince who sees directly into our hearts
And whom no imposter, however crafty, could ever deceive.
With his great mind, capable of discerning the truth,
He always penetrates the heart of the matter.
Nothing ever unbalances his wisdom,
And he always acts judiciously.
He honours the righteous with eternal glory,
But he never considers this zeal blindly.

His love for those who are truly pious does not prevent him
From regarding with horror all that frauds do to deceive.
This one was not likely to be able to take him by surprise,
As he had already caught many more skilful liars.] (5.7.1906–18)

The distance of the king from this scene provides an opportunity for an elaborate encomium, a portrait of the king by the Exempt that plays on the concept of unmasking, knowing the truth. Here the absent royal body occasions a tribute onstage that emphasizes the king's ability to see behind the mask; to have the courage to act; and to earn his subjects' love for doing so. The Exempt describes the sovereign's superior judgment, evident both in his ability to see through Tartuffe's hypocrisy and in his move to save Orgon, who had earlier proved his loyalty to the king. For the characters onstage, as for the audience, the sovereign exists as an image of a just and benevolent protector of his subjects.

Molière flatters the king with the *deus ex machina* [god emerging from the machine] ending, which uses the unmotivated and unanticipated royal intercession (one that has consequently been critiqued as deficient theatrical staging) to praise the king's just and able rule. Moreover, the godlike intervention of the king's (sudden) ability to save Orgon's family from ruin has direct parallels with the real spectacle of statecraft at Versailles and its unremitting propaganda. As playwright, of course, Molière masks, assigns fictional identities, to all his actors, an illusion that Tartuffe pushes to the breaking point through his incarnation of the imposter role. A man of the theatre himself, Molière explodes the hypocrite's identity only to magnify his own power of image-making in the form of an omniscient, disembodied (absent) king. Molière's sovereign is everything that Orgon is not: the king penetrates the truth and acts judiciously. Molière relies on the king to expose Tartuffe's false identity. Moreover, the playwright negates the hypocrite's evil with the Exempt's projection of an enduring image of the king's munificence. Sustaining the play of mirrors, this truth reflects back favourably on Molière, as the maker of the machine whose ultimate "deus" is the godlike absent monarch whose aura in the play supports the real monarchy's cultivation of the king's image. The king's power depends on his image; his image relies on repetition and imitation; and, the playwright demonstrates through his own role, imitation is inseparable from acting, artifice, and arbitrary actions. The latter three qualities are fault lines for the monarchy. Already the history of Molière's performance shows Louis XIV yielding to pressure before asserting his power. To compensate for the history of actions and reactions that occur as part of real statecraft, the king relies on the playwrights to burnish his image. The tragedies of Corneille and Racine challenge the integrity of the king's portrait, however, by exposing the State's arbitrary choices and the artificial harmonies that the sovereign imposes.

From Comedy to Tragedy: Second Acts in Corneille and Racine

Molière's comedy represents a happy ending not only for Orgon and his family but also for the real king, whose image the play glorifies. Depictions of the sovereign in tragedies are more complex, as befits a genre deemed more serious and defined by loss. In part the complexity relates to the design of the tragedies as a closed system of representation, one that moves from crisis to a final order. Dutch painters are far less concerned with unmasking a particular truth or imparting a single meaning to the scenes that they describe. Their works support multiple, and even contradictory, interpretations. Dutch genre paintings frequently develop competing spaces: the inside view provides views of the outside; within an interior, a staid musical performance in the foreground is juxtaposed with a lurid image on the wall. Dutch artists thus develop a sense of dual realities that function simultaneously.

Applied to the tragedies of Corneille and Racine, this way of seeing highlights interpretation as a process of recording scenes as memory traces; the audience retains image after image of what takes place onstage. The narrative aspect of theatrical production develops a sense of time as erasure: actions succeed one another; each scene replaces the one before. The imposition of order at the tragedy's close often depends on sequential time: the king executes his law; discordant actions are suppressed; order is restored; the audience takes solace in that order. Yet the audience perceives the actors onstage much as it does when it views a painting, retaining and "cataloguing" all elements. Whereas French court art encourages a distillation of elements into a celebration of monarchic power, Netherlandish realism in effect trains the viewer to subvert this process. The French audience arrived at the theatre armed with both the Ludovican episteme and the Dutch empirical orientation. The latter meant that the court's control of ideas was less than totalizing, however successful and moving the drama proved to be.

Conflict is inherent to theatrical performance. While the seventeenth-century audience certainly understood the conventions of the theatre and the aims of the playwrights, spectators were being asked, in many instances, to accept as law, for the good of the people, actions that involved denying the full truth of what they had witnessed. They recognized the harmony of the ending, yet they knew that it happened at the expense of other interests and as a result of particular choices that the sovereign made. The absolute quality of sovereign power, however, was very much the issue with which French court society contended. The idea of the king's law being "good for them" was contested, given the wars, the debts, the unequal dispensing of privileges, and the favouritism that Louis XIV showed.

It was never a question of the French audience really forgetting what actions a tragedy eliminates, subjugates, or otherwise defeats, any more than the characters onstage could ever forget the circumstances leading to their final scenes. The theatre audience, however, was accustomed to "reading" what it saw onstage as it would any other heroic narrative, literary or visual, in service of the Louis XIV. Dutch genre paintings rely on a different logic; they allow disparate elements of an image to coexist. Applied to the theatre, this model means that disruptive elements of the drama (external threats to the nation; defiance within the family; revolt and passion) remain vital even once order is restored. The theatre audience takes the full measure of the tragic cycle as part of a more complex understanding. At what cost, a spectator asks, does the sovereign's law restore harmony? Attuned to Netherlandish realist art that presents aggregates, complex wholes, the French would be more apt to see a tragedy's closure as arbitrary, as excluding details that continued to resonate. Realism encourages a cataloguing of all observable phenomena. Translated to the stage, the empirical emphasis of Dutch art destabilizes the idea of "oneness" and the artful syntheses through which only thoughts consistent with the sovereign's law/desire/order deserve to survive. The audience would be more inclined to recognize statecraft as involving as much theatre as balanced judgment, as much covering over as disclosure. The exercise of power is therefore susceptible to abuse. From *Horace*, through *Suréna*, and *Phèdre*, the slippage from benevolent justice to tyranny and misguided actions by the sovereign becomes all too evident.

Outside the theatre, and notably in conjunction with the presence of Northern realist art in their lives, the French had been conditioned to assemble what they observed without prejudice; to tolerate uncertainties, inconsistencies, and differences. Netherlandish paintings do not lead directly to discussions of dead lovers and quelled rebellions onstage, or at court. As a process for engaging in the world, for actively knowing what exists, and actively filtering those perceptions into a system that is independent of the narrative of absolutism that French artists and writers adopt in support of the monarchy, however, the visual experience empowers in seductive ways. The predominant intellectual force of classical theatre was consistent with the practice of subordinating all identities to that of the king. The numbers always favoured Louis: more art and theatre supported the king's image and the monarchy's interests than challenged them. Yet Northern realism was sufficiently part of the French cultural experience to have introduced a way of thinking that relied not on arbitrary exercises of power but rather on the observation, classification, and recording of information. That idea contained within it the potential for radical change, as it empowered beholders to know rather than simply to submit and be awed by what they saw.

Painting the Stage

Emanuel de Witte's *Interior with a Woman Playing a Virginal* presents an elaborately detailed scene of domestic life. This image demonstrates how Dutch genre paintings not only emphasize visual clues such as mirrors and perspectival effects but also unresolved elements of an elusive narrative.

De Witte's image offers a long perspective from front to back, across the rooms. The male head of household does not appear, although he was most likely the purchaser of the painting whose expansive architectural layout and beautifully rendered possessions would offer a most satisfying image of a burgher's success. The enfilade, or succession of rooms whose doors are all aligned along a single axis with the doors of the connecting rooms, provides a broad vista through the home. The viewer takes in the richly appointed decor, the calm, and the servant sweeping, all of which convey a positive image of domesticity, prosperity, and cleanliness.[11] The mistress, her back to the viewer, is playing a virginal. The gilt-framed mirror over her head, angled to maximize the light, does not reveal much of her face and none of her expression. Bathed in the window light as she plays the instrument, her superior social standing contrasts with that of the servant labouring at the opposite end of the home. The rooms are simply but richly appointed, including a marble floor, chandelier, and imported carpet. These features, while they suggest the owner's

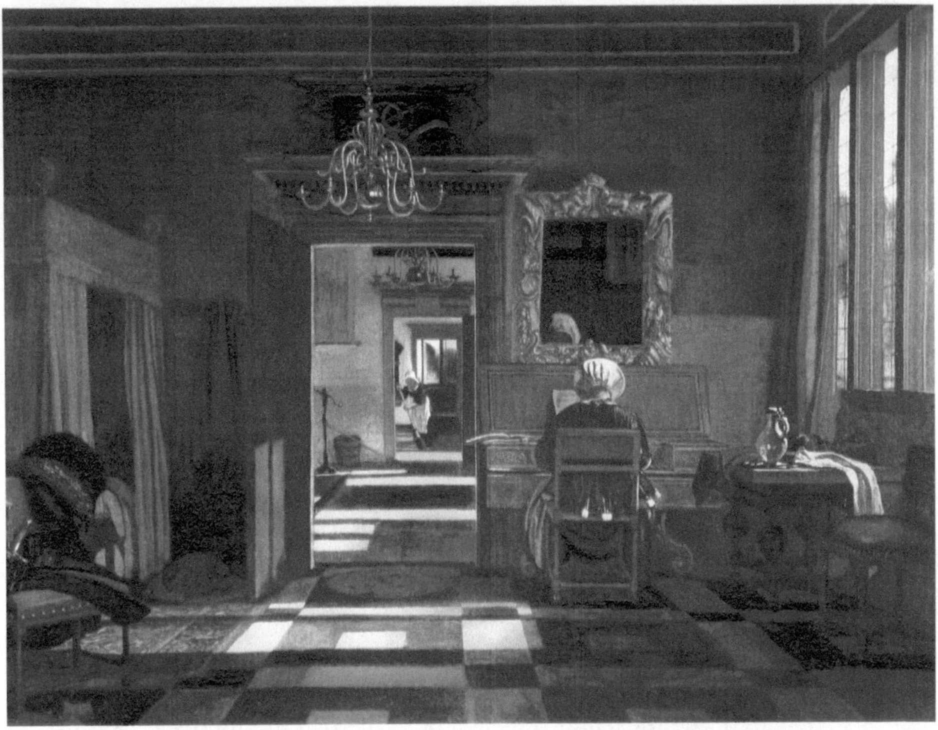

3.2. Emanuel de Witte. *Interior with a Woman at the Virginal*. Ca. 1660–70. 77.5 × 104.5 cm (30.51 × 41.14 in). Museum Boijmans van Beuningen, Rotterdam. Image courtesy Museum Boijmans van Beuningen, Rotterdam, The Netherlands / De Agostini Picture Library / Bridgeman Images. http://collectie.boijmans.nl/en/object/3594/Interior-with-a-Woman-at-the-Virginal/Emanuel-de-Witte.

material wealth, do so in an understated fashion that underscores the dignity and modesty of the lady and her important role in administering the household. Order and cleanliness reflect back the innocence of the soul. Music, however, is a call to love, and the two scores resting on the instrument, appropriate for a duo, suggest that there is more to the story. The viewer confronts two competing depictions: one of a proper burgher's home, the other of a home sullied by its lady. We look again, scrutinizing the objects more closely. The sword … Is that a soldier peeking out from the bed curtains? Indeed it is. His uniform and sword are lying on the chair; his coat hangs on the wall next to the bed, over the sleeping dog. In genre paintings soldiers frequently represent the interloper.[12] Here the implied sexual dalliance compromises the lady's honour. Nothing, and certainly not the dog, disturbs this second view.

De Witte's painting operates on two levels, and the beholder's ability to retain both is a critical aspect of the power of the image to convey information. The viewer inventories the image, cataloguing the various objects it contains. The ultimate determinate of the identity of those things depends on the category (fidelity/infidelity; order/disorder; cleanliness and godliness/dishonor and sin) that one assigns to it. Knowledge is an effect of the viewer's observation and classifications. This information proves useful to interpreting classical tragedy because as the plot advances the theatre audience similarly registers multiple identities based on binary relations (king/subject; male/female; love/duty).

French playwrights bind incidents together through a principle of internal necessity (unity of action) but also so that the plot appears complete, with its central conflict resolved. All parts of a play fit neatly into a whole, a social order controlled by the sovereign. Logically, the relation of part to whole, synecdoche, is consistent with a metaphorical emphasis on shared qualities, and the "analogic" French model discussed in chapter 1. In tragedy all surviving subjects submit to the king's authority; they are similar in their acceptance of his rule. The relation of part to whole, however, is more directly linked here to metonymy, where the association between things does not presume that they are similar. The same hero is glorified for his first action but vilified for his subsequent action. There is the rub. I argue that *Horace* retains the duality that characterizes de Witte's image. Like de Witte's painting, *Horace* offers two competing visions. Both meanings cohere, and, at the end, the play shows what the king would conceal. The painting helps us to visualize the theatrical experience as performed onstage.

Horace

With his two brothers, Horace enters the battle for Rome against his sister's lover Curiace, and his two brothers, who represent Albe. Proud to represent his country, Horace unequivocally dismisses Curiace's regret that such a battle pitches loved ones against each other. Horace remains fiercely dedicated to the code that links glory to the sacrifice of love for duty. He concentrates so fully on that glory, and on being recognized for his achievements (the more self-interested side of his heroic engagement), that he ultimately kills his sister Camille for her emotional provocation following his victory against the Curiaces.[13] Camille delivers an unchecked attack in which she curses Horace and the Roman ideal that he exemplifies:

Rome, l'unique objet de mon ressentiment!
Rome, à qui vient ton bras d'immoler mon amant!
Rome qui t'a vu naître, et que ton cœur adore!
Rome enfin que je hais parce qu'elle t'honore!

[Rome, the source of all of my resentment!
Rome, in whose name your arm just sacrificed my lover!
Rome, which witnessed your birth, and which your heart adores!
Rome, which I hate for honouring you!] (4.5.1301–4)[14]

Horace's defeat of the three Curiaces is a moment that touches the sublime, so perfectly does it capture the hero's willingness to sacrifice all affective ties in his successful battle against his foes. Unlike his brother-in-law Curiace, Horace relishes the battle that pits him against his family as a test of his superior ability. The hero willingly denies his connections to others, which choice, other characters argue, means that he denies the very qualities that make him human. Any good soldier, Horace maintains, can fight the enemy; true exceptionalism requires that a man be able and willing to kill "un autre soi-même" [an other self], the enemy who is also a beloved brother:

Hors de l'ordre commun il [le sort] nous fait des fortunes.
Combattre un ennemi pour le salut de tous,
Et contre un inconnu s'exposer seul aux coups,
D'une simple vertu c'est l'effet ordinaire,
Mille déjà l'ont fait, mille pourraient le faire,
Mourir pour le pays est un si digne sort
Qu'on briguerait en foule une si belle mort.
Mais vouloir au public immoler ce qu'on aime,
S'attacher au combat contre un autre soi-même,
Attaquer un parti qui prend pour défenseur
Le frère d'une femme et l'amant d'une sœur,

Et rompant tous ces nœuds s'armer pour la patrie
Contre un sang qu'on voudrait racheter de sa vie,
Une telle vertu n'appartenait qu'à nous.

[Fate has presented us with an exceptional challenge.
To combat an enemy for our collective well-being,
And to expose oneself to attacks from an unknown enemy
Is the ordinary effect of a simple virtue.
Thousands have already done this, and thousands more
could do as much.
To die for one's country is such an honourable end
That people would rush to meet such a beautiful death.
But to want to sacrifice for the public good what one loves,
To engage in combat against one's own family,
To attack an opposing side that takes as its defender
A wife's brother and a sister's lover,
And, denying all these connections, to arm oneself in defence
of one's country
Against blood that one would otherwise die to save,
Such a virtue belonged to us alone.] (2.3.436–49)[15]

The dilemma lies precisely in the fact that denial for a greater gain is arguably a qualified denial. The hero represses desire for family in order to satisfy a more intense desire for recognition. Horace relishes not only service to his nation but also personal glory. Vanity ultimately threatens what he achieved with distinction on the battlefield. His need for recognition as much as his sense of duty proves a formidable obstacle to his reputation.

Horace leaves the battlefield victorious, yet he is unable to distinguish clearly between the glory of the country he defends and his own personal glory. Arguably, these demands would be but two sides of the same coin, were it not for his sister Camille, who – erroneously, according to the codes governing society – insists on Horace's need to recognize sentimental attachments as well. Her offending behaviour notwithstanding, King Tulle judges Horace's murder of Camille to be a crime that no one, not even the gods, could excuse:

Cette énorme action faite presque à nos yeux
Outrage la nature, et blesse jusqu'aux dieux.
Un premier mouvement qui produit un tel crime
Ne saurait lui servir d'excuse légitime:

Les moins sévères lois en ce point sont d'accord;
Et si nous les suivons, il est digne de mort.

[This monstrous deed committed practically before our eyes
Is an outrage to nature and an offence even to the gods.
That an impulsive action produced such a crime
Cannot be considered a legitimate defence for him.
The least severe laws agree on this point,
And if we follow them, he should be condemned to die.] (5.3.1733–8)

Despite this explicit articulation of the law, however, the play's final act juxtaposes two actions that complicate any clear sense of an ending. The principal action occurs during a veritable trial in which the king, protecting his military advantage, exonerates the hero. The king ignores both State and religious precepts to defend his country. The second action concerns Tulle's regard for Camille. Tulle's speech condemns Horace but subjects him and all Romans to an imposed forgetting. They must ignore Horace's crime to preserve Rome:

Et l'art et le pouvoir d'affermir des couronnes
Sont des dons que le ciel fait à peu de personnes.
De pareils serviteurs sont les forces des rois,
Et de pareils aussi sont au-dessus des lois.
Qu'elles se taisent donc; que Rome dissimule
Ce que dès sa naissance elle vit en Romule:
Elle peut bien souffrir en son libérateur
Ce qu'elle a bien souffert en son premier auteur.
Vis donc, Horace, vis, guerrier trop magnanime:
Ta vertu met ta gloire au-dessus de ton crime.

[The art and the power to secure a kingdom
Are gifts that heaven accords only a very few.
Kings rely on such subjects for their strength,
And they are above the law.
Let the laws be silent, then; let Rome conceal
What from its birth it saw in Romulus:
Rome can tolerate in its liberator
What it also tolerated in its first author.
Live, then, Horace, you too magnanimous warrior:
Your virtue places your glory above your crime.] (5.3.1751–60)

Privileging the military capability necessary to defend Rome, Tulle effectively erases Horace's deplorable act of murder. The audience cannot but appreciate his judgment; he makes a pragmatic choice to protect country. The king's effort to consolidate power in defence of Rome rings true. Nonetheless, the characters, and with them the audience, engage in a trial of Horace that is also, implicitly, a trial of logic. Tulle imposes his interpretation of history as an exercise of memory that paradoxically conditions an obligatory forgetting. In his configuration of events Horace's victory against the Albans becomes the cause motivating forgiveness and the suppression of the crime:

Si d'ailleurs nous voulons regarder le coupable,
Ce crime, quoique grand, énorme, inexcusable,
Vient de la même épée et part du même bras
Qui me fait aujourd'hui maître de deux états.
Deux sceptres en ma main, Albe à Rome asservie,
Parlent bien hautement en faveur de sa vie:
Sans lui j'obéirais où je donne la loi,
Et je serais sujet où je suis deux fois roi.

[If, moreover, we want to consider the accused,
This crime, while great, monstrous, and inexcusable,
Comes from the same sword and results from the same arm
That today makes me master of two states.
I hold two sceptres: that of Albe and that of Rome.
They speak emphatically in favour of granting him life.
Without him I would obey, whereas now I execute the law,
And I would be a subject, while I am now twice king.] (5.3.1739–46)

In this speech Tulle reasserts the heroic code by eliminating the secondary, "different" deed that threatened Rome's hegemony. The image of Horace's murder of Camille, however, lingers through evocations of crime, the dead Camille, and Tulle's sense of the rule of law. The king champions the hero who possesses the courage, skill, and motivation to serve the nation. He applauds Horace's victory, however, without erasing the all too human image of Horace as a man unable, or unwilling, to control his emotions when the context shifts from the battlefield back to the family, which condemns him without excusing her.[16]

Tulle executes one more decision that allies his own emotion with his official recognition of the victim:

Je la plains; et pour rendre à son sort rigoureux
Ce que peut souhaiter son esprit amoureux,
Puisqu'en un même jour l'ardeur d'un même zèle
Achève le destin de son amant et d'elle,
Je veux qu'un même jour, témoin de leurs deux morts,
En un même tombeau voie enfermer leurs corps.

[I pity her, and to provide her tragic end
What her lover's spirit might desire,
Because on the same day the passion rooted in the same conviction
Brought to an end her own and her lover's destiny,
I want, so as to bear witness to their two deaths, on the same day and
In the same tomb, to have their bodies sealed.] (5.3.1777–82)

They will bury Camille beside her beloved Curiace. They will bury her opposition and thereby end her revolt. The audience, however, cannot forget Horace's violence against Camille. To ignore this crime, as Rome did Romulus's murder of his brother Remus in a disagreement over the proper site for building the city, amounts to the king's active suppression of knowledge, his deliberate abolishment of a memory. Tulle's order to recognize the hero requires everyone to "dissimulate," that is, conceal Horace's crime so that society can move forward, protected. The audience, however, learned what happened and does remember. The king's acknowledgment of Camille through a final reference to her burial with Curiace stands, for Corneille's audience, as a commemoration both of her, I have argued, and of the act of memory itself.[17]

While concealment is politically expedient, a rule that the characters onstage know they must obey, Corneille's audience cannot easily compress the images of Horace evoked onstage – the sublimely heroic Horace, Horace taunted by his sister into a heinous murder, and that negative hero accommodated by Tulle so that he appears again as the sublime Horace – into a single idea(l) even as it acknowledges the king's astute resolution of the crisis. Consistent with the classical emphasis on unity and reason, the audience will choose to recognize the benevolence and the power of the king's law. The will to choose, however, is very different from knowledge, the record of what has transpired. Order is restored: the rebellion represented by Camille's audacious (and therefore too masculine) intervention as well as by the overly sentimental and insufficiently heroic (and therefore too feminine) Curiace – this double imbalance – is set right and negated by the lovers' burial together.[18] This interpretation, moreover, privileges similarity as the monarchy's model for promoting the interests of the crown. Rome is saved at the expense of Albe; Horace wins out against Curiace; and Rome's hero, Horace, survives Rome's detractor, Camille: all *others* are eliminated.

Yet as he brings resolution to the crisis, Tulle portrays a decidedly dualistic society. In his speech the devoted Camille is coextensive with the politically reprehensible Camille; Horace the glorious hero survives with Horace the vain brother who kills his sister; the crime is protected, covered over, to fend off a future enemy even as the crime is acknowledged "jusqu'aux dieux" [even to the gods]. Tulle calls attention to all that separates the actual from the ideal. As with the sustained moral ambiguity of de Witte's painting, both of the play's storylines – that of the hero's victories and that of his crime – inform the audience's response. Tulle's exculpatory evidence involves a presentation of inculpatory evidence-the audience cannot understand the one without recognizing the other. The truth of that ambiguity resonates long after Camille's burial.

The king's judgment effectively creates a new law, or a new interpretation of extant moral and civil laws condemning the hero. Tulle's decision to excuse Horace's crime serves the interests of the State, however, and thus coincides with the basic function of law to maintain order and protect the nation. Although it is understandably prudent and efficacious, the decision to exonerate the hero is clearly arbitrary. Dissimulation, the covering up of the truth, runs up against the observations of the characters onstage as well as those of Corneille's audience. Both groups have witnessed the prelude and the aftermath of Camille's murder; they have seen the king vindicate the hero whose criminality the law affirms. Those who see the performance have learned about a resolution with which they well may agree, from a king whom they respect and admire. Nonetheless, it leaves parts of the equation unbalanced. How can a king oblige his subjects to ignore what they have witnessed, to forget what he himself has studied and labelled a crime?

Tulle acts as a prudent and generous leader, but the expectation that the audience's sense of Horace's crime be buried with Camille is all the more improbable given that as a final gesture the king honours her love for Curiace. Tulle identifies Horace as the murderer whose crime he then forgives. Camille will spend eternity with her lover. Yet funeral honours for her cannot erase the history that provoked her death. The performance of these rites, as commanded by the king, complicates his order to dissimulate, to bury the truth, since this burial is also an act of commemoration.[19] These ambiguities emerge directly from Corneille's play. Indeed, Tulle himself raises the issue of knowledge versus power, and he takes the side of power. His choice leaves the question of knowledge unsatisfied.

The audience's ability to understand the play finds a more consistent logic in Northern paintings that assemble eclectic objects without erasing the differences between them. In de Witte's painting the solution is not to deny the soldier's involvement with the wife of the owner of the house; nor is it to deny the apparent calm of a household in which the woman plays musical harmonies while the maid cleans. One act does not conceal the other; rather, the viewer's pleasure relates to identifying the pieces of the puzzle, that is, to discovering that the sordid story of the soldier's seduction of the mistress forms part of the story of the mistress's meticulously ordered household. If one considers Corneille's *Horace* as one perceives a Dutch painting, the "other" meanings – Camille's love for Curiace, Horace's inferior action, Tulle's arbitrary choice – all survive the final curtain.

Tragic Permutations: From *Horace* to *Suréna* to *Phèdre*

Vermeer's compositional format in *Lady Writing a Letter with Her Maid* helps to situate Corneille's organization of theatrical space in *Suréna*, the playwright's final work. Although it was considered a failure when initially performed, *Suréna* offers a compelling case for exposing the relations that underlie political power and knowledge.[20] Portraying the king as both a forceful ruler and a tyrant, this tragedy intriguingly problematizes the ideal of kingship and absolutism at a time when Louis XIV was engaged in fighting the Dutch. While the French would not have associated Vermeer's painting, or any particular Dutch genre painting, with *Suréna*, they would certainly have had Dutch art well within their purview, given France's military engagements. As befits the plots of love interests that play out in the face of an opposing power, moreover, the performances onstage mirror the dramas that Louis's subjects witnessed in real time as they vied for his attention and support. Familiarity with Dutch realist paintings would only have accentuated the audience's sense of the tension within the plays as they mirror the dramas at court. With *Lady Writing a Letter with Her Maid* Vermeer

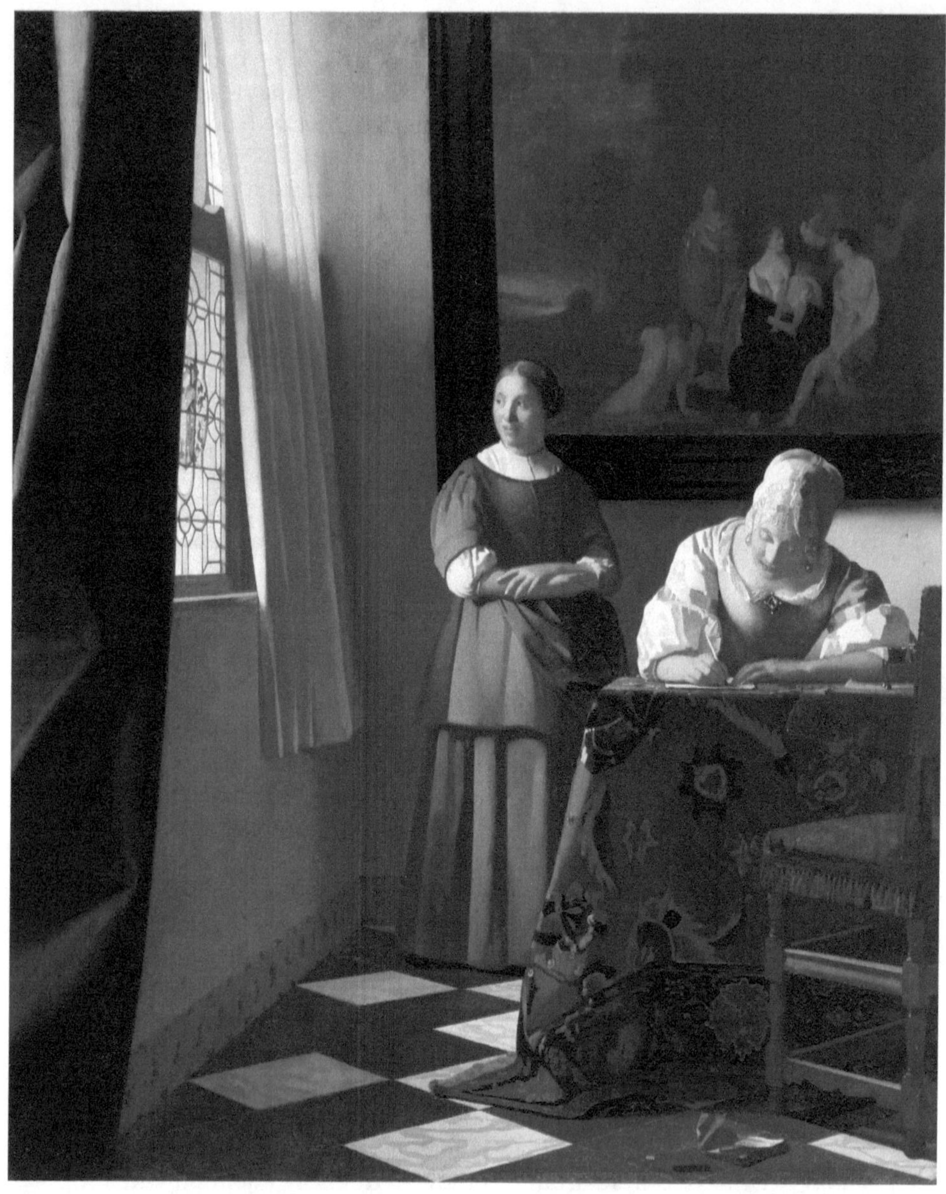

3.3. Johannes Vermeer. *A Lady Writing a Letter with Her Maid*. Ca. 1670. 71.1 × 60.5 cm (28 × 23.81 in). National Gallery of Ireland, Dublin. Image courtesy National Gallery of Ireland. https://www.nationalgallery.ie/woman-writing-letter-her-maid-johannes-vermeer.

creates a visually rich and multivalent work. Its compositional design has particular interest for *Suréna,* as the play develops both a love story and a political history. The calculated uncertainty of the image invites further comparisons of *Horace* with *Suréna,* which I consider together in a separate section to highlight how Corneille's tragic form evolves over the course of his career to degrade sovereign authority.

Like Vermeer, Corneille offsets the principal or frame narrative with a secondary narrative that it never entirely supplants. The audience compares primary and secondary histories in *Suréna* much as it does with the painting, whose various parts do not perfectly align. Vermeer creates an uneasy association of histories that is less than total and yet substantial: no single idea or identity can suffice to explain the full impact of the image based on the relation of the inserted painting to the primary image.

In ways that the patterns of elements in Vermeer's image help to conceptualize, Corneille expands the field of possible meanings by subjecting the tragic form to a series of permutations. I show how Corneille reconfigures patterns of elements critical to the outcome. These shifts demonstrate broader possibilities for knowledge than a strict dedication to a principle of analogy, or elimination of discordant elements in support of the king's position, would allow. Description here is cumulative, not reductive: the beholder looks not to eliminate elements that fail to substantiate an ideal but rather to identify and understand the relations between elements. The descriptive function has consequences for an audience of Racine's *Phèdre* as well, where it underscores the deficiency of the king's final position.

Suréna

Louis XIV, who was only a child when *Horace* was first staged, would eventually benefit from understanding the exercise of power and the role of the sovereign that Corneille conveys. The sense of order that emerges from the consistent elimination of difference is reinforced by Tulle's presence as a leader, who, unlike the hero, can recognize emotion without compromising his role as protector of the State. By the time Corneille ended his career with *Suréna,* however, the image of the king in the theatre had changed for the worse. Eurydice and Suréna fall victim to the will of King Orode and the machinations of his son Pacorus. Corneille seals the lovers' fate within a political drama that produces the murder of the hero and the death of the despairing Eurydice. In this tragedy love is always a eulogy to the couple's desire, part prayer and part exhortation. That passion would be destroyed by the manoeuvrings of the king were it not for the lyricism of the lovers' discourse and the justness of their cause. While the latter moves the audience, the former transports it. Language that touches the sublime transforms the lost love into something other, more ethereal and enduring. The political story appears to consume the love story. From the outset the lovers are victims exploited by the State. Their love for each other has no place in history, no chance to survive. The king, however, does not have the last word, as not only the lovers' suffering but also the aesthetic appeal of their interventions inform the audience's view of the machinations of power.

The formal patterns of the play extend to spatial relations, the separation of the private domain of the lovers and the public space involving their relations with the crown. Corneille triangulates the theatrical space just as he triangulates relations. The crisis involves two of King Orode's children as rivals for the lovers. Eurydice resists her obligation to marry Prince Pacorus, as her father's treaty with Orode stipulated. The king subsequently orders Suréna to wed his daughter, Princess Mandane. Vermeer's *Lady Writing a Letter with Her Maid* helps to elucidate how the audience perceives the relations between characters in terms of three spaces, two that are manifest, and the third, an *other, elsewhere* space [*ailleurs*], which the characters invoke in their laments.[21]

In *Lady Writing a Letter with Her Maid* Vermeer applies two compositional elements that have direct application to *Suréna*. The first element concerns the framing device, the relation of the inserted painting to the principal image. Vermeer creates intensity within the scene through this juxtaposition, which establishes two related, yet independent, narratives. Corneille similarly alternates two stories, the love of Eurydice and Suréna, and the political power that crushes them. The second element relates to the window, which opens the space of the room to the world outside. Providing natural light, the window designates the outdoors without revealing any specific objects. It creates a divide within in the image, the separation of interior and exterior spaces. Corneille's tragedy devotes considerable attention to the *ailleurs*, a space of love, and then of death. The viewer's appreciation of the finality of the ending is similarly broken, disrupted by the mournful lines pronounced first by the lovers and then in deference to their passing. Corneille balances the monarch's abuse of power with the lovers' elegiac verse.

Vermeer's art, therefore, parallels Corneille's lyricism, which touches the sublime.

In *Lady Writing a Letter with Her Maid* Vermeer presents a single scene rather than a full diachronic unfolding of events: the befores and the afters remain unknown even once the objects are mined for their iconographical significance. Vermeer's pair of female figures, the lady composing her letter and her maid, dominate the image. Neither looks at the other. The letter writing contextualizes the scene as a private moment of psychological intensity, as registered in the lady's expression. A crumpled page of a book on the floor, likely a letter manual, in the foreground forms a still life with a stick of sealing wax and a red seal, presumably removed from a letter received, to which the lady now responds.[22] The rejected page suggests the lady's dissatisfaction either with the letter she has just read or with her first draft of her own letter. Yet the lady herself looks calm, betraying no emotion as she writes, other than concentration. The maid, whose statuesque pose assigns her a certain dignity despite her role as servant, looks outside the home into the public space of the city where she will likely deliver her mistress's letter.

Vermeer enriches the space with a prominently displayed interior painting. The full image and the framed painting appear very dissimilar, the latter being biblical. They do, however, share characteristics. The inserted painting does not present an allegory of home, of women's space, of love, or prosperity, much less the epistolary form, although all these themes resonate. Like Vermeer's rendering of the lady and her maid, the large *Finding of Moses* painting on the rear wall emphasizes a woman's role.[23] It illustrates the moment in *Exodus* (2:1–10) where the Egyptian Pharaoh's daughter and her handmaidens discover the baby Moses in a basket among the reeds. The birth of Moses took place after the Egyptian ruler ordered all male Hebrew children to be drowned. After hiding him for three months, Moses's mother sent the baby down the Nile in a basket. The Pharaoh's daughter found him and saved him, raising Moses as her own son. Vermeer uses the biblical reference, which was very familiar to Dutch audiences as a story of divine providence and the reconciliation of opposing forces, to valorize the strong feminine emphasis in his image, ascribing to his lady the same attributes of compassion and independence assigned to the Pharaoh's daughter. Moreover, during the Dutch Revolt against Spain, artists and writers frequently compared William of Orange to Moses and the Dutch to the Israelites, God's chosen people.[24] The noble status of the Pharaoh's daughter corresponds with the social status of Vermeer's lady, although she is most likely a wealthy burgher's wife. In each case the presence of maid(s) highlights the superiority of the woman at the centre of the image.

As the viewer of Vermeer's image moves from the lady at her table to the maid standing on her right, and then to the Moses painting on the wall, there is much to decipher and no simple category in which to place what one identifies. Although specific details concerning the letter writing are left to the viewer's imagination, Vermeer clearly valorizes the act of contemplation, the mental activity (the lady's, the maid's, and the viewer's), and the many objects inside the room. The position and posture of the lady direct the viewer's attention to her letter writing; the maid carries the viewer's gaze outside; and the large painting that emerges in the space between the women and looms over them invites the viewer to consider its history. Triangulated in this way, the composition explodes the idea of frames and fixed knowledge, and therefore the notion of an integrated narrative. The elements of the painting present more than the sum of their parts.

Both Vermeer's *Lady Writing a Letter with Her Maid* and Corneille's *Suréna* take as their subject amorous relations, as letters in Dutch genre paintings frequently convey love, and often illicit love. The setting of Vermeer's image, a wealthy middle-class home, where the mistress is well attired in a green bodice with a broach, also has relevance for the play, where class identity subordinates Suréna to Orode and his son Pacorus. An outstanding general, Suréna defends kings but is not himself a king: "Cependant est-il roi, madame? Il ne l'est pas; / Mais il sait rétablir les rois dans leurs états" [However, is he a king, Madam? He is not; / But he knows how to restore kings to power] (1.1.59–60). Like the painting, the opening scene of Corneille's play involves Eurydice in a discussion with her maid of honour within an intimate setting. We might further associate Suréna with Moses, if only to suggest the value that the play, like the Egyptians in the Bible, accords to the *other* in Corneille's drama, the eponymous hero who, although a remarkable military leader, has no royal blood. The political drama in which Suréna and Eurydice appear as lovers functions much like the biblical allusion in Vermeer's image, that is, as the history that opposes the love story. Vermeer, however, does not use the framed painting to create an impenetrable seal for the love story, whereas Corneille's love story appears to be subsumed by the larger political drama that defeats the lovers. This sense of the whole, however, is fractured and fragmented in ways that the design of Vermeer's painting helps to clarify.

With *Lady Writing a Letter with Her Maid* the viewer's perception of the inserted painting's ebony frame is literally broken. Vermeer's perspective segments the image, revealing only the frame's left and bottom sides. The extension of the framed image beyond the picture plane breaks up the history recounted in the image, and further supports the idea of the moment depicted as part of a larger narrative whose full dimensions the viewer cannot know. The inserted painting does not set up a simple or complete parallel with the primary image of the lady writing her letter. The story of the finding of Moses does not provide all the information necessary to interpret her actions; the love story does not fit securely into its frame. In *Suréna* the political plot that frames the lovers' story similarly fails to contain it. The political calculus of containment ignores how the third "outside" space reframes the action leading to the lovers' deaths.

Eurydice announces to Ormène that she loves "elsewhere," confessing her love without identifying the name of her lover: "J'aime ailleurs" [I love elsewhere] (1.1.15).[25] Here *ailleurs* refers to Suréna. But *ailleurs* evokes more than a name. Opposing the patriarchal order, this *ailleurs* is a space of forbidden pleasure. *Ailleurs* represents experience not sanctioned by law, a space of passion, revolt, and loss. Corneille situates his lovers' story within the larger history of political manoeuvrings wrought by Orode and his son. The play, however, opens and closes with the love story of Eurydice and Suréna as it suffers the effects of the crown's machinations.

In a classic Cornelian choice, Suréna must elect either to privilege the realm of power or to remain faithful to Eurydice and dedicate himself to love. Rather than define love as the opposite of duty, however, the play encourages us to measure each of these terms against a third variable, the beauty of the lovers' discourse as it comes to be associated with meanings not contained by either the history that defeats the lovers, or their battles onstage. Corneille's lyricism assigns value to the lovers' plaints, elevating their struggles and even their deaths beyond the frame of the action. The exclusion of one term – duty or love – does not consolidate the hero's position or the king's, for both are measured against a passion so intense that the lovers' speech acquires a transcendent quality. The sublime in *Suréna* correlates with a poetic eulogizing of life and love, a grief so intense that it transports the characters, and with them the audience, away from the choice between a politically expedient marriage or an assassination. The transcendent power of the lovers' melancholic exchanges is, fittingly, punctuated with multiple references to an *elsewhere*. The lovers' lament fills a space beyond the king's rule; it describes a state of being that resonates for them from the start of the play, and that continues to affect the audience's view of sovereign power even once the elsewhere assumes the final cloak of death.

Suréna expresses the will to die rather than lose Eurydice. The hero's openness to death assumes a transcendent quality, which Eurydice echoes. The heroic sublime refers to the most beautiful utterances of the play, lines of devotion and lament that the lovers intone with great emotion as they confront their fate:

> Je sais ce qu'à mon cœur coûtera votre vue;
> Mais qui cherche à mourir doit chercher ce qui tue.
> Madame, l'heure approche, et demain votre foi
> Vous fait de m'oublier une éternelle loi:
> Je n'ai plus que ce jour, que ce moment de vie.
> Pardonnez à l'amour qui vous la sacrifie,
> Et souffrez qu'un soupir exhale à vos genoux,
> Pour ma dernière joie, une âme toute à vous.
>
> [I know what seeing you will cost my heart,
> But he who looks to die must seek out what kills.
> Madame, the hour is approaching, and tomorrow your vow
> Will make your obligation to forget me an eternal law.
> I only have this day, this moment of life.
> Forgive the love that sacrifices that life to you,
> And let my mournful sigh express before you,
> As my final joy, a soul devoted entirely to you.] (1.3.249–56)

Love and death are equivalent, all-consuming states. The hero accepts the choice he faces, and in that acceptance he denies Orode full power over him. Eurydice's response, similarly elegiac, opposes death, with its finality, to the desire to "toujours mourir" [always die]: "Je veux, sans que la mort ose me secourir, / Toujours aimer, toujours souffrir, toujours mourir" [I want, without death daring to save me / To always love, always suffer, always die] (1.3.267–8). The repetition of *toujours* [always] establishes the continuity of their love even in death, the elsewhere in which they will be united, always.

Fearing, without cause, that Suréna will lead the army to rebel against him, King Orode obliges the hero to abandon Eurydice. He believes that a royal marriage will keep Suréna's power in check. Prior to the play's opening scene, Suréna successfully defeated Orode's enemies, enabling him to retain power. The hero's subsequent challenge to the king, however, shows him to embody new values. Resisting Orode's order to marry his daughter, the hero obviously endangers his future, but he does not do so recklessly. He acts out of a deep commitment to Eurydice. Suréna's defiance of the king's demands is all the more reasonable because he resists a king who acts from a position of weakness. Suréna has proved his worth and has never been disloyal. Yet the king, aware of his own dependence on Suréna, attempts to subordinate him. The heroic code condemns the hero who refuses to sacrifice his love in service to the State. The king's own desperation, however, corrupts his judgment and erodes his effectiveness. Such is Corneille's, and also Suréna's, calculation.

Determined to resist Orode, Suréna fights not just this king and this marriage but also the power of the monarchy to impose its will on its subjects. Suréna has the determination to fight and the cleverness to foresee the consequences of his choices. By setting himself in opposition to the king, the hero risks his life. Nevertheless, he will not perish without having condemned the king in the eyes of the audience. The hero's position reflects not only his passion but also his reason, his critique of the king's political failings. Orode degrades his own position through his jealous persecution of the hero, risking as much militarily as he does morally and politically, which Suréna duly points out to Pacorus:

Qu'on veuille mon épée, ou qu'on veuille ma tête,
Dites un mot, Seigneur, et l'une et l'autre est prête:
Je n'ai goutte de sang qui ne soit à mon roi;
Et si l'on m'ose perdre, il perdra plus que moi.
J'ai vécu pour ma gloire autant qu'il fallait vivre,
Et laisse un grand exemple à qui pourra me suivre;
Mais si vous me livrez à vos chagrins jaloux,
Je n'aurai pas peut-être assez vécu pour vous.

[If one wants either my sword, or my head,
Say the word, Lord, and both are ready.
I have not one drop of blood that does not belong to my king,
And whoever dares to lose me, will lose more than me.

I have lived for my glory as much as it was necessary to live,
And I leave behind a great example for whoever
 will be able to follow me.
But if you release me to your jealous pains,
I will perhaps have not lived enough for you.] (4.4.1353–60)

After his initial resistance to his son's plot against Suréna, Orode agrees, intending to compensate for his own lack of military might and political clout by cruelly striking down the hero who threatens him – the valiant soldier on whom he depends.[26] Ineffectively assessing his own situation, Orode's behaviour weakens the State. Suréna's speech here will remain with the audience long after he is dead. Part of the force of this passage relates to the truth of what Suréna states and the illogic of the king's sacrifice of his greatest military asset. Part of the explanation for the hero's enduring influence rests with Corneille's association of the lovers and the sublime. The result is action that cannot easily be contained by the order of things that Orode sets in place.

The stress on the tragic form to restore order in the end is all the more evident when we consider it as a political performance structured to absorb the love interest. Although Corneille narrates an action from start to finish, the play's design resembles Vermeer's painting to the degree that it interrupts the political history, the frame story, of Suréna's defeat through repeated evocations of death, the ultimate elsewhere. Juxtaposing the framed biblical story with the window through which the maid gazes outside, Vermeer's image creates a dual perspective that reaches back in time to biblical history and forward to new knowledge of a world outside that is still obscure to the viewer, still to be uncovered by the maid who looks out at it. The painting's three major spaces – interior, framed, and exterior – cohere without coalescing. Similarly, Corneille's tragedy alternates between the history that concludes with Suréna's murder and Eurydice's mournful death at learning that he has been killed, and the ability of the lovers' story to move the audience. The heroic sublime unites the couple in death, the *ailleurs* of eternity, after Suréna's execution. Orode and his heir remain in control in the play's final moment. The State has successfully defeated the lovers. The State's imposition of law and the lovers' end are not, however, coterminous; they do not share the same boundaries in space, or the same boundaries in meaning. The lovers' story remains open to the afterlife, and to a knowledge that defies Orode's elimination of their resistance, their difference within the realm that he governs. Indeed, the lovers' story inspires further action. The play concludes not with the king's political triumph but rather with Palmis's anguished cry to the gods that the lovers' deaths be avenged: "Ne souffrez point ma mort que je ne sois vengée" [Do not allow me to die without having avenged this loss] (5.5.1738)! Palmis's plea for justice is one that history, with its record of violence, cannot answer alone. Justice requires the integration of the morals, the passion, and the commitment that the lovers, in their bodiless state, now embody *elsewhere*.

Reframing the Tragic: From *Horace* to *Suréna*

In addition to their experiences with the tragedies individually, dedicated viewers of Corneille's oeuvre familiar with both *Horace* and *Suréna* would associate the tragedies in a chain of images linking two heroes, two crises, two kings, and two tragedies. The tragic form, while stable, allows for permutations. Vermeer's *Lady Writing a Letter with Her Maid* offers an example of such reconfigurations via the floor pattern. The still life composed of the writing implements in the foreground is set off by a black tile. The floor features two patterns: a row of alternating black and white tiles follows a row whose sequence is three black tiles followed by one white tile. The concentration of black tiles in the foreground, while regular, presents more black tiles than any other visible area of the floor. The viewer may at first have the impression that a white tile is missing under the objects, as three other lines of white tile prominently traverse the image, two to the left and one to the right of the tile bearing the objects. The cross pattern of black tiles highlights the scattering of objects, adding to the impression of a charged or broken exchange between the lady and her lover.

Suréna both extends and modifies the patterns of *Horace* in ways that accentuate the tensions between the inner, personal story and the larger history in which it is contained. Suréna's "ordinary virtue" contrasts dramatically with Horace's exceptional commitment to serve his king and country.[27] Both Horace and Suréna fight heroically. Both heroes risk their hard-earned glory in the aftermath to war. Suréna's refusal to marry the woman chosen for him by the king parallels Horace's murder of Camille in that both are, officially, condemnable sequels to the initial victory. The plot takes the hero from a great military victory to a second and more personal challenge. Unlike Horace, however, Suréna rejects, on principle, the need to sacrifice love for duty. In place of the glory so coveted by Horace, Suréna, in complete lucidity, substitutes love. He does so, moreover, with the audience's blessing.

Is Suréna's crime equivalent to that of Horace? Suréna's resistance to the king's plans is decidedly an offence, a crime of *lèse-majesté*. The monarchy, however, appears less and less legitimate in *Suréna*, given the repressive actions of the king, including his subjection of the hero, who is his most valued general. Suréna's unwillingness to marry the king's daughter offends less than Horace's murder of Camille, both because the audience is touched by Suréna's passion and also because the hero thinks strategically in response to Orode's threats. As he observes to Eurydice, Suréna understands what thoughts motivate the king:

Madame, ce refus n'est point vers lui mon crime;
Vous m'aimez: ce n'est point non plus ce qui l'anime.
Mon crime véritable est d'avoir aujourd'hui
Plus de nom que mon roi, plus de vertu que lui;
Et c'est de là que part cette secrète haine
Que le temps ne rendra que plus forte et plus pleine.

[Madame, my offence to him is not this refusal;
You love me: nor is this what troubles him.
My real crime is having earned today
More of a reputation than my king, more virtue than he.
And from this success grows his secret hatred,
Which will only grow stronger and fuller with time.] (5.2.1509–14)

Suréna's death, as he predicts and desires, will have the effect of transforming the king into a tyrant. The audience sympathizes with Suréna and Eurydice not only because they love intensely but also because Suréna reasons so judiciously about the king's failings. If he dies, he wants there to be blood on the ruler's hands:

Si ma mort plaît au roi, s'il la veut tôt ou tard,
J'aime mieux qu'elle soit un crime qu'un hasard;
Qu'aucun ne l'attribue à cette loi commune
Qu'impose la nature et règle la fortune;
Que son perfide auteur, bien qu'il cache sa main,
Devienne abominable à tout le genre humain;
Et qu'il en naisse enfin des haines immortelles
Qui de tous ses sujets lui fassent des rebelles.

[If my death pleases the king, if he wants it sooner or later,
I prefer that it be a crime rather than an accident;
That no one attribute it to this common law
That nature imposes and that fortune rules.
I want its perfidious author, although he would
hide his hand,
To appear monstrous to all of humanity,
And that from this act be born the immortal hatred
That turns all his subjects into rebels.] (5.3.1607–14)

In *Suréna,* moreover, Corneille takes up a certain number of positions that he adopted in *Horace,* but he shifts them to characters with different profiles. These permutations serve to valorize Suréna as they affiliate him with the very humane fighter Curiace and also with the benevolent king Tulle. Curiace is a clear heroic second to Horace. Curiace dies on the battlefield, having earlier proved himself an unworthy aspirant of glory when he failed to express regret at needing to attack those whom he loves.[28] Like Curiace, Suréna rejects glory affiliated with a State that demands the sacrifice of love and human compassion. Suréna, however, does fight heroically, and he proves victorious, thus integrating Curiace's humanity into the heroic paradigm. Suréna challenges that paradigm by arguing that kings build their authority not through superior calculations but rather through violence, brute force. Royal power, he notes, often originates in horrible crimes: "[l]e parricide a fait la moitié de nos rois" [parricide produced half of our kings] (5.3.1640). With this phrase Suréna echoes not Curiace but rather Tulle, the benevolent king who excuses Horace. For anyone immersed in Corneille's theatre, Suréna's speech recalls Tulle's response to the hero's murder of his sister: "Qu'elles se taisent donc; que Rome *dissimule* / Ce que dès sa naissance elle vit en Romule" [Let the laws be silent, then; let Rome conceal / What from its birth it saw in Romulus] (5.3.1755–6; my emphasis).

Through association with Tulle, Suréna's speech assumes a positive valuation: he speaks like the good and just king who saved his country by sparing Horace. Suréna, however, proves as astute politically as Horace proves himself indifferent to the political process, at least to the degree that he attempts to deflect Tulle's call to defend himself. Asked to justify his murder of Camille, Horace recognizes the king's right to judge, yet he offers no substantial explanation for his action. His speech stands less as an exoneration of his conduct than as an oath to his king – a pledge that, in such circumstances, sounds more than a little vainglorious:

À quoi bon me défendre?
Vous [Tulle] savez l'action, vous la venez d'entendre;
Ce que vous en croyez me doit être une loi.
Sire, on se défend mal contre l'avis d'un roi,
Et le plus innocent devient soudain coupable,
Quand aux yeux de son prince il paraît condamnable.
C'est crime qu'envers lui se vouloir excuser:
Notre sang est son bien, il en peut disposer;
Et c'est à nous de croire, alors qu'il en dispose,
Qu'il ne s'en prive point sans une juste cause.
Sire, prononcez donc, je suis prêt d'obéir;
D'autres aiment la vie, et je la dois haïr. [...]
Je ne vanterai point les exploits de mon bras.

[What is the point of defending myself?
You [Tulle] know what I have done; you have just heard it described.
What you decide I must accept as law.
Your Majesty, one cannot easily defend oneself against
a king's judgment.
Even the most innocent becomes suddenly guilty,
When, in his prince's eyes, he appears to have committed the crime.
It is an offence against the prince even to want to justify oneself;
Our blood is his property, and he can dispose of it as he wishes.
And it is our responsibility to believe, when he does,
That he does not deprive himself of it without just cause.
Your Majesty, state your ruling; I am prepared to obey.
Others love life, and I must hate it. [...]
I will not boast about my accomplishments
on the battlefield.] (5.2.1535–46, 1573)

Horace condemns those who would judge him unworthy, recalling his early strategy to leave the battle in order to have his enemy chase him until they could no longer resist him (4.2). Self-serving, but not wrong, the hero tries to accomplish a rhetorical act equal to his military victory:

Votre majesté, sire, a vu mes trois combats:
Il est bien malaisé qu'un pareil les seconde,

Qu'une autre occasion à celle-ci réponde,
Et que tout mon courage, après de si grands coups,
Parvienne à des succès qui n'aillent au-dessous;
Si bien que pour laisser une illustre mémoire,
La mort seule aujourd'hui peut conserver ma gloire.

[Your Majesty witnessed my three battles:
It is very unlikely that another would equal them,
That another occasion would present a similar challenge,
And that all my courage, after such great battles,
Would not appear inferior to these earlier successes.
So that in order to preserve the memory of my greatness
Only death today can conserve my glory.] (5.2.1574–80)

Arguably, most people, as he claims, are capable of judging only the theatre of the war, its grand victories, and not the substance of heroic actions. Those who criticize him in this scene, however, are far more discerning. Camille did not represent the same threat to Horace as the Curiaces did on the battlefield. Thus, while Horace's conflict with her could, as he claims, be considered a battle that is inherently less spectacular, it was not less consequential. The real issue being debated here is not Camille as a lesser enemy but rather the fact that Horace murdered her. With the hero goes the glory and the future of the nation.

Suréna takes this debate further, condemning the crown's ineptitude and violence. He argues that dissimulation has long protected the evil corruption of those in power, pointing to the self-interest that motivates Orode and Pacorus to commit crimes that they never acknowledge:

Car enfin mes refus ne font pas mon offense;
Mon vrai crime est ma gloire, et non pas mon amour:
Je l'ai dit, avec elle il croîtra chaque jour;
Plus je les servirai, plus je serai coupable;
Et s'ils veulent ma mort, elle est inévitable.
Chaque instant que l'hymen pourrait la reculer
Ne les attacherait qu'à mieux *dissimuler*;
Qu'à rendre, sous l'appas d'une amitié tranquille,
L'attentat plus secret, plus noir et plus facile.

[For in fact my refusals do not constitute my offence;
My true crime is my glory, and not my love.

I said it; my crime will grow each day as my glory increases;
The more I serve them, the more I will be guilty.
And if they want my death, it is inevitable.
Each moment that the marriage could defer it
Would only make them *dissimulate* better,
And make, under the guise of a peaceful friendship,
The attack more secret, more evil,
and more effective.] (5.3.1650–8; my emphasis)

Suréna adopts the language of the benevolent king Tulle, calling a crime by its rightful name. He does so, however, not to exonerate Orode, as Tulle does Horace. Suréna does not attempt to justify the monarch's suppression of his true motives. He condemns Orode and Pacorus by exposing their machinations. This drama's *ex machina* factor includes no salutory *deus*, as in Molière's play. In *Suréna* dissimulation refers to Machiavellian manipulations, to an evil cover-up of motivations and strategies that protect the king without protecting the nation. It defines a plot against the hero that, while it ensures the king's power, crushes his subjects, thereby compromising the king's own image. Suréna provides a clear assessment of the State's abuses and miscalculations. He points to the fallacy of the ruler who would defeat his best military leader out of envy at his success and in full recognizes his own weakness. While initially outraged at the thought of killing Suréna, Orode comes to believe, as he expresses to Eurydice, that his failure to crush the hero would mean that he, Orode, would become his subject's subject:

Si votre Suréna m'a rendu mes états,
Me les a-t-il rendus pour ne m'obéir pas?
Et trouvez-vous par là sa valeur bien fondée
A ne m'estimer plus son maître qu'en idée,
A vouloir qu'à ses lois j'obéisse à mon tour"

[If your Suréna secured my states for me,
Did he do so only not to obey me?
And do you find it a sign of his value
That he would no longer respect me as his master except as an idea
And would now want me to obey his laws.] (5.1.1455–9)

Obedience, Orode insists, is a condition befitting the king's subjects; he will not be beholden to Suréna. The hero, however, defends the individual against the power of the State. He earns the right to do so because the king who asks for his loyalty at the same time abandons his own obligation to protect his subjects.

One cannot watch the last scene of *Suréna* without recognizing that, whatever Orode's power to support the hero's assassination, the king does not diminish Suréna's real value as a man of integrity who fights for his king and also for his own right to love Eurydice. Orode's actions are legitimate not only because he has the power to impose his will but also because in demanding that subjects submit to his authority he defends an aristocratic privilege, accepted practice, and the hierarchical organization of the court. Yet Orode compromises his own legacy by betraying his personal vulnerability; by yielding to his son, who is motivated as much by his desire for Eurydice as by political efficacy; and by permitting the death of the hero whose military skill is necessary to protect the country from its enemies. With the announcement of Suréna's death, therefore, the audience registers the fall of the hero as a measure of the king's own decline.

Horace and *Suréna* both stress resolution of the conflict via the ruler's assumption of power and elimination of challenges to his law, demands for obedience that have the effect of homogenizing society to the degree that all actors similarly accept the king's law, and the sacrifices of individual difference/desire that it imposes. Paired together, however, these plays reveal Corneille's reconfiguration of the familiar positions of hero, king, and rebel. While Corneille produced many dramas between these two tragedies, they suffice to suggest how the playwright carefully manipulates perspectives. Comparing how the two heroes situate themselves in relation to each other and to their kings, we see that Corneille continually fractures the space of the tragedy to rearrange fundamental elements. That volatility in turn equates with the sovereign's less-than-absolute hold at the end: his law orders society, but it does so at a price. Corneille tests the exercise of power, including both a benevolent application of authority (*Horace*) and its excesses (*Suréna*). The law that ensures sovereign rule in *Suréna* is a death sentence for the hero that scars the State's own image.

In *Horace* the similarities between opposing forces (Rome and Albe, masculine and feminine, self and other) order the play. The full cycle of actions depends on the elimination of the other: the enemy, and the feminine, and the sentimental. Yet the enemy is a mother (Albe), brother (Curiace), and sister (Camille). To kill them is not to surpass oneself, as Horace imagines, but rather, in his battle with Camille, to succumb to one's own baser instincts. *Suréna* takes the heroic paradigm and turns it, not on its head, but enough to interrupt the pattern whereby love sacrificed ensures extraordinary acts of heroism. Eurydice and Suréna do not embody power any more than, in the end, they embody love as a physical presence. They are guilty of resisting the king's will, and Suréna is defiant as he struggles to evade Orode's orders. The law that condemns the hero exists to protect the State. Suréna's story, however, continues to reflect unfavourably upon the king. Conveying their suffering, the couple's lamentation also offers its own consolation by giving form to grief. In death, the lovers enter a realm where sovereign law and rational logic no longer apply. From this *elsewhere* their poetry soars, imparting their deep and eternal devotion.

Consistent with the visual emphasis of Dutch genre paintings, which frequently return to the same themes (music making and letter writing are two examples), the theatre audience learns to attenuate the expectation that all is resolved, and that all is knowable. The shifts in the tragic form that the public observes from *Horace* to *Suréna* reinforce a new order of things that develops within the arts supporting the monarchy. These plays stand not only as independent works that support the sovereign's exercise of power but also as performances that challenge the monarchy's control of the public's imagination. *Phèdre* offers further evidence of the divide between myths supporting the king's portrait and descriptive evidence that confounds it.

Phèdre: The Abiding Loss

With Racine's *Phèdre,* descriptions, particularly those associated with death and the mourning process at the tragedy's close, diminish the portrait of the sovereign and the efficacy of the exclusionary law that seals the action by eliminating the forces opposed to it. Descriptions add beauty to the text. In Racine's tragedy aesthetic value accords with descriptions whose richness outshines the king's actions. Descriptive elements encourage interpretive strategies that favour a more complex and complete understanding of power and knowledge than can be distilled through a sense of resolution that derives from the king's final recognition of the truth.

During Thésée's absence his wife Phèdre makes advances to Hippolyte, her stepson, who rebuffs her. Falsely accused of the seduction, Hippolyte suffers the ultimate punishment when his father returns: Thésée implores Neptune to kill his son. Yet Hippolyte dies guilty not of loving Phèdre but of loving Aricie, the princess whom Thésée forbade him to marry out of fear of eventual retribution for earlier victories against her brothers. The king learns of Hippolyte's brutal death in a moving account by his governor, Théramène, after Phèdre has confessed to her crime and just before the poison she has swallowed takes her life.

Does the audience interpret Hippolyte's death as the direct consequence of Phèdre's evil? Is it a sign of Thésée's poor judgment and failure to apply well the very basic function that Descartes describes as "bon sens," the ability to distinguish between truth and falsity? The answer depends largely on whether one sees the drama as a history that restores order by ridding society of Phèdre's monstrous presence or as a story that builds layers of meaning without erasing traces of what came before.[29] We must consider whether the play maintains a rigorous support of sovereign law; whether, by showing Thésée's exercise of judgment to be wanting, the play fails to endorse the law fully; or whether both interpretations are valid. Once again, the problem builds from a dual structure: two forbidden loves and two deaths, played out through a series of parallel confessions. In the end, however, Thésée, although he blames Phèdre, confesses his error: "Et c'est sur votre foi [Phèdre] que je l'ai condamné" [And it is on your word (Phèdre) that I condemned him to die] (5.7.1620)! Thésée's shock and regret resonate with the audience but there is no ignoring his responsibility, his misplaced trust.

Racine's drama unfolds within a mythological world tempered by Jansenist beliefs in predestination as they meld to support the divine right of kings.[30] Predestination operates within the play as a self-regulating system. The elements of Phèdre's story work together to conserve a sense of fatality, a soul condemned from the start. As a frame structure for the tragedy, therefore, predestination implies a notion of irreversibility. Yet the audience detects discordances within the play, thoughts that cannot be stilled by Phèdre's demise. Moreover, through its description of both Hippolyte's response to love and of his death in the final act, the tragedy shifts away from myth and towards a reality effect that is all the more profound because the world it describes is in mourning.

In her first confession to Oenone, Phèdre recounts her concerted efforts to rid herself of her passion for Hippolyte:

> Athènes me montra mon superbe ennemi.
> Je le vis, je rougis, je pâlis à sa vue.
> Un trouble s'éleva dans mon âme éperdue.
> Mes yeux ne voyaient plus, je ne pouvais parler,

Je sentis tout mon corps et transir, et brûler.
Je reconnus Vénus, et ses feux redoutables,
D'un sang qu'elle poursuit tourments inévitables.
Par des vœux assidus je crus les détourner,
Je lui bâtis un temple, et pris soin de l'orner.
De victimes moi-même à toute heure entourée,
Je cherchais dans leurs flancs ma raison égarée.
D'un incurable amour remèdes impuissants!
En vain sur les autels ma main brûlait l'encens.
Quand ma bouche implorait le nom de la déesse,
J'adorais Hippolyte, et le voyant sans cesse,
Même au pied des autels que je faisais fumer,
J'offrais tout à ce dieu, que je n'osais nommer.
Je l'évitais partout. Ô comble de misère!
Mes yeux le retrouvaient dans les traits de son père.

[Athens showed me my superb enemy:
I saw him; I blushed; I turned pale at the sight of him.
A trouble arose in my lost soul.
My eyes could no longer see; I could not speak;
I felt my entire body freeze and then burn with fever.
I recognized Venus and her formidable fires,
The inevitable torments that she inflicts on her victims.
Through devoted prayers I thought that I could appease her:
I built her a temple, and took care to adorn it.
I remained there for long hours surrounded by sacrificed animals;
In their wounded sides I sought to regain my lost reason.
What ineffective remedies against an incurable love!
In vain I burned incense on the altars.
When my mouth pleaded, invoking the name of the goddess,
I worshipped Hippolyte, and seeing him incessantly,
Even at the foot of the altars that I set ablaze,
I was adoring this god whom I dared not name.
I avoided him everywhere. Oh, crowning misery!
My eyes discovered him in his father's features.] (1.3.272–90)

Phèdre performs a ritual sacrifice to appease Venus. Evidence of Phèdre's concerted efforts to combat her incestuous and adulterous desire for Hippolyte, the sacrifice, however, offers no relief. Phèdre sees in the animals' entrails no hope of a better future; she finds no escape from the goddess's persecution. In this expansive and plaintive recounting Phèdre underscores her lack of agency. She is the victim: her mind, under Venus's influence, plays tricks on her, causing her adoration of the goddess to morph into her adoration of Hippolyte.

In act 2 Hippolyte confesses his love to Aricie with words that sound as though they could have come from Phèdre, minus the invocation of Venus. While innocent of the crime of which Thésée accuses him – that is, of seducing Phèdre – Hippolyte stands guilty before Thésée, guilty in love. Like Phèdre, moreover, he resists his passion until he can resist it no more:

Contre vous, contre moi vainement je m'éprouve.
Présente je vous fuis, absente je vous trouve.
Dans le fond des forêts votre image me suit.
La lumière du jour, les ombres de la nuit,
Tout retrace à mes yeux les charmes que j'évite.
Tout vous livre à l'envi le rebelle Hippolyte.
Moi-même pour tout fruit de mes soins superflus,
Maintenant je me cherche, et ne me trouve plus.
Mon arc, mes javelots, mon char, tout m'importune.
Je ne me souviens plus des leçons de Neptune.
Mes seuls gémissements font retentir les bois,
Et mes coursiers oisifs ont oublié ma voix.

[Against you, against myself, I fight vainly;
When you are present, I flee you; when you are absent, I find you.
In the depths of the forest your image follows me.
The light of day, the shadows of night,
Everything displays before my eyes the charms that I try to avoid.
Everything conspires to make the rebellious Hippolyte succumb to you.
Now, the only fruit of my pointless labours,
I search for myself, but I can no longer find who I am.
My bow, my javelins, my chariot, everything troubles me;
I no longer remember Neptune's lessons.
In the woods only my moaning echoes,
And my idle steeds have forgotten my voice.] (2.2.541–52)

Hippolyte is as distraught as Phèdre and equally unable to combat his passion. He expresses the same failure to actualize what he intends. Yet within the mythological world that they inhabit Hippolyte's story now occurs without the gods; he does battle with himself, not with Venus, or with Neptune. Phèdre cannot escape Venus; Hippolyte has abandoned Neptune's teachings. Certainly, Racine encloses both characters within the tragic universe of myth – Hippolyte begins this scene by saying that the gods took his father: "Les dieux [le] livrent enfin à La Parque homicide" [The gods finally deliver (him) to the murderous Fates] (2.2.469). In contrast to Phèdre's many actions, however, Hippolyte's persistent inaction resonates within a world that seems, momentarily, to function without divine guidance. Hippolyte is effectively abandoned by the gods, thrown into a world of confusion in which he, like Phèdre, sees forbidden love in all things. Her efforts to build a temple to Venus are matched by his unmounted horses, by his despondency as expressed through his own choice not to ride. He exists within a secular world, a tragic family drama for which men and women bear responsibility. The gods and the monsters will soon act at the behest of Thésée, but they cannot erase the son's desire, disobedience, guilt, and regret regarding Aricie. These qualities shade his innocence; they nuance his portrait even as he goes to his death in the full glare of his father's unjust accusations.

Into the triangulated desire of Racine's universe Thésée, the father/king, plays out his anger through those same horses. These animals are signs of Hippolyte, signs of his filial guilt but also, and most revealingly, signs that the monarch responds not thoughtfully and with accurate judgment but rather mechanically, to punish. Thésée's justice, that is, continues the inexorable movement of kingship to eliminate those who challenge his law. The audience must ascribe moral responsibility to Thésée's actions, assess the proper exercise of reason by this king who survives in the aftermath of Hippolyte's death that Théramène movingly describes, the miserable end of the son "traîné par les chevaux que sa main a nourris" [dragged by the horses that would eat out of his hand] (5.6.1548).

A narrowly Jansenist reading would have us see Phèdre as the root of all evil, her suicide as final proof of that evil, and her elimination as the event that allows society, and with it the tragic form, to re-establish order. Racine's tragedy moves from a troubled beginning, to the paroxysm of the crisis, and then to resolution. Within that larger cycle of experience Thésée's final knowledge about Phèdre and his son marks a return to order. Thésée, however, stands accountable for his actions, for trusting Oenone and Phèdre rather than judge as he should. Thésée, we might say, *changed horses in midstream, backed the wrong horse,* and, having *put his cart before the horse,* in the end must *beat a dead horse.* He no doubt regrets not being more discerning and capable of seeing a *horse of a different colour*, a son whose love for his father involved a certain rebellion, but whose death, as evoked by Théramène's vivid images of the horses, neither Phèdre's confession nor her death can erase. Nor can Thésée's ultimate acceptance of Aricie alleviate all the grief and remorse that he expresses when he learns the truth.

Among the most celebrated passages in Racine's tragedy, Théramène's narration recounts events that have taken place offstage. Théramène's moving account of Hippolyte's death, as commanded by his father, functions as another *memento mori*, an occasion to reflect on mortality as that process implies a re-evaluation of the king's power. Consistent with a temporal emphasis on action, the narrative has a beginning, middle, and end: Hippolyte sets off; he meets the monster; he is killed when the monster frightens his horses; he is mourned by Théramène. As told by Théramène, however, this story is also remarkable for its hauntingly beautiful descriptions. He offers a portrait of a defeated hero whose cherished horses register his pain:

> A peine nous sortions des portes de Trézène,
> Il était sur son char. Ses gardes affligés
> Imitaient son silence, autour de lui rangés.
> Il suivait tout pensif le chemin de Mycènes.
> Sa main sur ses chevaux laissait flotter les rênes.
> Ses superbes coursiers, qu'on voyait autrefois
> Pleins d'une ardeur si noble obéir à sa voix,
> L'œil morne maintenant et la tête baissée
> Semblaient se conformer à sa triste pensée.
>
> [Scarcely had we left the gates of Troezen,
> He was on his chariot. His despondent guards
> Imitated his silence as they accompanied him.
> Immersed in his thoughts, he followed the road to Mycenae.
> His hand let the reins on his horses float freely.
> His superb steeds, which we used to see
> Full of such noble energy obey his voice,
> Now, with their sullen eyes and bowed heads,
> Seemed to mirror his sad thoughts.] (5.6.1498–1506)[31]

Théramène goes on to evoke the frightening apparition of the monster and the emotions of fear and loss. As he bears witness, he stresses the sensory qualities of the scene that he observed. He records its colours, its sounds, its frightful agony as registered in the "écailles jaunissantes" [yellowing scales] of the violent creature: "Indomptable taureau, dragon impétueux, / Sa croupe se recourbe en replis tortueux" [Untamable bull, impetuous dragon / Its tail coils onto itself in winding folds] (5.6.1518–20). Like an artist, Théramène paints the "image cruelle" [cruel image] of Hippolyte's final moments. Théramène sees, records, and condemns the world that took this precious life.[32] Indeed, the audience moved by his account would do well to ask whether Hippolyte, the lover of horses, does not outrun the events that seal his fate, so vital is the image that Théramène paints of him.

The proportion of action to description is reversed in Thésée's speech, which closes the play. Thésée has not seen Hippolyte die, and he produces no colours or sounds to evoke his son's death. The colour black, which absorbs all the light, captures Thésée's mood once Phèdre has confessed:

D'une action si noire
Que ne peut avec elle expirer la mémoire?
Allons, de mon erreur, hélas! trop éclaircis
Mêler nos pleurs au sang de mon malheureux fils.
Allons de ce cher fils embrasser ce qui reste,
Expier la fureur d'un vœu que je déteste.
Rendons-lui les honneurs qu'il a trop mérités.
Et pour mieux apaiser ses mânes irrités,
Que malgré les complots d'une injuste famille.
Son amante aujourd'hui me tienne lieu de fille.

[Would that memory
Of such a black act die with her.
Let us now, with my error, alas, all too clear,
Mix our tears with the blood of my unfortunate son.
Let us go embrace what remains of this dear son,
Expiate the fury of a vow that I now detest.
Let us give him the honours that he deserved all too well.
And to appease the angry spirits,
In spite of the plots of her unjust family,
Let his lover today assume her place as my daughter.] (5.7.1645–54)

This passage includes adjectives modifying nouns – "noire action" [black act]; "cher fils" [dear son]; "honneurs mérités" [honours deserved];

"mânes irrités" [the angry spirits] – but it reads like an elaboration of one mournful and inadequate action. Verbs punctuate the king's speech – "allons mêler nos pleurs" [let us mix our tears]; "embrassser ce qui reste" [embrace what remains]; "expier la fureur" [expiate the fury]; "rendre honneur" [give honour], and, most significantly, "Que ... [s]on amante aujourd'hui me tienne lieu de fille" [Let his lover today assume her place as my daughter]. Thésée's final words justify his substitution of the enemy lover Aricie for his son, with the emphasis on *lieu*, a rightful place in the familial and political hierarchy. Thésée admits his loss; he recognizes Hippolyte; and he acts to compensate for his own failed judgment. By adopting Aricie, the king restores order and he recognizes the love that his son felt for this woman. Modifying her status from enemy to family member, Thésée nevertheless leaves open the political exigencies of the crown and questions of legacy. After he accepts Aricie, there is no enemy, just as there is no more hidden truth. Nonetheless, the situation fails to account for an heir, other than Phèdre's two sons, whose eligibility has been poisoned, metaphorically, as the real poison entered their mother's veins. That same suicidal act also eliminated Thésée's power to punish Phèdre, the real monster, directly.

Théramène's devotion, far more paternal than Thésée's, points up the father's more jagged edges. Thésée's poor judgment diminishes him, as does Phèdre, who steals his thunder by taking her own life after she clarifies what he failed to see. Moreover, Théramène's plaintive tone, his poetic evocation of the monster, the dead hero, and his own emotions suggests the larger human as well as supernatural context against which Thésée's final action seems, unadornedly and deficiently, rooted in the here and now: "Aujourd'hui me tienne lieu de fille" [Today assume her place as my daughter]. Today cannot win out against eternity, any more than action can survive with impunity the depth and emotion conveyed through description. Thésée has learned the truth of his mistakes. The spectators have learned that truth and much more. No adoption will replace the son Thésée had murdered, either at the centre of the family or at the centre of the State. No history of this action can completely elude the seductive beauty of a masterfully detailed depiction of the loss that it produced. Conveying a heightened aesthetic awareness, Théramène's memories are effective counterweights to memories of the king's deeds. Thésée would have been wise to observe the horses, for observations not only yield the truth but also have the capacity, when the description is finely painted, to transform even a horrific loss into art that commands attention, and that inspires.

Power and the Imagination

Looking back from Thésée's beleaguered figure onstage towards the images that the court builds of Louis XIV as an immutable political force, Racine's audience sees a king whose well-oiled history machine every so often slips a gear. Political propaganda and court spectacle are intricately related, as scholars have long noted. While political actions on the world stage in Paris and at Versailles and theatrical performances onstage are distinct, the ability of the latter to mirror and reinforce the former has serious consequences. The production of knowledge shaped by the theatre depends on perceptions that the mind organizes in ways that, as Dutch art helps to explain, resist simple formulas. While it may be argued that the direct goal of the court's propaganda campaign to promote the king's image was political and not epistemological, the court endeavoured to restrict the flow of ideas to knowledge that it deemed beneficial to the monarchy's survival, and, more specifically, the king's glory. The theatre, via Dutch art, helps to understand how the choices that the court makes to promote its goals ultimately serve to construct a limited knowledge, one that is challenged by the audience's awareness of the manipulations involved. The theatre audience accustomed to "seeing the whole picture," as it does with Dutch art, develops a more intricate and nuanced understanding of the workings of power. Viewers ascribe a positive valence to their emotional response to the action. They also, without prejudice, perceive competing ideas. The appeal of lyrical prose, evocative imagery, and descriptions proves an able counterpoint to the restrictive order of things imposed by the monarchy as it tightens its grip on the public's imagination.

Systems of power and systems of knowledge are not the same. The adage "knowledge is power," however, certainly applies to French classical tragedy in its relation to the monarchy. The threat to the State is precisely that members of the audience may choose to recall what they have been asked to forget. Beauty, moreover, appears to be on the side of defiance to the court's hegemony, adding its seductive power to the alternative perspective, silently helping to shape a greater knowledge than the court's patronage of the arts allows. The theatre audience measures honest and judicious actions on the part of rulers against the struggles of those who thwart the law by seeking authenticity in human relations. The spectators assess actions that expose the corruption of those in power. They gain a sense of the incompleteness of any official interpretation that would bury divergent ideas along with the victims whose deaths are publicly mourned. The audience retains a sense that the monarchy is not inviolable; that a sovereign can rearrange his subjects' lives at will; and that the slope from revered sovereign to despot is indeed slippery. The theatre that celebrates the monarchy thus also serves as a cautionary tale for Louis XIV. In the next chapter the tragic cycle enters the actual history of the life and the death Louis XIV as marked by visual and textual portraits that define his legacy. This history of statecraft plays out like a five-act tragedy of Louis's rule.

4 In Death as in Life

The French monarchy fashioned the idea of Louis XIV's unlimited power in portraits of victory and prosperity. These images substituted for the king's mortal body, whose fate, of course, was to die. The French were keenly aware of this inevitability, all the more so on account of the inherent dangers of wars and the losses that France's army sustained, as well as the illnesses that beset the king and members of his royal family. Allegory remained a prominent feature of official French art of this period, and the Apollonian theme especially defined Versailles as the new Rome. Even in art that lacked an explicit reference to ancient gods or heroes, Louis XIV's image conveyed an exalted sense of accomplishment and enduring influence that extended the power and glory of the Ancients. The king's mortal body was never entirely eclipsed by the art and texts dedicated to him. This chapter explores objects from his reign that, while they continue to promote Louis's aura and authority, concern the king's decline and the monarchy's attempts to eulogize it. As king, Louis XIV was considered superior to all, a man who was much more than a man.[1] The line between the flesh and blood king and his image, as between the temporal and the eternal, however, becomes particularly evident when death approaches.[2]

I do not refer to specific critiques of Louis's military engagements, his lavish expenses, or questions of religious intolerance, including the Revocation of the Edict of Nantes in 1685, and other policies that led to Louis's decreased popularity during the final decades of his reign. The court's move to Versailles in 1682 coincided with the years of France's greatest influence, but by the mid-1680s, Louis XIV's power had begun to wane. Following the death of Colbert, Louis's chief minister, in 1683, France was drawn into increasingly costly wars. Debts mounted from these battles as well as from the expansion of Versailles and the splendours of court life there. The financial situation became more precarious, and an increased sense of corruption and financial fraud led to a marked dissatisfaction with Louis.[3] France, moreover, bore some of the negative effects of the migration of Huguenots to England, Holland, Germany, and America, including the loss of many artisans and merchants who had contributed to France's economy. These signs of conflict and deterioration serve as the background for the narrative of mourning that inserts itself into the court's visual and textual tributes to the king. We see the king's Roman armour begin to give way to the man who bares his flesh. As that vulnerable flesh succumbs to the weight of death, it becomes the subject of a still very royal, yet intriguingly empirical observation about life, posterity, and assembled identities.

While it would be an exaggeration to speak of the French appropriation of Dutch Golden Age paintings under Louis XIV, the consumption of Dutch art at Versailles and in Paris that continued over the course of his lifetime and in the decades following his death meant that the French were acculturated to art that broadened their vision and understanding beyond allegory. They had increasing exposure to art that took shape outside, both stylistically and epistemologically, the images and literature based on Louis's likeness to ancient gods and heroes so favoured by the monarchy. Dutch paintings took the French beyond an integrated model based on similarities, beyond the heroic court narrative of Louis's glory, to a more complete record of things; they present an elaborate description of specific and varied identities.

Building on the Dutch art that I presented in previous chapters, my references here to Northern realism, including three additional paintings by Steen, Rembrandt, and de Hooch, contribute to an expanded critical perspective of French court culture during this period. In this context *critical* denotes intellectual or cognitive processes related to the French reliance on likeness to promote the king, on the one hand, and the devotion of Netherlandish artists to cataloguing different objects, on the other. The French style continued to lead in royal palaces and the homes of the elite and had made its impression abroad as well. As Louis XIV's histories became less grand, however, the classificatory impulse of the Netherlandish realist artists increasingly had the potential to influence, as they largely rejected the allegories, myths, and histories on which much French court art was based. Such elaborate narratives appeared ever more *un*real to those who suffered the monarchy's troubles.

The French were still at pains to promote Louis XIV's image at Versailles and in Paris. Even when the king became the non-allegorized subject celebrated in a 1688 almanac, references to his declining years were inescapable. Almanacs were prints that contained a calendar as well as images celebrating a royal event of the previous year. Collectively, the various almanacs chronicle many important moments of Louis's reign. As a series, they integrate discrete histories into a larger narrative history of the king. Almanacs were not intended as objects for permanent display. Nonetheless, the effect of seeing, year after year, the succession of almanacs would have certainly reinforced the image of Louis XIV as larger than life and enduring. In this way the almanacs encapsulate the extensive propaganda campaigns conducted by the monarchy throughout his reign. His portrait was everywhere, yet the production of more and more images could not stave off thoughts of his eventual death.

The 1688 almanac features an event held to honour the king. Louis was firmly entrenched at Versailles when he returned to Paris for a celebration that was also an occasion for the city to bask in his royal light. The moment was all the more poignant because the king had been ill. I refer to this almanac to set the stage, as it were, for a presentation in this chapter that is broadly conceived to mirror the five-act structure of classical tragedy. Featuring the king and his exceptional general Turenne, my presentation of Louis's history evokes important aspects of classical tragedy: a focus on the king; the king's reliance on the hero's military skills; and the catharsis that tragedy produces through the experience of loss. Privileging issues of mourning and commemoration, the textual and visual objects that I assemble to shape this history convey the longevity of the king and the perfection of his image as well as his mortal condition. I conclude with a painting of Louis XIV made following his death, a post-mortem that preserves the Bourbon legacy.

Celebrations

In the almanac *Louis le Grand: L'amour et les délices de son peuple* [*Louis the Great: The Love and the Joy of His Subjects*] Louis XIV appears as himself, and he does so multiple times.[4] Even without recourse to allegory, this example suggests that French depictions of the king retain the emphasis on analogy: Louis is comparable to himself, as sole referent. Such reflexivity offers a further sign of Louis's power, or rather that of his image. As Louis concentrated his position in France and within Europe,

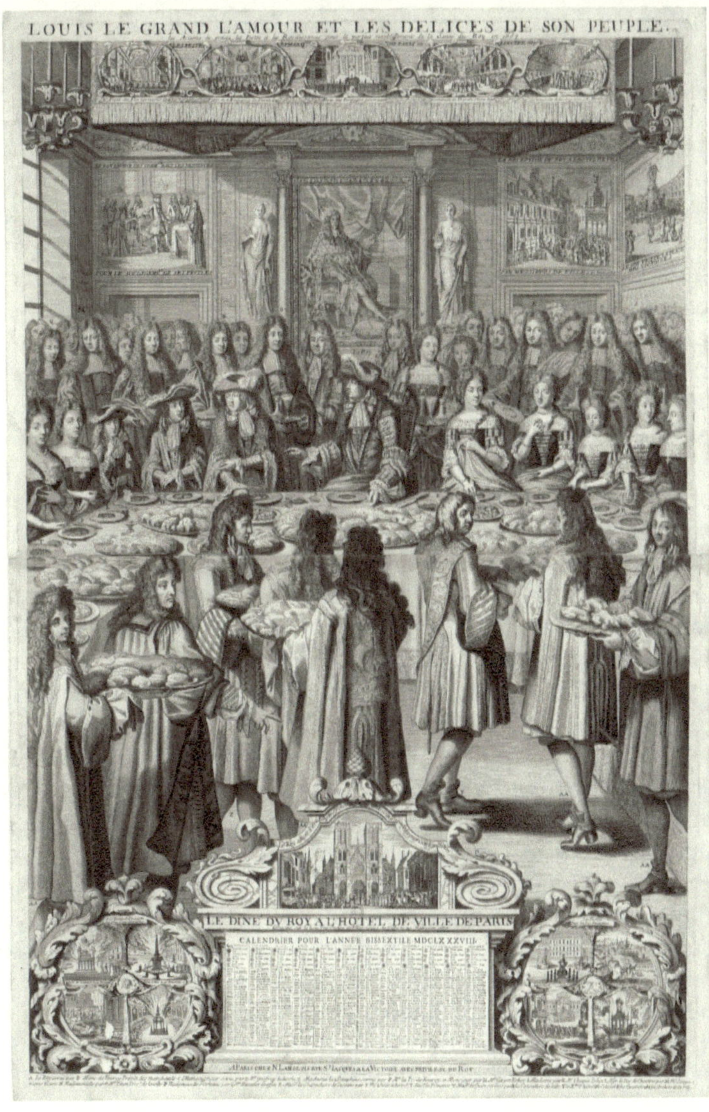

4.1. Pierre Lepautre. *Louis le Grand: L'amour et les délices de son peuple ou Les actions de graces, les festes et les rejouïssances pour le parfait retablissement de la Santé du Roy en 1687* [*Louis the Great: The Love and the Joy of His Subjects or The Gratitude, Celebrations, and Rejoicing for the Perfect Recovery of the King's Health in 1687*]. 1688. Engraving. Image courtesy Bibliothèque nationale de France. https://gallica.bnf.fr/ark:/12148/btv1b6945531s.

the spectre of death loomed larger. He aged, yet images continued to project his renown and his authority. Substituting for his mortal body, images that require no allusion to a god or ancient hero assert the monarch's unique status among men.

Louis le Grand: L'amour et les délices de son peuple celebrates the king's return to health following a precarious situation. The field of medicine enjoyed at least one moment of notorious success when Louis's famously situated fistula – his anal fistula – was successfully removed by surgical intervention, in four separate cuttings from 18 November through 10 December 1687.[5] The surgical procedure that Louis underwent had not achieved an entirely favourable or certain reputation prior to his effective, but protracted, treatment. The almanac recalls not the monarch's sickroom but rather the event held at Hôtel de Ville de Paris [Paris City Hall] in honour of His Majesty's recovery.

The almanac includes a large central image surrounded by a number of medallions, along with an explanatory text. Almanacs were propaganda tools that reached an audience outside the court, including members of the working class.[6] While not typical of court art exhibited at Versailles, this broadly circulated image of the Paris festivities offers a wonderful example of the analogic principle so essential to the court's campaign to promote Louis's image, albeit with a twist. Properly speaking, while based on a principle of similitude, this image is not classically allegorical, since, with the exception of two antique statues decorating the rear of the room, Louis XIV serves as the sole referent for the various images assembled on the page. More precisely, if the principal function of allegory is understood to be the expression of an abstract concept through reference to a corporeal object, then Louis is both that object and that idea. Louis is the featured subject of all the medallions. Indeed, the viewer sees so many images of Louis "in action" in connection to the various stages of his visit to Paris that the view of Louis seated at the table enjoying the meal at the Hôtel de Ville nearly eclipses the official framed portrait of the king that hangs over his head. Louis XIV is alive, and those who appear in the image, like the viewers of the almanac, revel in his presence. The viewer has every reason to believe that all is well in the realm.

The principal image in which the artist depicts the festivities in progress is surrounded by other images related to that reception, including events in Paris that preceded Louis's arrival at the Hôtel de Ville, his actual arrival there, and monuments constructed to honour him. Other medallions represent similar celebrations in France and abroad.[7] In addition to taking satisfaction in the king's return to Paris, the smaller images suggest homage to the king and recognition of the divine right through which he rules. Just above the rectangular space at the bottom of the almanac typically reserved for the calendar of the new year is an image of Louis's earlier visit to Notre Dame, where he offered thanks for his recovery. To the left of the king's portrait on the wall is an image depicting his good deeds to his people. These *mises en abîme* [embedded images] show Louis protected by God and protecting France. His singular power extends from the past, though the present, and into the future. The series of multiple Louis images contained within the almanac thus presents as complete a demonstration of the analogic principle in support of the monarchy as one could aspire to create. In France official court art relied on recurring patterns that bring perceptions back to a central subject, the king. This principle is in evidence here even as the narrative expands to include the various moments of Louis's Paris visit and celebration. Space does not so much conquer time in this rendering as master it by revealing all sequential actions to be tributes to Louis XIV.

The French maintained a strict hierarchy among those who accompanied and served the king. Louis XIV sits at the centre of the table with, to his right, Monseigneur (his son, Louis de France, the crown prince) and Monsieur (Philippe d'Orléans, the king's brother). Seated next to the king on his left are the crown princess (la Dauphine, Marie Anne Victoire) and Madame (Elizabeth Charlotte, *la Princesse Palatine*). Behind the king stand individuals authorized to serve the prince and princesses. M. de Fourcy, *le Prévôt des marchands*, the most important citizen of Paris, serves the king, and Mme de Fourcy serves the crown princess.[8] While those in attendance at the celebration are individualized, they wear similar clothes (save for the men's hats, which identify the royal family), and they sit and stand in symmetrical groups, further setting off the king's central position. The guests are served *à la française* [in the French style], with all courses being presented at the same time, as was the long-standing aristocratic custom. From his central position in the room the king does not look at the viewer. Rather, he is engaged in conversation with Monseigneur and Monsieur, which action establishes the primacy of the royal line.

The Dutch also had a tradition of scenes of celebration, although of a very different sort. As Jan Steen's boisterous *Dancing Couple* (1663) demonstrates, rejoicing was frequently recorded as festive, expansive, and lacking gravitas. The impact of such images relates to the fullness and

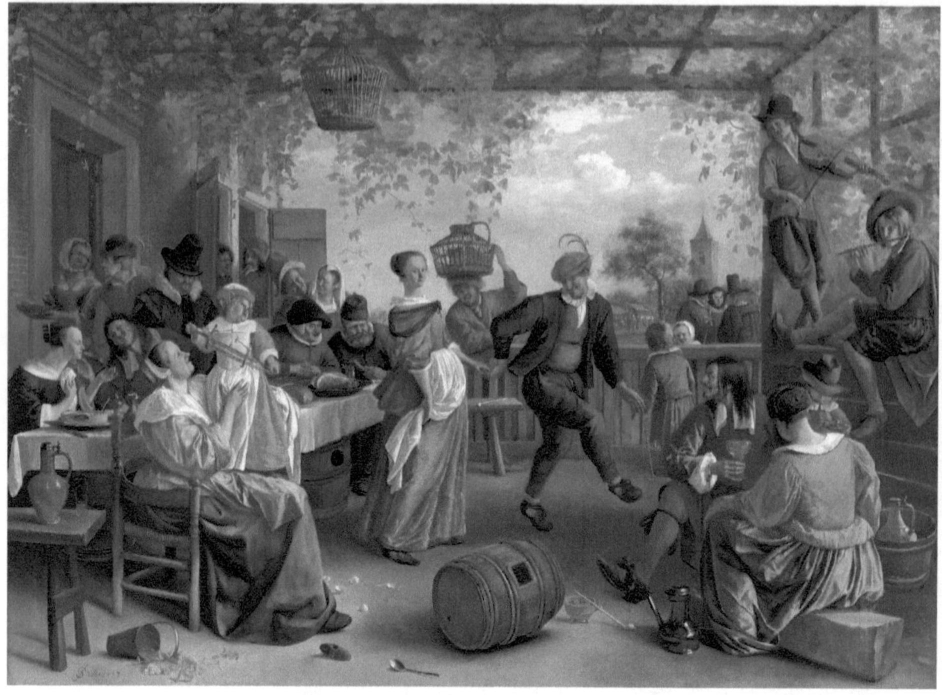

4.2. Jan Steen. *The Dancing Couple*. 1663. 102.5 × 142.5 cm (40.35 × 56.1 in). National Gallery of Art, Washington, DC. Image courtesy National Gallery of Art. https://www.nga.gov/content/ngaweb/Collection/art-object-page.1220.html.

variety of the depictions. Both the French almanac and Steen's painting are crowded with people and food. The Dutch image, however, resists symmetry and repetition in favour of an eclectic display of elements. Steen's image is expansive, full of varied details.[9] He displays different social classes, dress, activities, and objects to reveal the rich diversity of the scene, which depicts many sorts of people and objects, from birds in cages to the church in the distance. His work typifies the Dutch emphasis on variety and the assemblage of disparate elements.

In Steen's painting the meal has progressed enough for the revelry to have commenced. The Dutch celebrate a festival, called a kermesse, which appears, in the Bahktinian sense of carnival, to be a social equalizer.[10] The vine-covered trellis literally opens the festivities to the world outside, the area where tents have been set up for the fair. Taking place on a covered patio, this scene, with its music and dancing couple, and a man (said to be Steen himself) tickling the chin of an elegant guest as she drinks her wine, conveys the merriment of the party. To judge by her attire, this lady is quite demure. At the centre of the image, another woman, who appears by her dress to be of the same class as the other, dances with a man whose clothes identify him as a villager. The dancing lady indulges in the festivities far more than the woman being tickled at the table. In addition to food and wine, the image includes a spilled vase of flowers, a discarded shoe, an overturned barrel, a spoon, a pipe, and a brazier, which suggest the vitality, and in some cases the drunkenness, of the participants. While many "fractured" objects such as the cut flowers and broken eggshells serve as warnings against sensual pleasures and other earthly delights, the scene records the obvious pleasure enjoyed by the participants. The "spillage" of such objects also accentuates the dynamic quality of the scene, which depicts individual groups of figures as they engage in conversation and bits of seduction around the large table on the left as well as inside and outside the room on the right.

The contrast between the almanac and this image is significant. The Paris banquet for Louis XIV shows the meal as it commences. Although the individuals seated and standing around the table appear appropriately decorous, and some might say stiff, movement arguably does animate the scene. Trays of food on the table and, in the foreground, in the hands of the officers and *maîtres d'hôtel* in charge of serving the meal enliven this portrait of the royal family. They convey a mood of celebration through abundance as well as via protocol. The king engaged in conversation is a sign of his good health and apparent pleasure in receiving the honours paid to him. This image satisfies precisely because it records events as they happened, with Louis's presence at the table certifying his return to active life.

The almanac includes no eggshells, no broken items, no sign of Louis's illness or frailty. It does not have to include such signs, however, for death to be present. Both the "in situ" portrait of the king at the Hôtel de Ville and the king's framed image on the wall commemorate the king, but the official portrait of Louis hanging on the wall takes the viewer outside the moment depicted and into the historic record celebrating Louis's reign. That record is completed via the various vignettes that accompany the principle image. Only the monuments and the images survive Louis's actual visits, however, and even the survival of this almanac was an exception, since these prints were typically tacked on walls and then discarded. They were expected to come down as trash and not as part of the king's patrimony. Individually and collectively, the images of Louis in *Louis le Grand: L'amour et les délices de son peuple* suggest the health of the monarch, and of the monarchy, which can commemorate Louis in so many ways. Each medallion, though, is set off, marking conditions that have disappeared. The king is no longer in front of Notre Dame. He is no longer arriving at the Hôtel de Ville. The almanac describes foods he already consumed and gestures he already completed with people who are no longer gathered to honour him. The almanac's history of the king at the table, who is also the king in all the other images, ends much like the portrait on the wall. That status is double-edged. The image substitutes for the man and glorifies his accomplishments. Yet the almanac is a printed object held to the wall with no frame to protect it or mark its importance. The image of Louis XIV at the table has no frame beyond the edges of the paper on which it is printed. Louis is but a man, and although he survived his medical ordeal with the anal fistula, his life will eventually end. Indeed, as any empirical observation of the scene would verify, that man at the table is king, but that king is not his image. At least not yet.

The question is not what the French would have seen or understood in the almanac. They knew all too well that their king was aging and would eventually die. They understood the difference between the king's two bodies, his real corporeal presence and his image.[11] Rather, the issue is whether the French, when they contemplated how expertly the court introduced and replicated Louis's image – as if to defy not only all opposition to his ambitions for himself and for France but also time itself as it weighed on his body – were also drawn to look beyond the series of similar images to a deeper truth about their world. When Louis's subjects saw how the history of the king's eternal glory was constructed as if nothing else mattered, did they look critically at the art/artifice of the French court? Perhaps not. Still, whatever understanding the French garnered from their exposure to Dutch art – not only tavern scenes like Steen's but also genre scenes and still lifes – they had to have absorbed a sense of what separated the inclusiveness of that art and the artifice of the court's projection of Louis's image. Viewed from this perspective, the persistent reproduction of Louis XIV's portrait exposed a deeper need for them to look more closely at the things in their world, to understand what they observed before the meaning of such things, like their king, eluded them.

The idea motivating the production of Louis XIV's image appears to be that more is better: more images and more monumental images ensure the king's greater glory. Yet the more official images of Louis were commissioned over the course of his lifetime, the more such images refer to an aging king. Although Louis retains his forceful presence and his dignity in these images, he is allowed to mature in ways that retain his vigour. We recall that Rigaud completed his famous portrait of Louis, with his youthful legs (discussed in chapter 1) in 1701, when the king was sixty-three years old. Time, however, proves an ineluctable foe. The state of Louis's body, and with him, the state of France, requires that the French, along with their allies and their enemies, contrast the ideal of the man with Louis's perceived deficiencies as a leader in his advancing years.

The death of the sovereign was a fact of life, one that the court acknowledged time and time again. Preachers who eulogized Louis XIV insisted both on his virtue and constancy and also on the mortal state of this man whose body had abandoned him and released his soul to God. In his funeral oration for the king in La Sainte-Chapelle on 17 December 1715, Jean-Baptiste Massillon famously stated: "Dieu seul est grand, mes Frères et dans ces derniers momen[t]s surtout, où il préside à la mort des rois de la terre" [God alone is great, my brothers, and no more so than in these final moments, when he presides over the death of the kings of the earth].[12] In death Louis is but a man, and but one of many kings. His image has been fractured by history, felled by time. Yet as a king, and as a great king, Louis comes to embody the State as the state of his body yields first to its physical limits and then to the transcendence of ritual, in the form of relics, and of myth, as the autopsy unveils the truth of a splayed but spectacular corpse. It is a lesson of fatalities and the observances designed to compensate for them that the Maréchal Henri de Turenne (1611–75), whose excellence on the battlefield earned the king's respect and devotion, taught Louis well before he suffered the loss of his son, grandson, great-grandson, and other family members, and before he himself met his Maker. My presentation of Louis XIV's story thus begins with Turenne's.

The King and His General: A Spectacle in Five Acts

Turenne's distinguished service included many battles fought in the war against Holland. Turenne's death was a significant loss to the king, and the honours Louis XIV paid to Turenne presaged those that he himself would later receive. In this sense the image of Turenne served as a mirror in which to locate the king's victories and to validate his wars. I examine how three representations of Turenne reflect back upon the king's image: van der Meulen's painting of Arras, a commemorative fan, and a eulogy delivered to memorialize Turenne.

Death is not only an end but also a rupture. This is a truism. In the context of Louis XIV's reign, however, death was a singularly discordant experience. The monarchy's power was predicated on a master narrative of eternal glory; the court sought harmony in the unbroken repetition of tributes to the king and by the king to his loyal subjects. Death, however, means the destruction of parts, the wasting away of bodies. In particular, the death of a *grand homme* was a profoundly destabilizing event. Historical chronicles situate death within the context of a larger and often glorious sequence of events. Medicine could delay for significant periods the decline of the patient into the corpse. Church rituals contained the loss within salutary prayers and promises of the afterlife. Still, death disrupted the centres of authority in classical France. It challenged the monarchy by compromising the king's ability to lead in the absence of someone on whose skills he depended. It complicated a fundamental tenet of Cartesian science: the notion that humans, by virtue of their capacity to reason, are distinct from animals.[13] Once a man becomes a corpse, a machine whose parts have stopped working, the man/animal distinction appears less consequential. Not the mind – Descartes's *âme*, the *res cogitans* – but rather the Christian soul survives, part of the inscrutable workings of God. In death the mind – the site of perceptions and the inclinations of the will – ceases to function. Death represents the line dividing the known from the unknown, finite man from the infinite Creator. But a dead man does more than stir the passions of religious devotion. Even when one's faith is absolute, one cannot ignore the body's disintegration, the pull of the material world, forces of nature that can be measured as so many failed organs, so many calculable physical functions. Questions about the body in the classical period were increasingly answerable by science. Even objective scientific research, however, was never truly disinterested, tied as it was to the political needs of the State, which sponsored some projects at the expense of others.[14] The monarchy, science, and religion were three complementary yet contentious realms that regulated knowledge and power in seventeenth-century France. On the royal stage the deaths of Turenne, Louis XIV's respected and able general, and of the monarch himself played out as a drama of hearts and minds.

Act I: Turenne

Van der Meulen's painting of Louis XIV entering Arras discussed in chapter 2 establishes Turenne's prominence and value to the king. Louis appears on horseback behind the carriage, accompanied, on foot, by his brother, Philippe d'Orléans (Monsieur), and the Maréchal de Turenne. That trio, more than any single grouping within the painting, represents the centre of power, both political and military. Thanks to Turenne's success on the battlefield, France's inroads into the Spanish Netherlands were assured. His command during the Franco-Dutch War was critical. He defeated the forces at Turckheim, enabling the French to cross the Rhine. Turenne, however, was killed at Sasbach, an event that was the object of memorial commemorations both small and large as France mourned a hero.

The fan that commemorates Turenne's demise is a remarkable object both because of the history of its creation and because it portrays Turenne's dead body. Turenne captured Turckheim, a fortified town in Alsace, in January, 1675.[15] This victory was being celebrated in a commemorative fan commissioned in Turenne's honour when, in July of that same year, he died on the battlefield. While examining his army's position in Sasbach, northeast of Strasbourg, Turenne met with his artillery general Saint-Hilaire, whom he instructed to set the troops in position. Saint-Hilaire set off to do so, and when he returned, he called to Turenne's attention the movement of the enemy column. At that moment an apparently random canon shot hit both Saint-Hilaire, who lost his left arm, and Turenne, who perished.[16] Turenne's death was a tremendous loss for France, and for Louis XIV personally. The fan presents a complex battle scene, with cavalry preparing to breach the walls of the town, believed to be Turckheim. Turenne, sword aloft, enters on the left. Following the news of Turenne's death, the gorge (centre) of the fan was reconceived to memorialize him.[17]

In the redesigned fan gorge, Turenne, holding his sword aloft in the same commanding gesture as in the principal image, lies inert. Opinions may vary regarding the skill of the fan artist and the compromises required for him to accommodate the hero's unexpected passing. Indisputably, however, the image intrigues the viewer because it shows a dead body front and centre. The figures of the dead Turenne and his horse stand out not because they are badly positioned. Turenne's posture captures him somewhere between delicate slumber and brutal collapse, a pose that befits a fallen hero. What explains the viewer's sense

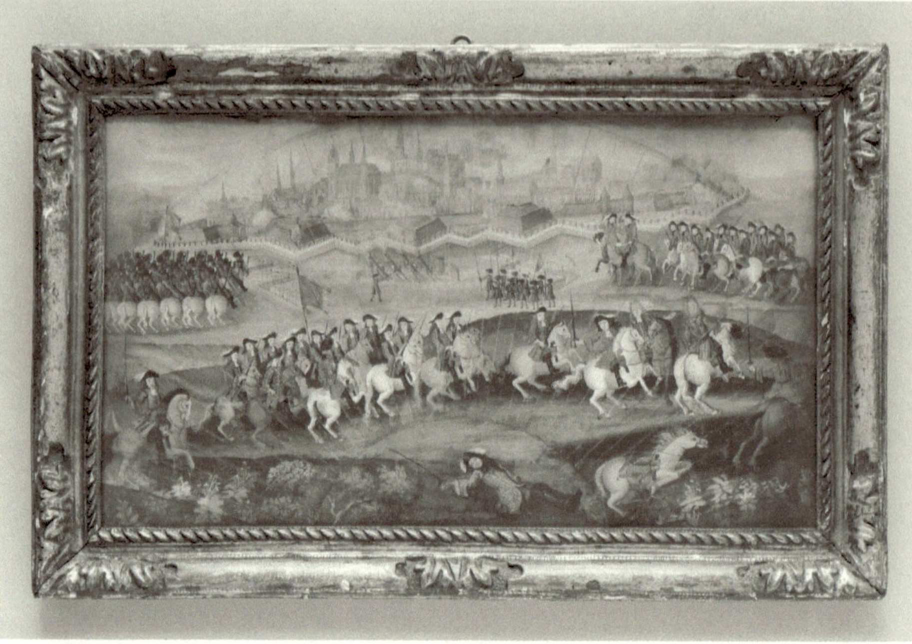

4.3. *Fan leaf painted in gouache commemorating the Death of the Vicomte de Turenne, Marshal of France, in 1675*. The Fan Museum, London. Image courtesy The Fan Museum, London. http://londonist.com/2009/10/from_the_fan_museum_war_peace.

of disproportion is that Turenne appears as a dead man, a corpse. A dead body, even one perfectly positioned to elicit the appropriate mix of emotion and tribute, disturbs by its very stillness. The artist avoids having Turenne lie in a supine position by elevating the ground under his torso. Turenne's body, however, lacks the very quality that defines the hero in the larger image, which shows men in action, soldiers worthy of Turenne as a man in command, a military leader capable of strategy and calculation, and a man fully exercising his reason.

We see a sanitized version of events. Turenne has been cleaned up and dressed in ceremonial uniform. Absent is Saint-Hilaire and/or his lost arm. Missing, too, is Saint-Hilaire's son, who discovered his injured father and who recorded the event. Seeing that his father had lost his arm, the son, in tears, threw himself onto the wounded man's chest. Saint-Hilaire's response to his son's gesture reveals his admiration for the fallen leader: "Ce n'est pas moi qu'il faut pleurer, dit celui-ci en montrant le corps de Turenne; c'est ce grand homme" ["It is not for me that you should be crying, he said, pointing to Turenne's body; it is for this great man"].[18] Most dramatically, however, the image juxtaposes the lifeless Turenne and his horse, still in motion. Indeed, the horse appears to be running out of the scene. The riderless horse evokes the ruptured bond between man and animal. Turenne here no longer harnesses the animal's energy. Recalling Descartes's mind/body dualism, moreover, we are struck by the fact that here the man has no brain function, unlike the horse. The animal still moves; he retains what Descartes describes as the machinelike qualities of the body, while the human Turenne has no comparable function. The dead figure is dressed in ways that identify Turenne as a *grand homme*. Yet the horse, rather than Turenne, remains capable of motion. Some of the awkwardness of the figure lying in the centre of the fan relates to our perception that the white horse has not only outridden but also outfunctioned his master. This scene offers a prelude to Louis's own death.

Act II: Honouring the Hero

Louis XIV ordered full public honours for Turenne, including burial at Saint-Denis, as was the custom for kings and distinguished persons since the Middle Ages. Turenne had served the king with distinction. Consistent with this tradition, moreover, Turenne's heart was preserved as a relic in the convent of the Carmelites on rue Saint-Jacques. The magnitude of national mourning was evident in public tributes that continued long after the burial, including one judged by Madame de Sévigné to be the most outstanding: the oration pronounced by the preacher Esprit Fléchier in Paris on 1 January 1676.[19]

Funerals heal the wounds of death through eulogies that offer portraits of the living. These texts, too, are sanitized, to the degree that controversial positions are typically elided, or corrected through contextualization that inspires praise.[20] In royal circles, moreover, praise of the dead courtiers serves as an occasion for lauding the king. Fléchier commends Louis XIV for recognizing his need for a seasoned commander like Turenne, who served as a model for the young king still learning about the art of war:

> Pour récompenser tant de vertus par quelque honneur extraordinaire, il fallait trouver un grand roi, qui crût ignorer quelque chose, et qui fût capable de l'avouer. Loin d'ici ces flatteuses maximes, que les rois naissent

habiles, et que les autres le deviennent; que leurs âmes privilégiées sortent des mains de Dieu, qui les crée, toutes sages et intelligentes; qu'il n'y a point pour eux d'essais, ni d'apprentissage; qu'ils sont vertueux sans travail, et prudents sans expérience. Nous vivons sous un prince, qui, tout grand, et tout éclairé qu'il est, a bien voulu s'instruire pour commander; qui, dans la route de la gloire, a su choisir un guide fidèle, et qui a cru qu'il était de sa sagesse de se servir de celle d'autrui. Quel honneur pour un sujet d'accompagner son roi, de lui servir de conseil, et, si je l'ose dire, d'exemple dans une importante conquête! Honneur d'autant plus grand, que la faveur n'y put avoir part; qu'il ne fut fondé que sur un mérite universellement connu, et qu'il fut suivi de la prise des villes les plus considérables de la Flandre.

[To reward so many virtues by some extraordinary honour requires a great king, one who felt that there were things that he did not know, and who was capable of admitting it. We are far here from the flattering formulas claiming that kings are born capable, and that others acquire their capabilities; that the kings' privileged souls emerge from the hands of God, who created them, already wise and intelligent; that for them no trial is required, no training; that they are virtuous without having to work at it, and prudent without needing any experience. We live under a king who, as great and as enlightened as he is, was determined to be educated about being a commander; who, on the road to glory, knew how to choose a faithful guide, and who believed that it was a sign of wisdom to benefit from the wisdom of others. What an honour it was for a subject to be chosen to accompany his king, to serve as his counsel, and, if I may say so, to serve as his example in an important battle! This honour was all the greater because no favour played a part in his selection; it was based only on his universally recognized merit; and this was followed by the capture of the most important cities in Flanders.] (20–1)

The burden of verbal description, like the visual portrait, is a significant one. Fléchier represents the loss of Turenne and what it means for Louis XIV, his court, and for France as a world power. Unlike the fan artist, Fléchier aims, ostensibly, to avoid depicting the corpse. He evokes the Maréchal's many professional accomplishments by insisting that they are too numerous for him to enumerate:

J'avoue, messieurs, que je succombe ici sous le poids de mon sujet. Ce grand nombre d'actions, dont je dois parler, m'embarrasse; je ne puis les décrire toutes, et je voudrais n'en omettre aucune. Que n'ai-je le secret de graver dans vos esprits un plan invisible et raccourci de la Flandre et de l'Allemagne! Je marquerais sans confusion dans vos pensées tout ce que fit ce grand capitaine, et vous dirais en abrégé, selon les lieux: ici il forçait des retranchements, et secourait une place assiégée; là il surprenait les ennemis, ou les battait en pleine campagne: ces villes, où vous voyez les lis arborés, ont été, ou défendues par sa vigilance, ou conquises par sa fermeté et par son courage. Ce lieu couvert d'un bois et d'une rivière, c'est le poste où il rassurait ses troupes effrayées après une honorable retraite: ici il sortait de ses lignes pour combattre, et d'un seul coup il prenait une ville, et gagnait une bataille: là distribuant ce qui lui restait de son propre argent, il achevait un siége [*sic*], et il allait en faire lever un en même temps.

[Your Majesty and Members of the Court, I admit that I am overwhelmed by my subject. The tremendous number of deeds of which I must speak confounds me; I cannot describe them all, yet I do not want to omit a single one. I wish that I knew how to imprint in your minds a small invisible map of Flanders and Germany! I would indicate without confusing you all that this great captain accomplished, and I would be able to explain to you in an abridged form, based on the locations: here he bore through the retrenchments and saved a place under siege; there he surprised the enemies, or fought them in the open countryside. These cities that you see lined with lilies were either defended by his vigilance or conquered by his determination and courage. This spot covered with woods and a river is the position from which he reassured his frightened troops following an honourable retreat. Here he left the ranks in order to fight, and with a single attack he took the city, and won the battle. There, distributing what remained of his own money, he completed a siege, and he went right on to start another one.] (13)

Fléchier paints a veritable landscape, *à la* van der Meulen, without naming a single site. Evoking a topographical map of battles, he constructs a list of possible, and likely known, circumstances related to the history of Turenne's victories. Fléchier's speech, however, remains in the category of things that describe without identifying. He communicates the essence of Turenne's military career, and of the man himself, as an ideal unhinged from any specific referents, that is, without elucidating geographical names for the events of the wars he fought.

The preacher, moreover, claims not to want to evoke the scene of Turenne's death:

> N'attendez pas, messieurs, que j'ouvre ici une scène tragique; que je représente ce grand homme étendu sur ses propres trophées; que je découvre ce corps pâle et sanglant, auprès duquel fume encore la foudre qui l'a frappé; que je fasse crier son sang comme celui d'Abel, et que j'expose à vos yeux les tristes images de la religion, et de la patrie éplorées. Dans les pertes médiocres, on surprend ainsi la pitié des auditeurs; et, par des mouvements étudiés on tire au moins de leurs yeux quelques larmes vaines et forcées. Mais on décrit sans art, une mort qu'on pleure sans feinte. Chacun trouve en soi la source de sa douleur, et rouvre lui-même sa plaie; et le cœur, pour être touché, n'a pas besoin que l'imagination soit émue.
>
> [Do not expect, distinguished member of the court, that I will begin to describe a tragic scene; that I will describe this great man as displayed on his own trophies; that I will reveal to you this pale and bleeding corpse around which the lightning bolt that hit him still gives off smoke; or that I will make his blood scream as if it were that of Abel, or that I expose before your eyes the sad images of religion and country both grief-stricken. In the case of ordinary losses these techniques serve to evoke the listeners' pity, and through these studied techniques one is able to extract at least some vain and forced tears. But one must describe without art a death that one sincerely mourns. Each one finds in himself the source of his suffering, and reopens by himself the wound this loss has produced; a heart, to be touched, does not require any flights of imagination to be moved.] (30)

There is no need, Fléchier states, to dramatize the sense of loss; the court's expression of grief requires no artificial prompts. Fléchier's speech touches the wound that pains all those present, including the king and members of the royal family. The preacher's rhetoric turns on a negation: I will not show; I will not describe the dead man. Fléchier evokes first a pale and bloodied body, then the dead body of Abel, treacherously killed by Cain, which story Christians interpret as evoking the martyrdom of Jesus. Fléchier's description thus summons up images of the fallen Turenne *qua* Christ. Paralipsis, the rhetorical device wherein the speaker brings up a subject by denying that it should be brought up, is a tool used to persuade. Prolepsis is an extreme kind of paralipsis that provides the full details of the acts one is claiming to pass over. I will not tell you a heroic tale, the tragic story of a pale and bloody body. I will make you, my audience, own the knowledge of that body by making you recognize what I deny describing. You know that body; you know that body is Turenne's. I heal you through words that extend the history of war and nationhood into the realm of faith and salvation, words that extend the image of the body of a man to the crucifix and the body of Christ. Turenne's corpse marks the liminal space between known and unknown, mortal and immortal. By denying the need to imagine the heroic scene, the preacher opts for the here and now, for the material loss that is Turenne's death to France. By evoking religious history, he promises salvation. The eulogy balances this essential tension.

Oratory relies on verbal flourishes that convince by enflaming the imagination, by jarring expectations. The priest's denial of the very tools that enable him to console his royal flock – I will not describe; you need not imagine – is but one example of how he keeps his audience's attention through inversion and reversal. To deny, artfully, the need to imagine death is to imagine it more deeply, with more layers of meaning – the hero, the king, the saviour, salvation. Rhetoric forms part of a paradigm that can include disputation, manipulation, and propaganda. Fléchier's oration clearly favours the interests of the Church and the monarchy, including, especially, the king and the royal family, the male members ("Messieurs" [His Majesty and distinguished members of the court]) whom he addresses at the outset of his oration. The preacher appeals directly to the suffering of those present, hoping to reinforce their faith via language that touches their hearts. They are wounded as Turenne was wounded and as Christ was wounded, and they must open themselves up to God. The preacher's words reach deep into the wound to touch the heart. As we shall see in the following account of Louis XIV's own demise, however, touching the heart of a great man is a grand gesture, one that forms part of the court's calculus for survival.

Act III: The King Is Dying

The Marquis de Dangeau, court diarist, recounts Louis's final days in excruciating detail.[21] Dangeau records the king's daily schedule, including the arrival of members of the royal family, among them the dauphin; the king's recommendations to them; the prayers. Successive visits to the king's chamber mark his progressive decline. Dangeau conveys his personal emotion in witnessing the king's demise, as well as the emotion that he observes both in the king and those in his inner circle. Yet

Dangeau also offers, if not a clinical account of disease equivalent to that which a doctor would present, an extensive chronicle of the ravages of the gangrenous leg that kills the king. Dangeau's sense of history and his emotions, the public as well as the private loss, are evident from the first line: "Je sors du plus grand, du plus touchant et du plus héroïque spectacle que les hommes puissent jamais voir" [I have just left the greatest, most moving, and most heroic scene that one could ever witness] (13).

Dangeau's account shows the ravages of death to be a dehumanizing process. Three different stages mark his account of the royal demise. The first is Louis's awareness of his state:

> Le roi, revenu de l'embarras qu'il eut dans l'esprit près d'un quart d'heure après son réveil et craignant de retomber dans un pareil état, pensa lui-même qu'il devoit recevoir le viatique sans attendre plus longtemps, et comptant de ce moment qu'il lui restoit peu d'heures à vivre, il agit et donna ordre à tout comme un homme qui va mourir, mais avec une fermeté, une présence d'esprit et une grandeur d'âme dont il n'y a jamais eu d'exemple.
>
> [Recovering from the confusion he was in about a quarter of an hour after waking, and fearing that he would again fall into this state, the king decided on his own that he should receive the last rites without further delay. Believing at that point that he had only hours to live, he acted and gave instructions as a man about to die, but with more firmness, presence of mind, and greatness of soul than the world has ever seen.] (15)

Dangeau quotes Louis observing to two *garçons de la chambre* [officers of the royal bedchamber], brothers from the Anthoine family: "Pourquoi pleurez-vous? Est-ce que vous m'avez cru immortel? Pour moi, je ne l'ai jamais cru être, et vous avez dû vous préparer depuis longtemps à me perdre dans l'âge où je suis" [Why are you crying? Did you think that I was immortal? I, for one, never thought so, and you should have started preparing yourselves to lose me a long time ago, given my age] (28).[22] The king knew that his death was imminent. Moreover, his claim to accept his fate suggests a certain courage that, whatever the truth of his emotions, he wants to model for the *garçons de la chambre* and those to whom they may speak of their experiences with him just prior to his death. Louis was aware that his body was failing, and in this short speech, despite expressing impatience (whether real or feigned) with the brothers' tears, he assumed responsibility for his image as he departed the world.

The second aspect of Dangeau's observations refers to the progression of the disease both physically and mentally. The king's gangrenous leg was manifestly incurable:

> Sur les dix heures [le 26 août 1715] on a pansé la jambe du roi, dans laquelle on lui a donné plusieurs coups de lancette et fait des incisions jusqu'à l'os; comme on a trouvé que la gangrène gagnoit jusque-là, il n'y a plus eu lieu de douter, même à ceux qui auroient le plus voulu se flatter, qu'elle vient du dedans et qu'on ne peut y apporter aucun remède.
>
> [At ten o'clock [26 August 1715] the king's leg was bandaged, following several cuts to lance it to the bone, since the gangrene was found to have spread that far. There is no longer any doubt, even among those who cling to hope, that the gangrene is coming from deep inside, and that there is no way he can be saved.] (22)

Mentally, the king was also declining. In sharp contrast to the capacities he demonstrated in his orders to the men in his service quoted above, Dangeau notes on 30 August: "Le roi a été toute la journée dans un assoupissement presque continuel et n'ayant quasi plus que la connoissance animale" [The king was sleeping nearly continuously throughout the day and he no longer had full mental capacities (literally: he only had an "animal consciousness")] (30). This portrait of the king precludes all idealization; the king had become a body, a machine, and was no longer capable of thought, language, and judgment:

> A dix heures et demie du soir on lui a dit les prières des agonisants, crainte qu'il n'expire pendant la nuit. La voix des aumôniers qui ont fait les prières a frappé la machine, qui pendant ces prières a dit à plus haute voix qu'eux l'*Ave Maria* et le *Credo* à plusieurs reprises, mais sans aucune connoissance et par la grande habitude que S.M. [Sa Majesté] a de les prononcer.
>
> [At 10:30 in the evening the prayers for the dying were said, fearing that he would expire during the night. The voice of chaplains who recited the prayers struck the machine, which during these prayers uttered, louder than they, the *Ave Maria* and the *Creed* several times, but without any awareness that he was doing so; rather His Majesty merely repeated prayers that he had said so often.] (31)

Portraying death as the destruction of both body and mind, Dangeau traces both the physical decline and the progressive confusion that overwhelmed Louis. Thus, Dangeau's reader knows that king's mind had gone out before his heart stopped beating. It is a testament to Dangeau's clinical observations that he does not take Louis's final recitation of prayers as a sign of divine intervention, a moment where Louis's *res cogitans* ceased to function and simply transmitted the word of God. Instead Dangeau insists on the fact that the king recited by rote; his brain functioned as a machine whose gears had not yet stopped moving. The machine stopped the following day, just days shy of Louis's seventy-seventh birthday.

Act IV: The Post-Mortem

Consistent with royal tradition, the king's heart and entrails were excised, and his body was buried in Saint-Denis.[23] The excision of the heart is a dramatic moment, a piece of royal theatre for the seven who officiated. The autopsy would appear to harmonize the conflicting interests of government, science, and religion, as members of the court, the medical community, and the clergy were all in attendance. Yet the opening of the body, the wound created to excise the heart and the viscera, is an act of violation. It fragments what was whole in the body (save for what was removed during the earlier surgeries) and exposes what is hidden there. Those in attendance, representatives of different centres of power and knowledge, together observe the body of the man they knew as king. What they see, however, is the cut that bisects the chest to expose the inner workings of the body/machine.[24]

According to Louis de Rouvroy, Duc de Saint-Simon, those present at the autopsy bore witness to a startling find. Louis's stomach and intestines were exceptionally large:

> Par l'ouverture de son corps qui fut faite par Maréchal, son premier chirurgien, avec l'assistance et les cérémonies accoutumées, on lui [au Roi] trouva toutes les parties si entières, si saines et tout si parfaitement conformé, qu'on jugea qu'il aurait vécu plus d'un siècle sans les fautes dont il a été parlé qui lui mirent la gangrène dans le sang. On lui trouva aussi la capacité de l'estomac et des intestins double au moins des hommes de sa taille; ce qui est fort extraordinaire, et ce qui était cause qu'il était si grand mangeur et si égal.

> [Inside the incision, which was made by Maréchal, the first surgeon, with the customary ceremonies, his [the king's] organs were found to be so intact, so healthy, and so perfectly normal that they thought he would have been able to live for more than a century, were it not for the problems already discussed that caused the gangrene to enter his blood. He was found to have a stomach and intestines more than twice as large as would be expected for a man of his size, which is really quite extraordinary, and which explains the fact that he was such a large and exceptional eater.][25]

Saint-Simon's account is consistent with the *procès-verbal de l'ouverture du corps* [official autopsy report], which notes that, while the heart was "très beau" [in very good shape] and other organs were also healthy, the intestines were "bien alterés avec inflammation surtout ceux du côté gauche, le gros intestin d'une dilation extraordinaire" [very altered with inflammation especially apparent on the left side, and the large intestine was exceptionally distended].[26] Saint-Simon, however, ascribes the large viscera to Louis's extraordinary life, as opposed to the pathology of his disease, recalling that the king had, among his many consuming passions, a voracious appetite. Saint-Simon establishes as real the mythic/heroic proportions of the man who was king. Blessed with an exceptional digestive tract, Louis is confirmed to be France's *plus grand homme*. While this notion harmonizes with the idea of the king's glory, the emphasis on size is exceptional. This discordancy occurs is not because the king falls short of expectations – he is appropriately *grand* – but rather because size should be the wrong measure of his worth, his grandeur/greatness. Louis le Grand's rule has depended on the cultivation of an image, his glorious image, rather than on his material existence, however outsized. Absolute power is infinite, and cannot be measured – not, certainly, in organs, and not even in time, the duration of Louis's life on earth. The return to material mortal existence at this final juncture impresses, even in a king so well endowed. The intestines, after all, recall not only the appetites that defined Louis's life but also the illness that brought about its end.

In death the king's body becomes, in the manner of Rembrandt's *Anatomy Lesson of Dr Nicolaes Tulp*, an object of study. Rembrandt's famous portrait of a dissection by the anatomist Dr Tulp privileges science with the cadaver offered for instruction, and again with the open book, likely Andreas Vesalius's *De humani corporis fabrica* [*Fabric of the Human Body*] (1543), in the bottom right-hand corner, which further emphasizes empirical study. Dr Tulp refers to the work of the great

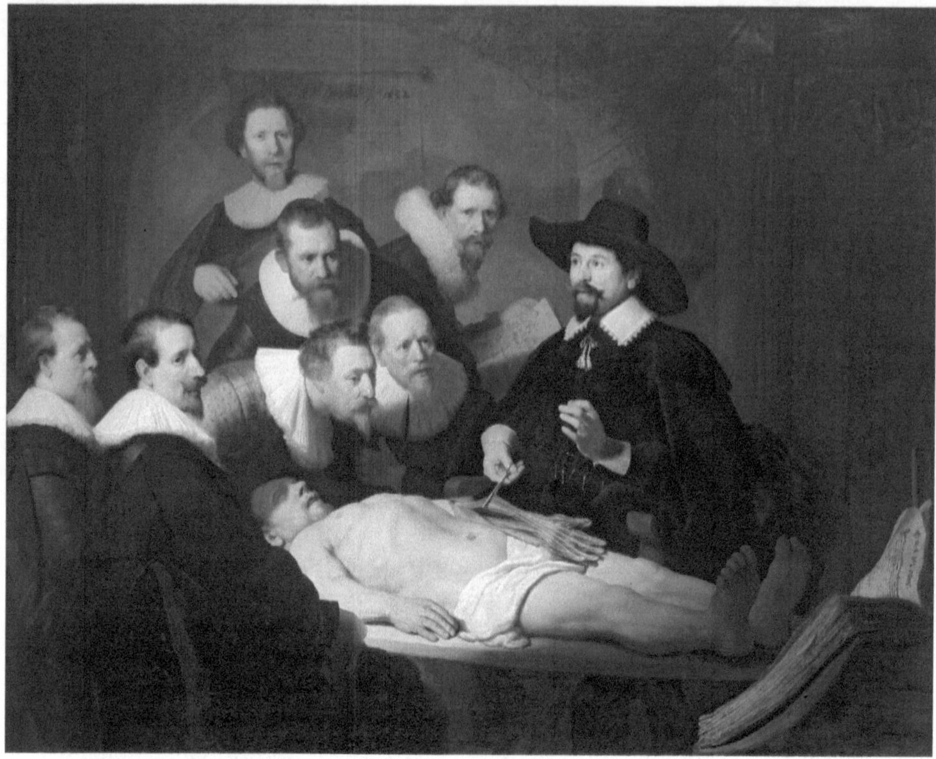

4.4. Rembrandt Harmensz. van Rijn. *The Anatomy Lesson of Dr Nicolaes Tulp.* 1632. 169.5 × 216.5 cm (66.73 × 85.24 in) Mauritshuis, The Hague. Image courtesy Mauritshuis, The Hague, The Netherlands/Bridgeman Images. https://www.mauritshuis.nl/en/explore/the-collection/artworks/the-anatomy-lesson-of-dr-nicolaes-tulp-146/.

Renaissance anatomist, which includes his own image, holding a dissected forearm. These references, or *mises en abîme*, do not, as they might in a royal image of Louis XIV, limit the viewer's knowledge to an earlier history. Evidence of scientific progress, the anatomy text evokes the history of science as it has evolved and continues to develop. Dissection reveals a knowledge that is new for the men in attendance; they have come to learn. While the members of the Guild of Surgeons, which commissioned the painting, are all engaged, they do not fix their gaze on the same thing. Some peer at the anatomy book, some at the body, one at the anatomist, and one, the man nearest the anatomist who appears to hold a list of their names, looks directly towards the viewer. Despite the closeness of the figures and the tight grouping around the cadaver, therefore, the painting opens itself up to different perspectives, another sign that the opening of the body serves a new knowledge. The expressions of the three members at the centre of the image nearest the corpse are particularly concentrated as Dr. Tulp uses forceps to identify muscles and tendons in the forearm, moving the fingers of his own left hand to show the movement they control.[27] The hand of the anatomist has the power to move the body, an action that would not be interpreted as usurping God's power but rather as demonstrating that science is consistent with God's plan.[28]

Dissections in Holland were public spectacles. In France the audience for the autopsy of Louis XIV was more restricted, and the king could not be a more different subject than the criminal whose cadaver served the cause of science in Holland. Nonetheless, the king's autopsy allowed for empirical findings. As had been the custom for centuries, the royal autopsy and embalming were established to meet the practical demands of preserving the body so that it could be viewed in its best, and least putrefied and pungent, state.[29] The remarkable circumstance in Louis XIV's case was not simply the information obtained from the dissection but also that Saint-Simon, whose critical evaluation of the king and his court are well in evidence in his *Mémoires*, nevertheless converts the empirical findings into a confirmation of the king's larger-than-life condition, as if science had come to serve not the cause of knowledge but that of myth. We are reminded that the book of record for the French court is not an anatomy lesson but rather the text scripted to promote the royal image. In this instance it is a portrait to which even Saint-Simon contributes. Still, the dissection itself is a medical as well as a political event. Heavy with verifiable observations of Louis's advanced gangrenous condition, the full autopsy report limits the court's recuperation of the king's royal body as an idea that entirely replaces the physical body. Louis is supersized, larger than life; but he is still a man whose large bowels have been empirically tested and whose interior portrait is one of pervasive decay.

In its careful elaboration of the various organs, the report offers hard science and nothing of the "ashes to ashes and dust to dust" vision of the natural cycle offered by the Church, a cycle whose repetitions establish continuity even as they identify the body's demise.[30] For continuity, and for salvation, the monarch sets in place other rituals. The king's body is wrapped and covered with a shroud, and the heart and the bowels (entrails) are embalmed. Louis's heart was placed in the church of Saint-Louis des Jésuites (currently the church of Saint-Paul-Saint-Louis) and his entrails were transported to Notre Dame Cathedral, where these relics connect him, and through him future worshipers, with the mystical and divine.

A long and venerable, and hence familiar, tradition, the harvesting of relics certainly remained an exceptional event in the lives of those who witnessed it. No science, no state, no religion, however codified its practices and however professional its practitioners, exists totally outside the wound of history. No one can peer inside the body of the king, through the cut of the chest and into the royal interior, without being moved. The common interests of science, the monarchy, and the Church, as they represent three distinct realms of knowledge and power, come together for the post-mortem activities. The splayed corpse, however, the wounded king/Christ/hero, is still very much a body. None can see the king's body in its most machine-like state without responding, and the expression is apt, *viscerally* – that is, with the emotion that Fléchier described as well as with knowledge of the internal organs of the body as science has exposed them. As Louis XIV's soul goes to meet his Maker, each realm of society will move, in predictable machine-like fashion, to re-establish its dominion. In the next century the cause of science and the advancement of knowledge through experiment (observation-based natural philosophy) will prove incompatible at critical junctures with both the monarchy and the Church.

Turenne as he was honoured to accompanying the king; the fan commemorating Turenne's victories that becomes a container for his dead body; a eulogy for him by Fléchier; an account of Louis's death by Dangeau, the king's autopsy recounted by Saint-Simon, and as included in the official report – these are all portraits of the mortal condition. Death causes one to stop and think. And in that moment of reflection order, reason, harmony – the hallmarks of rationalism – slip away, if only momentarily. The viewer/listener sees double: the general in the battle and the general in death; the man who was and the corpse that is; the image of two great men, Turenne and Louis le Grand, and the parts that made each tick. These things all register discontinuity, the shock of the person become a machine, and then of the machine grinding to a halt. The public thinks, not unlike Descartes, who thought and therefore knew that he existed: *Cogito ergo sum*. But it thinks with an added twist: the audience interprets the details that accumulate in these descriptions as so many weights placed in the scales of knowledge, scales still unbalanced as they consider the body, the mind, and the soul. Perceived mechanically as a function of its material properties, the dead body resists abstraction, the very energy that allowed Louis to rise above his mortal station as an image. To see that image rise again following Louis XIV's death will require the oratory of priests and the praise of historians. Not all, however, will be forthcoming.

Act V: Heirs Apparent

Portraits of Louis continued to be painted after his death, including the marvellous "Ventadour" portrait by the French School, *Louis XIV et sa famille* [*Madame de Ventadour with Portraits of Louis XIV and His Heirs*] (ca. 1715–20). The multigenerational portrait rejects much, although certainly not all, the allegorical trappings found elsewhere. Overall, this painting is structured more like the almanac in its emphasis on likeness. Instead of Louis XIV's own image appearing multiple times within the frame, here the successive generations mirror his image as a way of communicating his dynastic and, by extension, permanent legacy. For all its formal qualities, the French portrait is remarkably intimate, recalling Dutch genre paintings. While the Dutch also produced many family portraits, de Hooch's *Mother Lacing Her Bodice beside a Cradle* (1659–60) provides an interesting comparison to this French painting of the royal heirs, as both images accentuate the feminine nurturing role in a private setting. That intimacy, reinforced through the array of objects displayed in de Hooch's image, further suggests how the Dutch emphasis on cataloguing the things of their world offers a knowledge system capable of surviving the legacy of Louis XIV that the court so carefully orchestrates.

De Hooch shows a mother tending to an infant in a cradle; the family dog does much the same; a toddler contemplates the outdoors. The artist describes a private, feminine space. The maternal presence, evoking both nurture and closeness, is reinforced by the various objects that invite the viewer to inventory the home. The bed with its bed warmer, the cape on the hook, and other functional objects, including a table on which rest a cloth or carpet, a candle, and a pitcher, along with, in the other room, a chair and a table with a pot on it define the domestic space. Many items have been purchased, but in the home setting they do more than convey a certain level of material comfort. The objects

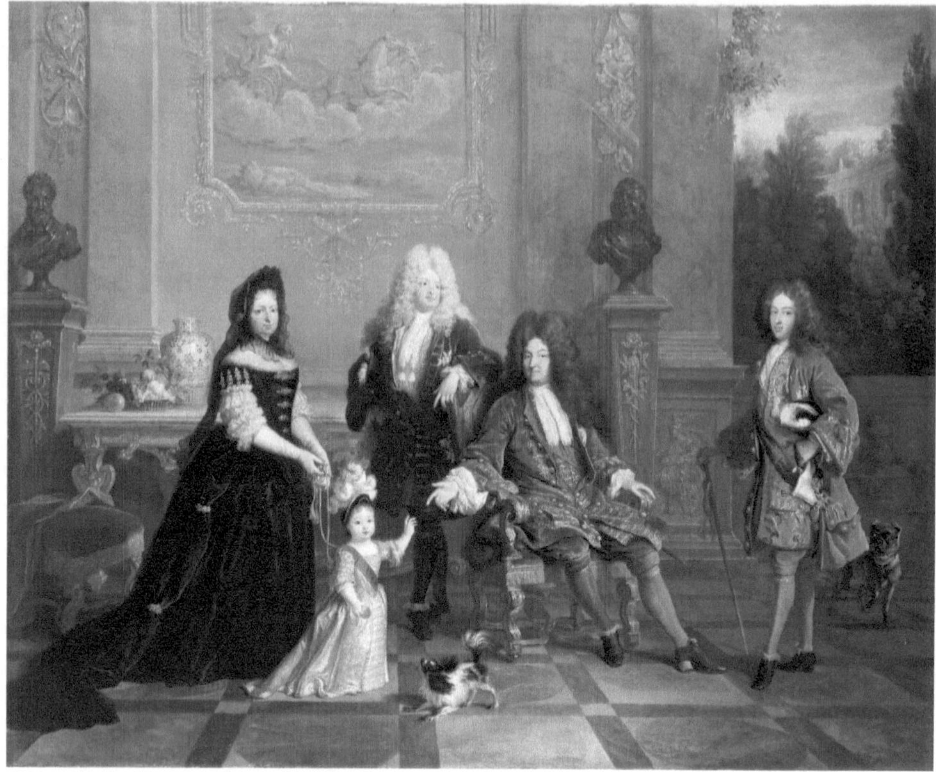

4.5. French School. *Louis XIV et sa famille* [*Madame de Ventadour with Portraits of Louis XIV and His Heirs*]. Ca. 1715–20. 127.6 × 161 cm (50.24 × 63.39 in). Wallace Collection, London. Image by kind permission of the Trustees of the Wallace Collection, London/Art Resource, NY. https://wallacelive.wallacecollection.org:443/eMP/eMuseumPlus?service=ExternalInterface&module=collection&objectId=65056&viewType=detailView.

help to identify the daily activities of the family while the father is out in the world. The woman's responsibilities include for caring for the children and maintaining the household.

The mother clearly anchors the scene. Not only the woman's size relative to the two children and the dog but also her red vest captures the viewer's attention, developing associations with the red cradle covering and the red cape hanging above her. The mother's open pose,

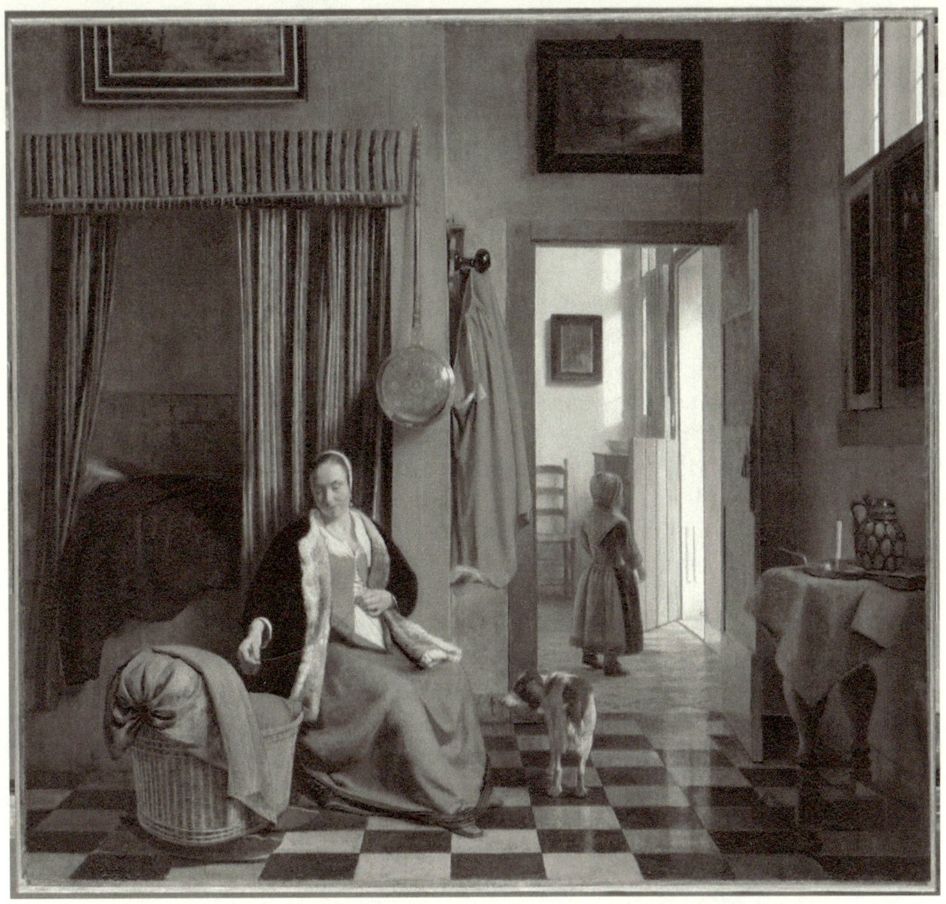

4.6. Pieter de Hooch. *Mother Lacing Her Bodice beside a Cradle*. Ca. 1663. Gemäldegalerie, Berlin. 95.2 × 102.5 cm (37.48 × 40.35 in). Photo bpk Bildagentur/Gemäldegalerie/Jörg P. Anders/Art Resource, NY. https://www.wga.hu/html_m/h/hooch/2/25hooch.html.

suggested by both her jacket and her loosely laced bodice (she has just nursed the baby), invites the viewer into the scene, even though her gaze turns discreetly away.

The maternal connection here quite literally exists as a string, or a lace from her bodice, that she extends towards the child in what would be a moment of fascination.[31] Teaching her baby to look and to see the string, to watch it move, she also offers comfort (as Freud would later say) by letting her baby experience how the string that moves away is also the string that, like the mother herself, always returns.[32] For the viewer, though, she offers a less secure knowledge. The viewer can imagine the older child, left foot slightly elevated, heading out the door letting in the sunlight. He is eager to explore the world, to see for himself what there is to see.

The overarching domestic theme notwithstanding, the composition relies on many discrete and discontinuous elements. The image is composed in such a way to oblige the viewer to consider the various objects individually and somewhat disjointedly. The viewer looks at *either* the cradle to the left *or* the child to the right. One cannot focus carefully on both the cradle and the older child together, as they are in opposite positions relative to the mother. The toddler, moreover, extends the viewer's thoughts outside the walls of the home to invisible portions of the city.

Even after mapping the composition in this way, the viewer might still feel a bit off course. The marble floor in the foreground and the tiled floor in the room behind it establish a perspective, only to lose it in the four framed objects, including two paintings, a mirror, and the window, which frame a space that is only partially exposed. The viewer cannot decipher the painting over the bed. The other painting over the doorway appears to be a landscape, another reminder of the life outside the home. A mirror hangs beneath it, but in the anteroom adjoining the main living space. De Hooch masters perspective to create the illusion of depth, affording the viewer knowledge of how parts of the house connect. Other things, however, do not connect as well, or, more accurately, stand out as pieces of a larger whole, parts of a dynamic scene whose energy the painter conveys by deliberately decentring and partitioning his composition. The mirror reflection could not be more natural, and yet it frames a part of a body in motion, exposing only the head of this child whose lifted foot suspends him in both time and space.

Noting the various segmented objects – the bottom portion of the painting, the head in the mirror, the door half open – one thinks not of likeness but rather of synecdoche, the part that substitutes for the whole. Even if the viewer understands from the bottom third of a painting that a full painting hangs in the room – that is, if the viewer can negotiate from parts to the whole in some key instances – the parts observed recall the parts still missing: the father, the city outside, etc. To refer to the *cradle* in order to describe the *baby*, moreover, is to neglect the fact that the cradle itself is an object of interest, irrespective of the baby it holds.

A viewer *sees* the whole of de Hooch's painting; it exists as a single visual field. Yet to *appreciate* the image, one must study its elements one by one. The painting makes the viewer aware of individual objects much like city maps from this period indicated monuments and other cultural points of interest. Orientation happens within the image, but it is not our modern cartographic one of indicating the directions, north and south, so as to learn to walk a straight path from point A to point B. Mapping de Hooch's image does not involve simply distinguishing the horizontals from the verticals, foreground from background, one object from the next. What I describe as *disorientation* refers to the fact that the viewer cannot *but* jump from one figure to the next, up to the toddler, and back down to the cradle, or the reverse. The viewer's gaze moves in and out of the two adjoining rooms to look inside them and the bed, and then inside the woman's open jacket. In this way the viewer assembles a view of the domestic space one item at a time. Precious items, such as the baby in the cradle, although essential to the experience that we observe, remain inscrutable. Is the toddler a he or a she? Both sexes wore skirts, and this child does not have an accessory such as a toy to identify it as male or female.[33] According to cultural norms, a boy would be more apt to emerge from the family nest into the world outside, as this toddler appears ready to do. He, however, could be a she who in the next step turns back to stand beside her mother.

In the *Ventadour* portrait of Louis XIV with Louis le Grand Dauphin, Louis, Duc de Bourgogne, and Louis, Duc d'Anjou, there is no question but that the toddler is a boy. This portrait takes the measure of six generations of royal heirs, from Henri IV through one of Louis's great-grandsons. A bust of Henri IV (1553–1610) appears on the left; a bust of Louis XIII (1601–43) appears on the right; Louis XIV (1638–1715) sits in the centre of the picture; Louis, the Grand Dauphin (1661–1711), stands with his left arm on the back of his father's chair; Louis, Duc de Bourgogne (1682–1712), Louis XIV's grandson, stands to his left. The child whom the king designates with his right hand is the future Louis XV (1710–74), who extends his left hand in a gesture that signifies his succession to the throne.[34]

Much separates de Hooch's maternal, domestic setting from the formality of Louis XIV and his heirs posing inside an imaginary palace setting. Yet three aspects of this portrait recall elements of de Hooch's painting: the positioning of the members of each generation in a circular pattern rather than a linear formation that would accentuate the direct line of descent; the child with the playful dog; and the protective role of his governess, Charlotte de La Motte Houdancourt, duchesse de Ventadour. History broke the dynastic line. In the unexpected rescripting of the Bourbon legacy, Louis XIV survived his son, his grandson, and two of his great-grandsons (the elder brothers of the child depicted here). The painting thus contains within it both the source of Louis's extended glory and the seeds of its destruction. Scholars believe that the painting was given to Madame de Ventadour, who is guiding the young prince with a lead (he is learning how to walk), as a tribute to her efforts to protect him from the doctors. Consistent with the custom of the day, they had wanted to bleed this child as they had many who died of the measles epidemic. She thus saved the future Louis XV, whose elder brother and father (and mother) died of measles, and whose grandfather had died of smallpox.

As with de Hooch's painting, this portrait links themes of nurture, intimacy, and legacy. The fruit basket functions as a still life within the painting, adding a temporal note that reinforces the idea of death and monarchic succession with the aging Louis XIV. Full to overflowing, with a piece of fruit on the table beside it, the fruit basket serves as both a sign of plenty and as a reminder of the transience of earthly existence. The painted still life and the individual fruits are *effets de réel*, realistic details that evoke actual pieces of fruit that the figures in the painting could see, touch, and eat. Those details resonate because real fruit will rot, and, like them, the great monarch, too, will die. The fruits reinforce, synecdochally, the idea of lineage: the fruit is a sign of the tree that produced it; the most important tree here is genealogical. The child holds a piece of fruit that identifies him as belonging to the majestic Bourbon tree as the successor to Louis XIV. This narrative is further enriched by two framed images on the back wall that offer different routes into myth and history, each with its evocation of lives stilled, lives to be celebrated and lives to be mourned. On the left, the Apollonian image is marked by the god's chariot. On the right, a palace garden scene similarly triggers associations that enrich our understanding of the royal family.

The image on the left recalls the Apollo fountain in the Garden of Versailles. The Ovidian myth of the sun god Apollo favours Louis's ambitions as the Sun King. Ovid's account includes a father/son drama that resonates with the history evoked in the portrait. Apollo's son Phaethon, attempting to prove to a doubting friend that he is indeed Apollo's son, approaches his father and asks to drive his chariot. Apollo tries to dissuade Phaeton, explaining how dangerous it would be for him to drive the chariot with its fiery steeds – not even Jupiter would attempt it. With reckless abandon, Phaeton ignores his father's admonitions and takes off. The horses speed out of control, scorching the earth as the chariot approaches. Earth implores Jupiter to intervene, and the king of the gods obliges, sending Phaethon out of the sky with a lightning bolt.[35]

The Apollo image conveys not only Louis's aspirations as the Sun King but also the importance of legacy and the challenges facing the French royal family. Given the date of the painting (1715–20), which likely follows Louis's own 1 September 1715 death, questions of legitimacy in Ovid are very much to the point. The painting is a dynastic work that celebrates Louis XIV via his ancestors and his descendants. The reference to Apollo suggests a more timeless history rooted in mythic struggles, whether with gods or supernatural figures, the father, or with nature itself. Indeed, following the measles epidemic of 1712, the history of the French monarchy had become its own myth. Louis XIV, a powerful king with three generations to succeed him, outlived many of his direct descendants.[36] The situation became so dire that the king passed an edict in July 1714 authorizing his legitimated bastards to succeed him after the princes of the blood.[37] The king's sun was clearly setting in the *Ventadour* portrait.

The other image on the back wall shows an arched structure, Roman-inspired, likely a grotto, with a fountain or statue, dominated by woods. The architectural monument communicates the great legacy of the ancients to which Louis's image would be forever bound. Evoking the landscape tradition, minus the subtleties of light and atmosphere, of Claude Lorrain and the colour palate of Poussin, this otherwise Roman view contributes to the sense of timelessness that these artists brought to France.

Neither the Apollonian allegory nor the landscape image overwhelms the history of Louis XIV's royal lineage. Indeed, the realistic portraits, which recall the fine details of Dutch genre painting, invite a different standard of evaluation. The French painting is commemorative, and a clear tribute to the king's glory. The inclusion, however, of Madame de Ventadour, a noblewoman who, while the likely recipient of the painting, was not in the line of succession, breaks the pattern of prospective male heirs to the throne, the Louis likenesses.[38] Moreover, this painting is a composite that includes two Louis heirs who were presumably dead at the time the painting was completed (Louis

XIV's son and his grandson) as was, most likely, Louis XIV himself.[39] The fact that this painting was, at least in part, a reconstruction of figures post-mortem belies the sense of destiny that it was intended to convey through the portraits of four generations. This royal portrait relies on resemblances ("the sons of Louis") to represent the value of the Bourbon dynasty to France. Although the portraits of multiple generations in the line of succession are signs of continuity, the notion that these historic figures on the canvas are copies of copies imparts added meaning, not all of it positive. All portraits are copies of originals. Here a further layer of separation between the original (each living members of the royal dynasty) occurs: the painted figures are copies of earlier portraits of the deceased members of the royal family. Assembled not from life but rather from other images, this dynastic portrait, or series of individual portraits, shares qualities with still lifes, and not only because so many of the figures represented were dead when it was created.

The bowl of fruit is the product of an invisible hand, likely that of a servant. The only other fruit appears in the hand of the surviving son, the heir-not-so-apparent in the depicted scene but already the ruler, most likely, at the time the painting was made. Still a toddler, saved because of the remarkable intervention of his governess, the prince holds an apple (or peach hard enough to play with) that entices the black and white dog. Consistent with iconography of the time, the dog's boisterousness suggests that the child requires continued guidance and education to make him a man/king.[40] The fate of the fruit, however, is to rot. The idea that Louis XIV, who ruled so long, died bereft of his son and grandson, heirs who had ensured his future – and his future image – resonates here as it does in a vanitas.

With Netherlandish still lifes even death can be looked at directly because the symbols of mortality are also objects in life that artists render with appealing accuracy. Flowers from different seasons appear in the same vase. Their enduring beauty is attributable not to any single flower, as all will die, but rather to the artist's image, which celebrates life as it bears witness to the transience of living things. The French image balances the history of the nation's losses with the busts and figures assembled for posterity. This history is reflected in the fruit that the child king holds, the apple that did, and yet did not, fall far from the tree that Louis XIV inherited from his father and grandfather; that he nurtured and watched grow, but whose branches began to fall before his own life cycle was complete.

In France the artistic emphasis on similar identities will be superseded over time by paintings that are more Dutch-inspired than Louis-inspired, images that train one's eye to find beauty, and meaning, in the display of objects such as bowls of fruit, as it will in Chardin's still lifes. In the remaining chapters I explore how the art historical transition in France from seventeenth-century history painting, portraiture, landscape, and still life to eighteenth-century genre painting and still lifes forms part of Louis XIV's legacy. It is a legacy complicated and enriched by the empirical emphasis of Dutch Golden Age art, which had profound implications for the structuring and recording of knowledge from Versailles through Enlightenment Paris. The Dutch remained a discrete part of that decor and that history.

PART THREE

Patterns of Change

5 The Great Reveal

During Louis's long reign the French were subjected to the court's propaganda along with direct critiques of the monarchy. At the same time, as earlier chapters have argued, the French were party to a vast cultural production that embraced different tendencies and intellectual orientations, including not only French works that expanded the Italian Renaissance tradition but also Netherlandish realist art as it evidenced a strong empirical orientation. Despite the firm hand of the monarchy in controlling the arts, French court culture was not monolithic. Part 1 identified Northern realist influences in France during Louis XIV's reign. Part 2 considered Dutch genre painting as a logic, or system, of possible relations that accentuates tensions played out on the classical stage and at the French court. Part 3 continues to interrogate the effects of empiricism within the arts by considering the question of legacy as both a material and an intellectual bequest of Louis XIV to his subjects.

How would French viewers experience the art that they encountered in private and royal collections? How would they consider examples of heroic depictions of Louis in conjunction with works by Poussin, on the one hand, and van Ruisdael, on the other? It would be too simple to state that Poussin, in favouring Arcadian landscapes; Le Brun, in depicting Louis crossing the Rhine to enter Holland; and van Ruisdael, in describing the fields of his native Haarlem, all emphasize nature, or even that all three artists to some degree accentuate realistic depictions. Let us look more closely at the lay of this land as evidenced in painting and texts associated with them.[1]

Poussin enjoys a somewhat paradoxical relationship at the heart of French seventeenth-century painting. Under Le Brun the Académie promoted the artist, circulating his works as engravings. Yet the monarchy understood that Poussin was not useful for the decoration of the royal palaces or for creating a "French type of painting," because, as Olivier Bonfait observes, his images sought to convey the emotion of each figure rather than to celebrate the hero in the centre of the group, the king.[2] Louis XIV's relationship to Poussin's work includes an intriguing history. The year 1665 marked Bernini's completion of his magnificent bust of Louis XIV. It also marked Bernini's failed attempt to secure a commission for the east facade of the Louvre, as well as his visit to the collection of the Duc de Richelieu (Armand Jean de Vignerot du Plessis, great-nephew of the cardinal).[3] Moreover, that same year, after losing a game of *paume* (an early form of tennis) to Louis XIV, the Duc de Richelieu presented the king with twenty-five paintings from his impressive art collection, including thirteen Poussins. Here royal history arguably degrades into sport and some high-stakes gambling.[4] Despite the fact that he spent much of his career in Rome, Poussin was revered by French artists. In Paris, and especially in the Académie royale de peinture et de sculpture, Poussin served as a critical reference until his emphasis on design and drawing was eventually superseded by the emphasis on colour that Rubens advocated.[5] At the time of Louis's acquisition of Poussin's paintings, there could be no doubt about the value of the artist's oeuvre for France's patrimony.[6]

The king emerges as the victor from his exchange with the duke. Yet if we look a bit further into the celebrated Poussin acquisition, different narrative strands for this history appear. One shows that for the king the contest was about winning at *paume* and of marking that victory by inflicting a penance on the duke. A more nuanced view describes how, rather than playing in order to win at sport, the king was playing in order to secure the duke's prized Poussin paintings and other art. We know that the duke was compensated for the paintings.[7] To imagine Louis as an art connoisseur, or even simply as a less discerning collector of valuable objects, elevates him above the rank of mere sports enthusiast. Nonetheless, it corrupts the king's image for people to think of him engaging in clever acquisitions for his collection. "Qui," asks Pierre Rosenberg, "mit au point l'habile stratagème (un grand n'était pas censé faire du commerce!) qui permit au souverain de s'en emparer et pourquoi celui-ci (ou qui parmi ses conseillers) décida-t-il d'acquérir en priorité ces œuvres? Nous l'ignorons" [Who ... came up with the clever strategy (a noble was not supposed to conduct business!) that allowed the sovereign to get hold of these works, and why did he (or one of his advisors) decide to prioritize the acquisition of these works?

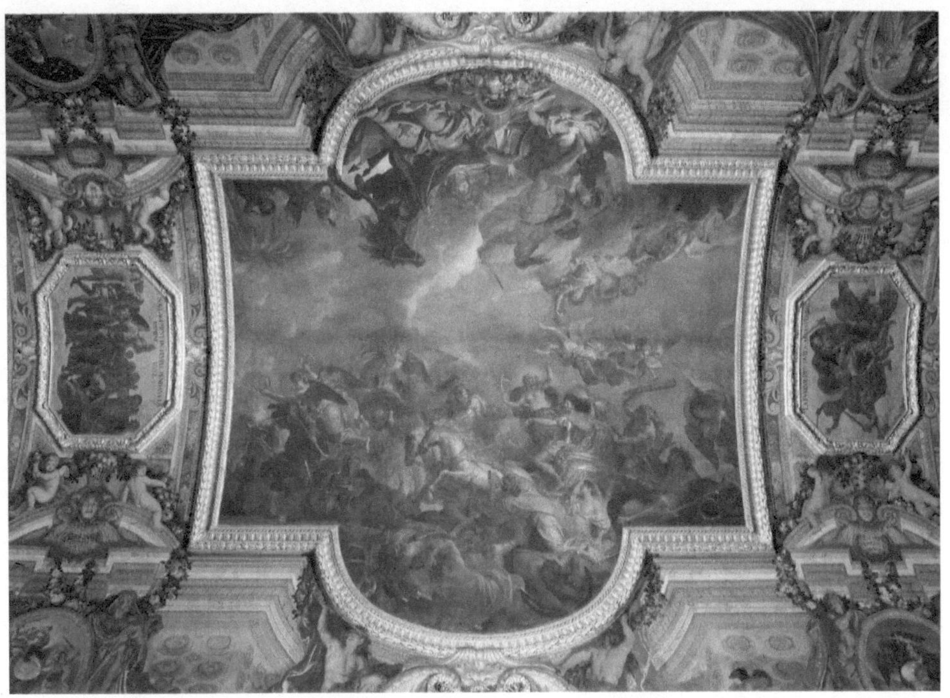

5.1. Charles Le Brun. *Le passage du Rhin en présence des ennemis, 1672* [*The Crossing of the Rhine in Front of the Enemies, 1672*]. Château de Versailles. Image courtesy Château de Versailles, France/Bridgeman Images. http://www.galeriedesglaces-versailles.fr/html/11/collection/c7.html.

We do not know].[8] We do not know, but at some fundamental level, it appears that art collecting has implicated Louis in something less grand than the simple projection of his glorious image.

Le Brun had only that glorious image in mind when he conceived the portrait of the king for *Le passage du Rhin en présence des ennemis, 1672* [*The Crossing of the Rhine in Front of the Enemies, 1672*]:

> Le roi est revêtu d'une armure et d'une tunique or; il est assis sur son char, tiré par deux chevaux blancs à crinière d'or, qui s'élance vers les Provinces-Unies. Regardant droit devant lui, il tient les rênes de la main gauche et brandit le [*sic*] foudre de la main droite. Les dessins préparatoires

conservés au musée du Louvre montrent que Charles Le Brun a soigneusement étudié la position du roi, en dessinant d'abord l'anatomie d'après le modèle vivant, puis le drapé séparément (inv. 29281 et 29288). L'artiste s'est efforcé de restituer l'élan, le dynamisme d'un épisode qui a été présenté comme un moment capital et héroïque de la guerre: "Les plus vives couleurs font remarquer le roi, la foudre à la main, les cheveux et son manteau agités par les vents, son char rapidement traîné par des chevaux fougueux" (*Mercure galant*, décembre 1684).

[The king wears armour and a gold tunic; he is seated in his chariot, led by two white horses with golden manes, which are bounding forward towards the United Provinces. Looking straight ahead, he holds the reins with his left hand and wields a thunderbolt in his right hand. The preparatory drawings for this work housed in the Louvre show that Charles Le Brun had carefully studied the position of the king, first drawing the anatomy from a live model, then draping it separately (inv. 29281 and 29288). The artist took pains to capture the thrust, the dynamic, of an event that was presented as a major heroic moment in the war: "The brightest colours make the king stand out, lightning in his hand, his hair and coat blowing in the wind, his chariot rapidly drawn by spirited horses" (*Mercure galant*, December 1684).][9]

The figures, including several allegories representing Holland (the navy, commerce, ambition, freedom, and several defeated cities), are so compactly presented that their energy has a "spill over" effect: the enemy is literally toppled. Le Brun's image so bursts with figures that, despite the title, and despite the fact that the battle involved crossing the Rhine, the river is invisible.[10] Ignoring the fact that the French actually met with little Dutch resistance, the painting honours Louis XIV, who is easily recognizable by his distinctive profile and because he is the only human figure in the image, by showing him doing battle against a formidable enemy force.

This painting contrasts markedly with much of Poussin's oeuvre, and nowhere more so than in *Un temps calme et serein* [*Landscape with a Calm*] (ca. 1650–1), which predates Colbert's 1660s projects for promoting Louis's image and the king's ambitious reconstruction of Versailles. This painting was not part of the royal collection: it is believed to have been owned first by Jean Pointel, a banker and silk merchant from Lyons based in Paris who devoted his art collection primarily to Poussin. The artist's politics date back to the Fronde, when he allied himself, via his

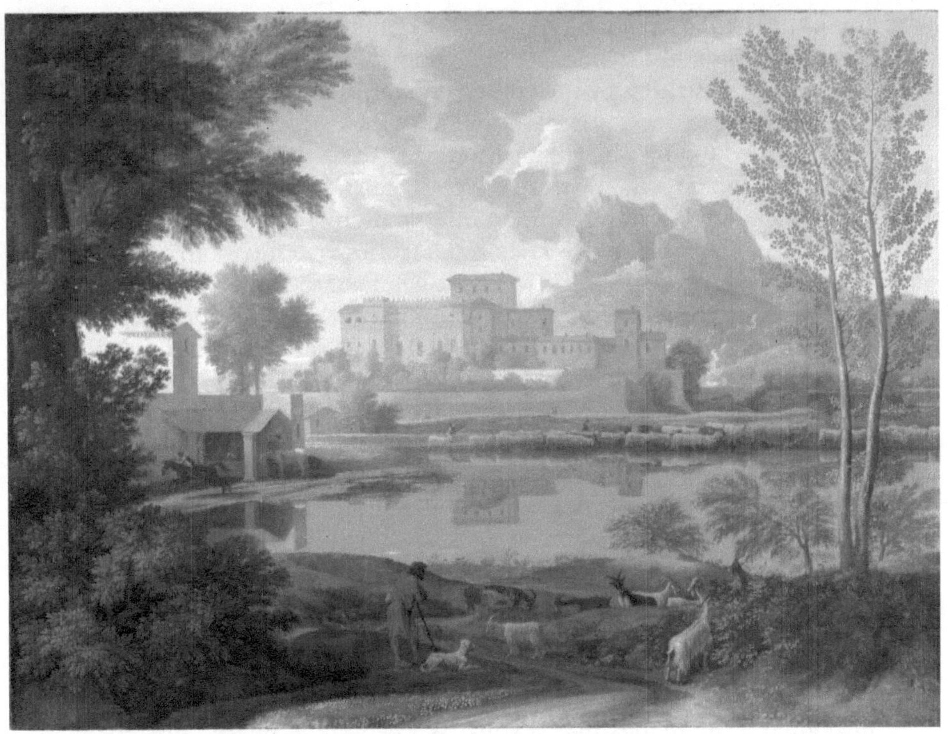

5.2. Nicolas Poussin. *Un temps calme et serein* [*Landscape with a Calm*]. Ca. 1650–1. 97 × 131 cm (38.19 × 51.57 in). J. Paul Getty Museum, Los Angeles. Image courtesy J. Paul Getty Museum. http://www.getty.edu/art/collection/objects/106381/nicolas-poussin-landscape-with-a-calm-un-temps-calme-et-serein-french-1650-1651/.

art, with the *noblesse de robe* [noblility of the robe] who had fought the crown during Louis's minority. Poussin painted from Rome, but his style came to define French classicism, with its emphasis on reason, symmetry, harmony, and clarity. The rational emphasis is evident in the architectural elements of his images as well as in his geometric organization of space. Scholars note, however, another, poetic side to his art. Along with a dominant rationalism, Poussin demonstrates a mythic reality, an eternal order.

Un temps calme et serein is remarkable for its lack of narrative emphasis.[11] As the Getty curators observe, Poussin "does not illustrate a story but rather evokes a mood. The ordered composition and clear, golden light contribute to the image's utter tranquility, while glowing, gem-like colors and fluid paint strokes enliven this scene of benevolent nature."[12] Poussin accentuates our view of the landscape via the gaze of the shepherd tending his goats. Moreover, the reflections of the buildings on the water, which stress the play of bright sunlight, emphasize phenomena involving no human intervention. The architecture, confirmation of the human presence, enters nature via the roofline, which appears to slip effortlessly into the ridgeline of the mountain cresting behind it, as this ridge in turn melds with the clouds above. These features contribute to the beholder's sense of serenity regarding the natural order.

The scene in the foreground, a circular composition with the shepherd dressed in red, his seated dog, and the standing goat, both white, is the core of a larger circular design that includes the shepherd's other goats. This scene is in turn ringed on the other side by two shepherds tending their rows of sheep and cattle as they follow the rounded contours of the water. The circles within circles convey the unending continuity of the shepherds' routine, the repeated actions that the calm weather has temporarily stilled, as the immobile shepherd in the centre foreground attests. The geometric forms ensure continuity, order, security. As we look from the shepherd in the foreground across the glistening water to the other shepherds and their herds, and then to the men on horses to the left, and on to the painting's larger frame of trees, sky, and buildings, Poussin's landscape invokes the enduring pastoral cycle, mythic time.

Yet there is movement. Herds on the far side of the water are quietly proceeding off to the right, and, more dramatically, the horse and rider is darting off to the left. These opposite movements suggest linear time as it weighs down on this otherwise story-less scene. Measured against the image's dreamy, languid quality, the darting horse seems all the more jolting because it takes the viewer's gaze beyond the frame of the painting. Indeed, in a painting that in so many ways describes the stillness of the natural setting absent an established historical or literary narrative, the horse's energy stands out because it so obviously opens a storyline. Where is this rider with the outstretched arm going, and why does he take off in such a hurry? Poussin's horseman bolts off to an unknown destination for an unknown cause. This figure strikes an odd note, as it disrupts the serenity of the scene dominated by the shepherd resting with his flock, and the unhurried movement of the pair of

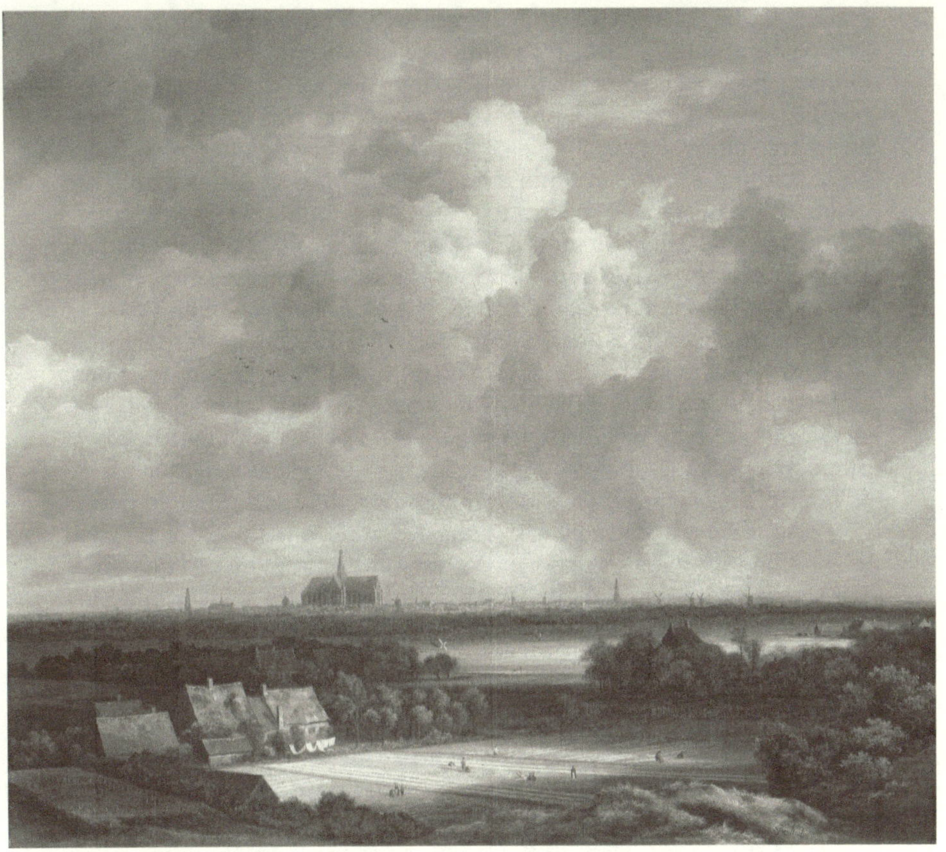

5.3. Jacob van Ruisdael. *View of Haarlem with Bleaching Grounds*. Ca. 1670–5. 55.5 × 62 cm (21.85 × 24.4 in). Mauritshuis, The Hague. Image courtesy Mauritshuis, The Hague, The Netherlands/Bridgeman Images. https://www.mauritshuis.nl/en/explore/the-collection/artworks/view-of-haarlem-with-bleaching-grounds-155/#.

herdsmen leading their sheep and cattle across the scene slowly enough that some animals bend down to drink the water.

Calm describes the weather as well as the slowed action of the figures other than the man on horseback. Yet nature, too, shows a sign of activity: we detect a volcano erupting off to the right, its fiery lava visible here and there along the mountain, where the white is interspersed with patches of glowing red.[13] The volcanic mountain, however, remains far enough in the distance that the animals exhibit no anxious movements. The pastoral setting includes prominent architectural elements, signs of man's power to master nature. The imposing building suggests temporality steeped in history but invulnerable to change; civilizing influences are coincident with a natural cycle of renewal and stasis. It is a scene without a hero, an unthinkable setting for a king determined to make his mark on history.

Ruisdael similarly represents a deep sense of calm, but with no animals and with an emphasis on human labour. The artist painted a series of Haarlem images based on the same theme. The Mauritshuis painting did not enter French collections, but the linen fields that it describes were a tourist attraction.[14] Some in France may well have heard these scenes described, as the French were among the many Europeans who shipped linen to Holland for bleaching. The French, moreover, certainly knew of the important production of landscape paintings emanating from Flanders and Holland.

Van Ruisdael's broad view dominates the image. His detailed depiction of workers, both male and female, setting out sheets of linen to be bleached by the sun plays out against the silhouette of Haarlem.[15] The shadows alternating with sunshine encourage the viewer to follow the light, to move steadily across the fields to the city beyond. Lines of white linen are laid out in parallel and perpendicular rows in both the near and the far fields, creating gridded spaces that resemble city maps. The viewer's perspective from the dunes encourages close observation of the setting: the intersecting rows of linen; the series of fields; the play of light and shadow. These discernible patterns are as important to the painting as are the meticulously detailed natural elements and the architectural features. Along with the labourers in the field, these recurring motifs engage the viewer. Like the artist, the viewer surveys, delimits, and categorizes the vast expanse of nature into knowable elements.

Ruisdael makes no final claim on eternity, beyond the endurance of nature itself. The soaring birds and the breaks in the billowing clouds that cover the sky, which occupies about two thirds of the image, emphasize movement and temporality.[16] The prominently displayed Saint-Bavo church stands as a monument not only to religion but also to the achievements of the men who constructed it centuries before, and to Ruisdael's contemporaries who had learned to value labour and industry. They held that God created the world but that the Dutch, as the windmills in the distance remind us, had taken the land back from the sea.[17] Ruisdael describes the fields, the industry, and the art that had allowed Holland to fulfil its destiny as an independent power in Europe.

Certainly, a king looking for a narrative to support his exploits and to disseminate his portrait would need to look beyond images such as these, and even the prestige of collecting them, to secure his place in history. To situate the image crossing the Rhine within the full panoply of images that Le Brun constructs to decorate the Galerie des Glaces [Hall of Mirrors] ceiling, it is important to recall that the Dutch, whose engagement with the French during the 1672–8 war the ceiling decor celebrates along with Louis XIV's earlier war in Flanders, are also responsible for a visual culture that challenged the allegorical model on which the French arts relied.

Le Brun's Ceiling Design for the Galerie des Glaces

Le Brun produced the magnificent ceiling of the Galerie des Glaces at Versailles from 1679 through 1684. The ceiling is an outstanding example of the monarchy's efforts to construct an elaborate visual narrative of Louis XIV's rise to glory. While the message of the king's infinite power remains constant in the ceiling design, both the history of its design and its final composition involve a number of variables. Louis rejected Le Brun's first proposal to represent him as Apollo as well as Le Brun's second proposal that he appear as Hercules. Instead, at the monarch's insistence, classical myth gave way to Louis's own history. Louis's image assumed pride of place in a series of scenes depicting his recent accomplishments: reforms in finance and justice, support for the arts, his personal rule, and France's wars against Spain and the Dutch Republic.[18] The shift from myth to Louis's accomplishments, however, did not occur without sustained allegorical support. France, Germany, Spain, and the United Provinces (Holland) are represented by female figures. The ceiling, moreover, is replete with other allegories. From abundance to the zodiac, the Palace of Versailles catalogues a long list of subjects, including fury, glory, and victory as well as nation-specific entries. Envy, representing the Spanish attitude towards the French, is a green emaciated female figure with snakes for hair.[19] To ensure that visitors correctly interpreted the images, they bear inscriptions.[20] Indeed, there are so many allegories and symbols that Louis ordered the publication of descriptions of the images so that members of the court and the general public could interpret them.[21] Nonetheless, on the path to glory Louis XIV divested himself of one fundamental layer of symbolic representation, namely, myth. Louis's appearance as himself legitimates his authority and cements his legacy via a new realism that is at once self-referential and imperial. Through his personal history, as glorified through the Versailles setting, his image ascends to the realm of the immortal gods.

The vaulted ceiling magisterially reinforces Louis's claims. There can be no mistaking the fact that the primary referent for the decor is the king. The fact that he emerges as a historical figure in his own right via a sequence of portraits increases the impact of these images on the visitors to the hall. The French victory, moreover, seems all the more impressive because the enemy Holland, on account of her global markets and resulting prosperity, proves a worthy opponent. The effect of Le Brun's ceiling would not be the same, however, if, as in the Versailles gardens, Ovid's *Metamorphoses* were the principal referent for the king and his success. The French had more associations with the Dutch than the ceiling projects via allegory. French visitors brought with them into the Galerie des Glaces a certain knowledge, ideas about the Dutch and, via Dutch art, an empirical grounding for processing what they observed.

As an expansive visual field comprising many discrete images, the ceiling serves as well as a container, an organizing system for the things and ideas that individual images represent.[22] Modelled after Italian ceilings, Le Brun's symmetrical design consists of a series of interconnected panels. Despite the triumphant narrative theme throughout, the history of Louis is segmented, literally, into parts. Nicolas Milovanovic explains that there exists no "sens de parcours du premier au dernier tableau" [no direct path leading from the first to the last painting]. Instead,

> il s'agit d'un système hiérarchisé mettant en relation plusieurs récits distincts (guerre de Hollande [1672–8], guerre de Dévolution [1667–8], gouvernement civil, quatre piliers de l'État) et s'organisant autour de la composition centrale, qui constitue la clef de l'ensemble du décor: la décision prise par Louis XIV en 1661 de gouverner par lui-même et d'acquérir la gloire par les armes face aux trois puissances rivales européennes – l'Empire, l'Espagne et les Provinces-Unies.
>
> [it is a hierarchical system that combines several distinct narratives (the Franco-Dutch War [1672–8], the War of Devolution [1667–8], civil government, four pillars of the State) that takes shape around the central panel, which is the focus of the entire design: the decision that Louis XIV made in 1661 to govern by himself and to acquire glory through wars against his three main European rivals: the Holy Roman Empire, Spain, and the United Provinces.][23]

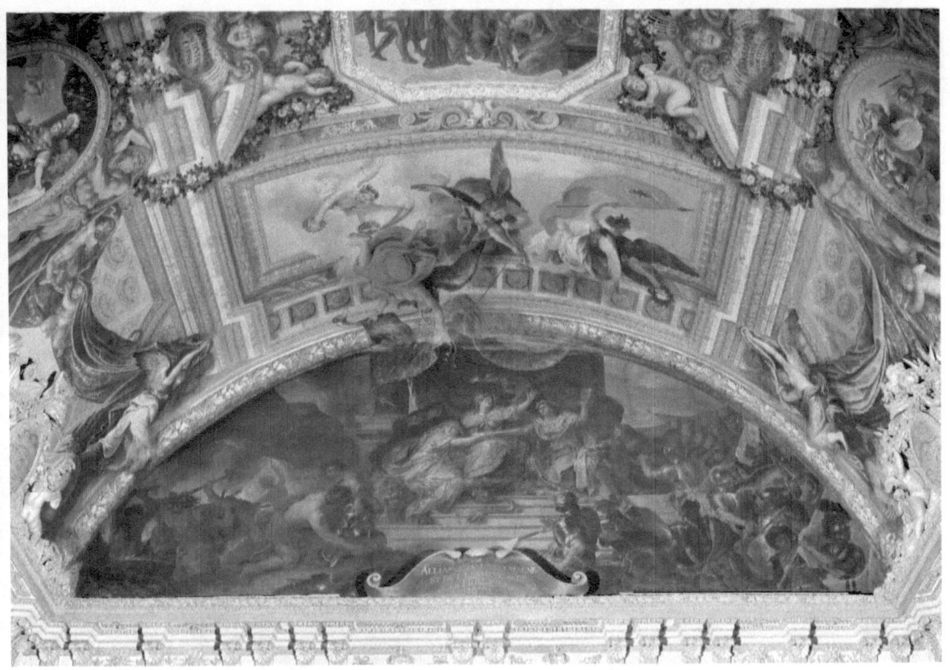

5.4. Charles Le Brun. *Alliance de l'Allemagne et de l'Espagne avec La Hollande, 1672*. [*Alliance of Germany and Spain with Holland, 1672*]. Château de Versailles. Image courtesy Château de Versailles, France/Bridgeman Images. http://www.galeriedesglaces-versailles.fr/html/11/collection/c1.html.

The hierarchical organization of the ceiling is consistent with the hierarchical structure of the court, with the king at the apex. Yet if we look at the design as a horizontal surface and concentrate on the relation of individual parts to each other, the absence of a "direct path" suggests a certain dynamism that supports the energy of the king's ambitions. It also establishes a certain classificatory ambiguity.

Despite the historical orientation of the design, which portrays highlights from the first eighteen years of Louis's reign, Le Brun does not respect a strict chronology. For example, moving from the Salon de la Guerre [War Salon] along the west (garden) side of the ceiling, the sequence of events is 1665, 1662, 1664, 1672, 1673, then back to 1664, 1662, etc. The ceiling design includes, at opposite ends, a

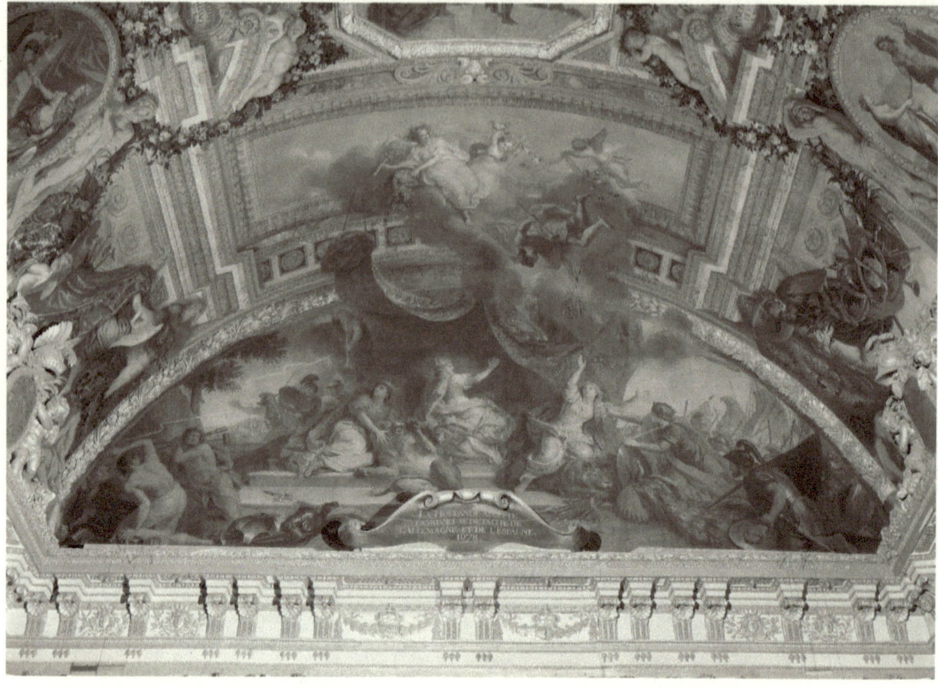

5.5. Charles Le Brun. *La Hollande accepte la paix et se détache de l'Allemagne, 1678*. [*Holland Accepts Peace and Separates from Germany, 1678*]. Château de Versailles. Image courtesy Château de Versailles, France/Bridgeman Images. http://www.galeriedesglaces-versailles.fr/html/11/collection/c32.html.

lunette (moon-shaped space) depicting the beginning and the end of the Dutch War. On the north end the lunette shows the 1672 alliance of Holland with Germany and Spain against France. At the south end the lunette depicts France's peace with Holland in 1678. Neither direction through the hall, however, affords a view of the lunette on the entering side unless the person entering the hall were to turn around. Whether visitors emerged into the hall from the north side or from the south side, the lunette on the side of that entrance would be located behind them.

Variability within the ceiling design is evident in other features. All visitors would not view the images in the same order or in the same combinations. One person might take in the east side first and then

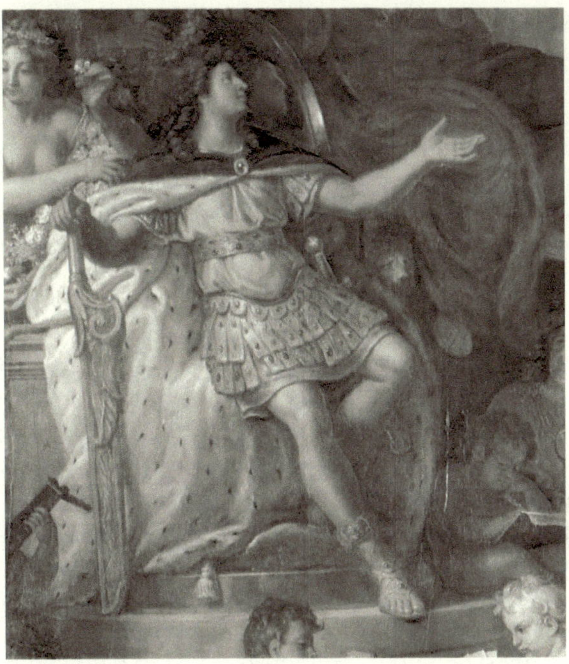

5.6. Charles Le Brun. *Le roi gouverne par lui-même, 1661* [*The King Governs by Himself, 1661*]. Detail. Château de Versailles. Image courtesy Château de Versailles, France/Bridgeman Images. http://www.galeriedesglaces-versailles.fr/html/11/collection/c17.html.

view the west side; another might look from east to west while moving across the hall; a third might select some from each side to examine closely; a fourth, particularly someone very familiar with the hall, might glance upward while crossing the hall without examining any image in detail. Each configuration creates a different narrative; each constructs a different portion of the history of Louis's reign. One could move beyond sets of contiguous images to consider together different series of images as dispersed throughout the ceiling. For example, in addition to selecting out the five narrative threads (four plus Louis's self-government) that Milovanovic identifies, one could piece together all the paintings that show Holland (there are six, and even more if one counts allegories for individual provinces or invasions); one could select those with Hercules (there are three); or one could reconstitute the images in chronological sequence. While each of these clusters supports the larger theme of Louis's glory, the process involves a reworking of the narrative.

The large central panel featuring the start of Louis XIV's self-rule, *Le roi gouverne par lui-même, 1661* [*The King Governs by Himself, 1661*], to which I referred in chapter 1 (image 1.5), orients the ceiling design both geometrically and thematically. This frame incorporates a pair of images: the larger one of Louis in Roman armour assuming command appears on the mirrored side of the hall, and, on the windowed side, there appears a smaller one of the enemies over whom Louis triumphs. In *Faste des puissances voisines de la France* [*The Spendour of the Neighbouring Powers of France*] Germany, Spain, and Holland are condemned for their pride in joining forces against France.

This dual configuration represents the complexity of the ceiling design. In order to account for the effect of the curve of the vault, the framed image is painted with a double orientation, that is, as two separate paintings to be viewed separately. If one were to look straight up from the image on one side and lean one's head back to see the image on the other side, it would appear upside down. The central cartouche dominates the design on account of its central position, its size, and its frameless division between images. The theme of Louis's self-rule assumes pride of place through an image of the king dressed as a Roman general. Louis appears on his throne surrounded by the Three Graces, who symbolize the gifts the heaven has granted him.[24]

As previous chapters have shown, French design favours the integration of elements. With the ceiling Le Brun constructs individual images as part of a single paradigm of Louis's glory. The artist structures his design through likenesses: Louis's experiences are all triumphs; Louis's history resembles that of the gods. Yet a visitor always perceives parts of the whole; panels of the ceiling that are visible from one perspective are hidden from another perspective in the hall. Viewers cannot take in the whole of the framed painting in a single examination: one side or the other eludes them. Balancing the central panel, two other smaller paintings, one the first major painting on the north side, the other the first major painting on the south side, also incorporate two reverse images within a single frame.[25] The ceiling is certainly grand, and no one can mistake the celebration of Louis's image through historic references. Depending on the position of the viewer in the room, the particular configuration of images on which the visitor focuses, and the degree to

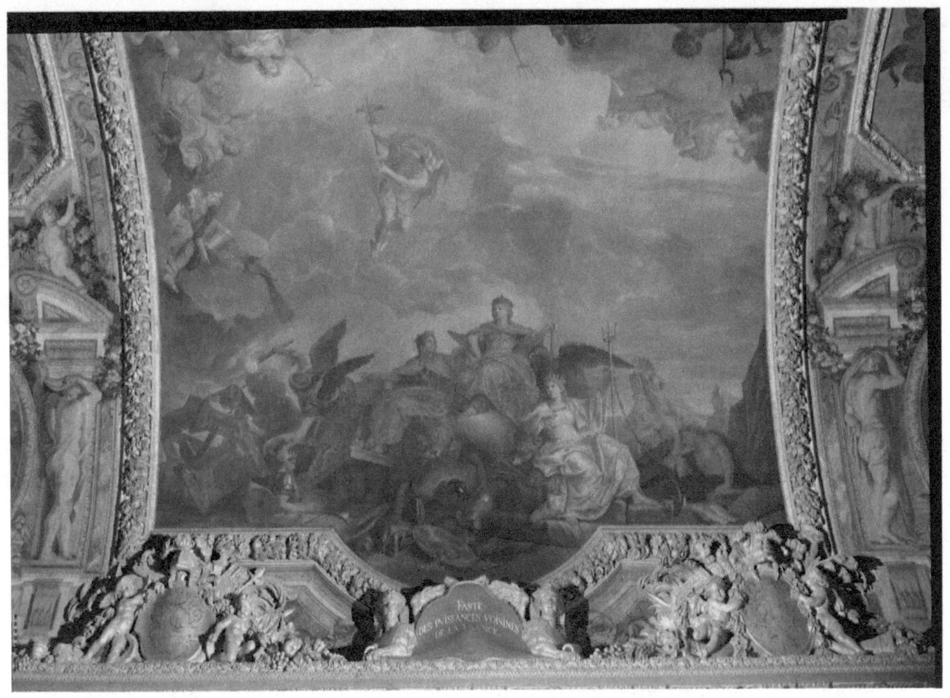

5.7. Charles Le Brun. *Faste des puissances voisines de la France* [*The Splendour of the Neighbouring Powers of France*]. Château de Versailles. Image courtesy Château de Versailles, France/Bridgeman Images. http://www.galeriedesglaces-versailles.fr/html/11/collection/c16.html.

which the visitor grasps the individual allegories, however, more or less of the images escapes the whole of Le Brun's design.

The ceiling contains no actual fault lines: Louis XIV serves over and over again as the heroic figure. The fluidity of the design, however, is a remarkable feature. Images remain subject to different manipulations by the viewers. What has been made can be undone, reconfigured. To the degree that each reconstructed narrative reinforces the idea of Louis's glory, the design works effectively to engage (some would say subjugate) the viewer to the court's expansive account of Louis's unparalleled success. Yet the viewer's active participation, which imitates that of Le Brun himself in designing the ceiling, also stresses an interpretive process that is more willed than fated. It reproduces the rational choices whereby Louis's image is made, not destined, to appear as a compelling, irrefutable ideal. Indeed, the viewer cannot but be impressed by the difference between Louis appearing as himself – the realism at the core of Le Brun's artistic choices – and all the allegories that populate his painted world. The artistry of the ceiling is effective, to be sure, as an object of splendour and celebration. It does not, however, erase divisions between the human and divine, mortal and immortal, essential and ornamental, any more than it erases the knowledge that Louis's crossing of the Rhine in 1672 was an easy victory.

One might think that few if any visitors would take the time for making specific connections between elements in various paintings. The fact, however, that he king ordered textual explanations to accompany the images suggests his commitment to having visitors study the images' details. Perhaps the courtiers awaiting the king as he walked from his private apartment to the chapel had occasion to think about such things as they sought an opportunity to make requests of him. Viewers who make associations between different images, study their inscriptions, and link the images in various groupings actively participate in the machinery of statecraft, the mechanics of promoting Louis XIV's image. Furthermore, they actively participate in the process of cataloguing information, not only as sequences in a narrative, but also as binaries: good and evil; French and Dutch; victor and vanquished; desire for what the Dutch possess and aversion for Dutch society.[26]

The first terms of the binary opposition (good, French, victor, desire) triumphs consistently over the second (evil, Dutch, vanquished, aversion). The viewer's engagement remains positive for the monarchy as long as Louis's subjects continue to trust that their interests are met through their support of him, or as long as they fear reprisal, which are two sides of the same coin. Were there no Dutch in the picture, literally and metaphorically, the knowledge that each combination of elements in the ceiling design celebrates Louis's power would be sufficient to consolidate the idea of Louis's glorious rule. The Dutch, however, are not simply the defeated enemy. They are foils to Louis and to France – proponents of a different society, different markets, and a different artistic tradition. In this context the French monarchy's depicted desire to conquer Holland is complex, involving a wish to rule, envy of Dutch markets, a wish to take pleasure in beautiful objects, and a need to impress and to dominate. What, exactly, does Louis XIV want? At the very least, the history narrated in Le Brun's ceiling attests to the spectacular transformation of the man who, though he would not be Apollo or Hercules, would still align himself with the great heroes of antiquity. Appearing in the ceiling a dozen times, always in Roman military armour, Louis's image remains cloaked in allusions.

The ceiling represents both Louis XIV's accomplishments and his grand ambitions to secure a place in history. In the central image commemorating Louis's self-government the king studies his own image reflected in Minerva's shield. Compressed into this image is wisdom and prudence, a combination of Minerva's qualities and her shield's function as a mirror reflecting back the idea that one should know oneself well (*Nosce te ipsum*, from the Delphic temple inscription).[27] One should know oneself well in order to act effectively. Those who gaze at the king here can legitimately ask nonetheless whether he can know himself except as an image, an image whose multiple representations, although they evoke an imposing history of victories, catch him in the act of dramatizing his own history, of posturing for posterity.

Looking into the Other Mirror

We can only imagine what Louis XIV, who so assiduously cultivated his image, would have thought as he stood before a Rembrandt self-portrait, *Portrait of the Artist at His Easel* (1660). Did Louis see the effects of the artist's bankruptcy registered in his facial expression? Rembrandt famously chronicled his image over time, a fascination that mirrors Louis's own appearance in the different stages of Le Brun's work. Rembrandt is far more modest, and, to judge by the intensity of his gaze, far more engaged in creating a penetrating study. As evident by the brushes, palette, and easel, his observations lead to his creation of a revealing portrait, and not merely his reflection, as is the case for Louis captured in Minerva's shield.

Louis XIV would find much to enjoy in Gerrit Dou's scene of a tooth extraction, *L'arracheur de dents* [*The Tooth Extraction*] (ca. 1630–5), and van Dyck's portrait of a wealthy burgher and his young son, *Portrait d'un homme de qualité avec son fils* [*Portrait of a Gentleman with His Son*] (ca. 1628–9). The king acquired these works from Everhard Jabach in 1671, as he did the de Heem still life, *Fruits et riche vaisselle sur une table*, discussed in chapter 1. These paintings, along with the Rembrandt self-portrait, formed part of the royal collection.[28] Certainly Louis XIV, or those who acted as his agents, saw in these works something arresting.

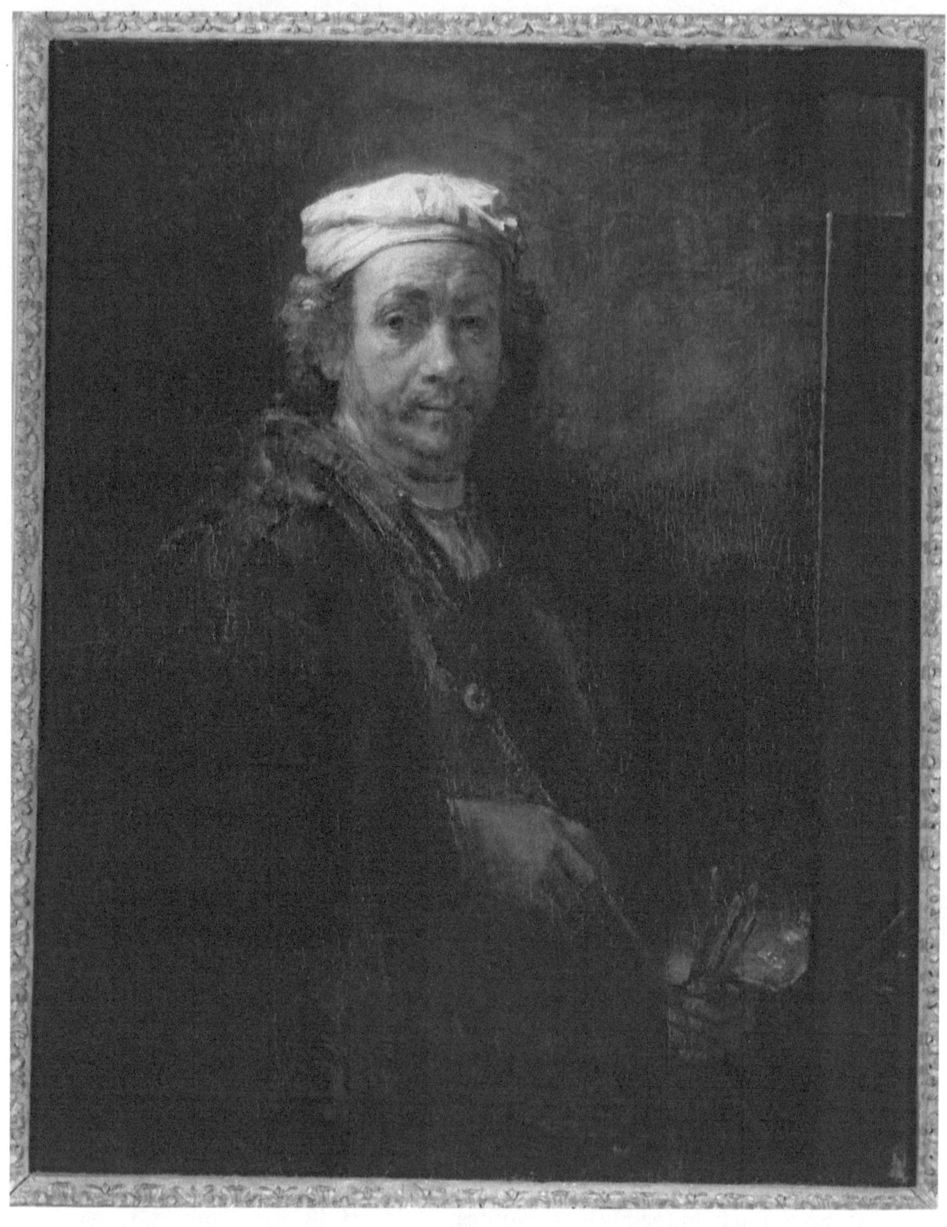

5.8. Rembrandt Harmensz. van Rijn. *Portrait de l'artiste au chevalet* [*Portrait of the Artist at His Easel*]. 1660. 111 × 85 cm (42.7 × 33.46 in). Musée du Louvre. Image courtesy Louvre, Paris, France/Bridgeman Images. https://commons.wikimedia.org/wiki/File:Rembrandt,_Auto-portrait,_1660.jpg.

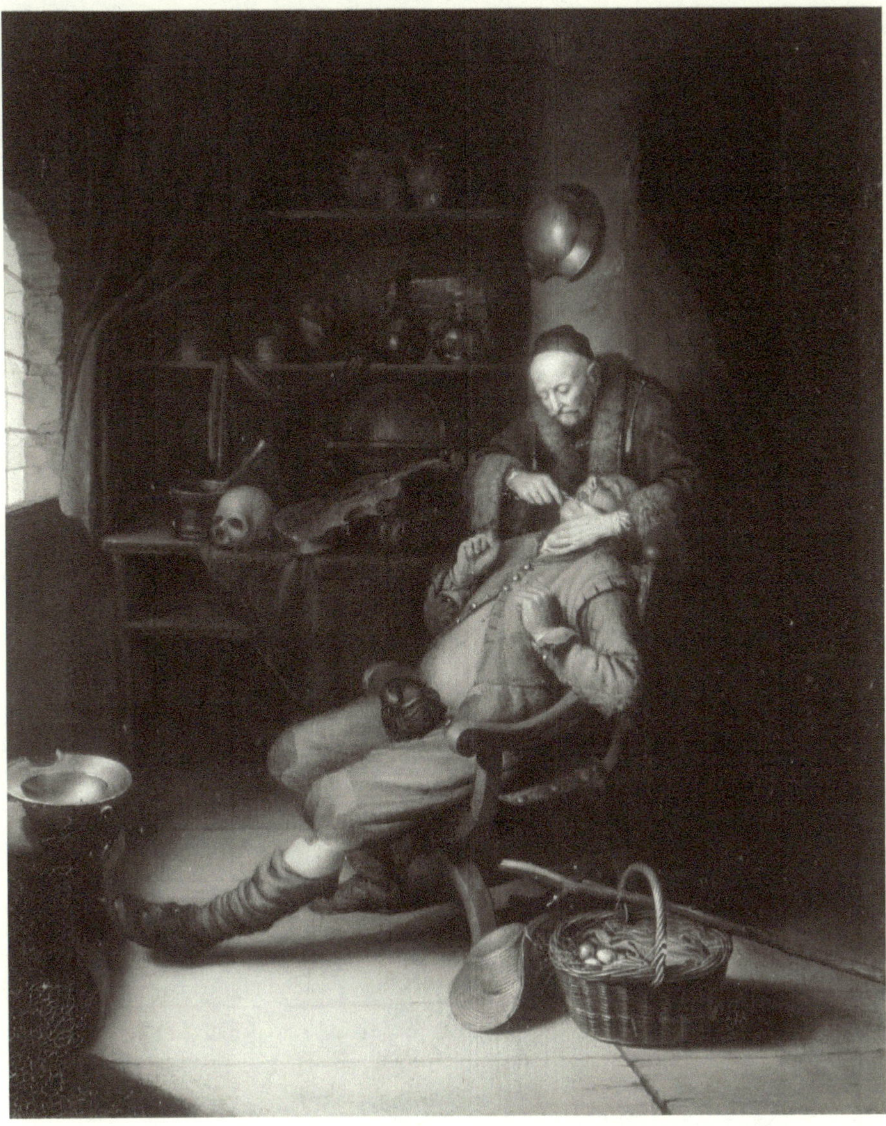

5.9. Gerrit Dou. *L'arracheur de dents* [*The Tooth Extraction*]. Ca. 1630–5. 32 × 26 cm (12.6 × 10.24 in). Musée du Louvre. Photo courtesy RMN-Grand Palais/ Art Resource, NY. https://commons.wikimedia.org/wiki/File:Gerard _Dou_-_The_Extraction_of_Tooth_-_WGA06635.jpg.

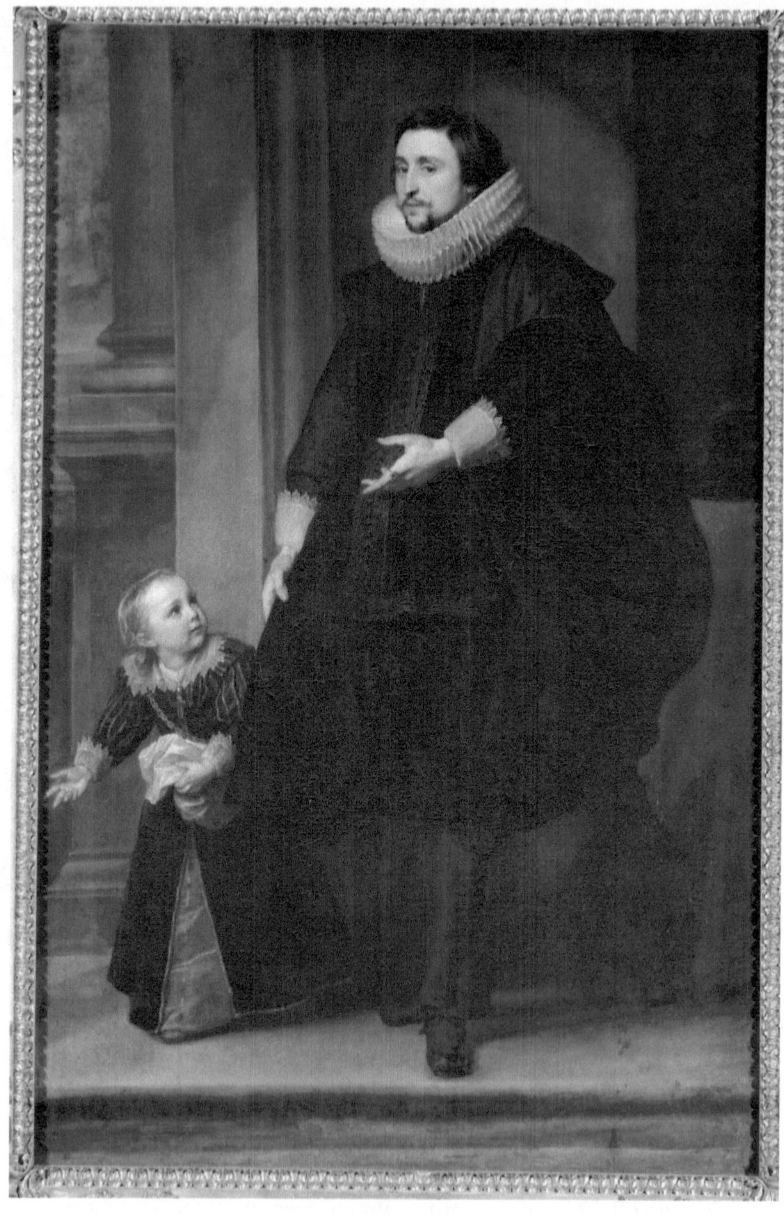

5.10. Antoon van Dyck. *Portrait d'un homme de qualité avec son fils* [*Portrait of a Gentleman with His Son*]. Ca. 1628–9. 204 × 137 cm (80.32 × 53.94 in). Musée du Louvre. Image courtesy Louvre, Paris, France/Bridgeman Images. http://cartelfr.louvre.fr/cartelfr/visite?srv=car_not_frame&idNotice=8781.

They conveyed both aesthetic qualities and market value as well as political advantages for owning them. The appeal of these works, like that of other seventeenth-century Netherlandish realist painting, originates in the richness of lives of men and women, however prosperous, with no claims to heroism other than what they accomplish themselves, and who recognized the authority of the regents, affluent local merchants, to govern rather than an absolute monarchy.

Dutch painters extend the viewer's line of vision past the vertical ascension of royalty, and outward towards the accumulation and display of things in the home of upper-middle-class burghers. Artists distil these objects, recording their utilitarian function within the home as well as the appeal of luxury items. Viewers take in bread and cheese that grace the table along with exotic lemons and Ming bowls; they observe the beauty of a pearl necklace as they do the tobacco pipe and brazier. Dutch paintings capture for all time the perfect essence of fortunes large and small in the richness of the moment that they describe. At these tables the king's image has no place. Perhaps when Louis looked deep into Rembrandt's eyes he saw that knowledge betrayed.

The Bourgeois Factor: The Power of Display

The aggregate display that characterizes Dutch realist art relates directly to the lives of the burghers of Holland's cities, where successful merchants enjoyed unprecedented wealth, as evident in the fine furnishings and art that they purchased. Short term, the history of Louis XIV's military victories during the Franco-Dutch War was far more consequential to France than was the success of the bourgeois at Versailles, whose influence as suppliers of both capital and services caused friction between them and the French nobles. Long term, however, the bourgeois would "rise" in France as well.

One ceiling painting stands out in this regard. Milovanovic describes the allegory for Holland in *Faste des puissances voisines de la France* [*The Splendour of the Neighbouring Powers of France*]:

> les Provinces-Unies sont peintes un degré en dessous de l'Espagne, avec une simple couronne comtale, pour marquer l'infériorité d'une République. L'allégorie est assise sur des ballots de marchandises pour signifier le commerce qui rend cet État florissant; elle tient de la main gauche le trident de Neptune et Téthys enchaînée pour montrer qu'elle s'est rendue maîtresse des mers, afin de favoriser son commerce.

> [the United Provinces is painted a bit beneath Spain, wearing a simple count's crown, to mark the inferior status of a republic. This allegory is seated on merchandise bundles to signify how the flourishing of this State was dependent on commerce; in her left hand she holds Neptune's trident and Tethys in chains to symbolize her [Holland's] domination over all the world's oceans in support of her own commercial ambitions.][29]

Evoking Holland's extensive international trade routes, this image ensures that, even defeated, the Dutch represented a formidable enemy who had generated tremendous financial advantage and, as the French well knew, had established a thriving middle class. The image favours the victors: Holland is shown defeated and prideful, an inferior republic lacking all the prestige and influence of a monarchy. The explicit signs of commerce in Le Brun's image are packages of merchandise, containers of goods, associated with the allegorical figure representing Holland. The boxes stacked under her are closed. Were these parcels open, the visitors would see the array of objects merchants imported from abroad. Closed, they show that Louis had thwartedan evil preoccupation with profit and commerce. Yet Louis went to war in part to make these parcels his own, to triumph over the system that created the routes responsible for bringing these goods to Europe. Presumably, whatever Dutch spoils Louis obtained through war were his to enjoy and celebrate. Why are merchandise and trade routes pejorative when associated with the Dutch but prized when captured by the French? What changed was not the content but the container. As long as France "framed" the story, in other words, the contents had value.

When the French who entered the Galerie des Glaces thought about the Dutch, they inevitably saw more in the ceiling than Le Brun's allegories. The French would have taken satisfaction in imagining this defeated adversary, but they knew much about the Dutch beyond their military engagements. Their ideas of Holland came not only from Louis XIV's justifications for wars against the enemy but also, during peacetime, from trade, including the art market, as well as from scientific exchanges that took people across borders. Dutch images in the royal collection, like those elsewhere, registered the ability of the Dutch to balance moral teachings with commerce, a commitment to tolerance as well as a fierce independence, and an openness to the world that had no currency in Louis's France, where the monarchy's efforts to impose its will were evident in affairs of state as in the arts cultivated to advance French interests.

Versailles served as a backdrop for spectacular imaginings, monumental architectural designs, and all form of tributes to the king with whose image his subjects' own fortunes rose or fell. The French were accepting of Louis XIV appearing "au naturel," that is, as himself in Roman costume in Le Brun's images. They would have found it awkward, no doubt, to see the real man exposed to the elements, that is, without armour, to all the deities and allegories that populate the ceiling panels. Although the Dutch were a God-fearing people preoccupied with sin without redemption, they nevertheless found satisfaction in the collection and display of material wealth, and in the art that made their possessions beautiful. Many French visitors to the Galerie des Glaces knew that Holland was overflowing with paintings, and that even people of modest means could own them. The French might have envied that access to art. Without abandoning their sense of the brilliance of Le Brun's ceiling design, they knew to respect the Northern tradition whose realism distilled the essence of things. The French would have admired Dutch images of fruits bursting with flavour alongside those beginning to rot, clouds rolling across the sky, and canals that wound their way through cities. Louis's courtiers had a sense of how Dutch artists captured the passage of time and the fragility of nature even as they engineered their cities and enlivened their markets. These ideas about the Dutch were far more nuanced than allegory could convey, even that painted by an artist as accomplished as Le Brun.

Thoughts of trade, merchandise, art, and the ascendency of the Dutch burghers certainly resonated with the French. During Louis XIV's reign the bourgeois in France were identified through their connections to commerce and finance, their active engagement in the world. Many bourgeois aspired to the privileges and power of the nobility. Drawn to the magnificence of court ceremonies that enhanced the power of the king, the more successful among them were eager participants in the spectacle that was Versailles, just as they were eager purveyors of the products required to decorate the palace and to dress the royals. Unsurprisingly, these bourgeois attempted to fill the power vacuum once Louis XIV's reign began to decline.[30] The Dutch had no direct influence on the rise of the bourgeoisie in France, events culminating in the French Revolution in 1789. Numerous factors endemic to France precipitated this rebellion, including conflicts over taxes between the monarchy and the nobility; tensions between the nobility and the bourgeoisie; debts that the monarchy had accumulated through wars and the expansion of Versailles; food shortages; and concerns about the effectiveness of Louis XVI. These issues are complex. By taking into account the presence of Dutch art during Louis's reign as part of a long view of early modern French culture, I do not pretend to find an explanation for France's social and political ills. I am, however, making the case that during the reign of Louis XIV the French idea of Holland was already connected, through its art, to a notion of empiricism, just as it was, more obviously, connected to global commerce, which was also a factor in the creation of Dutch art. Dutch burghers saw their lives validated in images that bore witness to their society and to their accomplishments, and that contributed to their sense of pride. The bundles of merchandise that Le Brun depicted with the allegory representing Holland, although a minor detail, supports other elements in the image. A chain of events had engaged the French in military battles against Holland, as this nation was involved in the construction of a society of considerable material wealth and as it participated in a visual culture that was more expansive and scientifically grounded than the arts that the French monarchy sponsored. The French at Versailles did not, of course, make these associations consciously or consistently as they absorbed the splendour of the Galerie des Glaces. But as the allegory of Holland met Louis XIV in Roman dress on Le Brun's ceiling, tensions between two systems of government, competing centres of trade, and the celebration of art as an inclusive record all persisted. Minerva, who in *Le roi gouverne par lui-même* points to Glory, is also associated with war, the arts, and commerce.[31] Minerva is well placed, therefore to reinforce the theme of war and France's victories against Holland in addition to all that continued to divide the two nations culturally. The detail of the merchandise, like the galloping rider in Poussin's image, opens the narrative to more than a single theme, or frame for knowledge. As van Ruisdael's image suggests, not individual labours so much as patterns of elements ensure that the full story will be told. Patterns explain how the viewer distils information into sets of relations, a system of human knowledge through which to make sense of the past and to fashion the future.

Off the battlefield a different world view was beginning to emerge that would define Louis XIV's legacy for the next century. In France that viewpoint saw nobles yield ground to the bourgeois. Over time allegory would give way in French art circles to Dutch-inspired genre paintings and still lifes that captured for eternity the appearance of things in the world. The next century saw the creation and publication of the *Encyclopédie,* a compendium of human knowledge that was the singular achievement of the Enlightenment. Edited by Denis Diderot and Jean Le Rond d'Alembert, the *Encyclopédie ou Dictionnaire raisonné des sciences, des arts et des métiers* [*Encyclopedia or Comprehensive Dictionary of the Sciences, Arts, and Trades*] appeared from 1751 to 1772 in seventeen volumes of text, eleven volumes of plates. It contained some seventy thousand articles written by 140 contributors, including the editors. The unparalleled level of detail in the *Encyclopédie* established the science of description as the unchallenged model for knowledge. Description was a science whose art the Dutch had already championed, and had already modelled for the French. In the next chapter I explore as part of Louis XIV's legacy important links between the descriptive emphasis of Dutch art and that of the *Encyclopédie*. My account of that legacy begins, and ends, with the tulip.

6 Legacies

La Bruyère: The Moral of the Tulips

With its critique of court society, especially its emphasis on the many behaviours that define the courtiers' relentless search for recognition and reward, La Bruyère's *Caractères* [*Characters*] (1688) bears witness to the decline of aristocratic values and the concomitant rise of the wealthy bourgeois in France. The financial resources of the successful bourgeois has affinities with the affluence of the burghers of the Dutch Republic. La Bruyère's portraits invite comparisons with Northern realist art because they make use of considerable empirical data. La Bruyère often incorporates lists of things, offsetting the court's cultivation of appearances with a decisively materialist emphasis.[1] Taking the measure of the courtiers via the objects that they display as proof of their worth, he continually shows the elite members of Louis XIV's court to be wanting. Such is the paradox of court society. Accumulation can signal loss. One's clothing can expose what it is intended to cover, namely, the blind ambition of those eager to please the monarch, his ministers, and others of superior rank. A bourgeois can exert more influence at court than a noble. Members of both classes offer disingenuous praise; promise friendship to rivals; and outmanoeuvre their challengers for prestige and privilege. In their efforts to please the king, courtiers therefore erase much of what defines them as individuals. Whatever their names, and whatever distinction their new watches, jackets, and shoes afford them, they appear in La Bruyère's text as characters, types.

Depicting the servile flattery, greed, and devotion to the whims of fashion that pervaded French court society, *Les caractères* provides a veritable taxonomy of Louis's court at Versailles and in Paris. La

Bruyère catalogues the many signs of dedicated self-interest in texts devoted to personal merit, matters of the heart, style, and other categories of social interaction.[2] Rather than support glory as a value intrinsic to the survival of the monarchy, that is, glory realized in service to the realm, members of court society promote themselves under the guise of generosity.[3] By 1688 the king's sun was setting, and a different order of things was taking shape around him.[4] Based on keen observation and meticulous classification, La Bruyère's texts challenge earlier assumptions, especially the idea that a society dependent on spectacle can sustain itself. Displaying the wit and daring required to expose what lies behind courtiers' roles on the court's stage, the moralist compiles a record of false virtues.

In "De la mode" ["Of Fashion"] a florist cultivates tulips not to know the abundance of nature so much as to experience a collector's pride in owning a piece of it, consistent with the court's prevailing vogue. Cultivation here equates growth – the expansion and perfection of the garden – with the abuse and ridicule of the gardener. The opening sentence condemns those who submit to the dictates of fashion: "Une chose folle et qui découvre bien notre petitesse, c'est l'assujettissement aux modes quand on l'étend à ce qui concerne le goût, le vivre, la santé et la conscience" [A foolish thing that reveals our pettiness is our slavish respect for fashion including even the food we eat, the way we live, matters of health, and matters of conscience].[5] A committed follower of the tulip craze, the florist ticks all the boxes laid out in this sentence. He sacrifices his well-being out of obsessive devotion to his prized possessions:

> Le fleuriste a un jardin dans un faubourg: il y court au lever du soleil, et il en revient à son coucher. Vous le voyez planté, et qui a pris racine au milieu de ses tulipes et devant *la Solitaire*: il ouvre de grands yeux, il frotte ses mains, il se baisse, il la voit de plus près, il ne l'a jamais vue si belle, il a le cœur épanoui de joie; il la quitte pour l'*Orientale*, de là il va à *la Veuve*, il passe au *Drap d'or*, de celle-ci à l'*Agathe*, d'où il revient enfin à *la Solitaire*, où il se fixe, où il se lasse, où il s'assit, où il oublie de dîner: aussi est-elle nuancée, bordée, huilée, à pièces emportées; elle a un beau vase ou un beau calice: il la contemple, il l'admire. Dieu et la nature sont en tout cela ce qu'il n'admire point; il ne va pas plus loin que l'oignon de sa tulipe, qu'il ne livrerait pas pour mille écus, et qu'il donnera pour rien quand les tulipes seront négligées et que les œillets auront prévalu. Cet homme raisonnable, qui a une âme, qui a un culte et une religion, revient chez soi fatigué, affamé, mais fort content de sa journée: il a vu des tulipes.

[The florist has a garden at his country home; he rushes there first thing in the morning and he returns at sunset. You would think that he was planted there, that he had taken root in the middle of his tulips. Standing before his *Solitaire* he opens his eyes wide; he rubs his hands; he bends down; he examines it more closely. It has never appeared so beautiful to him; his heart is filled with joy; he leaves it for the *Oriental* [woman], then goes over to the *Veuve* [widow]; and then on to the *Drap d'or* [cloth of gold], and from it to the *Agatha*, and finally returns to his *Solitaire*, where he sits down, where he grows tired, and where he forgets to eat dinner. This flower is magnificent in all its details; it is subtle, bordered, glimmering; it has a beautiful delicate shape or calyx. He contemplates it; he admires it. It is not God and nature that he admires in it; his thoughts go no further than the tulip bulb, which he would not sell for a thousand *écus*, and that he will give away for nothing when tulips are out and carnations come into fashion. This reasonable man, who has a soul, a place of worship, and a religion, arrives home tired and hungry but content with his day: he has seen tulips.] ("De la mode" 2.iv, 189; my emphasis)

Although he is not referenced here, Louis XIV, the grand arbiter of taste, also had a passion for tulips, and had the Grand Trianon filled with them.[6] These flowers were valued to excess not only in Holland, where people speculated wildly on tulip bulbs, but also in French high society during Louis's reign. La Bruyère's text suggests an overall collapse of values through the adoring gaze of the florist, who offers his tulips attention befitting a lover.[7] Even that assessment is qualified by the observation that the florist reveres his flowers in ways more properly reserved for religious practice.

The moralist, however, does not deride nature in deriding the man who excessively dedicates himself to his prized tulips. The florist starves his body as he starves his mind, more concerned with taste and fashion than with beauty or knowledge. Collecting tulips is a process of intellectual and physical deprivation. Observing that in future seasons these flowers will inevitably be replaced by another darling of horticultural fashion, La Bruyère accentuates the sense of ruin. Yet his description of the florist's garden shares a scientist's dedication to observation and recording. The emphasis on genus and species invokes botanical taxonomies and the idea of collecting as a proper means of assembling knowledge. La Bruyère attributes the deterioration of values that he describes to the vagaries of the marketplace rather than to nature or science. He encourages his reader to value judgments that are based not on the florist's idolatrous gaze upon his tulips but rather on the moralist's own careful observation of the florist.

Academic research was beyond the purview La Bruyère's text, which critiques the aimless self-absorption of the florist, the sole beholder of nature's splendour as he has assembled it in his garden.[8] Accurate description based on observation, however, was not beyond the moralist himself; these talents are evident in his clever portrait of the florist as it is throughout his collection of *caractères*. Portraying a man imprudently dedicated to flowers rather than to saving his soul before God, the moralist offers the literary equivalent of a Dutch vanitas: warning against material pleasures, his trenchant text nonetheless offers a source of immediate pleasure. Painted flowers outlast their real models; La Bruyère's wit elevates him above the foolishness that he depicts.

Dutch art, and Dutch tulips, continue to mediate the passage from the court of Louis XIV through the Enlightenment. La Bruyère's dedication to observation, definition, and categorization invites further connections with the scientific writing of the *Enclyclopédie*. Louis de Jaucourt, one of the principal contributors to the *Encyclopédie*, wrote on both tulips and Dutch art.[9] These texts provide an entry to questions of representation that concerned the editors of the *Encylopédie*.

Jaucourt: Light Itself

In an extensive article on the tulip Jaucourt explains:

> On divise généralement les tulipes en deux classes, prises du tems qu'elles fleurissent. La premiere classe est composée des tulipes printanieres, & la seconde des tulipes tardives. Il se trouve d'autres tulipes qu'on appelle méridionales, parce qu'elles fleurissent entre les printanieres & les tardives, mais il n'est pas besoin d'en faire une classe séparée.
>
> [Tulips are generally divided into two classes, depending on the time of year in which they bloom. The first class is composed of spring tulips and the second late tulips. There are other tulips called "southern" because they bloom between the spring tulips and the late tulips, but there is no need to consider them as a separate class.][10]

He specifies two seasons, spring and late spring, with the "southern" mid-season also mentioned. Even without the third class, one manages to classify all late tulips. Jaucourt's account integrates the geographical (zone) and the temporal (seasonal). Presumably the flowers in the mid group bloom later or earlier but share qualities with flowers of the other groups. For all this specificity, however, Jaucourt takes pains to note: "La classe des *tulipes* tardives est si nombreuse, qu'il n'est pas possible d'en faire une liste; il s'en trouve de si diversement colorées, qu'il est impossible aux Peintres d'en imiter la variété" [The class of late-blooming tulips is so large that it is impossible to make a complete list of what it contains; they are found in so many different colours that it is impossible for painters to imitate all their variations] [16:741]. From a classificatory point of view, the statement that one cannot classify everything is an admission that nature continues to outstrip science. While that limit proves frustrating to the encyclopedists, the value of their documentation is not in dispute. Jaucourt's article describes many other aspects of the tulip. Interestingly, he turns in the above passage to artists as the arbiters not of taste but of classification. He observes that even painters, who have mastered the ability to imitate nature, cannot imitate the diverse class of late-flowering tulips. The reader understands that these flowers are so prolific and cover such a vast geographical area that neither botanical artists, whose descriptive accuracy allows the identification of individual species, nor still life painters, especially in Holland, who depict many tulip species, have established a complete catalogue of the late tulips. Jaucourt provides knowledge both of what one observes and what escapes observation. Implying that the field of botany is always expanding, he also acknowledges the limited capacity of written description to record nature's abundance.

Elsewhere in the *Encyclopédie* Jaucourt engages with the question of description in connection with painting. His articles on the Ecole hollandaise [Dutch School], the Ecole flamande [Flemish School], and the Ecole allemande [German School] as well as the Ecole française [French School] speak directly to questions of representation as imitation. Articles on of the first three schools, which together make up the Northern tradition, offer a concise general description, followed by a list of painters and a very brief description of their art. Jaucourt identifies the depiction of realistic objects in a natural setting, the style characteristic of Flemish, Dutch, and German artistic traditions, in contradistinction to the French style as influenced by the Italians. The article on the Ecole hollandaise is most comprehensive regarding Northern art, and I restrict my comments to it.

Jaucourt characterizes his assessment as a synthesis of prevailing opinions that he judges to be most worthy of record:

> Voici, ce me semble, le précis des meilleures observations qui ont été faites sur les ouvrages de cette école, plus recherchés aujourd'hui qu'ils ne l'étoient sous le siecle de Louis XIV. Ils tiennent du goût & des défauts des Flamands & des Allemands, au milieu desquels vivoient les peintres de la Hollande. On les distingue à une représentation de la nature, telle qu'on la voit avec ses défauts; à une parfaite intelligence du clairobscur; à un travail achevé; à une propreté charmante; à une exactitude singuliere; à un art admirable dans la représentation des paysages, des perspectives, des ciels, des animaux, des fleurs, des fruits, des insectes, des sujets de nuit, des vaisseaux, des machines, & autres objets qui ont rapport au Commerce & aux Arts.
>
> [Here, it seems to me, is an account of the best observations made regarding the works associated with this school, more sought after today than they were during the century belonging to Louis XIV. They reflect both the taste and the defects of the Flemish and the Germans, among whom the Dutch painters lived. They are notable for their representation of nature, as one sees it, defects and all; for their perfect understanding of chiaroscuro; for the finish of their work; the appealing cleanness of their images; their exceptional precision; their talent in representing landscapes, perspectives, skies, animals, flowers, fruits, insects, night scenes, vessels, machines, and other objects related to commerce and the arts.] (Jaucourt, "École hollandaise" ["Dutch School"] [5:323])[11]

Jaucourt centres his appreciation of the Dutch on technique, on the skill and accuracy of their descriptions. The last part of the paragraph reads like a veritable taxonomy of elements in Dutch images. Many of the attributes that Jaucourt lists can be applied to a single Dutch painting: we easily recognize allusions to landscapes and still lifes. What Jaucourt does not say, but what we know to be true, is that his enumeration of the various characteristics of Dutch art coheres with the function of description in the *Encyclopédie*. The latter is conceived as a "dictionnaire raisonné des sciences, des arts et des métiers" [systematic dictionary of the sciences, arts, and crafts] that maps human knowledge via a series of subject headings, under which are classified individual articles that are subdivided into sections of vital information. The scope of Dutch art is far more restricted than that of the *Encyclopédie*. Nonetheless, the compositional design of Dutch images is compatible with the organization of the *Encyclopédie*. Both identify individual objects based on accurate observation, organizing them according to specific subjects in ways that highlight their particular attributes. While the details of objects serve to identify them, clusters of elements – relations between objects in the painting; relations between articles in the encyclopedia – determine the appropriate context(s) for assigning value to the objects. Multiple combinations of elements are possible.

Although he notes the increased popularity of Dutch works in the eighteenth century, Jaucourt criticizes them (along with Flemish and German paintings) for what he deems a lack of inspiration. The latter view reflects the traditional French preference, as defined by the Academy and applied by artists working for the crown, for art devoted to expansive histories. In the seventeenth century French academicians dismissed Netherlandish art as mimetic. This negative judgment has roots in the Italian Renaissance, when mere copying nature was judged as deficient. The *ut pictura poesis* principle adopted by the humanists meant that artists worked from nature in order to present an ideal. During the reign of Louis XIV, French art theory supported the same precepts, and academicians largely criticized Netherlandish artists for failing to meet the *poesis* criterion in their singular dedication to copying nature. Jaucourt's article thus reflects a long acculturation in France. It also reflects the eighteenth century's interest in emotions, as these were associated with forms of perception. Referring to the Abbé Du Bos, whose *Réflexions critique sur la poésie et sur la peinture* [*Critical Reflections on Poetry and Painting*] (1719) championed the affective qualities and emotional response to art consistent with a belief in the determining influence of temperaments, Jaucourt adds:

> Ces peintres flegmatiques & laborieux ont donc la persévérance de chercher par un nombre infini de tentatives, souvent réitérées sans fruit, les teintes, les demi-teintes, enfin toutes les diminutions de couleurs nécessaires pour dégrader la couleur des objets, & ils sont ainsi parvenus à peindre la lumiere même.

> [These phlegmatic and painstaking painters devote themselves to seeking, in innumerable attempts, often repeated without any noticeable improvement, the shades of colour, the half-tones, indeed all the subtle variations in hue necessary to soften the colour of objects, and they were thus able to paint light itself.] (5:323)

Jaucourt here invokes Sir William Temple, who, in his *Observations upon the United Provinces* (1672), determined that Holland's damp air and cold climate had the effect of chilling the Dutch brains, making them phlegmatic. The passions and their role in causation fall outside the scope of my study, but this reference makes clear that Jaucourt's assessment of Dutch artists was qualified by the sense that they were plodding and lacked a certain creative verve.

Dutch artists, Jaucourt re-emphasizes, are technically proficient. He notes the effort required for them to layer paint to achieve precise colour, an essential technique for rendering candlelight, reflections, and shadows. He alludes to the effects of warm light with which genre paintings suffuse rooms and the subtleties of weather conditions reflected in landscapes. Admiring the artists' "perfect understanding of chiaroscuro," the contrasting effects of light and shadow, Jaucourt observes that the Dutch are able to use colour to "peindre la lumiere même" [to paint light itself]. Artists in Holland who developed extensive gradations of light for dramatic effect include the Utrecht Caravaggisti, painters of the 1620s influenced by the art of Caravaggio such as Hendrick ter Brugghen, Gerard van Honthorst, and Dirck van Baburen, as well as Vermeer, Rembrandt, and Dou, among others. In Jaucourt's description "peindre la lumière même" applies to the physics of light as it relates to optics, the ability to depict convincingly the range of dark and light tones.[12]

Concurring with the Abbé Du Bos, however, Jaucourt criticizes the poverty of Dutch subjects, stating that artists are content to paint "une boutique, un corps-de-garde, ou la cuisine d'un paysan; leurs héros sont des faquins" [a shop, a guard, or a peasant's kitchen; their heroes are despicable men]. His prejudice for noble subjects – the histories of myth, literature, and religion that inspire greatness – is consistent with the established hierarchy of genres. Ordinary themes, however, are not the only reason for which Jaucourt qualifies his opinion of Dutch artists: "mais il ne faut pas chercher chez eux la beauté de l'ordonnance, de l'invention & de l'expression, qu'on trouve dans les ouvrages de France & d'Italie" [but one should not look to find the beauty of compositional design, invention and expression, that one finds in French and Italian works]. He believes that the Dutch lack inspiration:

> Mais ces peintres amusans ont assez mal réussi dans les autres parties de l'art, qui ne sont pas les moins importantes: sans invention dans leurs expressions, incapables pour l'ordinaire de s'élever au-dessus de la nature

> qu'ils ont devant les yeux, ils n'ont guere peint que des passions basses, ou bien une nature ignoble, & ils y ont excellé.
>
> [But these engaging painters were far less successful in other areas of their art, which are no less significant: with no invention in their expressions, unable typically to rise above what they see standing before them in nature, they painted virtually nothing but base passions, or an undignified nature, and they excelled at this.] (5:323)

Dutch artists are devoted practitioners of their art. Practice, however, does not make perfect. "Doing the same thing ten times over" cannot substitute for inspiration. Therefore, Jaucourt maintains, the Dutch fare poorly when compared to the Venetians:

> Nos Hollandois, au nombre desquels je n'ai garde de comprendre ici tous les peintres de leur nation, mais dans le nombre desquels je comprends la plûpart des peintres flamands, ont bien connu la valeur des locales couleurs, mais ils n'en ont pas sû tirer le même avantage que les peintres de l'école vénitienne. Le talent de colorier comme l'a fait le Titien, demande de l'invention, & il dépend plus d'une imagination fertile en expédiens pour le mélange des couleurs, que d'une persévérance opiniâtre à refaire dix fois la même chose.
>
> [Our Dutch, in which group I do not mean to include here all painters of their nation, but in which group I do include the majority of Flemish painters, understood how to paint the different values of local colours, but they were unable to do so as effectively as the painters of the Venetian school. The skill with colour exemplified by Titian requires invention, and it depends more on a fertile imagination capable of mastering the elements needed to create an effective mix of colours than on one's stubborn persistence in doing the same thing ten times over.] (5:323)

Asserting that Dutch painters were able to paint "la lumière même" [light itself], Jaucourt admires their ability to record the effects of light on objects and to capture the beauty that it bestows upon them. He declines, however, to recognize much beyond the technical mastery of Dutch artists. My analysis of Northern realist imagery has shown, however, that "light itself" should refer to more than physics. Dutch artists are, in fact, inspired; they produce a record of what they see and through that process they order knowledge. The objects that the artists capture in the light bear witness to their lives in ways that validate the resourcefulness of the Dutch nation; artists describe what Dutch society had built. To build in this sense refers to the perfection of lenses, the production of ships, and the development of commerce. It refers as well to art that catalogues, that cultivates a system of thought, and that associates power with empirical observation. Dutch images enlighten the beholder because they establish possibilities for knowing the world. The "ordinary" realism of Dutch artists challenged the authority of any institution that would impose a State spectacle to prevent subjects from looking outside the court for answers. It challenged the single-minded ideal of absolute power that the French monarchy of Louis XIV imposed in its patronage of the arts. The Dutch School leaves the shadows of the Sun King most emphatically, therefore, when articles such as Jaucourt's are understood to be constitutive parts of Enlightenment thought.

Diderot believed that the image, unlike language, has the capacity to describe nature directly by copying it faithfully. Artists imitate nature; imitation ensures accuracy. Yet, as the previous chapters have demonstrated, and our contemporary understanding of language asserts, visual language is complex.[13] With Netherlandish realist art the beholder's understanding is enriched by the intricate pairings, juxtapositions, cross-references, and unresolved elements of the image responsible for creating multiple levels of meaning. The beholder of Dutch genre paintings identifies objects and also comes to know them within varied and sometimes competing contexts. Dutch artists perfected the imitation of nature. Nevertheless, their images created comparisons, ambiguities, double entendres that expose how differences between objects preclude a simple understanding. The concept of description as imitation alone cannot account for these layers of meaning. The capacity of Dutch genre paintings, still lifes, and cityscapes to convey not only how individual things appear in nature but also multivalent relations made this art an outlier within French court culture during the reign of Louis XIV. Breaking through the court's singular focus on the king in both images and texts, the Northern realist emphasis on difference appears there as "la lumiere même," that is, an enlightened principle of reason and discovery.

The Art of the Science of Description

Diderot and d'Alembert designed a system for archiving the diverse texts and images that they and their collaborators prepared. They intended the *Encyclopédie* not only to record data but also to shape the reader's knowledge: they organized information according to a system of ideas reflecting their beliefs and values. The editors of the *Encyclopédie* expressed confidence in their ability to influence the future by assembling what they knew about the past and the present across diverse fields of study. Their texts greatly expand our understanding of the art and the science of classification. The editors specify the criteria for the articles to be included; they anticipate inevitable ambiguities and omissions; they create a vast network of cross-references (*renvois*); and they write with conviction about the liberating potential of knowledge to improve the world.

That mission was a rebuke of much of what the monarchy represented during the reign of Louis XIV politically as well as culturally. As expressed through its patronage of the arts, the monarchy sought to impose a singular knowledge; it cultivated one "absolute" narrative of Louis's greatness and tolerated but one narrative. Official court art largely failed to expand the French imaginary beyond the various iterations of the king's portrait. The empirical emphasis of the *Encyclopédie* project was consonant with the descriptive approach of Dutch Golden Age artists. Consistent with the vast amounts of information that had accrued in the sciences, trades, philosophy, and other fields, the encyclopedia offered detailed descriptions of observable phenomena and established practices. Texts and plates (illustrations) presented none of the aesthetic appeal of paintings, but the plates received ample attention as subjects in their own right. Dutch artists, I have argued, were archivists of a different sort. Their images record not only historic battles, guilds, civic associations, and other commemorations but also what the Dutch built on the land and the sea: fields, cities, markets, homes, shipping vessels, and the goods that filled them. If that list reads like an enumeration, it is because enumeration is what these artists did. Northern realism forms part of the cultural legacy of Louis's reign, one of its most consequential elements. Far more than French arts and letters in the seventeenth century, Dutch art anticipated modes of description in the eighteenth century.[14]

In his "Discours préliminaire" ["Preliminary Discourse"] (1751), d'Alembert develops the taxonomy of the *Encyclopédie* in terms of three functions: memory, which corresponds with history; reason, which grounds philosophy (including the science of God, the science of man, and the science of nature); and imagination (imitation of nature), which grounds artistic expression. Most notably, as Robert Darnton explains, d'Alembert's taxonomy privileges the science of man over divine science: humans alone can discover the keys of nature.[15] As Diderot observes in his article devoted to the topic, the encyclopedia is meant to include "tout ce qui a rapport à la curiosité de l'homme, à ses devoirs, à ses besoins, & à ses plaisirs" [all that relates to man's curiosity, his duties, his needs, and his pleasures] (Diderot, "Encyclopédie" [5:635]).[16] Articles related to *la terre* [earth/land], for example, cover the earth's geological history and its mineral composition as well as contemporary issues concerning the cultivation of the land, from the planting of individual species through directions for cooking, and the painting of landscapes. *Encyclopédie* entries thus run the gamut from the creation of the planet through "farm to table" production, and the art that captured views of it all. A table is a piece of furniture on which food is served. It is also a painted object on which artists display foodstuffs. In still lifes tables serve as supports for elaborate displays of items, from which image the idea of the encyclopedia as a compendium of information organized into sections (alphabetically, and also, within articles, according to set standards) becomes an easy extension. *Table* serves as a metaphor for the *Encyclopédie*'s classification of ideas, as in a table of elements. Even this description, however, ignores much about the construction of the table from wood; the cultivation of the forests, the effects of deforestation in Europe during the seventeenth century, notably in Holland; the different styles of painting; and the need for the *Encyclopédie* to present the most specialized knowledge for all subjects that it addresses. Something always, inevitably, escapes the established categories.

One of the problems that Diderot acknowledges in characterizing the vast *Encyclopédie* project relates to the many moving parts of the things that he and others describe. He identifies the challenge of communicating the various components of a machine, even with the addition of the plates.[17] His analysis of the editorial decisions regarding best practices for describing scientific devices and inventions points to the inevitability of machines, like the encyclopedists' descriptions of them, being outpaced by advances in design. Scientific progress dooms new machines to be replaced by newer, improved models. It follows that even up-to-date descriptions will eventually require revisions to incorporate the modifications. Full knowledge is always deferred. In practice, Diderot acknowledges, the *Encyclopédie* never arrives at its point of completion. Science advances faster than the authors can absorb the changes:

> Quand on traite des êtres de la nature, que peut-on faire de plus, que de rassembler avec scrupule toutes leurs propriétés connues dans le moment

où l'on écrit? Mais l'observation & la physique expérimentale multipliant sans cesse les phénomenes & les faits, & la philosophie rationelle les comparant entr'eux & les combinant, étendent ou resserrent sans cesse les limites de nos connoissances, font en conséquence varier les acceptions des mots institués; rendent les définitions qu'on en a données inexactes, fausses, incompletes, & déterminent même à en instituer de nouveaux.

[When examining beings from nature, what more can one do than to assemble carefully an account of all their known characteristics at the time one writes? But with observation and experimental physics always multiplying phenomena and facts, and with rational philosophy drawing comparisons between them, and reformulating them in different configurations such that the limits of our knowledge are continually being expanded or tightened, the accepted meaning of words is also continually changing. This makes the definitions that one assigned to them appear inexact, false, incomplete, thus requiring that new ones be established.] (Diderot, "Encyclopédie" [5:636A])

Thus, in addition to causal relations – how one part affects another; how one idea leads logically to the next – the *Encyclopédie* needs to account for sustained movement, including movement outside the linguistic "frame" or taxonomic structure that the editors design to contain it. What happens in terms of individual descriptions applies as well to the fluidity of categories (subject headings) that describe different phenomena, such as in the example of the table above. The *Encyclopédie* contains 166 entries with the word "terre" in the heading and no single category for containing them all.

Dutch art "removes the frame" to the world outside. Things appear unmediated, as they are in nature. The viewer identifies scenes of domestic life, city streets, etc. Within these "themes," or contexts, however, multiple classes of identities may be present (churches, people, animals, streets, pots, vegetables), and the relations between things will not always be stable or clearly defined (Is the mistress amused at the maid standing beside the empty pot or dismissive of her? Are those elegantly dressed women in a brothel? Who ate the missing piece of pie?). Still life paintings caution against indulging in worldly pleasures although the painting itself becomes a source of pleasure for the viewer. Artists associate good and evil, bread as Christ and bread as foodstuff, collecting as a source of material wealth and collecting as a source of knowledge. Association, however, does not mean the elimination of one term in favour of the other. The viewer sees only one object, the bread, but the composition requires that it be known in conjunction with other objects in the image; with iconography; with an aesthetic appreciation; and with commercial success. A vanitas evokes the owner's satisfaction in knowing that its moral message affirms his respectability, just as the display of such a beautiful image in his home announces his financial success and thereby offers him pleasure of another sort.

The allegories created by Le Brun in the Galerie des Glaces dress, literally and figuratively, Louis XIV in the armour of ancient military heroes. These images merge the present with the past to ensure a glorious future that never falters. Rather than an overriding narrative, Netherlandish artists create visual compositions that convey the reality effect of all things in the scene, whether a vast landscape or a market stall with fruits and vegetables. Dutch art inventories houses situated on streets and canals where commerce takes place; where lovers have taken their leave; where inserted paintings feature ships tossing in the sea and landscapes that register changes in the weather. All these differences cannot simply be eliminated – brushed under the table, as it were.

Diderot observes that branches of science proliferate as knowledge accumulates and more areas of specialization are recognized.[18] Furthermore, the effect of reading across several articles by following the cross-references means that each reader pursues a different and always partial understanding of the ever elusive whole.[19] The appearance of new volumes of the *Encyclopédie,* improved technologies requiring updated and ancillary descriptions, and the fact that one's path through the various volumes is limited only by one's curiosity and the time one dedicates to studying it ensure that no two readers have the same "book of knowledge." Moreover, Diderot's description of the function of cross-references shows his intent to establish for the whole of the *Encyclopédie* a system not unlike that which Dutch painters adopt for individual images:

> Je distingue deux sortes de renvois: les uns de choses, & les autres de mots. Les renvois de choses éclaircissent l'objet, indiquent ses liaisons prochaines avec ceux qui le touchent immédiatement, & ses liaisons éloignées avec d'autres qu'on en croiroit isolés; rappellent les notions communes & les principes analogues; fortifient les conséquences; entrelacent la branche au tronc, & donnent au tout cette unité si favorable à l'établissement de la vérité & à la persuasion. Mais quand il le faudra, ils produiront aussi un effet tout contraire; ils opposeront les notions; ils feront contraster les

principes; ils attaqueront, ébranleront, renverseront secretement quelques opinions ridicules qu'on n'oseroit insulter ouvertement. Si l'auteur est impartial, ils auront toujours la double fonction de confirmer & de réfuter; de troubler & de concilier.

[I distinguish two kinds of cross-references: those related to things, and the others to words. Cross-references of things clarify the object, indicating close connections between it and other objects very similar to it, along with less obvious connections with other things that seem to be unrelated to the object; they recall common ideas and analogous principles; they strengthen the consequences, tying the branch to the trunk; and they assign unity to the whole in a way that is favorable to the establishment of truth and persuasion. But when necessary, the cross-references attack; they undermine and secretly undercut opinions that one could not openly challenge. If the author is impartial, the cross-references will always have the double function of confirming and refuting; of disturbing and of reconciling]. (Diderot, "Encyclopédie" [5:642A])

Dutch artists demonstrate the same tendency to reveal and conceal, to multiply meanings by associating different objects that the viewer first perceives individually and then in multiple combinations, refining what one knows in ways that expand the range of meanings. Like the cross-references that Diderot and his collaborators set in place to develop a more complex body of knowledge and also to evade censorship, the design of Dutch images remains fluid despite all the attention that artists lavish on individual objects in order to identify them with precision.[20]

The editors of the *Encyclopédie* were well aware that mutability remained a central problem for their project to totalize knowledge, to build a compendium that excluded nothing pertinent to their subjects, and to describe in such a fashion that readers understood how all things functioned. The natural world and the academic word were constantly evolving. Moreover, as Joanna Stalnaker observes in her seminal work on description in the Enlightenment, the encyclopedists recognized the inability of the collection of encyclopedia articles and plates to provide adequate information that takes into account the need to acquire and then communicate technical expertise; improvement in machinery; the relationship of the text to the accompanying plates; and the limits of language, among other concerns. Stalnaker thus concludes: "the *Encyclopédie* was both a monument to human knowledge and a testament to it immense fragility."[21] Frustration in this regard does not, of course, equate with failure. Each step in the chain of information was a worthwhile accomplishment, even though a complete and totalizing knowledge proved, and would always prove, elusive. These obstacles inhibit but do not obscure what Diderot defines as the larger goal of expanding human knowledge to improve the quality of life for future generations:

> En effet, le but d'une *Encyclopédie* est de rassembler les connoissances éparses sur la surface de la terre; d'en exposer le système général aux hommes avec qui nous vivons, & de le transmettre aux hommes qui viendront après nous; afin que les travaux des siecles passés n'aient pas été des travaux inutiles pour les siecles qui succéderont; que nos neveux, devenant plus instruits, deviennent en même tems plus vertueux & plus heureux, & que nous ne mourions pas sans avoir bien mérité du genre humain.
>
> [In fact, the goal of an encyclopedia is to assemble various pieces of knowledge from across the globe; to discover the general system governing this knowledge and to reveal it to people with whom we are living, and to transmit it to those who will come after us; so that the work of previous centuries will not seem useless to future centuries; so that our descendants, by becoming better informed, at the same time become more virtuous and happy, and so that we will not die without having benefitted the human race.] (Diderot, "Encyclopédie" [5:635])

We assess the accomplishment of the *Encylopédie* by the expansive record that the encyclopedists assemble, including their reflections on the ideals and challenges that they experienced in realizing their objectives, and far less by what it fails to document.

Science, as Diderot describes it, outran the descriptive talents of the *philosophes*. Description could not keep pace with innovations; it needed to adapt to changes in nature; it needed to make allowances for future discoveries. Dutch realism, on the other hand, suspended time. Dutch art captures a moment, and an experience, between stasis and motion. Movement, Diderot advises, occurs on all levels. It involves the discoveries of new things and cataclysmic events, the reassignment of categories, the rewriting of texts, the development of new descriptive language, etc. Against this movement Netherlandish realist art presents the beauty of the things in the world, and that beauty endures. One of the qualities of art is to present the familiar in new ways, to shift

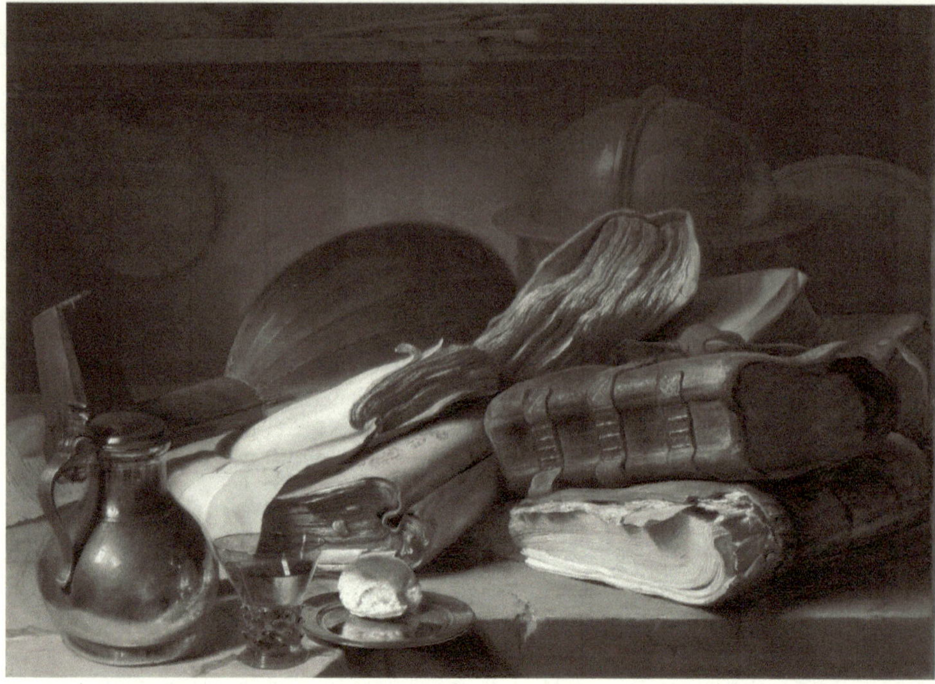

6.1. Jan Lievens. *Still Life with Books*. Ca. 1627–8. 91 × 120 cm (35.83 × 47.24 in). Rijksmuseum. Image courtesy Rijksmuseum. https://www.rijksmuseum.nl/nl/collectie/SK-A-4090.

perspective so that the unremarkable becomes remarkable. For Dutch artists the painterly impulse, too, is encyclopedic, an urge to create a repertory of materials, colours, forms. This approach to composition enhances the attention that the viewer pays to the qualities of each element in the image. The Dutch paint with their eyes. Their depictions of objects are similar to scientific descriptions of mechanisms and processes, as they are concerned with the identifying details. Yet their art takes the viewer well beyond functionality, as is evident in their many depictions of objects that record the effects of light on different textural surfaces. The Dutch idealization of their immediate world falls well short of the artistic ideal that French artists and writers sought in their support of Louis XIV. Nonetheless, Dutch art allows the viewer to appreciate how the real itself was, as the encyclopedists well knew, worthy of contemplation.

In Jan Lievens's *Still Life with Books* the record legers into which bills and other documents are meant to be held stand empty.[22] They are defined by little more than the materials of which they are made, their worn leather and parchment bindings and thick pages with no writing visible. Time has been effaced. No transactions are recorded. The books of life lie vacant, yet their curled pages and warped covers show all the effects of use. The overturned objects – the lute case that shows itself without the lute, the artist's palette in the shadows, and the pair of globes on which individual continents cannot be detected – signal the passage of time as erasure, death. Nor are the brushes applied to the palette. Art does not insulate against the tragedy that is the mortal condition.

Yet a piece of bread captures the viewer's eye, as it is holds the light near the centre of the horizontal ledge. Reflected on a pewter plate that juts out into the viewer's space, the bread imparts a sense of a life. Bread is both a religious symbol and, stripped down to is fundamental function as human sustenance, an icon of human existence. Here it basks in the light that sweeps across the image, releasing energy that counters the heaviness and wear of the objects. The reflections of both the bread on the plate and of the window and/or the candle on the pewter jug show vibrancy, as does the light that cuts through the glass standing between them. Life lies not in the represented objects but rather in the bits of colour that point to the light source outside the painting. The Dutch painter focuses on fleeting experience, but hints at something more: knowledge that might escape the attention of the viewer who concentrates only on the objects, and who seeks to assemble them into a grand narrative about the inevitability of death and the vanity of earthly pursuits. As a record of things – goods sold and purchased; art produced and consumed; foods and wine served and ingested – the painting speaks of the transitory nature of things. Yet the light tells another story. Although they are emptied of their contents, the containers (the lute case minus the lute, the palette without paint, the illegible globes) are not objects simply but painted objects made beautiful by the light. There is energy in that process, energy in the fact that, even as signs of the decay of material bodies, these reflections capture a moment in time, a process of recording that, in its emptiness, evokes experience still unidentified, still indefinite, but still evocative. Dutch artists create tensions like these repeatedly.

Lievens's still life draws connections between objects signifying death, the passage of time, and material existence. He depicts the sense of loss and destruction with objects whose curves and folds add a sensual quality. The overall monochromatic character of white, grey, and reddish brown is enhanced by the light reflected on polished surfaces, signs of inspiration. Lievens's painting is complex and richly inconsistent. The vanitas theme bears witness to transience and mortality. Yet the painting itself, an object created a decade before Louis XIV was born, was, and remains, admired. Ambiguity, paradox, and openness are all hallmarks of the visual language that the Dutch develop.

I am making a connection between Dutch compositions that position objects to reveal an assortment of tactile and visual qualities, on the one hand, and Diderot's emphasis on constructing a system with attention to its individual components, on the other. Diderot, however, argues that painting cannot fulfil this function. He believes that language alone has the power to establish logical connections, the basis for analytic thought, whereas painting records the world directly and uncritically:

> La peinture n'atteint point aux opérations de l'esprit; l'on ne distingueroit point entre des objets sensibles distribués sur une toile, comme ils seroient énoncés dans un discours, les liaisons qui forment le jugement & le syllogisme; ce qui constitue un de ces êtres sujet d'une proposition; ce qui constitue une qualité de ces êtres, attribut; ce qui enchaîne la proposition à une autre pour en faire un raisonnement, & ce raisonnement à un autre pour en composer un discours; en un mot il y a une infinité de choses de cette nature que la peinture ne peut figurer; mais elle montre du moins toutes celles qu'elle figure: & si au contraire le discours écrit les désigne toutes, il n'en montre aucune. Les peintures des êtres sont toûjours très incompletes; mais elles n'ont rien d'équivoque, parce que ce sont les portraits mêmes d'objets que nous avons sous les yeux. Les caracteres de l'écriture s'étendent à tout, mais ils sont d'institution; ils ne signifient rien par eux-mêmes. La clé des tableaux est dans la nature, & s'offre à tout le monde: celle des caracteres alphabétiques & de leur combinaison est un pacte dont il faut que le mystere soit revélé; & il ne peut jamais l'être completement, parce qu'il y a dans les expressions des nuances délicates qui restent nécessairement indéterminées.
>
> [Painting does not demonstrate the operations of the mind; one would not recognize in the objects distributed on a canvas the connections that form a judgement or a syllogism, as one would if these objects were expressed in language (discourse). One cannot tell which is the subject of a clause, what is an inherent quality of the object, an attribute; what links one clause to another to create a logical relation, and this relation to another so as to create an extended argument. Thus, there are countless things of this sort that a painting cannot represent. Yet a painting nonetheless does show all the relations that it depicts. Conversely, while written language elaborates

> all relations, it shows none of them. Paintings of beings and objects are always very incomplete; but they are not in the least ambiguous, because they are the portraits of what stands before our eyes. Written letters apply to everything, but they are devices; they do not signify anything in and of themselves. The key to paintings is in nature, and is available to everyone: that of the letters of the alphabet and their combinations is a pact whose secret must be uncovered. This secret, however, can never be entirely revealed because expressions contain subtle nuances that cannot be specified.] (Diderot, "Encyclopédie" [5:638])

Description in the natural sciences must strive for a completeness that eludes the art of painting. Images, Diderot affirms, go only so far in describing nature, and what they describe is too accessible, too apparent. No matter how technically proficient, art does not communicate fully the relations between objects; it does not reveal enough to analyse, debate, and affirm the function and purpose of phenomena. Language is best suited for communicating ideas because it is able to express logical connections. Yet language suffers from an inability to describe adequately. Language cannot paint, or show, what it describes with enough precision.

Without entering the debates concerning the function of language in which Diderot and his peers engaged, let us concede that no collection of art could substitute for the compilation of information contained and analysed in the *Encyclopédie*. Written texts allow for far more elaboration and nuance. Art, however, does more than imitate appearances. Dutch artists created a compendium of their world. They idealized what they saw, but they captured objects and settings in ways that made them instantly recognizable. Like texts, images are governed by a logic, or syntax, that orders knowledge. Dutch art, I have argued, differs from French court art precisely because Dutch artists do convey relations between objects in the painting. The "skies, animals, flowers, fruits, insects, night scenes, vessels, machines" to which Jaucourt refers are taxonomic divisions of the knowable world. The French court's elaboration of Louis XIV's portrait relies instead on a single category of identities. Louis resembles Apollo, the sun god of peace and the arts. Like Apollo, Louis fights France's enemies to achieve peace. Louis was also a patron of the arts; the arts supported the king's image via Apollonian themes. The arts respected the "oneness" law to promote the monarch's image.

Visual language contains no clauses, properly speaking. Paintings, however, do contain *propositions*, relations in which something is affirmed or denied. Indeed, the interest of many Dutch paintings is that the image both affirms and denies a proposition. Is the woman at the virginal virtuous? The woman is playing a musical instrument; music making is virtuous behaviour; therefore the scene describes the woman's virtue. Such syllogistic logic applies, as does: the (same) woman is playing music; she plays for a solider whose presence violates the sanctity of the home; therefore the woman playing music has lost her virtue. These descriptions apply not only to de Witte's painting discussed in chapter 3 but also to many other images.

Diderot observes that paintings cannot effectively establish a precise narrative. Lacking textual support (previous knowledge of the history being narrated), a viewer cannot always determine what the figures are doing:

> D'un autre côté, la peinture étant permanente, elle n'est que d'un état instantan[é]. Se propose-t'elle d'exprimer le mouvement le plus simple, elle devient obscure. Que dans un trophée on voye une Renommée les ailes déployées, tenant sa trompette d'une main, & de l'autre une couronne élevée au-dessus de la tête d'un héros, on ne sait si elle la donne ou si elle l'enleve: c'est à l'Histoire à lever l'équivoque.
>
> [On the other hand, although painting is permanent, it only describes one instant. If it sets about expressing the simplest movement, it becomes unclear. If on a trophy one sees Fame with her wings spread, holding her trumpet with one hand, and in the other a crown raised over the head of a hero, one cannot tell if she is giving it to him or taking it away: the history that inspired the painting determines which action it is.] (Diderot, "Encyclopédie" [5:638])

Dutch art has a deeply rooted iconographical tradition, but these paintings do far more than offer symbols based on Cesare Ripa's *Iconologia* and other symbolic systems.[23] The fact, moreover, that so many Dutch images, as Alpers has argued, have no mythical, biblical, or historical referents, means that much more is at stake than adapting established narratives. The type of "equivocation" to which Diderot points as a weakness becomes a strength in Dutch images, which operate on multiple registers. Northern realist art can convey, simultaneously, the plenitude of the moment and the sign of its decay. Still lifes summon death by celebrating life. Bollongier's *Floral Still Life* presents an exquisite arrangement of flowers, including several of the most celebrated Semper Augustus tulip, famous for being the most expensive flower sold during the Tulip Mania in Holland. The artist shows buds and full blooms, along with the insects that mark the end of the flowers' life cycle.

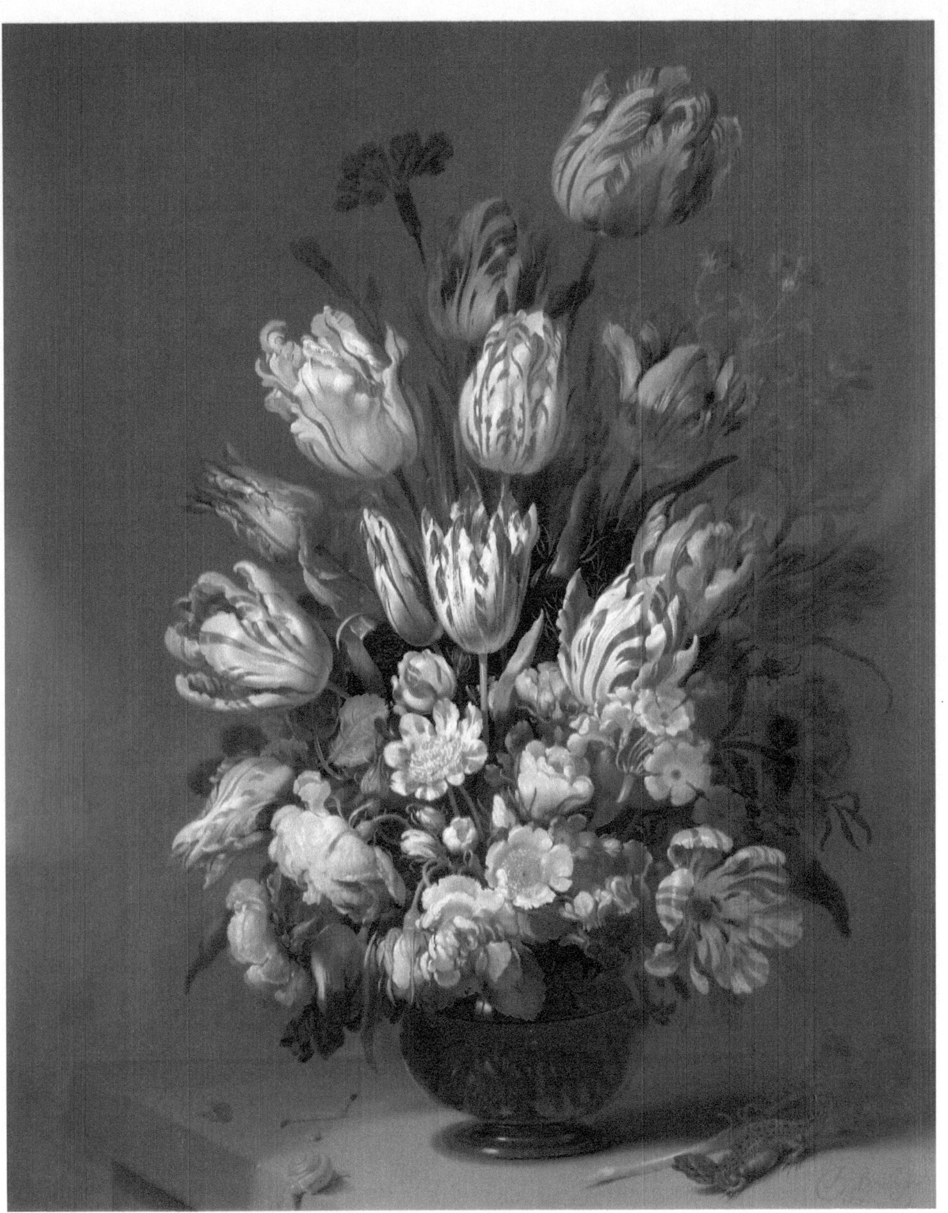

6.2. Hans Bollongier. *Floral Still Life*. 1639. 67.6 × 53.3 cm (26.61 × 20.98 in). Rijksmuseum. Image courtesy Rijksmuseum. https://www.rijksmuseum.nl/en/search/objects?q=+Bollongier++Floral&p=1&ps=12&st=Objects&ii=0#/SK-A-799,0.

Images like these show decline in ways that stress plenitude, enrichment. The fine, invisible line between abundance and deterioration marks the passage of time even as it exemplifies the ability of art to suggest what science cannot accurately measure: the actual experience of suspended time, concurrent stages of being, the before as it penetrates the after.

For a hero and for a king, one should always know whether the allegory Fame is giving glory or taking it away. Sometimes, however, the meaning lies with the transition from one valid state to another. What reveals the depth of experience is not the selection of either concept but rather a focus on the tension that exists between them. Dutch artists show the viewer that earthly things can change in the blink of an eye from sources of pride in one's success to the fear of moral condemnation, but they train the viewer to look deep into the painting. In these images abundance and blight, desire and fear of success coexist. Artists describe women who experience the thrill of illicit love and who know the teachings that condemn it; the beauty of material goods and the vanity of materialism; a mother's protective embrace and the child who trains his eyes on the world outside the home; daily routines immortalized through meticulously rendered compositions.

We do well therefore to look back at the influence of Dutch art not in terms of revolution or an exultant presence at court, but rather as a slow and steady infiltration of a system of ideas into the culture that developed around Louis XIV. It was not lost on the French that in Holland the influence of the royal family was largely supplanted by that of prosperous burghers, and that France's bourgeoisie contained many wealthy financiers and others with access to the king and his privileges. In the political theatre of the monarchy, the arts traced Louis's triumphant image year after year. Yet in Louis's France the ideas promulgated by Netherlandish realist art steadily "painted the light" in ways that undermined the court's attempts at controlling ideas, thereby anticipating a larger intellectual movement to come. Dutch art inhabited the French imagination, both as a material presence (for those who, increasingly as the century turned, directly viewed Dutch works) and (consistently from the start of Louis's reign) as an idea of a different society with strong bourgeois leanings and a penchant for recording what its citizens made, collected, and observed. In the French imaginary, although the French would not have described it in this way, Dutch art served as a repository for knowledge. Cataloguing objects, the Dutch reveal their world with special clarity. As painted objects – objects become ideas – the things of this world can be rearranged, controlled.

In a moving and passionate passage of the same article on the encyclopedia, Diderot explains his conviction that mankind must interpret nature, for without this intellectual engagement nature would remain silent, elusive:

> Une considération surtout qu'il ne faut point perdre de vûe, c'est que si l'on bannit l'homme ou l'être pensant & contemplateur de dessus la surface de la terre; ce spectacle pathétique & sublime de la nature n'est plus qu'une scene triste & muette. L'univers se taît; le silence & la nuit s'en emparent. Tout se change en une vaste solitude où les phénomenes inobservés se passent d'une manière obscure & sourde. C'est la présence de l'homme qui rend l'existence des êtres intéressante; & que peut-on se proposer de mieux dans l'histoire de ces êtres, que de se soûmettre à cette considération? Pourquoi n'introduirons-nous pas l'homme dans notre ouvrage, comme il est placé dans l'univers? Pourquoi n'en ferons-nous pas un centre commun? Est-il dans l'espace infini quelque point d'où nous puissions avec plus d'avantage faire partir les lignes immenses que nous nous proposons d'étendre à tous les autres points? Quelle vive & douce réaction n'en résultera-t-il pas des êtres vers l'homme, de l'homme vers les êtres?
>
> [One thing especially always to bear in mind is that if one banishes man or the thinking and contemplative being from the surface of the earth, this deeply moving and sublime spectacle of nature becomes a sad and silent scene. The universe stops speaking; silence and night take hold. Everything changes into a vast solitude where unobserved phenomena occur as though veiled or muffled. It is the presence of man that makes the existence of beings interesting; and what could one better propose in the history of these beings than to examine them in this way? Why not place man in our work as he is placed in the universe? Why not make him the centre of both? Is there a better point in the infinite space from which we could start to construct the immense lines that we are proposing to extend to all the other points? What a dynamic and pleasant reaction would result from this, both for beings as they connect with man, and man as he connects with them?] (Diderot, "Encyclopédie" [5:641])

Diderot holds that humans are the centre of knowledge, responsible for structuring the ideas that enable progress to occur. The ability to observe and to record what one observes is fundamental to science. The eyes that see and the hands that write rely on the mind's capacity to classify, that is, on the human ability to use the conventions of language to identify similar things and to indicate how they differ from other things. Although allegory dominates the arts cultivated by the crown during Louis XIV's reign, empiricism is manifestly present in seventeenth-century Netherlandish realism. Dutch Golden Age artists were committed to describing the world in precisely these ways, filling their images with an assortment of objects both ordinary and extraordinary. Their world came alive in their paintings.

Louis XIV's France stood at a considerable remove from Diderot's conviction that we animate an otherwise unknowable and unregulable world. The only man who appears to "make the earth move" in France is Louis, as supported by an army of artists devoted to creating his image as a projection of the monarchy's desire for power and influence. Nonetheless, as chapter 3 showed, Corneille and Racine both explored how the court could lose touch with the sublime. Devoid of lyricism and beauty, life under the monarchy becomes a spectacle of loss and mourning. These playwrights have shown how the "deeply moving and sublime spectacle" gives way to another depiction of the king's law as it suppresses revolt, otherness, difference, and as it fails to integrate layers of experience that connect his subjects with the infinite.

When we consider Netherlandish art from the vantage point of the court of Louis XIV, the judgment that Dutch artists paint ordinary and uninspired scenes, and that their art merely imitates, seriously underestimates the potential of realist images. These paintings enable the beholder to contemplate the world. For many Dutch artists the world is, admittedly, small and the view is very local. Their efforts appear microcosmic in comparison to the encyclopedists' attempts to organize and archive knowledge from all branches of intellectual endeavour. Nonetheless, the realism of Dutch artists, their detailed depictions of objects and places, shows their perspectives to be aligned with future empirical investigations into the workings of the world, including the knowledge assembled in the natural sciences and the liberal and mechanical arts (trades). In this way Dutch art disturbed the assumptions of the French court that included this art in its collections. The perfectibility of imitation that the Netherlandish artists demonstrated drew the beholder into the image, but the configurations of elements within the compositions confounded the sense, so prevalent in official French court art, that all elements in the work were subordinate to a single interpretation. Indeed, the capacity of Dutch art to "free" the beholder from the constraints of propaganda meant that in France, *avant la lettre*, it anticipated the efforts of the *Encyclopédie* that would enable readers to assemble knowledge. Such knowledge, the editors believed, would eliminate the abuses of absolutism and the monarchy's arbitrary exercise of power.

Referring to Francis Bacon, whose work inspired the ordering of knowledge in the *Encyclopédie*, and that of Descartes, Diderot observes:

> Tel est l'effet des progrès de la raison; progrès qui renversera tant de statues, & qui en relevera quelques-unes qui sont renversées. Ce sont celles des hommes rares, qui ont devancé leur siecle. Nous avons eu, s'il est permis de s'exprimer ainsi, des contemporains sous le siecle de Louis XIV.
>
> [This is the progress that results from the application of reason, progress that will overturn so many statues and that will set upright some that have been overturned. They are the statues of exceptional men who were ahead of their times. We have had, if we might say so, contemporaries who lived during the age of Louis XIV.] (Diderot, "Encyclopédie" [5:636a])

To this list of statues that the eighteenth century must set aright, we add those of Dutch artists of the seventeenth century. Their paintings were collected, viewed, and described by Louis XIV's contemporaries, and also by Diderot, whose ruminations about the arts extended their legacy. Thanks to them a magnificent bright red and white tulip, a Semper Augustus ["always venerable"], had emerged in the French imagination along with the fleur-de-lis to portray the age in which they lived.

As an art critic, Diderot had more to say about description, notably in the works of Chardin, whose still lifes retained many resonances of Dutch art. Diderot greatly admired Chardin's still lifes, and this commentary, to which I turn in my coda, offers a perspective on the history of ideas that mark the passage from the court of Louis XIV to the Enlightenment. In his discussion of the Salons, Michael Fried references Diderot's respect for the hierarchy of genres in which still lifes, landscapes, and genre paintings are classified below history paintings because they do not represent substantial human actions.[24] Yet Diderot upends this hierarchy with praise for "lesser genres," notably genre painting:

> je vois que la peinture de genre a presque toutes les difficultés de la peinture historique, qu'elle exige autant d'esprit, d'imagination, de poésie même, égale science du dessin, de la perspective, de la couleur, des ombres, de la lumière, des caractères, des passions, des expressions, des

> draperies, de la composition; une imitation plus stricte de la nature, des détails plus soignés; et que, nous montrant des choses plus connues et plus familières, elle a plus de juges et de meilleurs juges.
>
> [I see that genre painting has nearly all the complexities of history painting; that it demands as much intelligence, imagination, and even poetry; as much science of drawing, perspective, colour, shadows, light, character, passions, expressions, drapery, composition; a stricter imitation of nature, more accurate details; and that, in showing us better known and more familiar things, it has more judges and better judges.][25]

Indeed, Dutch Golden Age artists encourage us to consider their "ordinary" paintings as histories of another sort. They represent the significant human action of making sense ofthe world. Viewed within the context of the court culture that Louis XIV constructed with the support of artists, playwrights, and others, the anomalous Northern realist depictions affirm a commitment to knowledge rather than to ideology. Relying on empirical observation, classification, and display, Dutch realist paintings convey to the beholder the idea that illumination requires an abiding curiosity about the things of the world, and the sense that knowledge is as much an ongoing process as it is a final product.

Coda

Trompe L'oeil Illusions and the Thoughts They Inspire

Every innovation has its detractors. Every young generation has members of the older generation who see change as signalling the end of civilization as they know it. So it was, in France in the mid-eighteenth century, that many French artists, collectors, and philosophers confronted with anxious regret the increased appeal of seventeenth-century Dutch paintings for both nobles and bourgeois.[1] Salon tastes reflected the elite's desire to own Dutch cabinet paintings, as the smaller works were known. By the final years of the eighteenth century many wealthy members of the middle class had become devoted collectors of seventeenth-century Dutch works, and in French cities the market for less expensive Northern artists and copies of more costly works continued to expand. Mid-eighteenth-century French collectors often purchased French genre paintings to balance their collections of Dutch works.[2] In this environment French genre painters, themselves admirers of seventeenth-century Northern painting, found success by adapting the Northern techniques to a style explicitly their own. While it was impossible to deny the popularity of Dutch paintings, many decried their lowly subjects as well as their inflated prices. The vogue for still lifes and genre paintings by contemporary French artists who took their inspiration from seventeenth-century Northern realist art was equally concerning to those who defended the French academic tradition, as evident in the artist Jean-Baptiste Pierre's plaintive observation: "Mais quel travers ne pourroit-on reprocher à plusieurs artistes et amateurs devenus fanatiques de la Flandre, goût qui perdra la Peinture en France?" [But what has come over so many artists and admirers who have grown obsessed with Flanders, a taste that will be the death of painting in France?].[3]

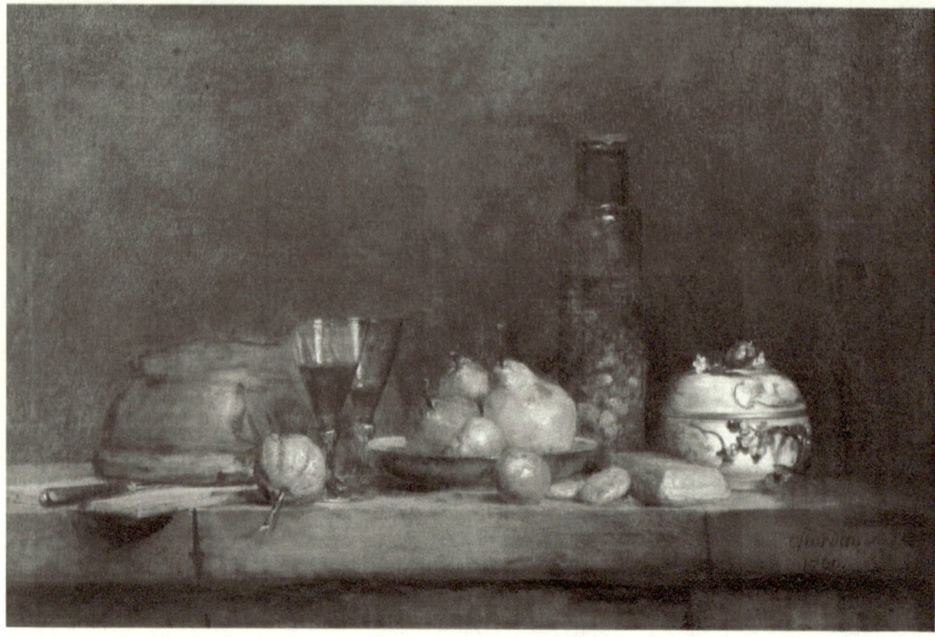

7.1. Jean-Baptiste-Siméon Chardin. *Le bocal d'olives* [*Still Life with Jar of Olives*]. 1760. 71 × 98 cm (27.95 × 38.58 in). Musée du Louvre. Image courtesy Louvre, Paris, France/Bridgeman Images. https://commons.wikimedia.org/wiki/File:Jean_Sim%C3%A9on_Chardin_-_Still-Life_with_Jar_of_Olives_-_WGA04777.jpg.

Chardin's still lifes and genre paintings exemplify the appeal of Netherlandish works for French artists during the eighteenth century. None other than Diderot attests to the impact of Chardin's oeuvre. In his capacity as art critic to the 1763 Salon, Diderot expresses his enthusiasm for the painter's still lifes.[4] I quote here a long passage from Diderot's article for the *Correspondance littéraire*, a cultural newsletter, in which he reviews Chardin's *Bocal d'olives* [*Still Life with Jar of Olives*]:

> C'est celui-ci qui est un peintre; c'est celui-ci qui est un coloriste.
>
> Il y a au Salon plusieurs petits tableaux de Chardin; ils représentent presque tous des fruits avec les accessoires d'un repas. C'est la nature même; les objets sont hors de la toile et d'une vérité à tromper les yeux.

Celui qu'on voit en montant l'escalier mérite surtout l'attention. L'artiste a placé sur une table un vase de vieille porcelaine de la Chine, deux biscuits, un bocal rempli d'olives, une corbeille de fruits, deux verres à moitié pleins de vin, une bigarade avec un pâté.

Pour regarder les tableaux des autres, il semble que j'aie besoin de me faire des yeux; pour voir ceux de Chardin, je n'ai qu'à garder ceux que la nature m'a donnés et m'en bien servir.

Si je destinais mon enfant à la peinture, voilà le tableau que j'achèterais. "Copie-moi cela, lui dirais-je, copie-moi cela encore." Mais peut-être la nature n'est-elle pas plus difficile à copier.

C'est que ce vase de porcelaine est de la porcelaine; c'est que ces olives sont réellement séparées de l'œil par l'eau dans laquelle elles nagent; c'est qu'il n'y a qu'à prendre ces biscuits et les manger, cette bigarade l'ouvrir et la presser, ce verre de vin et le boire, ces fruits et les peler, ce pâté et y mettre le couteau.

C'est celui-ci qui entend l'harmonie des couleurs et des reflets. Ô Chardin! ce n'est pas du blanc, du rouge, du noir que tu broies sur ta palette: c'est la substance même des objets, c'est l'air et la lumière que tu prends à la pointe de ton pinceau et que tu attaches sur la toile.

Après que mon enfant aurait copié et recopié ce morceau, je l'occuperais sur la *Raie dépouillée* du même maître. L'objet est dégoûtant, mais c'est la chair même du poisson, c'est sa peau, c'est son sang.

[This is the one who is a painter; this is the one who is a colourist.

At the Salon there are several small paintings by Chardin; nearly all of them present fruit with other components of a meal. They are completely natural; the objects exist outside the canvas and are so truthful that they deceive the eyes.

The one that you see while going up the staircase, in particular, deserves attention. On a table the artist placed an antique Chinese porcelain vessel, two cookies, a glass jar filled with olives, a basket of fruit, two glasses half filled with wine, a Seville orange with a pâté.

With the works of other painters, I seem to have to acquire new eyes to see them. With Chardin's paintings, I only have to rely on those that nature gave me and use them well.

If I were to want my child to become a painter, this is the painting that I would buy. "Copy that for me," I would tell him, "copy it for me again." Perhaps nature is not more difficult to copy than this image.

This porcelain vessel is clearly made of porcelain; these olives are really separated from the eye by the water that surrounds them; one merely has to reach for these cookies and eat them; this Seville orange to open and squeeze it; this glass of wine to drink it; these fruits to peel them; this pâté to cut through it with the knife.

This is the artist who understands the harmony of colours and reflections. Oh, Chardin! It is not white, red, black pigments that you grind on your palette; it is the very substance of the objects; it is the air and the light that you place on the tip of your brush and attach to the canvas.

Once my child had copied and recopied this piece, I would have him work on the gutted *Skate* by the same master. The object is disgusting, but it is the very flesh of the fish; it is its skin, its blood: the real thing would not affect one any differently.][5]

In his review of Chardin's new work, Diderot champions the painting as a model artistic endeavour: aspiring students should learn to imitate Chardin's image because it depicts things so convincingly that they appear real. Diderot does not attempt a narrative, an account of the various products placed on the table for a particular meal to be consumed by particular individuals. He inventories each item as proof of the painter's descriptive brilliance in recreating the colour, texture, and overall reality effect of the work.[6] For all his obvious emotion, Diderot presents a fairly scientific justification of his pleasure, offering a detailed description of the objects and their individual qualities (although he fails to say much more than that their appearance is so authentic that one is tempted to consume them).

Diderot refers to an earlier work by Chardin, *La raie* [*The Skate*], which features a dramatic gutted skate in the centre.[7] Two more ordinary fish are scattered on the table. A cat stands atop some oysters on the left, next to a plate holding scallions and, behind it, a jar of oil. On the right we see a pitcher, a jar, a pot and a pan, a knife angled out towards the viewer, which trompe l'oeil device recalls many Dutch still life paintings, and a utensil for cooking fish. Diderot again lists the items that he observes, replicating in language the visual inventory that Chardin had created. Diderot's catalogue of items suggests that the painting, its artistry notwithstanding, functioned for him as a system of identities. This enumeration indicates Diderot's dual reliance on observation and classification, even though in his explicit commentary he enthuses about the illusion that Chardin creates.

With *La raie*, however, the artist's descriptive accuracy, the intricacy of his image, does not suffice to account for the most outstanding feature of the painting: the gutted fish. While all the objects in the

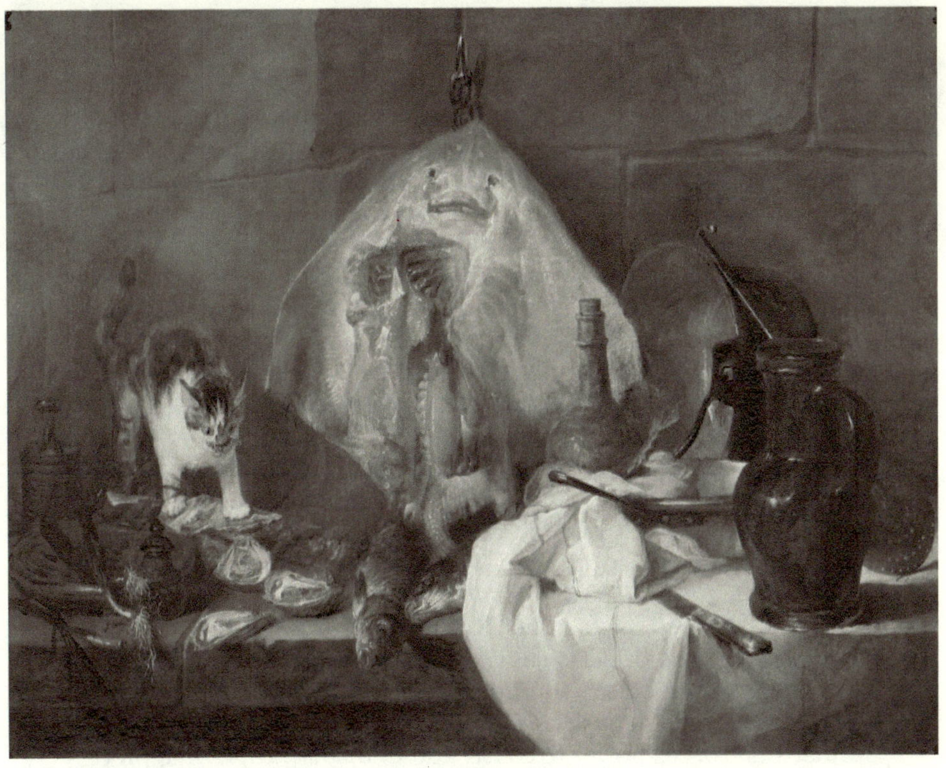

7.2. Jean-Baptiste-Siméon Chardin. *La raie* [*The Skate*]. Ca. 1725–6. 114 × 146 cm (44.88 × 57.48 in). Musée du Louvre. Image courtesy Louvre, Paris, France/Bridgeman Images. https://art.rmngp.fr/fr/library/artworks/jean-baptiste-simeon-chardin_la-raie_huile-sur-toile-ca7dffa4-958b-4cc5-9fca-b43a0d35008e.

still life suggest an empirical emphasis, the splayed fish takes us well beyond an ability to record the surface features of the objects. The exposed entrails of the skate remind us of dissection and Louis XIV's post-mortem.[8] It suggests connections between art and science that we can measure literally as depth perception: the viewer of Chardin's painting peers into the cavity of the fish, just as the officials attending to Louis's body studied his open chest cavity. Throughout Louis's reign the French public witnessed the monarchy's efforts to cover the body of the man with layers of heroic myths, a narrative armour through which to create the image of an all-powerful king, including the transposition of his final remains as relics. Chardin's fish was to be consumed by the viewer's eyes as an object destined for the stove, not as a religious symbol. His table of elements is a table set with things to be used in the preparation of a meal. That meal, however, is not being prepared. The haphazard *mise en place*, items assembled on the table, is an opportunity for the marauding cat that eyes the smaller fish, and not the bloody skate, which both fascinates and horrifies the viewer.

Diderot raises the standard of mimesis, signalling the quality of painted objects so evocative of the real things that they are instantly recognized. According to Diderot, however, the objects in the painting are more than simply naturalistic. They create the illusion, the false (but immensely satisfying) impression, that they are real. He describes effects similar to those of Netherlandish trompe l'oeil paintings that open up an image to suggest that it existed in three dimensions, appearing to share the viewer's space. Other Dutch Golden Age painters also created the illusion of the real through their precise renderings of things. But they, too, fell under the spell of illusion to the degree that they quietly mediated the cultural space allotted to the arts during the reign of Louis XIV. I refer here to the fact that Northern realism entered the French imaginary along with the expansive allegories that the monarchy commissioned. This process went largely undetected by the French, who viewed the Netherlandish works along with portraits of the king as further signs of his power to collect and to display art, as that process involved his efforts to control the flow of goods and ideas. The art that Louis XIV collected, artworks already recognized by others, assumed even greater value when attached to him. It followed that other members of the elite found Netherlandish art a natural part of court culture, art that had long been collected and valued.

Collecting art, like collecting generally, represents a desire to contain and to order. The French understood the realist images from Flanders and Holland to fit in with French and Italian works as part of the display of wealth and power as well as taste. In the French context, Netherlandish realist art represented the same totalizing instinct of the monarchy, the same efforts to identify things as being part of the king, "like" Louis, and therefore contributing to his glory. This notion was in part an illusion, however, because, as my analyses of Dutch paintings have shown, realist descriptions exposed, by virtue of their difference from official French court art, the spectacle of the propaganda machine that moved the arts under the court's patronage. The monarchy created a portrait of the king that was omnipresent but that fact did not ensure the full suspension of disbelief necessary to support its ambitions and ideals. Real portraits of the king were highly visible, yet they cultivated an illusion of power. Dutch art, on the other hand, empowered the viewer via knowledge of the world.

Holland, I have argued, was both a real enemy to the French during the reign of Louis XIV and an idea: a nation that France was dedicating to defeating, and a society that existed in the French imagination as enviably enriched through trade, including many luxury and exotic items that burghers collected as signs of their wealth, their curiosity about the world, and their aesthetic discernment. The French knew that Louis's court set the style for Europe. Many of the richly appointed Dutch Golden Age paintings were designed to appeal to the tastes of wealthy Dutch burghers, who, like the bourgeois in France, wanted to acquire for themselves the aura of power, some of it certainly associated with the French court.[9] From the French vantage point, many themes of Dutch paintings were of lesser importance, and they served in this way to validate for the French a sense of their own superior tastes and way of life. Yet the French continued to collect Northern realist works during Louis's reign, less than they did French and Italian works, but as part of prestigious royal and private collections that continued to expand. The distinctive features of Netherlandish realism resonated in the minds of the French even when they were most preoccupied by the splendorous artwork and elaborate histories developed in praise of Louis XIV. I have argued that as the French elite absorbed the various objects in these paintings, that is, as they registered the descriptive details that were the hallmark of Netherlandish realist art, they also absorbed the patterns of things in the image. The patterns correlate with patterns of thoughts and categories of knowledge. The French monarchy had but one real subject, one pattern, and innumerable layers with which to dress it. With Dutch art the potential for meaning, for the possible relations between things, grew exponentially through the more natural and deliberately random design of their compositions.

For Louis XIV's France the conquest of power was consonant with the manipulation of ideas. The monarchy endeavoured to fill its cultural space with myths and grand narratives through which the real king, possessing a real body destined one day to be studied and dissected, was virtually eclipsed, replaced by his glorious image. Against that sleight of hand, the allegorical hand of many painters and writers working in service to the crown, Dutch art offered a radically different intellectual orientation. Dutch art took the French elsewhere, but not towards ancient heroes. Onstage this *ailleurs* belonged to French tragedy; it was a space of death and lamentation that echoed well after the final act concluded. Within royal palaces and cities emblazoned with works commemorating Louis XIV, Dutch art directed the French towards a space in which people engaged in everyday activities, a world that appeared at once authentic and contingent. The much-vaunted capacity of Dutch art to imitate was, most dramatically for the French court, a disruption to the tightly ordered, singularly predictable logic that the monarchy sought to impose. The French court mythologized the king; Northern realist artists honed their skills to capture and to valorize the real. They cultivated an art of describing that was also a science of knowledge. Committed to recording on the canvas what they observed, to creating the illusion that what they described was real, Netherlandish artists encouraged the beholder to attend to things, and to consider the patterns, structures, and functions that explain the relations between them. The science of description involved more than a privileged subject. It included genre paintings of doctors and the sick with their hurting teeth, and it involved perspectival devices that enabled Dutch artists to perfect their techniques of spatial representation and *enfilade* rooms. Most dramatically, however, the science of description engaged art as a system of knowledge. The science of art refers to categories of ideas that *allowed the world to speak*, as Diderot himself would later see.

Dutch visual culture mediated how the French saw themselves and how they saw the culture that the monarchy built. Louis XIV, his ministers, chief painter, architects, and others in his service actively created a theatre, a visual and textual spectacle, in which nobles, bourgeois, and foreign visitors to the court were expected to conduct their lives. Court culture was based on a logic that continually turned on the figure of the king. During the seventeenth century Dutch painters instead committed to depicting "objects in the light." They presented an interpretation of the world that was as epistemologically open and expansive as the French model was closed and contained. The empirical orientation of Dutch art produced a record of things that was both more grounded and ultimately more determinate than the allegories through which the French advanced the interests of the monarchy. In France the illusion was that the Dutch difference was not really consequential.

Netherlandish realist art challenged the basic assumptions of French court propaganda, namely, the efficacy, over time, of its efforts to sustain the singular paradigm of Louis XIV's absolute supremacy. Dutch artists contributed another vision and another way of cataloguing knowledge, one that would come to be associated with the Enlightenment project. As evident in the conceptualization of the *Encyclopédie*, the *philosophes* assembled knowledge in ways that resisted many prevalent ideas, both political and philosophic, and they developed a new critical apparatus for doing so. It was not a minor sidenote of that process that some of the new ways of thinking ultimately undermined the authority of the monarchy – its real power, and not simply its attempts to harness power through propaganda and patronage of the arts.

No one can mistake Chardin's fruit or fish or other objects in his beautiful still life with the olive jar, its fruits, glasses, and porcelain – all the domestic elements that Diderot elaborates in his description – for a seventeenth-century Dutch work. Chardin's style is distinct. Nonetheless, the story of his cleverness in being admitted to the Académie involved just such confusion over his early still lifes of the skate and the buffet. Placing these paintings in the vestibule rather than in the examination room, as was the custom, Chardin brought his work to the attention of the examiners outside of the space, and outside the context, reserved for the evaluation. Two judges who saw Chardin's paintings before the examination commenced believed them to be the work of a Flemish master.[10]

Diderot praises the illusionistic realism that Chardin in fact shares with his Dutch predecessors. Like the Dutch, Chardin exhibits an uncanny ability to render on the canvas the tactile qualities of objects. Diderot applauds the painting whose illusion is so complete that it requires no effort on the part of the viewer to comprehend it: his eyes register and his mind instantly recognizes the objects that the image contains. Chardin perfected, albeit with a deliberately less refined style, the technique of Dutch painters a century earlier. Diderot suggests that Chardin's paintings evoke the experience of sensory perception – what it feels like for the viewer to experience them.

Within Diderot's description, moreover, the painted objects exist as ideas. They have been translated into visual language, and that translation is rife with challenges, as Diderot explains in his article on the encyclopedia:

> Un vocabulaire universel est un ouvrage dans lequel on se propose de fixer la signification des termes d'une langue, en définissant ceux qui peuvent être définis, par une énumération courte, exacte, claire & précise, ou des qualités ou des idées qu'on y attache. Il n'y a de bonnes définitions

que celles qui rassemblent les attributs essentiels de la chose désignée par le mot. Mais a-t-il été accordé à tout le monde de connoître & d'exposer ces attributs? L'art de bien définir est-il un art si commun? Ne sommes nous pas tous, plus ou moins, dans le cas même des enfans, qui appliquent avec une extrème précision, une infinité de termes à la place desquels il leur seroit absolument impossible de substituer la vraie collection de qualités ou d'idées qu'ils représentent? De-là, combien de difficultés imprévues, quand il s'agit de fixer le sens des expressions les plus communes? On éprouve à tout moment que celles qu'on entend le moins, sont aussi celles dont on se sert le plus.

[A universal vocabulary is a work in which one proposes to set the meaning of terms of a particular language by defining those terms that can be defined, through a short, exact, clear, and precise enumeration either of the characteristics or the ideas that one assigns to them. The only good definitions are those that bring together the essential attributes of the thing designated by the word. But does everyone know and agree on these attributes? Is the art of defining well as common as all that? Aren't we all, more or less, in the same situation as children, who apply with extreme precision innumerable terms in place of which it would be absolutely impossible for them to substitute a true collection of the characteristics or ideas that the terms represent? Thus we are moved to ask: How many unanticipated difficulties can ensue, when we try to set the meaning of the most common expressions? We always feel that the ones that we understand the least are also those that we use the most often.] (Diderot, "Encyclopédie" [5:635])

Despite what he deems the deficiencies of language, Diderot dedicates a textual description to replicating his impressions as a viewer standing before Chardin's image. The translation from the painted object to the beholder's idea (mental image) occurs also because Chardin presents not objects, but rather painted objects that appear as the artist has arranged them and shown them to reflect and absorb the light. For this, too, antecedents existed in seventeenth-century Netherlandish paintings.

Diderot has Chardin outdo even Parrhasius, who deceived the very skilled artist Zeuxis with a trompe l'oeil curtain: "crachez sur le rideau d'Apelle et sur les raisins de Zeuxis. On trompe sans peine un artiste impatient et les animaux sont mauvais juges en peinture" [spit on Apelles's curtain and on Zeuxis's grapes. It is easy to deceive an

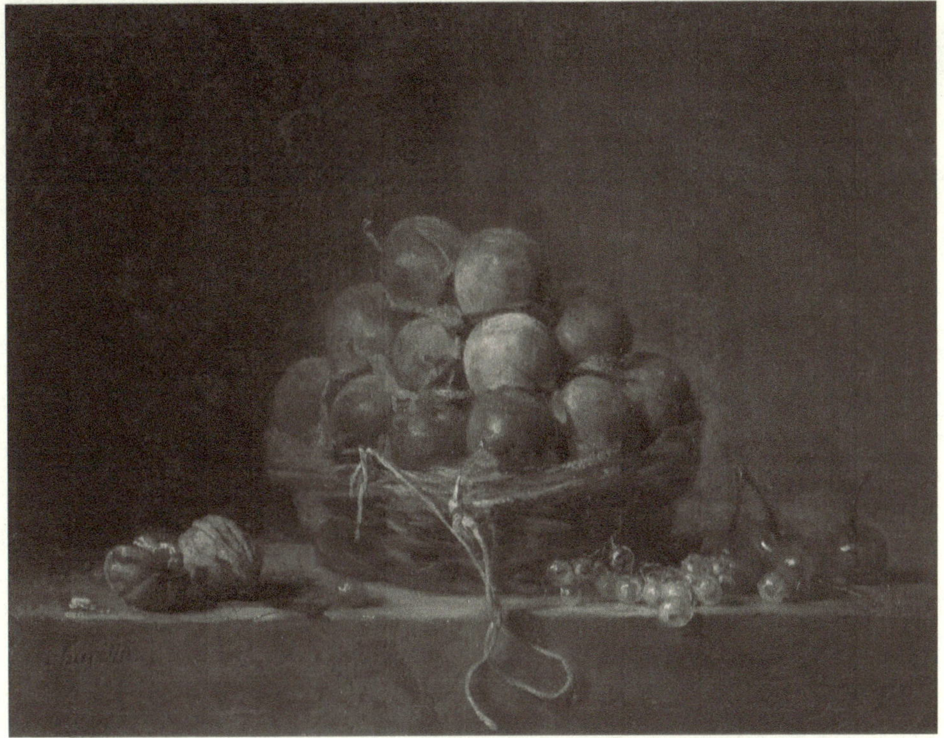

7.3. Jean-Baptiste-Siméon Chardin. *Panier de prunes* [*Basket of Plums*]. 1765. 32.4 × 41.9 cm (12.76 × 16.5 in). Chrysler Museum of Art, Norfolk, Virginia. Image courtesy Ed Pollard, Chrysler Museum of Art. http://chrysler.emuseum.com/objects/23379/basket-of-plums;jsessionid=34D5512806EC27B8CEE5DC8C008285DC?ctx=02e81828-b3e4-45ec-827d-32a821d60182&idx=0.

impatient artist and animals are poor judges of painting] ("Salon de 1763" 196).[11] When Zeuxis, whose own still life was so realistic that birds tried to eat the grapes, attempted to open the curtain on Parrhasius's (not Apelles's) painting, he discovered that it was an integral component of the image, a painted object.[12] Even the disgusting flesh of the skate becomes the subject of Diderot's praise because it creates the illusion that it is real. As a painted object, however, the fish conveys an essence, an idea that, while it recalls an actual skate, delivers a sense of wonder, magic, beauty, and, via the vivisection, disgust – but also a sense of discovery. Diderot's revulsion at the real fish is transformed into admiration before the painted image that evokes the same visceral response, in all senses of the term. Emphasizing Chardin's ability to copy the world, Diderot expresses his approval of the art that appears to substitute for the real. His palpable delight in the process through which his perception of the painted object makes it knowable is a tribute to the empirical rigour of the art. The viewer sees the fish as it would appear in an actual kitchen, but with a greater intensity because the painter has isolated it, exposed its internal organs, and captured its colours and textures. The same descriptive function applies to the olives in the jar and the objects surrounding it; they replicate not only the appearance of real objects but also the beholder's experience of them as things to be seen, touched, smelled, tasted, and heard as they make contact with glasses, plates, and pans.

Chardin's *Panier de prunes* [*Basket of Plums*] resonates for similar reasons. This painting, or a replica that the artist made, which is in private hands, was exhibited at the 1765 Salon.[13] In writing about this image Diderot again called attention the authenticity of Chardin's still life, correlating the painted fruit in the basket with real fruit. Diderot also noted the detail of the string handle, one of many realistic touches in the image. We further observe that the string underscores the humble nature of the image, despite the arrangement of plums into an artful pyramid shape. It also evokes the role of the creator: the artist who paints the string, the person who made the basket, the person who carried it, and the viewer whose mind moves from one of these agents to the other. The simplicity of this image is, like fine Dutch paintings, deceptive. Chardin lavishes attention on the effects of the light, which modify the shading of the fruit. The opalescent white currents evoke pearls because of the way the artist captures their lustrous sheen.[14] Yet Chardin's plum still life has none of the lavishness of de Heem's *Fruits et riche vaisselle sur une table*. Chardin captures in miniature, and thus effectively controls, the world as one might live it, if one shared his sensibilities.

Even French academics recognized the effectiveness of images that precisely imitate the real. Roger de Piles, the leading theoretician of the Academy, observed in 1708: "plus la Peinture imite fortement & fidelement la nature, plus elle nous conduit rapidement & directement vers sa fin, qui est de séduire nos yeux" [the more that painting imitates nature emphatically and faithfully, the more it leads us rapidly and directly towards its goal, which is to seduce our eyes].[15] We have seen that Netherlandish realism not only "seduces the eyes" but also entices the mind. Dutch Golden Age art invites the viewer to experience the pleasure of things meticulously portrayed through a reliance on geometric perspective and the effective use of line, colour, and volume. Like Dutch artists, Chardin in his still lifes allows one to be so absorbed in the scene that it appears real, yet he presents a very particular combination of elements that gives definition to ordinary experience. With *Panier de prunes* the intrinsic connection between nature and culture is subsumed into a work of art that uses description as a strategy for knowing. The invisible hand that pulls the string and places it *just so* is the hand of a master who dares the viewer not to examine the skate closely; who engages the viewer with the various textures of oranges, water, olives, and paté; and who seduces the viewer through the sculptured beauty of a basket of perfect plums.

What seduces, as Diderot's own reaction demonstrates, is the artist's combination of imitation and inspiration. That same reality-based illusion did not sustain itself in the culture that grew around Louis XIV. The court created and disseminated an idealized image of the king. His courtiers knew how spectacle worked, and they had much to gain from the illusion. Nonetheless, many criticized the king, his policies, and the cultivation of appearances that corrupted relations and obscured the truth. These voices penetrated some of the court's pomp to expose the art of statecraft, the manipulation of identities that occurred in the actual political theatre that was Versailles. More discretely, and with no intent to critique, Dutch art likewise exposed the French to another way of seeing and understanding what they saw.

Crowning Glories has focused on the contribution of realist painting from Flanders and Holland to the French imaginary during Louis XIV's reign. Although the artists and the dealers who sold Netherlandish realist works to French collectors intended no revolution and started none during this period, this art occupies a significant place within the history of knowledge as it extends from seventeenth-century court culture to the *Encyclopédie* in the eighteenth century. Perceived as a system for ordering thoughts, Northern realist art effectively refashioned the order of things imposed by French court culture. Whether they viewed Dutch paintings directly or heard them described; whether they simply accepted *as French* the realist techniques that Flemish artists like van der Meulen produced to record Louis XIV's history; or whether they noted the particular success of Flemish art in France, Louis's subjects regularly encountered a way of recording the world that relied on direct observation. The French courtier did not need to attend directly to the formal techniques of painting or literature to perceive how in France the arts grounded in myth and history differed from Dutch scenes of private homes and even exuberant tavern scenes, all remarkable for their mimetic precision. Unless they were artists, the French were likely unconcerned with the compositional design of images, and even artists knew that their success depended on pleasing the monarch by adopting the themes and styles that he and his ministers judged appropriate to honour him. Yet the history of ideas leading to the Enlightenment would demonstrate unequivocally that Netherlandish art focused on individual identities and a naturalistic technique formed part of the legacy of this period for France, just as it did for Flanders and Holland.

Art is not science, but the arts, too, record and catalogue information. Devoted to describing their world, Northern painters reinforced the impulse to see and to order perceptions. As we move from Dutch realism to Chardin's fish, olives, and plums, we are tracing a path away from the spectacle of Versailles and its gardens. Some Netherlandish paintings in France's royal palaces proved uncontroversial and unremarkable, while others, such as de Heem's *Fruits et riche vaisselle sur une table* garnered great acclaim. The very "ordinary" scenes that the French associated with the Northern realist tradition, including still lifes, portraits, landscapes, cityscapes, and genre scenes, also, extraordinarily, became part of Louis XIV's legacy. Examples of this tradition were discussed by French connoisseurs, academicians, strollers in Paris markets, and tourists alike. Seventeenth-century Dutch art continued inexorably, but not without resistance, to encourage the French towards Enlightenment thought. Rooted in observations of the real, Dutch art edged French court society towards the broad perspective and the bold ambitions of Diderot and his contemporaries. Let there be no illusion about that.

Notes

Introduction

1 Peter Burke, *The Fabrication of Louis XIV* (New Haven, CT: Yale University Press, 1992) analyses these and other examples of the king's image that explain the relationship between art and power. The king's image has been the subject of much scholarly attention since the seminal work by Ernst Kantorowicz, *The King's Two Bodies: A Study in Medieval Political Theology* (Princeton, NJ: Princeton University Press, 1957). Other critical studies include Louis Marin, *Le portrait du roi* (Paris: Editions de Minuit, 1981); Jean-Marie Apostolidès, *Le roi-machine: Spectacle et politique au temps de Louis XIV* (Paris: Editions de Minuit, 1981); Hélène Merlin Kajman, *L'absolutisme dans les lettres et la théorie des deux corps: Passions et politique* (Paris: Honoré Champion, 2000); Mitchell Greenberg, *Baroque Bodies: Psychoanalysis and the Culture of French Absolutism* (Ithaca, NY: Cornell University Press, 2001); Nicolas Milovanovic and Alexandre Maral, eds., *Louis XIV: L'homme et le roi* (Paris: Skira Flammarion, 2009); Joël Cornette, *La mort de Louis XIV 1er septembre 1715: Apogée et crépuscule de la royauté* (Paris: Gallimard, 2015).

2 Norbert Elias argues that Louis XIV asserted his authority by manipulating the social hierarchy through which members of the elite derived their sense of identity and importance (*La société de cour* [Paris: Flammarion, 2008]). See also Jay M. Smith, *The Culture of Merit: Nobility, Royal Service, and the Making of Absolute Monarchy in France, 1600–1789* (Ann Arbor: University of Michigan Press, 1996).

3 See Louis de Rouvroy, Duc de Saint-Simon, *Mémoires complets et authentiques du Duc de Saint-Simon*, 20 vols (Paris: Hachette, 1856–8), vol. 13, ch. 5: http://rouvroy.medusis.com/docs/1305.html; English,

vol. 11, ch. 78: http://www.gutenberg.org/ebooks/3875?msg=welcome_stranger#link2HCH0078.

4 See John Michael Montias, *Vermeer and His Milieu: A Web of Social History* (Princeton, NJ: Princeton University Press, 1989).

5 Inherited from antiquity and codified by André Félibien, secretary of the *Académie royale de peinture et de sculpture* [The Royal Academy of Painting and Sculpture], the hierarchy of genres ranked history painting first (religious, mythological, or contemporary history), followed by portraiture, genre painting, landscapes, and still lifes. See André Félibien, *Conférences de L'Académie royale de peinture et de sculpture, pendant l'année 1667* (Paris: F. Léonard, 1668).

6 Mariët Westermann refers to the long seventeenth century ending in 1718 with the publication of Arnold Houbraken's biographies of Dutch and Flemish artists (*A Worldly Art: The Dutch Republic 1585–1718* [New Haven, CT: Yale University Press, 2005], 10).

7 The Spanish Netherlands refers to the States of the Holy Roman Empire in the Low Countries held by the Spanish Crown during the period 1581–1714.

8 Hans Vlieghe explains that while the designation "Flemish" refers to the cultural life of all the Southern Netherlands, southern "Flemish" and northern "Dutch" artists were closely associated: "the artists who were active in the Southern Netherlands between 1585 and 1700 must have felt that only to a limited extent did they belong to an artistic tradition that was any different from that in the Northern Netherlands. This is most clearly shown by the fact that both branches of the history of art of the Low Countries are regarded as a single entity by seventeenth-century art-historiography" (*Flemish Art and Architecture, 1585–1700*, trans. Alastair and Cora Weir [New Haven, CT: Yale University Press, 2004], 1). He further notes that some artists worked in both parts of the Netherlands, and that many travelled to Rome, with which city they were identified for parts or all of their careers.

9 By the time Louis XIV moved the court to Versailles, works by Italian artists, especially Venetian and Bolognese, dominated the royal collection along with paintings by Poussin, who was the best represented among the French artists. Netherlandish works, however, had a comparatively small but distinct role in the royal collection. See Arnauld Brejon de Lavergnée, ed., *L'inventaire Le Brun de 1683: La collection des tableaux de Louis XIV* (Paris: Editions de la Réunion des musées nationaux, 1987); and Antoine Schnapper, *Curieux du Grand Siècle: Collections et collectionneurs dans la France du XVIIe siècle*, vol. 2, *Œuvres d'art* (Paris: Flammarion, 2005).

10 I am working at the intersection of history, art history, literature, and epistemology. I remain indebted to Christopher Braider's earlier study of the importance of pictorial naturalism in shaping a model of understanding based on empirical observation, *Refiguring the Real: Picture and Modernity in Word and Image, 1400–1700* (Princeton, NJ: Princeton University Press, 1993). Braider masterfully analyses the critical role of Northern "descriptive art" in Western experience from the Renaissance onwards. His study dedicates scant attention to the image of Louis XIV. I offer a concentrated view of the French court during Louis's reign, examining how Northern descriptive art subverts the monarchy's hold on power and knowledge.

11 See Burke, *Fabrication*. The "Petite Académie" [Small Academy], which became the Académie royale des inscriptions et médailles [Royal Academy of Inscriptions and Medals] upon its official creation by Colbert in 1663, had the express mission of establishing the inscriptions and mottos for the monuments and medals issued to honour Louis XIV. The Academy's charter represents the clear ambitions of the court to promote the king's objectives and image. Many other works produced in this period also supported the monarchy's goals. Classical playwrights Corneille, Molière, and Racine all celebrated the king's law, as I discuss in chapter 3. Although Louis XIV never appeared as a character in these plays, the sovereign's role was unmistakably tied to the consolidation of power under the French king, who was the privileged referent for these dramas.

12 This approach is consistent with current investigations into the French court of Louis XIV that integrate developments from different fields, including literature, philosophy/science, and art, as well as studies of foreign influences that affect how the French see themselves, their modes of expression, and their capacity for conceptualizing the world. See Faith E. Beasley, *Versailles Meets the Taj Mahal: François Bernier, Marguerite de la Sablière, and Enlightening Conversations in Seventeenth-Century France* (Toronto: University of Toronto Press, 2018).

13 Michel Foucault, *Les mots et les choses: Une archéologie des sciences humaines* (Paris: Gallimard, 1990); Peter Burke, *A Social History of Knowledge: From Gutenberg to Diderot* (Cambridge: Polity Press, 2000); Ann Blair, *Too Much to Know: Managing Scholarly Information before the Modern Age* (New Haven, CT: Yale University Press, 2010); Jacob Soll, *The Information Master: Jean-Baptiste Colbert's Secret State Intelligence System* (Ann Arbor: University of Michigan Press: 2011).

14 In a recent study of forms that organize both the arts and political life, Caroline Levine, *Forms: Whole, Rhythm, Hierarchy, Network* (Princeton,

NJ: Princeton University Press, 2017), analyses how shapes, patterns, and relations of part to whole challenge conventional analytic models in literary and cultural studies.

15 See John Loughman and John Michael Montias, *Public and Private Spaces: Works of Art in Seventeenth-Century Dutch Houses* (Zwolle, Netherlands: Waanders, 2001).

16 Marin, *Portrait du roi*; Burke, *Fabrication*.

17 Balthasar de Monconys, *Journal des voyages de Monsieur de Monconys ... où les sçavants trouveront un nombre infini de nouveautez, en machines de mathématique, expériences physiques, raisonnemens de la belle philosophie, curiositez de chymie, et conversations des illustres de ce siècle ... publié par le Sr de Liergues, son fils*. 3 parts. Lyon: H. Boissat and G. Remeus, 1665–6, II,149.

18 Elisabeth de Bièvre observes that the baker was probably Hendrik van Buyten, whose estate was one of the largest in Delft at the time. He owned a Vermeer as well as works by other Delft painters. De Bièvre further notes that a few days after this visit Monconys purchased *Woman in a Window* by Dou (*Dutch Art and Urban Cultures 1200–1700* [New Haven, CT: Yale University Press, 2015], 161).

19 The shared influences and rivalries of these artists was the subject of a recent exhibition. See Adriaan E. Waiboer, ed., with Arthur K. Wheelock, Jr. and Blaise Ducos, *Vermeer and the Masters of Genre Painting: Inspiration and Rivalry* (New Haven, CT: Yale University Press, 2017).

20 Schnapper, 23, notes that Félibien criticized the "attachment exclusif et excessif à la nature" [exclusive and excessive dedication to imitating nature], while Abraham Bosse admired it. Schnapper adds that although the French were divided over the proper approach to history paintings, they agreed that Northern realism lent itself well to landscapes.

21 This idea builds on the empirical emphasis of Francis Bacon, in England, and the scientific method of René Descartes, in France.

22 On tobacco, see Julie Hochstrasser, *Still Life and Trade in the Dutch Golden Age* (New Haven, CT: Yale University Press, 2007), 171–87.

23 Foucault's seminal analysis of Velázquez's *Meninas* in *Les mots et les choses* sets the stage for his essentially discursive analysis of the classical episteme. See my *Classical Model: Literature and Knowledge in Seventeenth-Century France* (Ithaca, NY: Cornell University Press, 1996), 24–43.

24 In an innovative and compelling study, Christopher Braider focuses on subjectivity as it emerges from Descartes's mind-body dualism to present a more chaotic and less monolithic concept of the classical period (*The Matter of Mind: Reason and Experience in the Age of Descartes* [Toronto: University

of Toronto Press, 2011]). I share an abiding sense that any "single model" understanding of the classical age in France neglects essential tensions that shape knowledge in this period (see my *Classical Knowledge*and *Tables of Knowledge: Descartes in Vermeer's Studio* [Ithaca, NY: Cornell University Press, 2006]). Studying the French/Dutch dynamic within French culture during Louis's reign, *Crowning Glories* interrogates an epistemological dilemma that emerges from a comparison of two distinct forms of logical inquiry that coexisted within the French court: the French analogic model and the Northern realist model based on differences.

25 I analyse images and texts independently, considering each example to function as a system of thought. Questions concerning narrative sources for pictorial compositions have long intrigued scholars. Exploring the semiotic relation of images to texts, Norman Bryson argues that Le Brun's codification of expressions served as a model for painting through the eighteenth century (*Word and Image: French Painting of the Ancien Régime* [Cambridge: Cambridge University Press, 1983]). Studying Rembrandt's pictorial and narrative influences, Svetlana Alpers demonstrates reciprocal prioritization: images influence other images; texts influence images (*Rembrandt's Enterprise: The Studio and The Market* [Chicago: University of Chicago Press, 1995]).

26 See Simon Schama, *The Embarrassment of Riches: An Interpretation of Dutch Culture in the Golden Age* (New York: Vintage, 1997).

27 The French emphasis on narrative refers to histories both real and fictional that comprise multiple events. It also includes portraits of the king, all of which refer either explicitly or implicitly to ancient gods and heroes, that is, to a long tradition of glorious deeds that shapes the image of Louis XIV. Not only Netherlandish still lifes but also genre paintings convey themes without referencing a specific sequence of events. Action depicted in genre paintings is typically limited in focus and it serves to inform ideas such as vanity, love, motherhood, music, letter writing, etc. as part of a description of daily life.

28 See Martin Kemp, *The Science of Art: Optical Themes in Western Art from Brunelleschi to Seurat* (New Haven, CT: Yale University Press, 1992) and *Visualizations: The Nature Book of Art and Science* (Oxford: Oxford University Press, 2000); and, for Dutch Golden Age painting, Svetlana Alpers, *The Art of Describing: Dutch Art in the Seventeenth Century* (Chicago: University of Chicago Press, 1984). I return below to her seminal study.

29 See M.M. Slaughter, *Universal Languages and Scientific Taxonomy in the Seventeenth Century* (Cambridge: Cambridge University Press, 1982); and Eric Jorink, *Reading the Book of Nature in the Dutch Golden Age, 1575–1715*, trans. Peter Mason (Leiden: Brill, 2010).

30 Louis XIV, "Supplément pour l'année 1666," in *Mémoires pour l'instruction du dauphin*, ed. C. Dreyss, vol. 2 (Paris: Didier, 1860), 15: https://books.google.com/books?id=flv8brYaWaoC&printsec=frontcover&vq=ob%C3%A9issance&source=gbs_ge_summary_r&cad=0#v=onepage&q=ob%C3%A9issance&f=false.

31 As Braider enumerates, this period "remained an era of ceaseless cultural combat, pitting Cartesians against Thomists, *précieux* against classicists [*Querelle des femmes*], *esprits forts* [*libertines*] against *honnêtes gens* ... Jansenists against Jésuits, *anciens* against *modernes*" (*Matter of Mind*, 17).

32 With the expansion of Versailles, the magnificence of royal spectacle affected all the arts. See Robert W. Berger, *A Royal Passion: Louis XIV as Patron of Architecture* (Cambridge: Cambridge University Press, 1994); Philippe Beaussant, *Les plaisirs de Versailles: Théâtre et musique* (Paris: Fayard, 1996); Chandra Mukerji, *Territorial Ambitions and the Gardens of Versailles* (Cambridge: Cambridge University Press, 1997); Claire Goldstein, *Vaux and Versailles: The Appropriations, Erasures, and Accidents that Made Modern France* (Philadelphia: University of Pennsylvania Press, 2008); Jacques Levron, *La cour de Versailles aux* XVIIe *et* XVIIIe *siècles* (Paris: Perrin, 2010), Gaëlle Lafage, *Charles Le Brun décorateur de fêtes* (Rennes: Presses Universitaires de Rennes, 2015).

33 François Duc de La Rochefoucauld, *Maximes et Réflexions morales* (1664), 2: https://fr.wikisource.org/wiki/Maximes.

34 Jean de La Bruyère, "Des femmes" 48.VIII, p. 113, Les caractères *ou* Les moeurs de ce siècle *précédé des* Caractères *de Théophraste, traduits du grec par La Bruyère*, ed. Robert Garapon (Paris: Classiques Garnier 1969), https://fr.wikisource.org/wiki/Les_Caract%C3%A8res/Des_femmes. See Louise Horowitz, *Love and Language: A Study of the Classical French Moralist Writers* (Cleveland: Ohio State University Press, 1977); Louis van Delft, *Le moraliste classique: Essai de définition et de typologie* (Geneva: Droz, 1982); Michael Moriarty, *Taste and Ideology in Seventeenth-Century France* (Cambridge: Cambridge University Press, 1988).

35 Not only did France incur substantial debts from Louis XIV's wars but also many nobles resented being excluded from substantive political decisions as the king consolidated his power.

36 See Philip Conisbee, ed., *Georges de La Tour and His World* (New Haven, CT: Yale University Press, 1996); Jacques Thuillier, *Georges de La Tour* (Paris: Flammarion, 2003); and Dalia Judovitz, *Georges de La Tour and the Enigma of the Visible* (New York: Fordham University Press, 2017).

37 Alpers, *Rembrandt's Enterprise*, demonstrates that the great master of the Dutch Golden Age far exceeded "the art of describing," the title of her

groundbreaking 1984 book, which function subtends my analysis of the formation of knowledge.

38 See Michael Werner and Bénédicte Zimmermann, "Beyond Comparison: *Histoire croisée* and The Challenge of Reflexivity," *History and Theory* 45, no. 1 (February 2006): 30–50, https://www.jstor.org/stable/3590723.

39 Tulip Mania in Holland, which scholars consider the first case of an economic bubble, produced speculation on tulip bulbs at exorbitant levels, followed by a dramatic collapse of the market in February 1637. See Anna Pavord, *The Tulip: The Story of a Flower That Has Made Men Mad* (London: Bloomsbury, 2004).

Chapter 1

1 See Eric Coatalem, ed., *La nature morte française au XVIIe siècle/17th-Century Still Life Painting in France* (Dijon: Editions Faton, 2015); Helen Chastain Sowa, *Louise Moillon, Seventeenth-Century Still Life Artist: An Illustrated Biography* (Chicago: Chateau Publications, 1998); and Michel Faré, *Le grand siècle de la nature morte en France: Le XVIIe siècle* (Fribourg: Office du livre, 1974).

2 Hilliard T. Goldfarb, "Meditations on Still Life Painting in Seventeenth-Century France," in Coatalem, 26–9 (French trans. "Méditations sur la peinture de la nature morte en France au XVIIe siècle," J. Faton, 10–25). On Picart, see Faré, 84–98.

3 Alexis Merle du Bourg, *Peter Paul Rubens et la France 1600–1640* (Villeneuve-d'Ascq, France: Presses Universitaires de Septentrion, 2004), 124–5, dates the van Boucle *Marchande de fruits* as 1635–45 based on the woman's French-styled clothing. Comparing several paintings from the period devoted to the fruit market theme, Merle du Bourg characterizes van Boucle's style as more restrained and therefore more French (Alexis Merle du Bourg, "Major Northern Influence," in Coatalem, 383–4, and in French with illustrations, "L'apport substantiel du Nord," 366–7).

4 See https://www.louvre.fr/en/oeuvre-notices/table-desserts for information concerning the iconographical allusions contained in the painting.

5 Schama underscores the Dutch urge to classify, evidence for which he finds in a range of items from scientific taxonomies, including a tulip classification system, through paintings. My analysis of Dutch Golden Age paintings builds on a notion of classification that I developed in *Tables of Knowledge*. I study paintings by Vermeer and his contemporaries to demonstrate that if, as Descartes famously postulated, truth can be acquired through the a rigorous application of the scientific method, the

recording of truth, the description of what science uncovers, is a far more vexed and uncertain undertaking.

6 For a detailed study of individual collectors and collections during this period, see Schnapper.

7 Colbert served as minister in 1661–83, an expansive role that included Surintendant des Bâtiments, arts et manufactures [Director-General of Building, Arts, and Factories] (1664–83) and Contrôleur général des finances [Controller-General of Finances] (1665–83), among other governmental functions.

8 When in 1662 Colbert took over as a representative of the crown, it became officially known as La Manufacture Royale des Meubles de la Couronne [Royal Factory of Furniture for the Crown].

9 Thomas W. Gaehtgens, "The Arts in the Service of the King's Glory," in *A Kingdom of Images: French Prints in the Age of Louis XIV, 1660–1715*, ed. Peter Fuhring, Louis Marchesano, Rémi Mathis, and Vanessa Selbach (Los Angeles: Getty Publications, 2015), 5.

10 Colbert also oversaw an extensive publishing project known as the Cabinet du Roi [King's Cabinet] (ca. 1665–70) to circulate prints of the works in the king's collection (excluding portraits of the king and the royal family). He commissioned skilled French printmakers to produce hundreds of large and detailed engravings of the royal collections and accomplishments. Beginning in 1670, some of these print series were combined with descriptive texts and published as books, while others were bound without textual commentary and distributed.

11 Moving beyond the iconographical tradition, Alpers argues that scientific advances with optical devices (microscopes, lenses, camera obscura) help to explain the descriptive emphasis of seventeenth-century Dutch artists (*Art of Describing*). Rather than illustrate an existing narrative from myths and histories, Dutch art presents the world to the viewer seemingly *in situ*, but with a heightened emphasis on the colours and textures of objects. I posit that the integrity of Dutch images depends not only on the accuracy of the painter's imitation but also on the open patterns of objects, often dispersed throughout the image with deliberate randomness, through which the viewer comes to know the world.

12 Leon Battista Alberti, *De pictura and De statua*, ed. and trans. Cecil Grayson (London: Phaidon, 1972). See also Louis Marchesano and Christian Michel, eds., *Printing the Grand Manner: Charles Le Brun and Monumental Prints in the Age of Louis XIV* (Los Angeles: Getty Publications, 2010).

13 André Félibien, *Conférences de l'Académie royale de peinture et de sculpture* (Paris: François Léonard, 1668; reprint London: David Mortier, 1705), https://gallica.bnf.fr/ark:/12148/bpt6k98018158.

14 French art theory required reverence for the classics. This *grand goût* generally caused the French to look down on Netherlandish art. Frans Grijzenhout notes that Roger de Piles made allowances for Rubens, the great colorist who favored lofty subjects, and, to a lesser degree, Rembrandt, for his chiaroscuro ("Between Reason and Sensitivity: Foreign Views of Dutch Painting, 1660–1800," in *The Golden Age of Dutch Painting in Historical Perspective*, ed. Frans Grijzenhout and Henk van Veen, trans. Andrew McCormick [Cambridge: Cambridge University Press, 1999], 13–14).

15 See Neil De Marchi and Hans J. Van Miegroet, "Comment les tableaux des anciens Pays-Bas ont envahi le marché parisien/How Netherlandish Paintings Came to Paris," in *Rubens, Van Dyck, Jordaens et les autres: peintures baroques flamandes aux musées royaux des beaux-arts de Belgique/ Flemish Baroque Paintings from the Royal Museums of Fine Arts of Belgium* (Paris: Musée Marmottan, 2012), 28–47/2–19.

16 Schnapper, 88–89 and 91–95. See also Neil De Marchi and Hans J. Van Miegroet, "Novelty and Fashion Circuits in the Mid-Seventeenth-Century Antwerp-Paris Trade," *Journal of Medieval and Early Modern Studies* 28, no. 1 (Winter 1998): 201–46.

17 Schnapper observes that initially Louis manifested little interest in painting. As the royal collection grew, however, and plans for Versailles developed, the arts became increasingly engaging for the king (286–87).

18 Charles Le Brun, *L'inventaire Le Brun de 1643: La collection des tableaux de Louis XIV*, ed. Arnauld Brejon de Lavergnée (Paris: Réunion des Musées nationaux, 1987). For a comparative study of the various schools represented, see Brejon de Lavergnée's introduction.

19 Olivier Bonfait, "Les collections picturales des financiers à la fin du règne de Louis XIV," *XVIIe siècle* 151 (avril-juin 1986): 125–51.

20 Ibid., 132. Bonfait specifies that the "Northern School" refers to painters from Flanders and Holland. He compares the financiers' collections to those of the *parlementaires*, who collected principally Italian and French works.

21 Ibid., fig. 8, "Le goût pictural dans les collections parisiennes d'après les inventaires après décès: A. Noblesse et bourgeoisie: 1710–1720" ["Pictorial Tastes in Parisian Collections according to Post-Mortem Inventories: A. Nobility and Bourgeoisie: 1710–1720"],146. Bonfait indicates that bourgeois collections included 42 per cent works by French artists; 28 per cent by Italian artists; and 30 per cent by Northern artists, whereas noble collections contained 33 per cent works by French artists; 22 per cent works by Italian artists, and 44 per cent works by Northern artists.

22 Ibid., fig. 5, "La fréquence des thèmes dans les collections financières et parlementaires" ["Number of Paintings Ranked by Subject in the Collections of Financiers and *Parlementaires*"], 144.

23 Maxime Préaud observes that prints included "scholarly compositions and monumental portraits, which served as indexes of one's wealth and integration into superior social milieus," and also lesser-priced almanacs "primarily intended for the bourgeoisie rather than the lower classes" ("Printmaking under Louis XIV," in Fuhring et al., *Kingdom of Images*, 13). Referring to the Cabinet du roi, Préaud explains that prints served to disseminate advances in science and also as diplomatic gifts (11).

24 Thomas W. Gaehtgens, "Genre Painting in Eighteenth-Century Collections," in *The Age of Watteau, Chardin, and Fragonard: Masterpieces of French Genre Painting*, ed. Colin B. Bailey (New Haven, CT: Yale University Press, 2003), 80. Gaehtgens argues that the popularity of these works explains in part the increased production of French genre paintings in the eighteenth century.

25 Sophie Raux observes that since the since the fifteenth century the largest segment of the market corresponded not to commissioned work or patronage, which were the province of the upper class, but rather to a more expansive distribution among various classes at home and abroad, notably in Paris ("Circulation, Distribution, and Consumption of Antwerp Paintings in the Markets of the Southern Netherlands and Northern France [1570–1680]," in *Moving Pictures: Intra-European Trade in Images, 16th–18th Centuries*, ed. Neil De Marchi and Sophie Raux [Turnhout, Belgium: Brepols, 2014], 94). In the early sixteenth century, Antwerp supported an "*on spec* market at both the local and international level" (Raux 97). By the end of that century Antwerp painters who "engaged in wholesale exports ... brought unprecedented diversity to picture type, genre, quality, and price" (Raux, 116–17).

26 Bonfait, "Collections picturales de financiers," 131, indicates that the presence of royal portraits in financiers' and magistrates' collections was "considerable" [considerable], with the king's portrait appearing in half of the inventories.

27 Westermann describes as "wordly" Dutch artists' depictions of their society and land "with an unprecedented concern for a 'reality effect'" (7). The Dutch were also worldly in the sense of belonging to a global economy. See Michael North, *Art and Commerce in the Dutch Golden Age*, trans. Catherine Hill (New Haven, CT: Yale University Press, 1997); and Schama.

28 See Jonathan Israel's comprehensive history of Holland, *The Dutch Republic: Its Rise, Greatness, and Fall 1477–1806* (Oxford: Oxford University Press, 1995).

29 Jonathan Israel notes that the French fought the British on the borders of New York and Canada; the Dutch captured Pondicherry, India, from the French in 1693 and held it until 1699; and the French and Spanish fought in the Caribbean ("The Emerging Empire: The Continental Perspective, 1650–1713," in *The Origins of Empire: British Overseas Enterprise to the Close of the Seventeenth Century. The Oxford History of the British Empire*, vol. 1, ed. Nicholas Canny [Oxford: Oxford University Press, 2001], 441).

30 See Israel, *Dutch Republic*; Joël Cornette, *Le roi de guerre: Essai sur la souveraineté dans la France du Grand Siècle* (Paris: Payot, 2010); and Hervé Hasquin, *Louis XIV face à l'Europe du Nord: L'absolutisme vaincu par les libertés* (Brussels: Editions Racine, 2005).

31 See Eric Sluijter, "On Brabant Rubbish, Economic Competition, Artistic Rivalry, and the Growth of the Market for Paintings in the First Decades of the Seventeenth Century," trans. Jennifer Kilian and Katy Kist; footnotes by author, *JHNA* 1, no. 2 (Summer 2009): https://jhna.org/articles/brabant-rubbish-economic-competition-artistic-rivalry-growth-market-paintings-first-decades-seventeenth-century/.

32 Westermann notes that although William I's sons built up "a fine Stadhouder's court in the Hague" whose "splendor made claims for the Oranges as natural rulers of the Dutch Republic, the Stadhouders were always dependent on the finances and political designs of the States-General, controlled primarily by the upper-middle-class regents from the cities rather than land-based nobles" (*Worldly Art*, 21).

33 J.L. Price, *Culture and Society in the Dutch Republic during the 17th Century* (London: Batsford, 1974), 141–2. See also Loughman and Montias; John Michael Montias, *Artists and Artisans in Delft: A Socio-Economic Study of the Seventeenth Century* (Princeton, NJ: Princeton University Press, 1982); North; Schama; and Westermann.

34 See Nicole de Reynies, "Les lissiers flamands en France au XVIIe siècle, et considérations sur leurs marques," in *Flemish Tapestry Weavers Abroad: Emigration and the Founding of Manufactories in Europe*, ed. Guy Delmarcel (Leuven, Belgium: Leuven University Press, 2002), 208–11.

35 Representation in this way conditions a response; it shapes knowledge.

36 Northern artists also had a tradition of allegorical expression and significant religious painting. Yet even these, as Jan Brueghel the Elder's *Allegory of Spring* (1616) exemplifies, can offer a veritable catalogue of nature. Examining the extensive flora represented in this image, Anna

Pavord observes that the scene "shows similar tulips growing in a garden border. There is just one of each kind, including a showy bicolour splayed open to show the regular markings of red round the edges of the white petals. Fleurs-de-lys, tree peonies, anemones, a grand *Fritillaria imperialis*, and aquilegias are the tulips' companions" (82).

37 Alpers argues that Dutch artists record the world on the surface of the canvas much like the retina of the eye records visual stimuli (*Art of Describing*, chapter 2). A painting does not function literally as a copy of the retinal image or of the real. Effects of colour, including light and shadow, as well as the selection and arrangement of objects in the painting, must be adjusted to heighten the "reality effect."

38 Alpers contrasts the descriptive function of Dutch art with the narrative tradition devoted to scenes from myths, the Bible, and history (*Art of Describing*).

39 http://collections.chateauversailles.fr/?permid=permobj_5d962739-2716-402c-9832-20497a55523e#f4bbc9cd-0252-498a-842c-bc238ec546ed.

40 Ibid.

41 See Claudia Salvi, *D'après nature: La nature morte en France au XVIIe siècle* (Waterloo, Belgium: La Renaissance du livre, 2000); Thierry Bajou, *La peinture à Versailles, le XVIIe siècle* (Paris: Réunion des musées nationaux, 1998); and Thierry Bajou, *Les peintres du roi, 1648–1793* (Paris: Réunion des musées nationaux, 2000).

42 See Louis Marin, *La parole mangée et autres essais théologico-politiques* (Paris: Klincksieck, 1986); Abby E. Zanger, *Scenes from the Marriage of Louis XIV: Nuptial Fictions and the Making of Absolutist Power* (Stanford, CA: Stanford University Press, 1997).

43 http://collections.chateauversailles.fr/#0526b6cd-b4a7-41e4-88f4-9531dcda4252.

44 Julie Hochstrasser, "'Still-staende dingen': Picturing Objects in the Dutch Golden Age," in *Early Modern Things: Objects and Their Histories, 1500–1800*, ed. Paula Findlen (New York: Routledge, 2013), 111–12.

45 See Sam Segal, *Flowers and Nature: Netherlandish Flower Painting of Four Centuries* (The Hague: SDU Publishers, 1990); Norbert Schneider, *Still Life: Still Life Painting in the Early Modern Period* (Cologne: Taschen, 1999). Recent scholarship has devoted considerable attention to seeing beyond the vanitas and *memento mori* themes of still lifes. See Norman Bryson, *Looking at the Overlooked: Four Essays on Still Life Painting* (Cambridge, MA: Harvard University Press, 1990); Hanneke Grootenboer, *The Rhetoric of Perspective: Realism and Illusionism in Seventeenth-Century Dutch*

Still-Life Painting (Chicago: University of Chicago Press, 2006); Eddy de Jongh, *Questions of Meaning: Theme and Motif in Dutch Seventeenth-Century Painting*, trans. Michael Hoyle (Leiden: Primavera Pers, 2000); Hochstrasser, "Still-staende"; Hochstrasser, *Still Life*; and Paul Taylor, *Dutch Flower Painting, 1600–1720* (New Haven, CT: Yale University Press, 1995).

46 Paul Taylor emphasizes the value that artists placed on the space within an image by separating individual objects from each other ("The Concept of *Houding* in Dutch Art Theory," *Journal of the Warburg and Courtauld Institutes* 55 (1992): 210–32), https://www.jstor.org/stable/751425.

47 For a meticulous analysis of the use of space in Dutch painting, see Martha Hollander, *An Entrance for the Eyes: Space and Meaning in Seventeenth-Century Dutch Art* (Berkeley: University of California Press, 2002).

48 On nudes in Dutch art, see Klaske Muizelaar and Derek Phillips, *Picturing Men and Women in the Dutch Golden Age: Paintings and People in Historical Perspective* (New Haven, CT: Yale University Press, 2003).

49 I study this pair of paintings in *Tables of Knowledge*, 124–6.

50 Marin, *Portrait du roi*, affirms: "Le roi n'est vraiment roi, c'est-à-dire monarque, que dans des images [The king is only really a king, that is, a monarch, in images] (12).

Chapter 2

1 Deidre Nansen McCloskey argues that ethical virtues explain the expansion of the middle class in seventeenth-century Holland (*Bourgeois Equality: How Ideas, Not Capital or Institutions, Enriched the World* [Chicago: University of Chicago Press, 2016], 326–55).

2 The classical period reflected the influence of Descartes, for whom cognition refers not to an inherent ontological order but rather to the activity of the human intellect, which reproduces reality as thought, representation. See Descartes's discussion of *mathesis universalis* in *Regulae*, IV, AT 371–9, *Rules for the Direction of the Mind*, in *Philosophical Writings of Descartes*, trans. John Cottingham, Robert Stoothoff, and Dugald Murdoch, vol. 1 (Cambridge: Cambridge University Press, 1999), 15–20.

3 The basic patterns that emerge function as the grammar, or set of rules, governing the mind's organization of individual identities/thoughts. See Foucault, *Mots et les choses*.

4 Recent scholarship on the Enlightenment addresses questions of cognition and metaphor. See Sean Silver, *The Mind Is a Collection: Case Studies in Eighteenth-Century Thought* (Philadelphia: University of Pennsylvania

Press, 2015); and Brad Pasanek, *Metaphors of Mind: An Eighteenth-Century Dictionary* (Baltimore: Johns Hopkins University Press, 2015). I locate the importance of such issues in France a century earlier.

5 See Isabelle Richefort, ed. *Adam-François van der Meulen: Peintre flamand au service de Louis XIV* (Rennes: Presses Universitaires de Rennes, 2004).

6 See Julie Anne Plax, "Seventeenth-Century French Images of Warfare," in *Artful Armies, Beautiful Battles: Art and Warfare in Early Modern Europe*, ed. Pia F. Cuneo (Boston: Brill, 2002), 131–55.

7 In his memoirs van der Meulen lists fourteen paintings under the title *Conquêtes du roi*, which were painted for Marly. The cycle was expanded to twenty plus works with the addition of paintings by van der Meulen and his followers. Robert Wellington argues that some paintings in this cycle were made after prints, while other prints were made after paintings. He further notes that prior to Louis XIV's initial 1686 visit to Marly, where several of van der Meulen's paintings were already hung, the artist had re-released the catalogue of his engravings, which work garnered him the enthusiastic praise of the *Mercure galant* ("The Cartographic Origins of Adam Frans van der Meulen's Marly Cycle," *Print Quarterly* 28, no. 2 [June 2011]: 146–7, https://www.jstor.org/stable/43826143). See Richefort, 98–118.

8 Wellington observes: "On the vertical axis of the painting the skyline has been raised considerably, which in turn causes the horizon line to lower, allowing for a picturesque treatment of sky, lending the painting the appearance of a pastoral scene with atmospheric observations reminiscent of Claude Lorrain's idealized arcadian landscapes" (147).

9 Richefort, 101.

10 Ibid., 181.

11 After taking Douai, Louis XIV went to meet the queen, who had remained with the court at the Château de Compiègne. Departing from Bapaume, the royal procession arrived in the afternoon of 22 July 1667 southeast of Arras in Beaurains and Achicourt.

12 For sartorial details of the royal style, see Jeanne Button and Stephen Sbarge, *History of Costume, in Slides, Notes and Commentaries*, vol. 4 (Valley Stream, NY: Trinity Media Resources, 1975), Yale University Visual Resources Collection, http://findit.library.yale.edu/catalog/digcoll:1845470; and Joan DeJean, *The Essence of Style: How the French Invented High Fashion, Fine Food, Chic Cafes, Style, Sophistication, and Glamour* (New York: Free Press, 2006).

13 A system that supports only similar identities cannot (logically) tolerate a system that supports differences. The reverse proposition is not false,

however: a category of similar things can well exist as a class of things within a catalogue of differences.

14 Patel modified the site, anticipating the construction of the Grand Canal.

15 The viewer of van der Heyden's painting would not necessarily know that he created an image of Amsterdam's old town centre by combining views of the old Haarlemmersluis, a lock on the Nieuwezijds Voorburgwal, with a row of houses located on the Herengracht canal. The exquisite urban setting, and the sense of civic pride that its architecture and canal engenders, appealed to buyers. See Peter C. Sutton, ed., *Jan van der Heyden (1637–1712)* (New Haven, CT: Yale University Press, 2006); and Ariane van Suchtelen and Arthur K. Wheelock, Jr., eds, *Dutch Cityscapes of the Golden Age* (Zwolle, Netherlands: Waanders Publishers, 2008).

16 See Alpers, *Art of Describing*, ch. 4, 119–68.

17 Georg Braun and Franz Hogenberg, *Civitates orbis terrarum* (Cologne: 1572), http://historic-cities.huji.ac.il/mapmakers/braun_hogenberg.html. Maps included accounts of the city's history, commerce, and enough other details to present what has been called an armchair traveller's compendium. Jan Micher, *Bird's Eye View of Amsterdam* (ca. 1652, Amsterdam Museum, https://commons.wikimedia.org/wiki/File:Jan_Micker_-_Bird%27s_Eye_View_of_Amsterdam_(ca._1652).jpg) offers a cartographic view of Amsterdam inspired by Cornelis Anthonisz's *View of Amsterdam* (1532). Artists who paint street scenes, however, tend to present a more restricted perspective.

18 Similarly, Vermeer's *Little Street* features but the one street, and only a very little bit of it. Although the viewer sees houses behind the one in front of which children play, the private alley where the maid places her brooms does not lead through to any of them (ca. 1658 [54.3 x 44 cm (21.4 x 17.3 in)], Rijksmuseum, https://www.rijksmuseum.nl/en/search/objects?q=Vermeer+Little+STreet&p=1&ps=12&st=OBJECTS&ii=6#/SK-A-2860,3). Several of van der Heyden's cityscapes offer more bustling scenes of streets. I found none, however, that depicted more than two streets intersecting or bordering both sides of a canal, and certainly nothing resembling a street grid.

19 For the history of the landscape through the cityscape, see Sutton, *Jan van der Heyden*, 29–31.

20 Alpers observes: "the world depicted in Dutch pictures often seems cut off by the edges of the work or, conversely, seems to extend beyond its bounds as if the frame were an afterthought and not a prior defining device" (*Art of Describing*, xxv).

21 On the tableau, see Michael Fried, *Absorption and Theatricality: Painting and Beholder in the Age of Diderot* (Chicago: University of Chicago Press, 1988);

and Tili Boon Cuillé, *Narrative Interludes: Musical Tableaux in Eighteenth-Century French Texts* (Toronto: University of Toronto Press, 2006).

22 Blaise Ducos describes Jabach's strategies and political finesse in France: "il est amené à adopter ce que l'on peut nommer des 'conduites impériales,' volontairement calquées sur ce qui s'observe à la cour du roi. De même que le souverain s'entoure d'artistes (français et étrangers), et charge l'Académie royale de peinture et de sculpture d'œuvrer à la gloire de son image, Jabach emploie les meilleurs peintres de son temps à faire son portrait et constitue une collection unique de dessins et de peintures (Holbein, Rubens, van Dyck ...). Le public visé par Jabach est la cour de France, mais aussi le monde européen du collectionnisme, sur lequel il projette son ombre" [he comes to adopt what one could call "imperial behaviours," volontarily built on what one sees at the king's court. Just as the sovereign surrounds himself with artists (French and foreign), and charges the Royal Academy of Painting and Sculpture to promote his glorious image, so Jabach commissions the best painters of his day to do his portrait, and develops a unique collection of drawings and paintings (Holbein, Rubens, van Dyck ...). The public that Jabach attempts to impress is the French court, but also the world of European collectors, onto which he casts his long shadow.] ("Erasme, Rubens, van Dyck: La logique impériale d'Everhard Jabach," *Un Allemand à la cour de Louis XIV: De Dürer à van Dyck, la collection nordique d'Everhard Jabach* [Paris: Musée du Louvre, 2013], 26).

23 Vicomte de Grouchy, "Everhard Jabach, collectionneur parisien (1695)," *Mémoires de la Société de l'Histoire de Paris et de l'Ile-de-France*, vol. 21 (1894), 217–92, https://gallica.bnf.fr/ark:/12148/bpt6k6434807w/f221.item.

24 Schnapper, 273.

25 My interpretation relies on Keith Christiansen's detailed description of the painting in the Metropolitan Museum of Art (2015) catalogue entry: https://www.metmuseum.org/art/collection/search/626692; and also his "What's That? A Closer Look at Objects in the Jabach Portrait," https://www.metmuseum.org/blogs/now-at-the-met/2014/whats-that.

26 See Jan Baptist Bedaux, *Pride and Joy: Children's Portraits in the Netherlands 1500–1700*, ed. Jan Baptist Bedaux and Rudi Ekkart (New York: Harry N. Abrams, 2001), 27–8.

27 Diego Velázquez, *Las meninas*, 1656, 318 x 276 cm (125.2 x 108.66 in), Prado Museum, https://www.museodelprado.es/coleccion/obra-de-arte/las-meninas/9fdc7800-9ade-48b0-ab8b-edee94ea877f. Stephan Wolohojian notes that there is no evidence that either Le Brun or Jabach had seen *Las*

Meninas (*A Grand Tableau: Charles Le Brun's Portrait of the Jabach Family* [New York: Metropolitan Museum of Art, 2017], 22–3).

28 Bedaux explains that Dutch portrait painters frequently associated children and dogs, who similarly require training to reign in natural tendencies (*The Reality of Symbols: Studies in the Iconology of Netherlandish Art 1400–1800* [The Hague: Gary Schwartz, SDU Publishers, 1990], 110; 113).

Chapter 3

1 In my *Classical Model* I analyse how closure in classical texts is consistently disrupted. See also John D. Lyons, *Kingdom of Disorder: The Theory of Tragedy in Classical France* (West Lafayette, IN: Purdue University Press, 1999); Richard Goodkin, *Birth Marks: The Tragedy of Primogeniture in Pierre Corneille, Thomas Corneille, and Jean Racine* (Philadelphia: University of Pennsylvania Press, 2000); Christopher Braider, *Indiscernible Counterparts: The Invention of the Text in French Classical Drama* (Chapel Hill: North Carolina Studies in the Romance Languages and Literatures, 2002); Hélène Bilis, *Passing Judgment: The Politics and Poetics of Sovereignty in French Tragedy from Hardy to Racine* (Toronto: University of Toronto Press, 2016).

2 Governed by the three unities (action, time, and place), French classical tragedy achieves balance in five, typically symmetrical, acts that take place around a central crisis within a twenty-four-hour cycle in a single location. The conflict introduced in the first two acts typically peaks in the third, and is resolved in the final two acts, hence the formula *exposition, nœud, dénouement* [opening, crisis, denouement]. Although the denouement marks loss, it provides, as Aristotle theorized, for catharsis, the purging of the passions. The king's law determines the fate of the hero and restores order.

3 In a similar vein, Mukerji argues that military techniques evident in the design of the Versailles gardens and elsewhere subtended the glorification of Louis and his expansionist policies.

4 See my *Royal DisClosure: Problematics of Representation in French Classical Tragedy* (Birmingham, AL: Summa Publications, 1987) and *Classical Model.* I am developing a concept of visual memory that expands the notion of closure that I applied in these earlier studies.

5 For a study of cognition that focuses on knowledge of others in a social context, see Richard E. Goodkin, *How Do I Know Thee: Theatrical and Narrative Cognition in Seventeenth-Century France* (Evanston, IL: Northwestern University Press, 2015).

6 Molière, *Le Tartuffe*, version de 1664 reconstruite par Georges Forestier et Isabelle Grellet, http://www.moliere.paris-sorbonne.fr/Tartuffe_1664_reconstruit.pdf.

7 Molière, *Le Tartuffe* (1669), http://www.theatre-classique.fr/pages/programmes/edition.php?t=../documents/MOLIERE_TARTUFFE.xml. All references are to this edition.

8 For more on performance and the social implications of *Tartuffe*, see Jacques Guicharnaud, *Molière, une aventure théâtrale:* Tartuffe, Dom Juan, Le Misanthrope (Paris: Gallimard, 1963); Ralph Albanese, Jr, "Une lecture idéologique du dénouement de *Tartuffe*," *Romance Notes* 16, no. 3 (1975): 623–35; James F. Gaines, *Social Structures in Molière's Theat*er (Columbus: Ohio State University Press, 1984); Patrick Dandrey, *Molière ou l'esthétique du ridicule* (Paris: Klincksieck, 1992); Larry F. Norman, *The Public Mirror: Molière and the Social Commerce of Depiction* (Chicago: University of Chicago Press, 1999).

9 See my discussion of Molière's placets in "Petitions for Justice: Molière's *Tartuffe* Viewed in the Mirror of Pierre de Lancre's Witches," in *Theatrum Mundi: Studies in Honor of Ronald W. Tobin*, ed. Claire L. Carlin and Kathleen Wine (Charlottesville, VA: Rookwood Press, 2003), 92–9.

10 Jean-Pierre Cavaillé signals the king's equivocation: "Louis XIV doit cette fois céder aux pressions d'un groupe suffisamment puissant pour contrarier son goût, son 'plaisir,' mais aussi, et par là même, capable de mettre en cause la nature absolue de son pouvoir" [Louis XIV now must yield to the pressures of a group sufficiently powerful to go against his taste, his "pleasure," and also, therefore, capable of challenging the absolute nature of his power] ("Hypocrisie et imposture dans la querelle du *Tartuffe* (1664–1669): *La lettre sur la comédie de l'imposteur* (1667)," *Les Dossiers du Grihl* (1997), 10, https://journals.openedition.org/dossiersgrihl/292?lang=en). See François Rey and Jean Lacouture, *Molière et le roi: L'affaire* Tartuffe (Paris: Seuil, 2007).

11 The painting features what the Dutch call a see-through doorway, a *doorkijkje*. The room's architectural details contribute to the idealization of the scene. C. Willemijn Fock indicates that the arrangement of four consecutive living spaces, with doors all aligned *en enfilade*, did not occur in Dutch city dwellings of the period ("Semblance or Reality? The Domestic Interior in Seventeenth-Century Dutch Genre Painting," in *Art and Home: Dutch Interiors in the Age of Rembrandt*, ed. Mariët Westermann [Zwolle, Netherlands: Waanders Publishers, 2001], 83–7).

12 See Richard Helgerson, *Adulterous Alliances: Home, State, and History in Early Modern European Drama and Painting* (Chicago: University of Chicago Press, 2000).

13 On Horace's relation to Camille, see Goodkin, *Birth Marks*, 62–77.

14 Pierre Corneille, *Horace* (1641), http://www.theatre-classique.fr/pages/programmes/edition.php?t=../documents/CORNEILLEP_HORACE.xml. All references are to this edition.

15 For more on the sublime in Corneille, see Emma Gilby, *Sublime Worlds: Early Modern French Literature* (London: Legenda, 2006). John D. Lyons, *Tragedy and the Return of the Dead* (Evanston, IL: Northwestern University Press, 2018) examines tragedy, Burke's sublime, and Freud's uncanny.

16 Even Le Vieil Horace berates the hero, arguing that Camille was best punished by hands other than his: "Je ne plains point Camille: elle était criminelle; / Je me tiens plus à plaindre, et je te plains plus qu'elle: / Moi, d'avoir mis au jour un cœur si peu romain; / Toi, d'avoir par sa mort déshonoré ta main. / Je ne la trouve point injuste ni trop prompte; / Mais tu pouvais, mon fils, t'en épargner la honte: / Son crime, quoique énorme et digne du trépas, / Était mieux impuni que puni par ton bras" [I do not pity Camille: she acted criminally; / I consider myself more deserving of pity, and I pity you more than I do her: / I, for having brought into this world a heart so little Roman; / You, for having through her death, dishonoured your hand. / I do not find it unjust or too quick to strike; / But, my son, you could have spared yourself the shame: / Her crime, while egregious and while she deserved to die, / Was better left unpunished than punished by your arm] (5.1.1411–18).

17 See my *Classical Model*, 43–58.

18 See Mitchell Greenberg, *Subjectivity and Subjugation in Seventeenth-Century Drama and Prose: The Family Romance of French Classicism* (Cambridge: Cambridge University Press, 1992); John D. Lyons, *The Tragedy of Origins: Pierre Corneille and Historical Perspective* (Stanford, CA: Stanford University Press, 1996); Merlin-Kajman, 90–101; Susan Maslan, "The Dream of the Feeling Citizen: Law and Emotion in Corneille and Montesquieu," *SubStance* 35, no. 1 (2006): 69–84, https://www.jstor.org/stable/3685636; Claude Haas and Michael E. Auer, "The Dramaturgy of Sovereignty and the Performance of Mourning: The Case of Corneille's *Horace*," in *Walter Benjamin's Hypothetical French "Trauerspiel,"* ed. Hall Bjørnstad and Katherine Ibbett, spec. issue *Yale French Studies* 124 (2013): 121–34, https://www.jstor.org/stable/23646045?seq=1#page_scan_tab_contents.

19 Tulle addresses the family's suffering, advising the elder Horace to attend to his daughter's burial, in order "to purify the sacrifice" they would make to the gods: "Mais nous devons aux dieux demain un sacrifice; / Et nous aurions le ciel à nos vœux mal propice, / Si nos prêtres, avant que de sacrifier, / Ne trouvaient les moyens de le purifier: / Son père en prendra

soin; il lui sera facile / D'apaiser tout d'un temps les mânes de Camille" [But tomorrow we owe the gods a sacrifice; / And the heavens will not be favourably disposed towards our vows / If our priests, before making the sacrifice, / Do not find a way to purify it: / Her father will take care of this; it will be easy for him / To appease both them and at the same time Camille's spirits] (5.3.1771–6).

20 Some older aristocrats were more approving, but the young court that had assembled around Louis XIV seemed to prefer love to duty: the plays of Racine with their emphasis on the affairs of the heart had won out over Corneille's duty-bound heroes.

21 To emphasize epistemological relations, I am proposing a very different connection between the theatre and art than Georges Forestier, who associates Corneille's tragedy with Poussin's *Paysage avec Orphée et Eurydice* (1650–51, Musée du Louvre). Forestier shows "comment Corneille a été comme nécessairement conduit dans *Suréna* à assimiler le mythe d'Orphée et le rêve pastoral" [how Corneille was unavoidably led in *Suréna* to assimilate the Orpheus myth and the pastoral dream] ("Corneille et la tragédie: Hypothèses sur l'élaboration de *Suréna*," *Littératures classiques* 16 [1992]: 153).

22 Some critics have referred to a letter or a book on the floor that may be a manual for letter writing. See Peter Sutton, ed., *Love Letters: Dutch Genre Paintings in the Age of Vermeer* (London: Frances Lincoln, 2003).

23 Jacques Foucart identified Lely as the artist of this painting ("Peter Lely, Dutch History Painter," *Hoogsteder-Naumann Mercury* 8 [1989]: 17–26). See Arthur K. Wheelock, Jr, *Vermeer & the Art of Painting* (New Haven, CT: Yale University Press, 1995), 156–62.

24 See Lisa Vergara, "Women, Letters, Artistic Beauty: Vermeer's Theme and Variations," in Sutton, *Love Letters*, 57–8.

25 Pierre Corneille, *Suréna* (1654), http://www.theatre-classique.fr/pages/programmes/edition.php?t=../documents/CORNEILLEP_SURENA.xml. All references are to this edition.

26 Serge Doubrovsky observes that Suréna's execution "se produira au moment précis où deux séries causales indépendantes convergeront, où Orode et Pacorus uniront des ressentiments différents [d'un roi faible et d'un rival insatisfait] en un assassinat unique" [will occur precisely at the point when two independent causal sequences converge, when Orode and Pacorus will unite their different resentments [that of a weak king and that a thwarted rival] in one assassination] (*Corneille et la dialectique du héros* [Paris: Gallimard, 1963], 463).

27 *Suréna* reminds us of other heroes of classical tragedy. Georges Forestier observes that "au dénouement de *Suréna*, c'est comme si c'était Rodrigue

qui mourait" [at the end of *Suréna* it is as though Rodrigue were dying] (142). Ellen M. McClure examines Suréna's role as ambassador for the Parthians to the kingdom of Eurydice's father prior to the start of the action (*Sunspots and the Sun King: Sovereignty and Mediation in Seventeenth-Century France* [Urbana and Chicago: University of Illinois Press, 2006], 240–9).

28 "Nous serons les miroirs d'une vertu bien rare: / Mais votre fermeté tient un peu du barbare, / Peu, même des grands cœurs, tireraient vanité / D'aller par ce chemin à l'immortalité [We will mirror a very rare virtue: / But your determination seems rather barbaric, / Few, even very brave hearts, would pride themselves / In adopting this path to immortality] (2.3.455–8).

29 On myth and its connections to monstrosity in *Phèdre*, see Roland Barthes, *Sur Racine* (Paris: Seuil, 1963); Sara Melzer, "Myths of Mixture in *Phèdre* and the Sun King's Assimilation Policy in the New World," in *Racine for the Next Millennium*, ed. Harriet Stone, spec. issue *L'Esprit Créateur* 38, no. 2 (Summer 1998): 72–81, https://doi.org/10.1353/esp.2010.0025; Mitchell Greenberg, *Racine: From Ancient Myth to Tragic Modernity* (Minneapolis: University of Minnesota Press, 2010); Sylvaine Guyot, *Racine et le corps tragique* (Paris: PUF, 2014).

30 See Philippe Sellier, "Le jansénisme des tragédies de Racine: Réalité ou illusion?," *Cahiers de l'Association Internationale des Etudes Françaises* (1979) 31: 135–48, https://doi.org/10.3406/caief.1979.1190.

31 Jean Racine, *Phèdre* (1697), http://www.theatre-classique.fr/pages/programmes/edition.php?t=../documents/RACINE_PHEDRE.xml. All references are to this edition.

32 This passage has been labelled baroque since Leo Spitzer's iconic analysis "The 'Récit de Théramène,'" *Linguistics and Literary History: Essays in Stylistics* (Princeton, NJ: Princeton University Press, 2015), 87–134. See Amy Wygant's analysis, "Leo Spitzer's Racine," *MLN* 109, no. 4 (Sept. 1994): 632–49, https://www.jstor.org/stable/2904967. I argue, however, that the text's baroque qualities are essential to the audience's understanding of Hippolyte's death. Description connects the son's death with the sublime, as it does the lovers Suréna and Eurydice.

Chapter 4

1 Louis's motto, "*nec pluribus impar*," literally, "not unequal to many [suns]," suggests that, like the sun, with which the motto was associated, Louis lights up/rules the world. As the king of all kings, he was "le premier des hommes et peut-être plus qu'un homme" [the first among men

and possibly more than a man] (Onésime Reclus, *Le plus beau royaume sous le ciel* [Paris, Hachette, 1899], 3), http://gallica.bnf.fr/ark:/12148/bpt6k1031624.

2 See Antoine Vallot, Antoine Daquin, and Guy-Crescent Fagon, *Journal de santé de Louis XIV*, ed. Stanis Perez (Grenoble: Jérôme Millon, 2004). See also Stanis Perez, *La santé de Louis XIV: Une biohistoire du Roi-Soleil* (Paris: Tempus Perrin, 2010).

3 On financial debt and corruption during Louis's reign, see Gary B. McCollim, *Louis XIV's Assault on Privilege: Nicolas Desmaretz and the Tax on Wealth* (Rochester, NY: University of Rochester Press, 2012); and Guy Rowlands, *The Dynastic State and the Army under Louis XIV: Royal Service and Private Interest 1661–1701* (Cambridge: Cambridge University Press, 2002).

4 "Louis le Grand, l'amour et les délices de son peuple: les actions de graces, les festes et les rejouissances pour le parfait rétablissement de la santé du roy en 1687" ["Louis the Great, The Love and the Joy of His Subjects, the Thanks, Celebrations, and Delight for the Perfect Return of the King's Health in 1687"], in *Almanachs parisiens 1661–1716*, ed. Brigitte Montclos (Paris: Musée Carnavalet, 1998), 60–1.

5 A fistula is an abnormal passageway from one organ to another or from one organ to the body's surface.

6 Maxime Préaud explains that, with the exception of some almanacs that were collected, these large sheets were destined for cabarets, artisans' workshops, and schoolrooms; rarely did they appear in private homes ("Printmaking under Louis XIV," in *A Kingdom of Images: French Prints in the Age of Louis XIV, 1660–1715*, ed. Peter Fuhring, Louis Marchesano, Rémi Mathis, and Vanessa Selbach [Los Angeles: Getty Publications, 2015], 12). Originally the calendar constituted the almanac's main focus, but as the years passed the images gained importance, especially among the bourgeois for whom they were "primarily intended" (Préaud 13). The almanacs thus served to disseminate the encomium of Louis XIV.

7 Montclos identifies the series of medallions: "Le haut de la feuille est occupée par un dais sur la retombée duquel cinq vignettes énumèrent 'Les festes remarquables de Paris en janvier 1687': fêtes du Parlement, de l'Académie de peinture, des Fermiers généraux, les illuminations du pont Notre-Dame et la clôture des actions de grâce à Notre-Dame [At the top of the page is a canopy showing five vignettes of 'The Remarkable Celebrations in Paris in January, 1687': Celebrations by Parliament, The Academy of Painting, The Tax-Farmers General, The Illuminations on Notre Dame Bridge, and The Closing Prayers of Thanksgiving at Notre Dame]" (60).

8 For a full list of those in attendance, see https://gallica.bnf.fr/ark:/12148/btv1b69455315.

9 See https://www.nga.gov/collection/art-object-page.1220.html.

10 Mikhail Bakhtin, *Rabelais and His World*, trans. Hélène Iswolsky (Bloomington: Indiana University Press, 2009).

11 On the king's two bodies, see Kantorowicz; and Marin, *La parole mangée*. On Louis XIV's death, see Francis Assaf, *La mort du roi: Une thanatographie de Louis XIV* (Tübingen: Gunter Narr Verlag, 1999); and Gérard Sabatier and Béatrix Saule, eds., *Le roi est mort: Louis XIV, 1715* (Paris: Tallandier, 2015).

12 Jean-Baptiste Massillon, "Oraison funèbre de Louis le Grand, roi de France," *Oraisons funèbres: Massillon, Fléchier, Mascaron, précédées de* L'essai sur l'oraison funèbre *par Villemain* (Paris: Garnier Frères, 1875), 134, https://gallica.bnf.fr/ark:/12148/bpt6k6483277j/f1.image.r=Oraison%20fun%C3%A8bre%20de%20Louis%20XIV%20MASSILLON.

13 Descartes did not believe animals to possess a soul. Philosophers now regard the question of consciousness for animals as more vexed, and it remains a controversial topic. My point is that, consistent with Descartes's notion that animals do not possess a soul, the human corpse from which the soul has been released and the animal corpse from which there was believed to be no soul are similarly lacking consciousness.

14 E. Stewart Saunders notes: "Having originated as a response to the political context of the intellectual community of France, the Royal Academy of Sciences (1666) and the technical institutions that were created after it now responded to the needs of the state ... Whatever may have been Colbert's dedication to the enrichment of the mind, there is little doubt that his greatest enthusiasm was for those aspects of mathematics, mechanics, and astronomy that would improve the art of navigation" ("Louis XIV: Patron of Science and Technology," *Libraries Research Publications*, Paper 46, https://docs.lib.purdue.edu/lib_research/46).

15 Turenne conducted what was considered unconventional warfare: a winter battle that employed a novel strategy. He feigned an attack on two sides of the Imperial army, centre and right, and then proceeded to attack successfully the enemy's exposed left flank. See Jean Bérenger, *Turenne* (Paris: Fayard, 1987); and John A. Lynn, *The Wars of Louis XIV: 1667–1714* (Harlow, UK: Longman Publishing: 1999).

16 See Andrew Michael Ramsay, *Histoire du Vicomte de Turenne, Maréchal général des armées de France*, vol. 2 (Paris: Vve Mazières et J.-B. Garnier, 1735), https://gallica.bnf.fr/ark:/12148/bpt6k86571z/f4.image.r=Histoire%20du%20Vicomte%20de%20Turenne,%20

%20Mar%C3%A9chal%20g%C3%A9n%C3%A9ral%20des%20arm%C3%A9es%20de%20France.langEN, which contains an account of Turenne's death, including letters by Mme de Sévigné and the sermon by Fléchier.

17 Pamela Cowen explains the fan's history: "The body of Turenne dressed in red, bedecked with gold, lies on what would have been the gorge of the fan. This demonstrates that the original design could not have been intended to commemorate his death. Moreover, the lower part of the leaf, both left and right, has been over-painted in a darker colour ... To draw attention to the dead hero the heads of two of the riders in the group on the right have also been over-painted, so that the man in blue has his head at a very unusual angle, and both have now been painted without hats, which would not be expected during military operations" (*A Fanfare for the Sun King: Unfolding Fans for Louis XIV* [London: Third Millennium Publishing, 2003], 69).

18 H. Léon Lecestre, ed., *Mémoires de Saint-Hilaire [fils] 1661–1678*, vol. 1 (Paris: Libraire Renouard, 1903), 208–9, https://catalogue.bnf.fr/ark:/12148/cb34024395n.

19 Marie de Rabutin-Chantal, Marquise de Sevigné, *Correspondance*, ed. Roger Duchêne and Jacqueline Duchêne, vol. 2 (Paris: Gallimard, Bibliothèque de la Pléiade, 1974), 28 March 1676. Sévigné did not hear Fléchier's oration, as she was not in Paris at the time, but after reading his text she pronounced it superior to Mascaron's. Sévigné wrote several letters concerning Turenne's death that confirm her sense of the enormity of France's loss. See John D. Lyons, *Before Imagination: Embodied Thought from Montaigne to Rousseau* (Stanford, CA: Stanford University Press, 2005), 135–42.

20 Esprit Fléchier skilfully acknowledges exisiting conficts by describing how Turenne won the praise of those who opposed him: "C'est la destinée des grands hommes d'en être attaqués, et c'est le privilége [*sic*] de M. de Turenne d'avoir pu la vaincre. L'envie fut étouffée, ou par le mépris qu'il en fit, ou par des accroissements perpétuels d'honneur et de gloire: le mérite l'avait fait naître, le mérite la fit mourir. Ceux qui lui étaient moins favorables, ont reconnu combien il était nécessaire à l'état: ceux qui ne pouvaient souffrir son élévation, se crurent enfin obligés d'y consentir; et n'osant s'affliger de la prospérité d'un homme qui ne leur aurait jamais donné la misérable consolation de se réjouir de quelqu'une de ses fautes, ils joignirent leur voix à la voix publique, et crurent qu'être son ennemi, c'était l'être de toute la France" [It is the destiny of great men to be attacked; and it is the privilege of M. de Turenne to have won out over his critics. Envy was stifled, either by his scorn for it or by his relentless

path to honour and glory: merit marked his birth; merit marked his death. Those who were less favourably disposed towards his rise were in the end obliged to recognize it; and, not daring to burden themselves with challenging the success of a man who would never have granted them the satisfaction of being able to delight in any of his faults, they joined their voices with those of the public and believed that to be his enemy was to be the enemy of all of France] (*Oraison funèbre de Turenne* [Paris: Jules Delalain, 1851], 23, https://gallica.bnf.fr/ark:/12148/bpt6k57883027).

21 See Philippe de Courcillon Dangeau, Marquis de, *Mémoire sur la mort de Louis XIV par le Mis de Dangeau* (Abrégé du Journal du Marquis de Dangeau), ed. Eudoxe Soulié and Louis Dussieux (Paris: Didot Frères, 1858), https://gallica.bnf.fr/ark:/12148/bpt6k55404p.

22 See also Anthoine, les frères [garçons de la chambre de Louis XIV], *La mort de Louis XIV: Journal des Anthoine*, ed. Edouard Drumont (Paris: A. Quantin, 1880), rpt. Charleston, SC: BiblioBazaar: 2008.

23 Louis XIV's entrails were presented to Notre Dame on 4 September. On 6 September his heart, like that of his father Louis XIII, was presented to the Eglise Saint Paul-Saint Louis, rue Saint-Antoine, in Paris.

24 Jonathan Sawday describes the fascination and horror that one feels as one peers into the body even as this knowledge, appropriated over time by the Church, meant that the order of nature revealed through dissection became a sign of the order of God (*The Body Emblazoned: Dissection and the Human Body in Renaissance Culture* [London: Routledge, 1995]).

25 Saint-Simon, vol. 12, ch. 15, http://rouvroy.medusis.com/docs/1215.html.

26 Anthoine, 77–8; cited in Assaf, 187.

27 Scientists continue to debate the accuracy of Rembrandt's depiction of the forearm.

28 See Dolores Mitchell, "Rembrandt's 'The Anatomy Lesson of Dr. Tulp': A Sinner among the Righteous," *Artibus et Historiae* 15, no. 30 (1994): 145–56, https://www.jstor.org/stable/1483478.

29 See Philippe Charlier, "Autopsie et embaumement," in *Le roi est mort*, ed. Gérard Sabatier et Béatrix Saule (Paris: Tallandier, 2015), 42–9.

30 "All came from the dust and all return to the dust" (*Ecclesiastes* 3:20).

31 De Hooch depicts the family without the husband, whose commerce most likely allowed for the purchase of the items in the painting and also perhaps for the commission of the painting itself.

32 Modern readers are reminded of Sigmund Freud's description of the child game of fort/da in *Beyond the Pleasure Principle*, trans. C.J.M. Hubback (London: International Psycho-Analytical Press, 1922, https://www.libraryofsocialscience.com/assets/pdf/freud_beyond_the_pleasure_principle.pdf.

33 Saskia Kuus observes that subtle differences in dress served to identify boys and girls, although many inconsistencies in such patterns exist ("Children's Costume in the Sixteenth and Seventeenth Centuries," in Bedaux and Ekkart, eds., *Pride and Joy*, 73–83). See also Annemarieke Willemsen, "Images of Toys: The Culture of Play in the Netherlands around 1600," in Bedaux and Ekkart, eds., *Pride and Joy*, 61–72.

34 https://wallacelive.wallacecollection.org:443/eMP/eMuseumPlus?service=ExternalInterface&module=collection&objectId=65056&viewType=detailView.

35 The Apollo myth offers no exact parallel with Racine's *Phèdre*, but the son's fatal chariot ride also presents similarities with Hippolyte's story. Both Ovid and Racine depict runaway horses that precipitate the son's demise. Unlike Racine's Hippolyte, Phaeton dies solely as the result of his actions. He boasts to his friend and fails to accept his father's warning. While guilty of loving Aricie, Hippolyte is innocent of seducing Phèdre, the crime for which Thésée orders him killed. Two fathers require mediation by the gods; two fathers survive the violent deaths of their sons; two fathers, strangely, provide a context for understanding Louis XIV as the sun sets on his reign. In Ovid the king, Jupiter, acts decisively and hits his target. In this respect he is very unlike Thésée, who mistakenly punishes his son rather than his guilty wife. Jupiter, however, commits adultery with Callisto, impregnating her with a son, which violence casts a shadow on his success in thwarting Phaeton's violence.

36 Louis, Duc de Bretagne (25 June 1704–3 April 1705) died of convulsions; Louis, Duc de Bretagne (8 January 1707–8 March 1712) died of measles; Louis XV de France (15 February 1710–10 May 1774) alone survived.

37 The line of succession extended first to Louis-Auguste de Bourbon, Duc de Maine, legitimated in 1673, and then to Louis Alexandre de Bourbon, comte de Toulouse, legitimated in 1681, followed by their legitimate male children.

38 See Rosalind Savill, Stephen Duffy, and Joanne Hedley, eds., *The Wallace Collection* (London: Scala Publishers, 2006); and John Ingamells, ed., *The Wallace Collection Catalogue of Pictures*. vol. 3: *French before 1815* (London: Paul Holberton Publishing, 1985), 170–5.

39 The Wallace Collection catalog, indicates that the age of the sitters is not consistent with a precise moment in time.

40 See Jan Baptist Bedaux, introduction, in Bedaux and Ekkart, eds., *Pride and Joy*, 19–22.

Chapter 5

1 My discussion of Le Brun's ceiling relies on the documentation edited by Nicolas Milovanovic at the Château de Versailles, *Versailles, la galerie*

des Glaces, Catalogue iconologique, coproduction RMN – EPV (Versailles: Château de Versailles, 2008) (hereafter *Versailles Catalogue*), which provides detailed information about the allegories and the inscriptions. See http://www.galeriedesglaces-versailles.fr/html/11/collection/galerie.html and http://www.galeriedesglaces-versailles.fr/html/11/rechercher/page_recherche.html as well as links for individual paintings.

2 Olivier Bonfait, *Poussin et Louis XIV: Peinture et monarchie dans la France du Grand Siècle* (Paris: Hazan, 2015), 164–5.

3 Brejon de Lavergnée mentions Bernini's visit to Richelieu's collection (66).

4 See Pierre Rosenberg, "Les Poussin de Louis XIV," in *Louis XIV: L'homme et le roi*, ed. Nicolas Milovanovic and Alexandre Maral (Paris: Skira Flammarion, 2009), 83–93.

5 The debate, which resembled the earlier one in Florence (drawing) and Venice (colour), was characterized as the *Poussinists versus the Rubenists.*

6 Bonfait, *Poussin et Louis XIV* traces the arc of Poussin's career from his active court role as the king's first painter through the end of Louis's reign, when Poussin's commissions were largely from private clients.

7 Rosenberg indicates that Richelieu received market value: 50,000 livres, about 2,000 livres per painting ("Les Poussin," 86).

8 Ibid.

9 Milovanovic, ed. "Le passage du Rhin en présence des ennemis, 1672," *Versailles Catalogue*, http://www.galeriedesglaces-versailles.fr/html/11/selection/page_notice-ok.php?myPos=1&compo=c7.

10 Milovanovic, ibid., notes that Louis crossed the river with his troops where the water was very low and the Dutch resistance "quasi inexistante" [practically non-existent].

11 See Todd Olson, *Poussin and France: Painting, Humanism, and the Politics of Style* (New Haven, CT: Yale University Press, 2002), 232–3; and Anthony Blunt, *Nicolas Poussin* (London: Pallas Athene, 1967).

12 http://www.getty.edu/art/collection/objects/106381/nicolas-poussin-landscape-with-a-calm-un-temps-calme-et-serein-french-1650-to-1651/.

13 In an attempt to link this painting more closely with its pendant *L'orage* [*The Storm*], Louis Marin speculates that a spewing mountain on the right might explain why the man on horseback tears off: "Serait-ce ce feu de montagne, et la nuée qui en est le signe, que le cavalier *devine* pour le fuire au galop?" [could this mountain fire and cloud of smoke that points to it explain what the rider senses and why he rides off at a galop?] (*Sublime Poussin* [Paris: Seuil, 1995], 143). This interpretation seems all the more implausible, however, given that the rider takes off in the wrong direction. See T.J. Clark, *The Sight of Death: An Experiment in Art Writing* (New Haven, CT: Yale University Press, 2006), 84–5.

14 A combination of pride in Haarlem's bleaching fields and a sense of their beauty brought visitors from the city, including foreigners.

15 The bleaching of linen was central to Haarlem becoming a leading textile centre, thanks in part to its location near the Spaarne river (for water), the dunes (for drying), and also to dairy farms (for buttermilk). Linen from elsewhere, including France, was shipped to Haarlem for bleaching. In the first stage the linens were soaked in lye for about a week. During the second stage, boiling potassium lye was poured over the already-soaked linens. After that, the linens were removed from the liquid and washed to remove the lye. The linens were later placed in wooden containers filled with buttermilk, where they remained for five or six days. Then the moist linens were laid over grass in the field to absorb the summer sunlight, becoming brighter and softer. Depending on the weather, the process could take five to six months, at which point the linen was dried on the sandy dunes. See Linda Stone-Ferrier, "Views of Haarlem: A Reconsideration of Ruisdael and Rembrandt," *Art Bulletin* 67, no. 3 (1985): 417–36, https://www.jstor.org/stable/3050960.

16 Seymour Slive rejects an emblematic reading in favour of a realistic depiction of the scene (*Jacob van Ruisdael: Master of Landscape* [New Haven, CT: Yale University Press, 2005], 12–14).

17 "God created the earth, but the Dutch created Holland" is a familiar Dutch adage.

18 The events depicted on the ceiling extend from the Treaty of the Pyrénées in 1659, which ended with a weakened Spanish crown and arrangements for Louis XIV's marriage to Marie-Thérèse of Spain, through the Treaty of Nijmegen in 1679, which marked the end of France's six-year war with the Dutch.

19 Milovanovic, ed. "Envie," *Versailles Catalogue*, http://www.galeriedesglaces-versailles.fr/html/11/selection/page_notice-ok.php?myPos=1&compo=c36.

20 Paul Tallemant completed the original inscriptions in Latin, working in collaboration with Le Brun. These texts were quickly replaced by French inscriptions composed by François Charpentier. Boileau and Racine wrote a final series (Milovanovic, Introduction, *Versailles Catalogue*, http://www.galeriedesglaces-versailles.fr/html/11/collection/intro.html).

21 The Galerie des Glaces and the adjoining Salon de la Paix [Peace Salon] and the Salon de la Guerre [War Salon] together contain more than 250 allegories and more than 2,000 symbols (Pierre Arizzoli-Clémentel, Avant-Propos, *Versailles Catalogue*, ed. Milovanovic, http://www.galeriedesglaces-versailles.fr/html/11/collection/propos.html). See also

François Charpentier, *Explication des tableaux de la galerie de Versailles* (Paris: Muguet, 1684), http://catalogue.bnf.fr/ark:/12148/cb30224844x.

22 The frame shapes also serve to catalogue events: "La signification des sujets est également historique, avec plusieurs niveaux de discours: les principales compositions traitent de la guerre de Hollande. Les ovales et les octogones montrent les principaux actes du gouvernement civil. Les octogones qui flanquent la composition centrale évoquent la guerre de Dévolution (première guerre menée par le roi mais de moindre importance que la guerre de Hollande). Les quatre ovales centraux, de plus grandes dimensions que les autres et d'une technique différente (huile sur toile marouflée au lieu d'huile sur plâtre), montrent les quatre fondements du gouvernement de Louis XIV: la Justice, les Finances, le Commerce et les Arts. [The themes are also historic, with several layers of meaning: the principal compositions describe the Franco-Dutch War. The ovals and the octagons show the principal acts of civil government. The octagons on either side of the central composition evoke the War of Devolution (the first war led by the king, but of lesser import than the Franco-Dutch War). The four central ovals, which are larger than the others and which utilize a different technique (marouflage, oil applied to canvases that were pasted onto the ceiling, instead of oil being applied directly to the plaster), show the four foundations of government under Louis XIV: Justice, Finance, Commerce, and the Arts] (Milovanovic, introduction, *Versailles Catalogue*, http://www.galeriedesglaces-versailles.fr/html/11/collection/intro.html).

23 Milovanovic, ibid.

24 Milovanovic, ed., "*Le roi gouverne par lui-même, 1661*," *Versailles Catalogue*, http://www.galeriedesglaces-versailles.fr/html/11/collection/c17.html.

25 *Prise de la ville et de la citadelle de Gand en six jours, 1678* [*The Capture of the City and the Citadel of Ghent in Six Days*, 1678] is framed with *Mesures des Espagnols rompues par la prise de Gand* [*Actions of the Spanish Thwarted by the Capture of Ghent*]; *Le passage du Rhin en présence des ennemis, 1672* [*The Passage of the Rhine in Front of the Enemies, 1672*] appears with *Le roi prend Maëstricht en treize jours, 1673* [*The King Takes Maestricht in Thirteen Days, 1673*].

26 For the "récit du roi" [narrative of the king], see Marin, *Portrait*, 47–107.

27 See Hall Bjørnstad's reading of Louis's reflection in Minerva's shield, "'Plus d'éclaircissement touchant la grande galerie de Versailles': Du nouveau sur les inscriptions latines," *XVIIe siècle* 243 (2009): 321–43, https://www.cairn.info/revue-dix-septieme-siecle-2009-2-page-321.htm.

28 The Louvre database lists the provenance with Jabach, although scholars have discussed whether the Rembrandt self-portrait came from de La

Feuille, who worked in Amsterdam. See Ernst van de Wetering, ed., *A Corpus of Rembrandt Paintings IV: Self-Portraits* (Dordrecht: Springer, 2005): 514–15.

29 Milovanovic, ed., "Faste des puissances voisines de la France," *Versailles Catalogue*, http://www.galeriedesglaces-versailles.fr/html/11/selection/page_notice-ok.php?myPos=8&compo=c16.

30 Referring to the bourgeois who gained influence in the 1670s once the king's power declined, Apostolidès argues that Colbert, in the reformed financial administration that he established, and others effectively replaced the king, who became but a "roi-machine" [king-machine], a hollow presence.

31 In *L'ordre rétabli dans les finances, 1662* [*Financial Order Restored, 1662*] Minerva fights those who misused France's finances.

Chapter 6

1 Louise Horowitz describes the courtiers collapsing under the weight of the many objects included in the *Caractères* ("Things Thick and Thin: The Material of *Les Caractères*," *French Review* 64, no. 1 [Oct. 1990]: 12–18), https://www.jstor.org/stable/395660. See also David M. Posner's examination of La Bruyère, *The Performance of Nobility in Early Modern European Literature* (Cambridge: Cambridge University Press, 1999, 181–210.

2 In *The Classical Model*, 112–29, I find similar taxonomic evidence for La Rochefoucauld's maxims. Both moralists provide lists of court behaviors that resemble elaborate classificatory systems.

3 See Michael Moriarty, "La Bruyère: Virtue and Disinterestedness," *French Studies* 68, no. 2 (1 April 2014): 164–79, https://academic.oup.com/fs/article-abstract/68/2/164/607475?redirectedFrom=fulltext.

4 Burke notes that in 1688 Louis XIV was fifty years old; was in poor physical condition; and "[i]n politics too there was a downward trend. The second half of the long period of personal rule was less successful than the first. It was a period of neither peace nor victory" (*Fabrication*, 108–9).

5 La Bruyère, "De la mode," *Les caractères*, 2.188–9, https://fr.wikisource.org/wiki/Les_Caract%C3%A8res/De_la_mode.

6 Pavord documents the Versailles plantings under Louis XIV, including a reference to this text by La Bruyère (83–4). On Louis's influence on court fashions, see DeJean, *Essence*.

7 Most of the species, like the genus *tulipe* itself, are feminine: Orientale [Oriental woman], la Veuve [widow], Agathe [Agatha], and Solitaire [solitary woman].

8 Alice Stroup provides a thorough history of advances in botanical science under Louis XIV (*A Company of Scientists: Botany, Patronage, and Community at the Seventeenth-Century Parisian Royal Academy of Sciences* [Berkeley: University of California Press, 1990]). Botany and chemistry had traditionally focused on medical uses of plants. The Académie pursued these fields to determine the anatomical and chemical basis by which plants might be classified. Scientists investigated which salts and oils were produced by the plant and which were absorbed from the earth through the roots. They hoped to find empirical verification of the corpuscular theory of natural philosophy.

9 Frank A. Kafker and Serena L. Kafker specify that for volumes VIII–XV Jaucourt "wrote between one-quarter and one-half of the articles per volume and, for the last two volumes of letterpress, over fifty per cent of each. At times spending thirteen or fourteen hours a day surrounded by as many as four or five personal secretaries, he compiled one article after another, the total eventually reaching over seventeen thousand – about one-quarter of all the articles in the seventeen volumes of letterpress" (*The Encyclopedists as Individuals: A Biographical Dictionary of the Authors of the* Encyclopédie [Oxford: Voltaire Foundation, 1988], 176, https://artflsrv03.uchicago.edu/philologic4/kafker/navigate/1/60/).

10 "Tulipe" ["Tulip"] p. 16:740, https://artflsrv03.uchicago.edu/philologic4/encyclopedie1117/navigate/16/3820/. All references are to Denis Diderot and Jean le Rond d'Alembert, eds., *Encyclopédie, ou dictionnaire raisonné des sciences, des arts et des métiers, etc.*, ed. Robert Morrissey and Glenn Roe, University of Chicago: ARTFL Encyclopédie Project (Autumn 2017 Edition), http://encyclopedie.uchicago.edu/. Subsequent references to the *Encyclopédie* refer to this edition and appear parenthetically in the body of my text, with the original volume page numbers provided by ARTFL. I retain ARTFL spelling but alter some punctuation.

11 http://artflsrv02.uchicago.edu/cgi-bin/philologic/getobject.pl?c.4:596:15.encyclopedie0513.

12 In seventeenth-century Holland the mastery of light relates as well to the artists' dedicated attention to perspectival techniques, including in some instances the use of a camera obscura. Artists honed their skills, perfecting the accurate portrayal of three-dimensional space through perspectives that take the viewer through a series of doors and rooms towards the canals or courtyards outside.

13 See, in addition to my *Classical Model* and *Tables of Knowledge*, comparative studies of early modern art, literature, and philosophy by Braider; Judovitz; David Marshall, *The Frame of Art: Fictions of Aesthetic Experience, 1750–1815* (Baltimore: Johns Hopkins University Press, 2005); and Suzanna

Berger, *The Art of Philosophy: Visual Thinking in Europe from the Late Renaissance to the Early Enlightenment* (Princeton, NJ: Princeton University Press, 2017).

14 Joanna Stalnaker presents an original analysis of how, before literary writing really separated from scientific writing in the nineteenth century, descriptive techniques adapted from natural history both aided and complicated the work of the encyclopedists (*The Unfinished Enlightenment: Description in the Age of the Encyclopedia* [Ithaca, NY: Cornell University Press, 2010], 1–27).

15 In the *Discours préliminaire* (https://encyclopedie.uchicago.edu/node/88) d'Alembert models his tree of knowledge on that proposed by Bacon (*The Advancement of Learning*, 1605, book 11). Robert Darnton explains two significant changes: d'Alembert placed reason ahead of imagination and he placed the science of man above the science of nature (*The Great Cat Massacre and Other Episodes in French Cultural History* [New York: Basic Books, 1984], 191–213).

16 http://artflsrv02.uchicago.edu/cgi-bin/philologic/getobject.pl?c.4:1252.encyclopedie0513.

17 Scholars cite Diderot's article on the stocking machine, whose large number of parts complicated his description. Stalnaker observes that neither the written description nor the plate sufficed alone to explain the machine; nor could one simultaneously say in words and show in pictures how the parts of the machine fit together and moved to produce the stocking. The text necessarily separated out individual steps of movements that were fluid; and the image described parts that covered one another (see her discussion of machines, 99–123). See also Jacques Proust, "L'article *Bas* de l'*Encyclopédie*," in *Langue et langages de Leibniz à l'Encyclopédie*, ed. Michèle Duchet (Paris: 10/18, 1977), 245–78.

18 The article "Histoire naturelle" ["Natural History"] emphasizes changes that occurred within science, with advances spawning new branches of study: "Mais plus on a acquis de connoissances, plus on a été porté, & même nécessité, à les diviser en différens genres de Science. Cette division n'est pas toujours exacte, parce que les Sciences ne sont pas si distinctes qu'elles n'ayent des rapports les unes avec les autres; qu'elles ne s'allient & ne se confondent en plusieurs points, soit dans les généralités, soit dans les détails" [But the more one acquires knowledge, the more one is inclined, and even required, to divide this information among different types of science. This division is not always exact, however, because the sciences are not so distinct that they have no relation to one another; that they do not have certain points in common, regarding either their general

characteristics or their specific details] (8:226), http://artflsrv02.uchicago.edu/cgi-bin/philologic/getobject.pl?c.7:929:1.encyclopedie0513.

19 For more on slippage and the subversion of meaning in the *Encyclopédie*, see Jacques Proust, "Diderot et le système des connaissances humaines," *Studies on Voltaire and the Eighteenth Century* 256 (1988): 117–27; Wilda Anderson, *Diderot's Dream* (Baltimore: Johns Hopkins University Press, 1990); David W. Bates, "Cartographic Aberrations: Epistemology and Order in the Encyclopedic Map," in *Using the* Encyclopédie*: Ways of Knowing, Ways of Reading*, ed. Daniel Brewer and Jule Candler Hayes, *Studies on Voltaire and the Eighteenth Century* 2002: 5 (Oxford: Voltaire Foundation, 2001), 1–20; and Julie Candler Hayes, *Reading the French Enlightenment: System and Subversion* (Cambridge: Cambridge University Press, 2006).

20 Unlike Le Brun's ceiling in the Galerie de Glaces, however, no hero unites the Netherlandish images, individually or collectively; nor is there the equivalent of the allegory of Holland to call that unity into question.

21 Stalnaker, 117.

22 See Arthur K. Wheelock, Jr., ed., *Jan Lievens: A Dutch Master Rediscovered* (New Haven, CT: Yale University Press, 2008).

23 Cesare Ripa, *Iconologia, or Moral Emblems* (1593), https://openlibrary.org/books/OL24131257M/Iconologia_or_Moral_emblems.

24 Fried, 130–1. See also Gillian B. Pierce. *Scapeland: Writing the Landscape from Diderot's* Salons *to the Postmodern Museum* (Amsterdam: Rodopi, 2012), 63–109.

25 Denis Diderot, *Essais sur la peinture*, in *Oeuvres esthétiques de Diderot*, ed. Paul Vernière (Paris: Bordas, 1988), 725–7.

Coda

1 Although Dutch genre painting clearly provided inspiration to eighteenth-century French genre painters, many factors influenced the popularity of these later works. Jörg Ebeling refers to shifts in Parisian society that contributed to the increased demand, including the entrance of wealthy members of the haute bourgeoisie into the Paris elite, and the fact that many of the genre paintings, although they depicted aristocratic settings, were acquired by bourgeois who sought a more aristocratic lifestyle ("Upwardly Mobile: Genre Painting and the Conflict between Landed and Moneyed Interests," in *French Genre Painting in the Eighteenth Century*, ed. Philip Conisbee [New Haven, CT: Yale University Press, 2007], 73–89).

2 Bailey notes: "Not infrequently were genre painters called upon to produce pendants or companion pieces to Northern examples; more generally, their work would be expected to adorn the walls of collections in which Dutch and Flemish Old Masters predominated and set the visual tone" (19). Christian Michel affirms the tremendous influence of Dutch and Flemish art, including that of Flemish painters living in Paris, on eighteenth-century French painters (*Le "célèbre Watteau"* [Geneva: Droz, 2008)], 180–81). See also Jacques Foucart, "L'influence des peintres nordiques du XVIIe siècle sur les Français du XVIIIe siècle: Pastiche et création," in *Au temps de Watteau, Fragonard et Chardin: Les Pays Bas et les peintres français du XVIIIe siècle*, ed. Jacques Foucart et al. (Lille: Musée des Beaux-Arts, 1985), 15–20.

3 "Jean-Baptiste Pierre to Abel-François Poisson de Vandières, Marquis de Marigny Marigny," draft of letter dated 4 June 1772; ctd. in Colin B. Bailey, "Surveying Genre in Eighteenth-Century French Painting," in *The Age of Watteau, Chardin, and Fragonard: Masterpieces of French Genre Painting*, ed. Colin B. Bailey (New Haven, CT: Yale University Press, 2003), 19n167. See also Pierre Rosenberg, ed., *Chardin: 1699–1779* (Cleveland: Cleveland Museum of Art, 1979); Pierre Rosenberg and Hélène Prigent, eds., *Chardin: La nature silencieuse* (Paris: Gallimard, 1999); and Pierre Rosenberg, ed., *Chardin* (New Haven, CT: Yale University Press, 2000).

4 The Salon was the exhibition organized by the Académie royale de peinture et de sculpture. This event attests to the enduring power of the arts under Louis XIV, as the Académie, created in 1648, was bound by its original statutes to exhibit a painting by each of its members. Beginning 1751, the Salon was held every other year.

5 Denis Diderot, "Salon de 1763," *Salons*, ed. J. Assézat and M. Tourneux, vol. X (Paris: Garnier, 1763), 194–6, https://fr.wikisource.org/wiki/Salon_de_1763.

6 Kate E. Tunstall analyses contradictions that critics have noted between Diderot's theories of art and his philosophy ("Diderot, Chardin et la matière sensible," *Dix-huitième siècle* 1/2007 (n° 39): 577–93, https://www.cairn.info/revue-dix-huitieme-siecle-2007-1-page-577.htm). See also Groottenboer, 21–25; Claudia Moscovici, *Romanticism and Postromanticism* (Lanham, MD: Lexington Books, Rowman & Littlefield, 2010), ch. 3, https://fineartebooks.wordpress.com/2010/12/17/diderots-salons-art-criticism-of-greuze-chardin-boucher-and-fragonard/; and René Démoris, "Diderot et Chardin: La voie du silence," in *Fabula/Les colloques, Littérature et arts à l'âge classique 1: Littérature et peinture au XVIIIe siècle, autour des Salons de Diderot*, ed. René Démoris, http://www.fabula.org/colloques/document635.php.

7 The *Raie* served as Chardin's submission piece for the *Académie* along with *Le buffet* [*The Buffet*], 1728, 194 x 129 cm (76.38 x 50.79 in), Musée du Louvre, https://commons.wikimedia.org/wiki/File:Jean_Sim%C3%A9on_Chardin_-_The_Buffet_-_WGA04741.jpg. *Le buffet* features a dog in the foreground looking up longingly at a pyramid of fruits on a table.

8 Throughout the eighteenth century scientific illustration cultivated interest in the inner workings of bodies and machines. Gautier d'Agoty's lifelike dissected corpses (*Myologie complète en couleur*, 1746) express an artistic vision. Buffon's *Histoire naturelle* (1749), accompanied by Daubenton's descriptions, depicts views of skeletons and organs. *Encyclopédie* plates show the internal mechanisms of machinery. I thank Tili Boon Cuillé for her help with these references.

9 For the French design influence in Holland and distinctive features in seventeenth-century French decor, see Joan DeJean, *The Age of Comfort: When Paris Discovered Casual – and the Modern Home Began* (New York and London: Bloomsbury, 2010); Nicolas Milovanovic, *Du Louvre à Versailles: Lecture des grands décors monarchiques* (Paris: Les Belles Lettres, 2005); Peter Thornton, *Seventeenth-Century Interior Decoration in England, France, and Holland* (New Haven, CT: Yale University Press, 1978).

10 Thomas Crow relates this celebrated story of Chardin's academic début ("Chardin at the Edge of Belief: Overlooked Issues of Religion and Dissent in Eighteenth-Century French Painting," in *French Genre Painting in the Eighteenth Century*, ed. Philip Conisbee [New Haven, CT: Yale University Press, 2007], 92).

11 Pliny, "An Account of Painting and Colours," *Natural History*, trans. John Bostock and H.T. Riley, bk. 35, ch. 36, http://www.perseus.tufts.edu/hopper/text?doc=Perseus%3Atext%3A1999.02.0137%3Abook%3D35%3Achapter%3D36.

12 Pliny, "Account," also relates a story of two different painters. In Protogenes's absence, Apelles drew a single line on a large panel that this artist had been painting. When Protogenes returned and noticed this fine line on his panel, he knew his visitor had been Apelles.

13 Jefferson C. Harrison, ed., *The Chrysler Museum Handbook of the European and American Collections: Selected Paintings, Sculpture and Drawings* (Norfolk, VA: Chrysler Museum, 1991): 56, 75.

14 Denis Diderot, *Essais sur la peinture*, in *Œuvres esthétiques de Diderot*, ed. Paul Vernière (Paris: Bordas, 1988).

15 Goldfarb, 29. Goldfarb cites Roger de Piles, *Cours de peinture par principes* (Paris: Jacques Estienne, 1708), 3, http://gallica.bnf.fr/ark:/12148/bpt6k1051278h/f21.image.r=Roger%20de%20Piles.

Bibliography

Albanese, Ralph, Jr. "Une lecture idéologique du dénouement de *Tartuffe*." *Romance Notes* 16, no. 3 (1975): 623–35.

Alberti, Leon Battista. *De pictura and De statua*. Edited and translated by Cecil Grayson. London: Phaidon, 1972.

Alpers, Svetlana. *The Art of Describing: Dutch Art in the Seventeenth Century*. Chicago: University of Chicago Press, 1984.

– *Rembrandt's Enterprise: The Studio and the Market*. Chicago: University of Chicago Press, 1988.

Anderson, Wilda. *Diderot's Dream*. Baltimore: Johns Hopkins University Press, 1990.

Anthoine, les frères. *La mort de Louis XIV: Journal des Anthoine*. Edited by Edouard Drumont. Paris: A. Quantin, 1880; rpt. Charleston, SC: BiblioBazaar, 2008.

Apostolidès, Jean-Marie. *Le roi-machine: Spectacle et politique au temps de Louis XIV*. Paris: Editions de Minuit, 1981.

Arizzoli-Clémentel, Pierre. Avant-Propos. *Versailles, la Galerie des Glaces, Catalogue iconographique*. Edited by Nicolas Milovanovic. http://www.galeriedesglaces-versailles.fr/html/11/collection/propos.html.

Assaf, Francis. *La mort du roi: Une thanatographie de Louis XIV*. Tübingen: Gunter Narr Verlag, 1999.

Bailey, Colin B. "Surveying Genre in Eighteenth-Century French Painting." In *The Age of Watteau, Chardin, and Fragonard: Masterpieces of French Genre Painting*. Edited by Colin B. Bailey. New Haven, CT: Yale University Press, 2003. 2–39.

Bajou, Thierry. *Les peintres du roi, 1648–1793*. Paris: Réunion des musées nationaux, 2000.

– *La peinture à Versailles, le XVIIe siècle*. Paris: Réunion des musées nationaux, 1998.

Bakhtin, Mikhail. *Rabelais and His World*. Translated by Hélène Iswolsky. Bloomington: Indiana University Press, 2009.

Barthes, Roland. "L'effet de réel." *Communications* 11, no. 1 (1968): 84–9. http://www.persee.fr/doc/comm_0588-8018_1968_num_11_1_1158.

– *Sur Racine*. Paris: Seuil, 1963.

Bates, David W. "Cartographic Aberrations: Epistemology and Order in the Encyclopedic Map." In *Using the* Encyclopédie*: Ways of Knowing, Ways of Reading*. Edited by Daniel Brewer and Julie Candler Hayes. *Studies on Voltaire and the Eighteenth Century* 2002:5. Oxford: Voltaire Foundation, 2001. 1–20.

Beasley, Faith E. *Versailles Meets the Taj Mahal: François Bernier, Marguerite de la Sablière, and Enlightening Conversations in Seventeenth-Century France*. Toronto: University of Toronto Press, 2018.

Beaussant, Philippe. *Les plaisirs de Versailles: Théâtre et musique*. Paris: Fayard, 1996.

Bedaux, Jan Baptist. *The Reality of Symbols: Studies in the Iconology of Netherlandish Art, 1400–1800*. The Hague: Gary Schwartz, SDU Publishers, 1990.

Bedaux, Jan Baptist, and Rudi Ekkart, eds. *Pride and Joy: Children's Portraits in the Netherlands 1500–1700*. New York: Harry N. Abrams, 2001.

Bérenger, Jean. *Turenne*. Paris: Fayard, 1987.

Berger, Robert W. *A Royal Passion: Louis XIV as Patron of Architecture*. Cambridge: Cambridge University Press, 1994.

Berger, Susanna. *The Art of Philosophy: Visual Thinking in Europe from the Late Renaissance to the Early Enlightenment*. Princeton, NJ: Princeton University Press, 2017.

Bièvre, Elisabeth de. *Dutch Art and Urban Cultures 1200–1700*. New Haven, CT: Yale University Press, 2015.

Bilis, Hélène. *Passing Judgment: The Politics and Poetics of Sovereignty in French Tragedy from Hardy to Racine*. Toronto: University of Toronto Press, 2016.

Bjørnstad, Hall. "'Plus d'éclaircissement touchant la grande galerie de Versailles': Du nouveau sur les inscriptions latines." *XVIIe siècle*, no. 243 (2009): 321–43. https://www.cairn.info/revue-dix-septieme-siecle-2009-2-page-321.htm.

Blair, Ann. *Too Much to Know: Managing Scholarly Information before the Modern Age*. New Haven, CT: Yale University Press, 2010.

Blunt, Anthony. *Nicolas Poussin*. London: Pallas Athene, 1995.

Bonfait, Olivier. "Les collections picturales des financiers à la fin du règne de Louis XIV." *XVIIe siècle* 151 (avril-juin 1986): 125–51.

– *Poussin et Louis XIV: Peinture et monarchie dans la France du Grand Siècle*. Paris: Hazan, 2015.

Braider, Christopher. *Indiscernible Counterparts: The Invention of the Text in French Classical Drama*. Chapel Hill: North Carolina Studies in the Romance Languages and Literatures, 2002.

– *The Matter of Mind: Reason and Experience in the Age of Descartes*. Toronto: University of Toronto Press, 2011.

– *Refiguring the Real: Picture and Modernity in Word and Image, 1400–1700*. Princeton, NJ: Princeton University Press, 1993.

Braun, Georg, and Franz Hogenberg. *Civitates orbis terrarum*. Cologne: 1572. http://historic-cities.huji.ac.il/mapmakers/braun_hogenberg.html.

Brejon de Lavergnée, Arnauld, ed. *L'inventaire Le Brun de 1683: La collection des tableaux de Louis XIV*. Paris: Editions de la Réunion des Musées Nationaux, 1987.

Bryson, Norman. *Looking at the Overlooked: Four Essays on Still Life Painting*. Cambridge, MA: Harvard University Press, 1990.

– *Word and Image: French Painting of the Ancien Régime*. Cambridge: Cambridge University Press, 1983.

Burke, Peter. *The Fabrication of Louis XIV*. New Haven, CT: Yale University Press, 1992.

– *A Social History of Knowledge: From Gutenberg to Diderot*. Cambridge: Polity Press, 2000.

Button, Jeanne, and Stephen Sbarge. *History of Costume, in Slides, Notes and Commentaries*. Vol. 4. Valley Stream, NY: Trinity Media Resources, 1975. Yale University Visual Resources Collection. http://findit.library.yale.edu/catalog/digcoll:1845470.

Cavaillé, Jean-Pierre. "Hypocrisie et imposture dans la querelle du *Tartuffe* (1664–1669): La *Lettre sur la comédie de l'imposteur* (1667)." *Les dossiers du Grihl*, 1997. https://dossiersgrihl.revues.org/292?lang=en.

Charlier, Philippe. "Autopsie et embaumement." In *Le roi est mort: Louis XIV- 1715*. Edited by Gérard Sabatier and Béatrix Saule. Paris: Editions Tallandier, 2015. 42–9.

Charpentier, François. *Explication des tableaux de la galerie de Versailles*. Paris: Muguet, 1684. http://catalogue.bnf.fr/ark:/12148/cb30224844x.

Christiansen, Keith. Metropolitan Museum of Art. Catalogue entry. https://www.metmuseum.org/art/collection/search/626692.

– "What's That? A Closer Look at Objects in the Jabach Portrait." Metropolitan Museum of Art. 11 September 2014. https://www.metmuseum.org/about-the-museum/now-at-the-met/2014/whats-that.

Clark, T.J. *The Sight of Death: An Experiment in Art Writing*. New Haven, CT: Yale University Press, 2006.

Coatalem, Eric, ed. *La nature morte française au XVIIe siècle/17th-Century Still Life Painting in France*. Dijon: Editions Faton, 2015.

Conisbee, Philip, ed. *Georges de La Tour and His World*. New Haven, CT: Yale University Press, 1996.

Corneille, Pierre. *Horace*. 1641. http://www.theatre-classique.fr/pages/pdf/CORNEILLEP_HORACE.pdf.

– *Suréna*. 1675. http://www.theatre-classique.fr/pages/programmes/edition.php?t=../documents/CORNEILLEP_SURENA.xml.

Cornette, Joël. *La mort de Louis XIV 1er septembre 1715: Apogée et crépuscule de la royauté*. Paris: Gallimard, 2015.

– *Le roi de guerre: Essai sur la souveraineté dans la France du Grand Siècle*. Paris: Payot, 2010.

Cowen, Pamela. *A Fanfare for the Sun King: Unfolding Fans for Louis XIV*. London: Third Millennium Publishing, 2003.

Crow, Thomas. "Chardin at the Edge of Belief: Overlooked Issues of Religion and Dissent in Eighteenth-Century French Painting." In *French Genre Painting in the Eighteenth Century*. Edited by Philip Conisbee. New Haven, CT: Yale University Press, 2007. 90–104.

Cuillé, Tili Boon. *Narrative Interludes: Musical Tableaux in Eighteenth-Century French Texts*. Toronto: University of Toronto Press, 2006.

Dandrey, Patrick. *Molière ou l'esthétique du ridicule*. Paris: Klincksieck, 1992.

Dangeau, Philippe de Courcillon, Marquis de. *Mémoire sur la mort de Louis XIV par le Mis de Dangeau* (Abrégé du Journal du Marquis de Dangeau). Edited by Eudoxe Soulié and Louis Dussieux. Paris: Didot Frères, 1858. https://gallica.bnf.fr/ark:/12148/bpt6k55404p.

Darnton, Robert. *The Great Cat Massacre and Other Episodes in French Cultural History*. New York: Basic Books, 1984.

DeJean, Joan. *The Age of Comfort: When Paris Discovered Casual – and the Modern Home Began*. New York and London: Bloomsbury, 2010.

– *The Essence of Style: How the French Invented High Fashion, Fine Food, Chic Cafes, Style, Sophistication, and Glamour*. New York: Free Press, 2006.

De Jongh, Eddy. *Questions of Meaning: Theme and Motif in Dutch Seventeenth-Century Painting*. Translated by Michael Hoyle. Leiden: Primavera Pers, 2000.

Delft, Louis van. *Le moraliste classique: Essai de définition et de typologie*. Geneva: Droz, 1982.

De Marchi, Neil, and Hans J. Van Miegroet. "Comment les tableaux des anciens Pays-Bas ont envahi le marché parisien/How Netherlandish Paintings Came to Paris." In *Rubens, van Dyck, Jordaens et les autres: Peintures baroques flamandes aux musées royaux des beaux-arts de Belgique/Flemish Baroque Paintings from the Royal Museums of Fine Arts of Belgium*. Paris: Musée Marmottan, 2012. 28–47/2–19.

– "Novelty and Fashion Circuits in the Mid-Seventeenth-Century Antwerp-Paris Trade." *Journal of Medieval and Early Modern Studies* 28, no. 1 (Winter 1998): 201–46.

Démoris, René. "Diderot et Chardin: La voie du silence." In *Fabula/Les colloques, littérature et arts à l'âge classique 1: Littérature et peinture au XVIIIe siècle, autour des Salons de Diderot*. Edited by René Démoris. http://www.fabula.org/colloques/document635.php.

Descartes, René. *Philosophical Writings of Descartes*. Translated by John Cottingham, Robert Stoothoff, and Dugald Murdoch. Vol. 1. Cambridge: Cambridge University Press, 1999.

Diderot, Denis. *Essais sur la peinture*. In *Oeuvres esthétiques de Diderot*. Edited by Paul Vernière. Paris: Bordas, 1988.

– "Salon de 1763." *Salons*. Edited by J. Assézat and M. Tourneux. Vol. X. Paris: Garnier, 1763. 159–226. https://fr.wikisource.org/wiki/Salon_de_1763.

Diderot, Denis, and Jean le Rond d'Alembert, eds. *Encyclopédie, ou dictionnaire raisonné des sciences, des arts et des métiers, etc*. Edited by Robert Morrissey and Glenn Roe. Chicago: University of Chicago, ARTFL Encyclopédie Project. Spring 2016 Edition. http://encyclopedie.uchicago.edu/.

Doubrovsky, Serge. *Corneille et la dialectique du héros*. Paris: Gallimard, 1963.

Ducos, Blaise. "Erasme, Rubens, van Dyck: La logique impériale d'Everhard Jabach." In *Un Allemand à la cour de Louis XIV: De Dürer à van Dyck, la collection nordique d'Everhard Jabach*. Paris: Musée du Louvre, 2013. 11–28.

Ebeling, Jörg. "Upwardly Mobile: Genre Painting and the Conflict between Landed and Moneyed Interests." In *French Genre Painting in the Eighteenth Century*. Edited by Philip Conisbee. New Haven, CT: Yale University Press, 2007. 73–89.

Elias, Norbert. *La société de cour*. Paris: Flammarion, 2008.

Faré, Michel. *Le grand siècle de la nature morte en France: Le XVIIe siècle*. Fribourg: Office du livre, 1974.

Félibien, André. *Conférences de l'Académie royale de peinture et de sculpture, pendant l'année 1667*. Paris: F. Léonard, 1668; reprint London: David Mortier, 1705. https://gallica.bnf.fr/ark:/12148/bpt6k98018158.

Fléchier, Esprit. *Oraison funèbre de Turenne*. Paris: Jules Delalain, 1851. https://gallica.bnf.fr/ark:/12148/bpt6k57883027.

Fock, C. Willemijn. "Semblance or Reality? The Domestic Interior in Seventeenth-Century Dutch Genre Painting." In *Art and Home: Dutch Interiors in the Age of Rembrandt*. Edited by Mariët Westermann. Zwolle, Netherlands: Waanders Publishers, 2001. 83–101.

Forestier, Georges. "Corneille et la tragédie: Hypothèses sur l'élaboration de *Suréna*." *Littératures classiques* 16 (1992): 141–68.

Foucart, Jacques. "L'influence des peintres nordiques du XVIIe siècle sur les Français du XVIIIe siècle: Pastiche et création." In *Au temps de Watteau, Fragonard et Chardin: Les Pays Bas et les peintres français du XVIIIe siècle.* Edited by Jacques Foucart et al. Lille: Musée des Beaux-Arts, 1985. 15–20.

– "Peter Lely, Dutch History Painter." *Hoogsteder-Naumann Mercury* 8 (1989): 17–26.

Foucault, Michel. *Les mots et les choses: Une archéologie des sciences humaines.* Paris: Gallimard, 1990.

Freud, Sigmund. *Beyond the Pleasure Principle.* Translated by C.J.M. Hubback. London: International Psycho-Analytical Press, 1922. https://www.libraryofsocialscience.com/assets/pdf/freud_beyond_the_pleasure_principle.pdf.

Fried, Michael. *Absorption and Theatricality: Painting and Beholder in the Age of Diderot*. Chicago: University of Chicago Press, 1988.

Fuhring, Peter, Louis Marchesano, Rémi Mathis, and Vanessa Selbach, eds. *A Kingdom of Images: French Prints in the Age of Louis XIV, 1660–1715*. Los Angeles: Getty Publications, 2015.

Gaehtgens, Thomas W. "The Arts in the Service of the King's Glory." In *A Kingdom of Images: French Prints in the Age of Louis XIV, 1660–1715*. Edited by Peter Fuhring, Louis Marchesano, Rémi Mathis, and Vanessa Selbach. Los Angeles: Getty Publications, 2015. 1–8.

– "Genre Painting in Eighteenth-Century Collections." In *The Age of Watteau, Chardin, and Fragonard: Masterpieces of French Genre Painting*. Edited by Colin B. Bailey. New Haven, CT: Yale University Press, 2003. 78–89.

Gaines, James F. *Social Structures in Molière's Theater*. Columbus: Ohio State University Press, 1984.

Gilby, Emma. *Sublime Worlds: Early Modern French Literature*. London: Legenda, 2006.

Goldfarb, Hilliard T. "Meditations on Still Life Painting in Seventeenth-Century France." In *La nature morte française au XVIIe siècle/17th-Century Still Life Painting in France*. Edited by Eric Coatelem. Dijon: Editions Faton, 2015. 26–9. (French trans. J. Faton, "Méditations sur la peinture de la nature morte en France au XVIIe siècle." 10–25.)

Goldstein, Claire. *Vaux and Versailles: The Appropriations, Erasures, and Accidents that Made Modern France*. Philadelphia: University of Pennsylvania Press, 2008.

Goodkin, Richard. *Birth Marks: The Tragedy of Primogeniture in Pierre Corneille, Thomas Corneille, and Jean Racine*. Philadelphia: University of Pennsylvania Press, 2000.

– *How Do I Know Thee: Theatrical and Narrative Cognition in Seventeenth-Century France*. Evanston, IL: Northwestern University Press, 2015.

Greenberg, Mitchell. *Baroque Bodies: Psychoanalysis and the Culture of French Absolutism*. Ithaca, NY: Cornell University Press, 2001.

– *Racine: From Ancient Myth to Tragic Modernity*. Minneapolis: University of Minnesota Press, 2010.

– *Subjectivity and Subjugation in Seventeenth-Century Drama and Prose: The Family Romance of French Classicism*. Cambridge: Cambridge University Press, 1992.

Grijzenhout, Frans. "Between Reason and Sensitivity: Foreign Views of Dutch Painting, 1660–1800." In *The Golden Age of Dutch Painting in Historical Perspective*. Edited by Frans Grijzenhout and Henk van Veen. Translated by Andrew McCormick. Cambridge: Cambridge University Press, 1999. 11–28.

Grootenboer, Hanneke. *The Rhetoric of Perspective: Realism and Illusionism in Seventeenth-Century Dutch Still-Life Painting*. Chicago: University of Chicago Press, 2006.

Grouchy, Vicomte de. "Everhard Jabach, collectionneur parisien (1695)." *Mémoires de la Société de l'Histoire de Paris et de l'Ile-de-France* 21 (1894): 217–92. https://gallica.bnf.fr/ark:/12148/bpt6k6434807w/f221.item.

Guicharnaud, Jacques. *Molière, une aventure théâtrale:* Tartuffe, Dom Juan, Le Misanthrope. Paris: Gallimard, 1963.

Guyot, Sylvaine. *Racine et le corps tragique*. Paris: PUF, 2014.

Haas, Claude, and Michael E. Auer. "The Dramaturgy of Sovereignty and the Performance of Mourning: The Case of Corneille's *Horace*." *Walter Benjamin's Hypothetical French "Trauerspiel."* Edited by Hall Bjørnstad and Katherine Ibbett. Special issue of *Yale French Studies* 124 (2013): 121–34. https://www.jstor.org/stable/23646045?seq=1#page_scan_tab_contents.

Harrison, Jefferson C., ed. *The Chrysler Museum Handbook of the European and American Collections: Selected Paintings, Sculpture and Drawings*. Norfolk, VA: Chrysler Museum, 1991.

Hasquin, Hervé. *Louis XIV face à l'Europe du Nord: L'absolutisme vaincu par les libertés*. Brussels: Editions Racine, 2005.

Hayes, Julie Candler. *Reading the French Enlightenment: System and Subversion*. Cambridge: Cambridge University Press, 2006.

Helgerson, Richard. *Adulterous Alliances: Home, State, and History in Early Modern European Drama and Painting*. Chicago: University of Chicago Press, 2000.

Hochstrasser, Julie. *Still Life and Trade in the Dutch Golden Age*. New Haven, CT: Yale University Press, 2007.

– "'Still-staende dingen': Picturing Objects in the Dutch Golden Age." In *Early Modern Things: Objects and Their Histories, 1500–1800*. Edited by Paula Findlen. New York: Routledge, 2013. 105–24.

Hollander, Martha. *An Entrance for the Eyes: Space and Meaning in Seventeenth-Century Dutch Art*. Berkeley: University of California Press, 2002.

Horowitz, Louise. *Love and Language: A Study of the Classical French Moralist Writers*. Cleveland: Ohio State University Press, 1977.

– "Things Thick and Thin: The Material of *Les Caractères*." *French Review* 64, no. 1 (October 1990): 12–18. https://www.jstor.org/stable/395660.

Ingamells, John, ed. *The Wallace Collection Catalogue of Pictures III: French before 1815*. 4 vols. London: Paul Holberton Publishing, 1985.

Israel, Jonathan I. *The Dutch Republic: Its Rise, Greatness, and Fall 1477–1806*. Oxford: Oxford University Press, 1995.

– "The Emerging Empire: The Continental Perspective, 1650–1713." In *The Origins of Empire: British Overseas Enterprise to the Close of the Seventeenth Century. The Oxford History of the British Empire*. Vol. 1. Edited by Nicholas Canny. Oxford: Oxford University Press, 2001. 423–44.

Jorink, Eric. *Reading the Book of Nature in the Dutch Golden Age, 1575–1715*. Translated by Peter Mason. Leiden: Brill, 2010.

Judovitz, Dalia. *Georges de La Tour and the Enigma of the Visible*. New York: Fordham University Press, 2017.

Kafker, Frank A., and Serena L. Kafker. *The Encyclopedists as Individuals: A Biographical Dictionary of the Authors of the* Encyclopédie. Oxford: Voltaire Foundation, 1988. https://artflsrv03.uchicago.edu/philologic4/kafker/navigate/1/60/.

Kantorowicz, Ernst. *The King's Two Bodies: A Study in Medieval Political Theology*. Princeton, NJ: Princeton University Press, 1957.

Kemp, Martin. *The Science of Art: Optical Themes in Western Art from Brunelleschi to Seurat*. New Haven, CT: Yale University Press, 1992.

– *Visualizations: The Nature Book of Art and Science*. Oxford: Oxford University Press, 2000.

Kuus, Saskia. "Children's Costume in the Sixteenth and Seventeenth Centuries." In *Pride and Joy: Children's Portraits in the Netherlands 1500–1700*. Edited by Jan Baptist Bedaux and Rudi Ekkart. New York: Harry N. Abrams, 2000. 73–83.

La Bruyère, Jean de. Les caractères *ou* Les mœurs de ce siècle *précédé des* Caractères *de Théophraste, traduits du grec par La Bruyère*. Edited by Robert Garapon. Paris: Classiques Garnier, 1969. https://fr.wikisource.org/wiki/Les_Caract%C3%A8res_(Garapon).

Lafage, Gaëlle. *Charles Le Brun décorateur de fêtes*. Rennes: Presses Universitaires de Rennes, 2015.

La Rochefoucauld, François, Duc de. *Maximes et Réflexions morales* (1664). https://fr.wikisource.org/wiki/Maximes.

Le Brun, Charles. *L'inventaire de Le Brun 1643: La collection des tableaux de Louis XIV*. Edited by Arnauld Brejon de Lavergnée. Paris: Réunion des Musées nationaux, 1987.

Lecestre, H. Léon, ed. *Mémoires de Saint-Hilaire [fils] 1661–1678*. 6 vols. Paris: Libraire Renouard, 1903–16. https://catalogue.bnf.fr/ark:/12148/cb34024395n.

Levine, Caroline. *Forms: Whole, Rhythm, Hierarchy, Network*. Princeton, NJ: Princeton University Press, 2017.

Levron, Jacques. *La cour de Versailles aux* XVIIe *et* XVIIIe siècles. Paris: Perrin, 2010.

Loughman, John, and John Michael Montias. *Public and Private Spaces: Works of Art in Seventeenth-Century Dutch Houses*. Zwolle, Netherlands: Waanders, 2001.

Louis le Grand: L'amour et les delices de son peuple, ou Les actions de graces, les Festes et les Rejouïssances pour le parfait retablissement de la Santé du Roy en 1687. http://gallica.bnf.fr/ark:/12148/btv1b6945531s.

Louis XIV. *Mémoires pour l'instruction du dauphin*. Edited by C. Dreyss. 2 vols. Paris: Didier, 1860. https://books.google.com/books?id=flv8brYaWaoC&printsec=frontcover&vq=ob%C3%A9issance&source=gbs_ge_summary_r&cad=0#v=onepage&q=ob%C3%A9issance&f=false.

Lynn, John A. *The Wars of Louis XIV: 1667–1714*. Harlow, UK: Longman Publishing, 1999.

Lyons, John D. *Before Imagination: Embodied Thought from Montaigne to Rousseau*. Stanford, CA: Stanford University Press, 2005.

– *Kingdom of Disorder: The Theory of Tragedy in Classical France*. West Lafayette, IN: Purdue University Press, 1999.

– *The Tragedy of Origins: Pierre Corneille and Historical Perspective*. Stanford, CA: Stanford University Press, 1996.

– *Tragedy and the Return of the Dead*. Evanston, IL: Northwestern University Press, 2018.

Marchesano, Louis, and Christian Michel, eds. *Printing the Grand Manner: Charles Le Brun and Monumental Prints in the Age of Louis XIV*. Los Angeles: Getty Publications, 2010.

Marin, Louis. *La parole mangée et autres essais théologico-politiques*. Paris: Klincksieck, 1986.

– *Le portrait du roi*. Paris: Editions de Minuit, 1981.

– *Sublime Poussin*. Paris: Seuil, 1995.

Marshall, David. *The Frame of Art: Fictions of Aesthetic Experience, 1750–1815*. Baltimore: Johns Hopkins University Press, 2005.

Maslan, Susan. "The Dream of the Feeling Citizen: Law and Emotion in Corneille and Montesquieu." *SubStance* 35, no. 1 (2006): 69–84. https://www.jstor.org/stable/3685636.

Massillon, Jean-Baptiste. "Oraison funèbre de Louis le Grand, roi de France." In *Oraisons funèbres: Massillon, Fléchier, Mascaron, précédées de L'Essai sur l'oraison funèbre par Villemain*. Paris: Garnier Frères, 1875. 134–68. https://gallica.bnf.fr/ark:/12148/bpt6k6483277j/f1.image.r=Oraison%20fun%C3%A8bre%20de%20Louis%20XIV%20MASSILLON.

McCloskey, Deidre Nansen. *Bourgeois Equality: How Ideas, Not Capital or Institutions, Enriched the World*. Chicago: University of Chicago Press, 2016.

McClure, Ellen M. *Sunspots and the Sun King: Sovereignty and Mediation in Seventeenth-Century France*. Chicago: University of Illinois Press, 2006.

McCollim, Gary B. *Louis XIV's Assault on Privilege: Nicolas Desmaretz and the Tax on Wealth* Rochester, NY: University of Rochester Press, 2012.

Melzer, Sara. "Myths of Mixture in Phèdre and the Sun King's Assimilation Policy in the New World." In *Racine for the Next Millennium*. Edited by Harriet Stone. Special issue. *L'Esprit Créateur* 38, no. 2 (Summer 1998): 72–81. https://doi.org/10.1353/esp.2010.0025.

Merle du Bourg, Alexis. "Major Northern Influence/L'apport substantiel du Nord." In *La nature morte française au XVIIe siècle/17th-Century Still Life Painting in France*. Edited by Eric Coatalem. Dijon: Editions Faton, 2015. 382–9/362–81.

– *Peter Paul Rubens et la France 1600–1640*. Villeneuve-d'Ascq, France: Presses Universitaires de Septentrion, 2004.

Merlin-Kajman, Hélène. *L'absolutisme dans les lettres et la théorie des deux corps: Passions et politique*. Paris: Honoré Champion, 2000.

Michel, Christian. *Le "célèbre Watteau."* Geneva: Droz, 2008.

Milovanovic, Nicolas. *Du Louvre à Versailles: Lecture des grands décors monarchiques*. Paris: Les Belles Lettres, 2005.

Milovanovic, Nicolas, ed. *Versailles, la Galerie des Glaces: Catalogue iconographique*. Coproduction EPV - RMN. Versailles: Château de Versailles, 2008. http://www.galeriedesglaces-versailles.fr/html/11/accueil/index.html.

Milovanovic, Nicolas, and Alexandre Maral, eds. *Louis XIV: L'homme et le roi*. Paris: Skira Flammarion, 2009.

Mitchell, Dolores. "Rembrandt's 'The Anatomy Lesson of Dr. Tulp': A Sinner among the Righteous." *Artibus et Historiae* 15, no. 30 (1994): 145–56. https://www.jstor.org/stable/1483478.

Molière. *Le Tartuffe*. 1669. http://www.theatre-classique.fr/pages/pdf/MOLIERE_TARTUFFE.pdf.

– *Le Tartuffe*. Version de 1664 reconstruite par Georges Forestier et Isabelle Grellet. http://www.moliere.paris-sorbonne.fr/Tartuffe_1664_reconstruit.pdf.

Monconys, Balthasar de. *Journal des voyages de Monsieur de Monconys ... où les sçavants trouveront un nombre infini de nouveautez, en machines de mathématique, expériences physiques, raisonnemens de la belle philosophie, curiositez de chymie, et conversations des illustres de ce siècle ... publié par le Sr de Liergues, son fils.* 3 parts. Lyon: H. Boissat and G. Remeus, 1665–6. http://gallica.bnf.fr/ark:/12148/btv1b8608278p.

Montclos, Brigitte, ed. *Almanachs parisiens 1661–1716*. Paris: Musée Carnavalet, 1998.

Montias, John Michael. *Artists and Artisans in Delft: A Socio-Economic Study of the Seventeenth Century*. Princeton, NJ: Princeton University Press, 1982.

– *Vermeer and His Milieu: A Web of Social History*. Princeton, NJ: Princeton University Press, 1989.

Moriarty, Michael. "La Bruyère: Virtue and Disinterestedness." *French Studies* 68.2 (1 April 2014): 164–79. https://academic.oup.com/fs/article-abstract/68/2/164/607475?redirectedFrom=fulltext.

– *Taste and Ideology in Seventeenth-Century France*. Cambridge: Cambridge University Press, 1988.

Moscovici, Claudia. *Romanticism and Postromanticism*. Lanham, MD: Lexington Books, Rowman & Littlefield, 2010. Chapter 3. https://fineartebooks.wordpress.com/2010/12/17/diderots-salons-art-criticism-of-greuze-chardin-boucher-and-fragonard/.

Muizelaar, Klaske, and Derek Phillips. *Picturing Men and Women in the Dutch Golden Age: Paintings and People in Historical Perspective*. New Haven, CT: Yale University Press, 2003.

Mukerji, Chandra. *Territorial Ambitions and the Gardens of Versailles*. Cambridge: Cambridge University Press, 1997.

Norman, Larry F. *The Public Mirror: Molière and the Social Commerce of Depiction*. Chicago: University of Chicago Press, 1999.

North, Michael. *Art and Commerce in the Dutch Golden Age*. Translated by Catherine Hill. New Haven, CT: Yale University Press, 1997.

Olson, Todd. *Poussin and France: Painting, Humanism, and the Politics of Style*. New Haven, CT: Yale University Press, 2002.

Pasanek, Brad. *Metaphors of Mind: An Eighteenth-Century Dictionary*. Baltimore: Johns Hopkins University Press, 2015.

Pavord, Anna. *The Tulip: The Story of a Flower That Has Made Men Mad*. London: Bloomsbury, 2004.

Perez, Stanis. *La santé de Louis XIV: Une biohistoire du Roi-Soleil*. Paris: Tempus Perrin, 2010.

Pierce, Gillian B. *Scapeland: Writing the Landscape from Diderot's* Salons *to the Postmodern Museum*. Amsterdam: Rodopi, 2012.

Piles, Roger de. *Cours de peinture par principes*. Paris: Jacques Estienne, 1708. http://catalogue.bnf.fr/ark:/12148/cb311123215.

Plax, Julie Anne. "Seventeenth-Century French Images of Warfare." In *Artful Armies, Beautiful Battles: Art and Warfare in Early Modern Europe*. Edited by Pia F. Cuneo. Boston: Brill, 2002. 131–55.

Pliny. "An Account of Painting and Colours." In *Natural History*. Translated by John Bostock and H.T. Riley. Bk. 35. Chapter 36. http://www.perseus.tufts.edu/hopper/text?doc=Perseus%3Atext%3A1999.02.0137%3Abook%3D35%3Achapter%3D36.

Posner, David M. *The Performance of Nobility in Early Modern European Literature*. Cambridge: Cambridge University Press, 1999.

Préaud, Maxime. "Printmaking under Louis XIV." In *A Kingdom of Images: French Prints in the Age of Louis XIV, 1660–1715*. Edited by Peter Fuhring, Louis Marchesano, Rémi Mathis, and Vanessa Selbach. Los Angeles: Getty Publications, 2015. 9–14.

Price, J.L. *Culture and Society in the Dutch Republic during the 17th Century*. London: Batsford, 1974.

Proust, Jacques. "L'article *Bas* de l'*Encyclopédie*." In *Langue et langages de Leibniz à l'*Encyclopédie. Edited by Michèle Duchet. Paris: 10/18, 1977. 245–78.

– "Diderot et le système des connaissances humaines." *Studies on Voltaire and the Eighteenth Century* 256 (1988): 117–27.

Racine, Jean. *Phèdre*. 1697. http://www.theatre-classique.fr/pages/programmes/edition.php?t=../documents/RACINE_PHEDRE.xml.

Ramsay, Andrew Michael. *Histoire du Vicomte de Turenne, Maréchal général des armées de France*. Paris: Vve Mazières et J.-B. Garnier, 1735. https://gallica.bnf.fr/ark:/12148/bpt6k86571z/f4.image.r=Histoire%20du%20Vicomte%20de%20Turenne,%20%20Mar%C3%A9chal%20g%C3%A9n%C3%A9ral%20des%20arm%C3%A9es%20de%20France.langEN.

Raux, Sophie. "Circulation, Distribution, and Consumption of Antwerp Paintings in the Markets of the Southern Netherlands and Northern France (1570–1680)." In Moving Pictures*: Intra-European Trade in Images, 16th–18th Centuries*. Edited by Neil De Marchi and Sophie Raux. Turnhout, Belgium: Brepols, 2014. 93–122.

Reclus, Onésime. *Le plus beau royaume sous le ciel*. Paris: Hachette, 1899. http://gallica.bnf.fr/ark:/12148/bpt6k1031624.

Rey, François, and Jean Lacouture. *Molière et le roi: L'affaire* Tartuffe. Paris: Seuil, 2007.

Reynies, Nicole de. "Les lissiers flamands en France au XVIIe siècle, et considérations sur leurs marques." In *Flemish Tapestry Weavers Abroad:*

Emigration and the Founding of Manufactories in Europe. Edited by Guy Delmarcel. Leuven, Belgium: Leuven University Press, 2002. 203–26.

Richefort, Isabelle, ed. *Adam-François van der Meulen: Peintre flamand au service de Louis XIV*. Rennes: Presses Universitaires de Rennes, 2004.

Ripa, Cesare. *Iconologia, or Moral Emblems* (1593). https://openlibrary.org/books/OL24131257M/Iconologia_or_Moral_emblems.

Rosenberg, Pierre. *Chardin*. New Haven, CT: Yale University Press, 2000.

– "Les Poussin de Louis XIV." In *Louis XIV: L'homme et le roi*. Edited by Nicolas Milovanovic and Alexandre Maral. Paris: Skira Flammarion, 2009. 83–93.

Rosenberg, Pierre, ed. *Chardin: 1699–1779*. Cleveland: Cleveland Museum of Art, 1979.

– Rosenberg, Pierre, and Hélène Prigent, eds. *Chardin: La nature silencieuse*. Paris: Gallimard, 1999.

Rowlands, Guy. *The Dynastic State and the Army under Louis XIV: Royal Service and Private Interest 1661–1701*. Cambridge: Cambridge University Press, 2002.

Sabatier, Gérard, and Béatrix Saule, eds. *Le roi est mort: Louis XIV, 1715*. Paris: Tallandier, 2015.

Saint-Simon, Louis de Rouvroy, Duc de. *Mémoires complets et authentiques du Duc de Saint-Simon*. 20 vols. Paris: Hachette, 1856–8. http://rouvroy.medusis.com/; English: http://www.gutenberg.org/files/3875/3875-h/3875-h.htm#link2HCH0078.

Salvi, Claudia. *D'après nature: La nature morte en France au XVIIe siècle*. Waterloo, Belgium: La Renaissance du livre, 2000.

Saunders, E. Stewart. "Louis XIV: Patron of Science and Technology." *Libraries Research Publications*. Paper 46. https://docs.lib.purdue.edu/lib_research/46.

Savill, Rosalind, Stephen Duffy, and Joanne Hedley, eds. *The Wallace Collection*. London: Scala Publishers, 2006.

Sawday, Jonathan. *The Body Emblazoned: Dissection and the Human Body in Renaissance Culture*. London: Routledge, 1995.

Schama, Simon. *The Embarrassment of Riches: An Interpretation of Dutch Culture in the Golden Age*. New York: Vintage, 1997.

Schnapper, Antoine. *Curieux du Grand Siècle: Collections et collectionneurs dans la France du XVIIe siècle*. 2 vols. Paris: Flammarion, 2005.

Schneider, Norbert. *Still Life: Still Life Painting in the Early Modern Period*. Cologne: Taschen, 1999.

Segal, Sam. *Flowers and Nature: Netherlandish Flower Painting of Four Centuries*. The Hague: SDU Publishers, 1990.

Sellier, Philippe. "Le jansénisme des tragédies de Racine: Réalité ou illusion?" *Cahiers de l'Association Internationale des Etudes Françaises* no. 31 (1979): 135–48. https://doi.org/10.3406/caief.1979.1190.

Sevigné, Marie de Rabutin-Chantal, Marquise de. *Correspondance*. Edited by Roger Duchêne and Jacqueline Duchêne. 3 vols. Paris: Gallimard, 1974.

Silver, Sean. *The Mind Is a Collection: Case Studies in Eighteenth-Century Thought*. Philadelphia: University of Pennsylvania Press, 2015.

Slaughter, M.M. *Universal Languages and Scientific Taxonomy in the Seventeenth Century*. Cambridge: Cambridge University Press, 1982.

Slive, Seymour. *Jacob van Ruisdael: Master of Landscape*. New Haven, CT: Yale University Press, 2005.

Sluijter, Eric. "On Brabant Rubbish, Economic Competition, Artistic Rivalry, and the Growth of the Market for Paintings in the First Decades of the Seventeenth Century." Translated by Jennifer Kilian and Katy Kist; footnotes by the author. *JHNA* 1, no.2 (Summer 2009). https://jhna.org/articles/brabant-rubbish-economic-competition-artistic-rivalry-growth-market-paintings-first-decades-seventeenth-century/.

Smith, Jay M. *The Culture of Merit: Nobility, Royal Service, and the Making of Absolute Monarchy in France, 1600–1789*. Ann Arbor: University of Michigan Press, 1996.

Soll, Jacob. *The Information Master: Jean-Baptiste Colbert's Secret State Intelligence System*. Ann Arbor: University of Michigan Press, 2011.

Sowa, Helen Chastain. *Louise Moillon, Seventeenth-Century Still Life Artist: An Illustrated Biography*. Chicago: Chateau Publications, 1998.

Spitzer, Leo. "The 'Récit de Théramène.'" *Linguistics and Literary History: Essays in Stylistics*. Princeton, NJ: Princeton University Press, 2015. 87–134.

Stalnaker, Joanna. *The Unfinished Enlightenment: Description in the Age of the Encyclopedia*. Ithaca, NY: Cornell University Press, 2010.

Stone, Harriet. *The Classical Model: Literature and Knowledge in Seventeenth-Century France*. Ithaca, NY: Cornell University Press, 1996.

– "Petitions for Justice: Molière's *Tartuffe* Viewed in the Mirror of Pierre de Lancre's Witches." In *Theatrum Mundi: Studies in Honor of Ronald W. Tobin*. Edited by Claire L. Carlin and Kathleen Wine. Charlottesville, VA: Rookwood Press, 2003. 92–9.

– *Royal DisClosure: Problematics of Representation in French Classical Tragedy*. Birmingham, AL: Summa Publications, 1987.

– *Tables of Knowledge: Descartes in Vermeer's Studio*. Ithaca, NY: Cornell University Press, 2006.

Stone-Ferrier, Linda. "Views of Haarlem: A Reconsideration of Ruisdael and Rembrandt." *Art Bulletin* 67, no. 3 (1985): 417–36. https://www.jstor.org/stable/3050960.

Stroup, Alice. *A Company of Scientists: Botany, Patronage, and Community at the Seventeenth-Century Parisian Royal Academy of Sciences*. Berkeley: University of California Press, 1990.

Suchtelen, Ariane van, and Arthur K. Wheelock, Jr, eds. *Cityscapes of the Golden Age*. Zwolle, Netherlands: Waanders Publishers, 2008.

Sutton, Peter C., ed. *Jan van der Heyden (1637–1712)*. New Haven, CT: Yale University Press, 2006.

– *Love Letters: Dutch Genre Paintings in the Age of Vermeer*. London: Frances Lincoln, 2003.

Taylor, Paul. "The Concept of *Houding* in Dutch Art Theory." *Journal of the Warburg and Courtauld Institutes* 55 (1992): 210–32. https://www.jstor.org/stable/751425.

– *Dutch Flower Painting, 1600–1720*. New Haven, CT: Yale University Press, 1995.

Thornton, Peter. *Seventeenth-Century Interior Decoration in England, France, and Holland*. New Haven, CT: Yale University Press, 1978.

Thuillier, Jacques. *Georges de La Tour*. Paris: Flammarion, 2003.

Tunstall, Kate E. "Diderot, Chardin et la matière sensible." *Dix-huitième siècle* vol. 39 (2007): 577–93. https://www.cairn.info/en-savoir-plus.php?ID_REVUE=DHS.

Vallot, Antoine, Antoine Daquin, and Guy-Crescent Fagon. *Journal de santé de Louis XIV*. Edited by Stanis Perez. Grenoble: Jérôme Millon, 2004.

Vergara, Lisa. "Women, Letters, Artistic Beauty: Vermeer's Theme and Variations." In *Love Letters: Dutch Genre Paintings in the Age of Vermeer*. Edited by Peter C. Sutton. London: Frances Lincoln, 2003. 50–62.

Vlieghe, Hans. *Flemish Art and Architecture, 1585–1700*. Translated by Alastair and Cora Weir. New Haven, CT: Yale University Press, 2004.

Waiboer, Adriaan E., ed., with Arthur K. Wheelock, Jr, and Blaise Ducos. *Vermeer and the Masters of Genre Painting: Inspiration and Rivalry*. New Haven, CT: Yale University Press, 2017.

Wellington, Robert. "The Cartographic Origins of Adam Frans van der Meulen's Marly Cycle." *Print Quarterly* 28, no. 2 (June 2011): 142–54. https://www.jstor.org/stable/43826143.

Werner, Michael, and Bénédicte Zimmermann. "Beyond Comparison: *Histoire croisée* and the Challenge of Reflexivity." *History and Theory* 45, no. 1 (February 2006): 30–50. https://www.jstor.org/stable/3590723.

Westermann, Mariët. *A Worldly Art: The Dutch Republic 1585–1718*. New Haven, CT: Yale University Press, 2005.

Wetering, Ernst van de, ed. *A Corpus of Rembrandt Paintings IV: Self-Portraits*. Dordrecht: Springer, 2005.

Wheelock, Arthur K., Jr, ed. *Jan Lievens: A Dutch Master Rediscovered*. New Haven, CT: Yale University Press, 2008.

– *Vermeer & the Art of Painting*. New Haven, CT: Yale University Press, 1995.

Willemsen, Annemarieke. "Images of Toys: The Culture of Play in the Netherlands around 1600." In *Pride and Joy: Children's Portraits in the Netherlands 1500–1700*. Edited by Jan Baptist Bedaux and Rudi Ekkart. New York: Harry N. Abrams, 2000. 61–72.

Wolohojian, Stephan, Melinda Watt, and Michael Gallagher, eds. *A Grand Tableau: Charles Le Brun's Portrait of the Jabach Family*. New York: Metropolitan Museum of Art, 2017.

Wygant, Amy. "Leo Spitzer's Racine." *MLN* 109, no. 4 (September 1994): 632–49. https://www.jstor.org/stable/2904967.

Zanger, Abby E. *Scenes from the Marriage of Louis XIV: Nuptial Fictions and the Making of Absolutist Power*. Stanford, CA: Stanford University Press, 1997.

Index

Page numbers in bold refer to illustrations